F. Liszt

George Sand

Berlioz

Beethoven

Goethe

Thomas F. Barnum

Ch. Gounod

Byron

Rousseau

Marie Thérèse

Thomas Hardy

Beaumarchais

Voltaire

Eug. Delacroix

Chateaubriand

Gq. Mazzini

Pleasures

of

Music

'Nobody is ever patently right
about music.'

VIRGIL THOMSON

EDITED & WITH A NEW PREFACE BY
JACQUES BARZUN

PLEASURES

of

MUSIC

*An Anthology of Writing
about Music and Musicians
from Cellini to Bernard Shaw*

THE UNIVERSITY OF CHICAGO PRESS

THE UNIVERSITY OF CHICAGO PRESS, CHICAGO 60637
CASSELL AND CO., LTD., LONDON

93 92 91 90 89 88 87 86 85 84   9 8 7 6 5 4 3

Cloth ISBN: 0-226-03856-4
Paper ISBN: 0-226-03854-8
LCC Card Number: 77-73691

CONTENTS

The Musical Life

APROPOS OF INSTRUMENTS

Fantasies and Confessions

Correspondence

323. Johannes Brahms, 326. Charles Baudelaire, 329. Emmanuel Chabrier, 332. Sydney Smith, 333. Giuseppe Verdi, 334. Franz Schubert, 337.

Maxims and Good Stories

The editor's acknowledgments to holders of copyright and publishing rights are made in the list of Sources and Acknowledgments, pp. 365–71.

PREFACE 1977

※

THIS anthology was first put together 25 years ago under the prompting of a pair of circumstances, one personal and one general. In 1950 I had just published *Berlioz and the Romantic Century* and in its long preparation had come across many good things about music said or written by authors and musicians of every kind. I thought these good things should be collected as wholes or excerpts and translated if necessary.

The general circumstance was due to the advent of the long-playing disc. It virtually created a new public for writings about music. Up to that time, the experienced reader of books tended to keep away from print dealing with musical subjects, thinking it "special," probably filled with technical terms and enigmatic snippets from scores. As for the relatively few persons who "knew music," they were either listening to it or playing it. They had no time for books. It was in fact a question whether they could read words other than a handful of Italian ones ending in -o and -mente.

What recording on discs, seconded by broadcasting, accomplished was to greatly enlarge the musical repertory and to make it known to thousands of unassuming people as yet untouched by the opposing prejudices of Hear Nothing and Read Nothing. The newcomers, like Lydia the Lady of the Aroostook, "wanted to know." They got to know the music by playing the disc and they got the habit of reading about music by scanning the commentary on the back of the jacket.

This innocent practice established without argument that one's experience of music could be enhanced, organized, solidified by the use of words—preferably wise, accurate, and enlivening words. What was thus quietly overcome was not only the needless division between readers and listeners, but also the previous, rather snobbish, doctrine that each art must be taken pure, without soiling admixture from the other arts: "Literature has nothing to do with Music"—as if song, Greek drama, church ritual, and modern opera were not admixtures, which together constitute the greater part of all the music our civilization has produced.

"Yes, yes, but we didn't mean that; we meant reading words *about* music—interpretation, appreciation, commentary, comparison—all the literary froth that isn't strict analysis ('He then modulates harshly to the distant key of E♭ minor')."

Well, to say nothing of the practice of the Greeks and the Chinese, who are always so useful in critical debates, many western European musicians since the Renaissance have found it pleasant or necessary to write about their art, and their writings in many genres have usually been other than the so-called technical analysis which describes with assorted adverbs the tonal goings-on.

Some of these doubly gifted artists have argued about the aims and powers of music, or defined the pleasures of hearing, performing, and discussing it. Others have told us of the arduous life it entails, or explained their works and theories in autobiographies. Instrumentalists have descanted on sound and the mechanics of producing it; or, when travelling, have given their friends news of the foreign musical scene in letters. Nearer to us, long-eared writers, such as Hoffmann of the Tales, Balzac, Hardy, Bernard Shaw, have composed fiction about music and musicians. Finally, a large fund of legends, anecdotes, and bons mots has gathered about this most sociable of the arts, whose devotees are no less talkative than other men.

Pleasures of Music in its original form drew on all these sources. In the present edition, I have thought it desirable to leave out the fiction which made up the first part. My reason is this: a good anthology is ideally for the bedside; it should be possible to lift and hold it easily for browsing while lounging or lying down. To this end the size and shape of the book should contribute. Hence the omission of some 130 pages, including an Introduction full of wit and wisdom but no longer required in these days of total enlightenment about art and criticism.

Yet mindful of avid readers and solicitous about their hunger, I have kept in the List of Sources on p. 365 the authors and titles of the thirteen pieces of fiction that once formed the substantial hors d'oeuvre to the main course.

Criticism

ROMAIN ROLLAND

Making the Rounds

Rolland's novel in many volumes, Jean-Christophe, deals chiefly with the experiences of a young German musician in Paris at the turn of the century—1900 to 1910.

O F his own accord, Théophile Goujart came a few days later to seek out Christophe in his garret. He seemed not at all upset at finding him in such poor surroundings. He was on the contrary, most charming, and said to him, 'I thought you might enjoy hearing a little music from time to time, and since I have press tickets for everything, I've come to pick you up.'

Christophe was delighted. He was touched by the kind thought and returned effusive thanks. Goujart seemed quite different from what he had been the first night. In tête-à-tête he put on no side; he was easygoing, almost shy, and eager to learn. Only in front of others did he automatically resume his superior airs and dogmatic tone. To be sure, his eagerness to learn had a practical motive. He showed no curiosity about anything except the current scene, but he wanted to know what Christophe thought of a score just received, of which he himself could scarcely give an account since he was barely able to read notes.

They went together to a symphony concert. The entrance was common to the hall and to a casino. By a tortuous corridor one reached a windowless auditorium where the atmosphere was stifling. The seats were narrow and too close together. Part of the audience was standing, blocking the exits—French lack of comfort throughout.

A man who seemed to be cankered by incurable boredom was conducting at top speed one of the Beethoven symphonies, as if he could hardly wait to get it over with. From the neighbouring casino the strains of the cabaret show's bumps and grinds came and mingled with the funeral march of the *Eroica*. The concert audience kept straggling in, settling down, and staring at one another. As soon as they had stopped coming, they began leaving. Christophe was exerting all his powers of concentration to follow the work through the distractions of this county fair. By dint of strenuous effort he was even beginning to enjoy parts of it—for the orchestra was competent and Christophe had long been deprived of symphonic music—when Goujart seized his arm and, in the middle of a movement, said to him, 'Time for us to go. We're due at another concert.'

Christophe frowned but did not answer. He followed his guide, who took him halfway across Paris and brought him to another hall, redolent of the stable.[1] There, on other days of the week, they gave pantomimes and cheap plays. For music in Paris is like those penniless workmen who go halves on a single room—when one gets out of bed, the other comes from his work into the warmed sheets. In this hall as in the other, no fresh air, of course. Since the days of the Sun King Louis XIV, the French have deemed it unhealthful, and the sanitary code of theatres, as formerly that of Versailles, is that the air should be kept unbreathable.

A noble-looking, white-haired man was unleashing with the gestures of a lion tamer an act from a Wagnerian opera. The poor beast—that is to say, the act—resembled those menagerie animals who are petrified by the footlights and who must be whipped if they are to remember that they were once wild beasts. Some large female Philistines and a gaggle of little geese were witnessing this show with a smile on their lips. After the wild beast had roared and the tamer had bowed, and both had been rewarded by the spectators' making a rumpus, Goujart attempted to take Christophe with him to a third concert. But this time Christophe clamped both hands on the arms of his seat and declared he would not budge. He was sick and tired of rushing from place to place to catch a morsel of opera here and some crumbs of symphony there. In vain did Goujart try to explain that music criticism in Paris was a trade in which it was more important to see than to listen. Christophe retorted that music

[1] The author seems to have taken as his models the Pasdeloup and Lamoureux Concerts, housed respectively in the Cirque d'Hiver (the stable) and the Casino de Paris. The two conductors, again, are Lamoureux at the Cirque and his son-in-law Chevillard at the Casino; though the two societies did not flourish concurrently.

was not made to be taken on the run, between cabs, that it required a more collected mood. This hash of concerts gave him nausea; he wanted only one at a time.

He was in fact astonished at this proliferation of music. Like most Germans, he believed that in France the art occupied but a secondary place. He expected that it would be served to him in very small portions, though exquisite. As it was, he had his choice, to begin with, of no less than fifteen concerts in one week. There was at least one each evening and sometimes two or three—at the same hour and in opposite quarters of town. As for Sunday, there were always four, all at the same hour. Christophe marvelled at this greediness and gaped at the size of the programmes. He had thought hitherto that his compatriots enjoyed a monopoly of these debauches of sound, which had so often disgusted him in Germany. Now he saw that the Parisians could easily match them in this form of guzzling: two symphonies, one concerto, one or two overtures, one act from opera —all indiscriminately mixed: German, Russian, Scandinavian, French; champagne, ginger beer, ale and wine, the public gulped them down at a sitting without turning a hair. Christophe wondered that these French lightweights had such strong stomachs. But he had missed the point. They needed no stomachs, for they were sieves; nothing stayed with them.

Christophe was not long in noticing that this vast amount of music boiled down in fact to very little. At every concert he found again the same names and the same pieces. These copious programmes revolved in one narrow circle: virtually nothing before Beethoven; almost nothing after Wagner. And in between, what gaps! It seemed as if music were equivalent to five or six celebrated Germans, three or four Frenchmen and (ever since the Franco-Russian alliance) half-a-dozen Muscovite numbers. Nothing from the older French composers. Nothing from the great Italians. Nothing from the German titans of the seventeenth and eighteenth centuries. Nothing from contemporary German music—with the sole exception of Richard Strauss who, being shrewder than the rest, came each year to impose his new works on the Paris public. No Belgian music, no Czechish, and what was most astounding, no French music by contemporaries.

Yet of the French school everybody spoke in mysterious terms, as of a thing that was revolutionizing the world. Christophe kept watching for a chance to hear this music, for his inquiring mind was broad and unprejudiced; he was consumed by the desire to hear something new and to admire the works of genius. But despite his efforts he did not manage to hear the modern French, for he did not include under that head some three or four little pieces, of fine texture but coldly and carefully complicated, which had hardly held his attention.

JEAN-CHRISTOPHE IN PARIS (1908)

G. K. CHESTERTON

Music with Meals

ANEWSPAPER comment on something I recently wrote has given me a momentary illusion of having really got hold of what is the matter with modernity. For that serpent is as slippery as an eel, that demon is as elusive as an elf. But for the moment I thought I had him—or at least a perfect specimen of him. I wrote recently to the effect that music at meals interferes with conversation. And certain people at once began to discuss whether music at meals interferes with digestion. And in that one detail I seemed to have caught the very devil himself by the tail.

Those who read my article know that I never even mentioned digestion. I never even thought of it. It never crosses my mind while I am eating meals. It certainly never crosses my mind when I am listening to music. Least of all did it ever cross my mind while I was writing that particular article. And the idea that it should cross anybody's mind, not to say occupy anybody's mind, in connection with the other controversy seems to me a compendium of all the dullness, baseness, vulgarity, and fear that make up so much of the practical philosophy of this enlightened age. What I complained of was not that music interfered with animal assimilation, but that it interfered with human speech, with the talk of taverns like the Tabard or the Mermaid, with the talk of Dr. Johnson or Charles Lamb, with the *Noctes Ambrosianae* or the Four Men of Sussex; with all the ancient Christian custom of men arguing each other's heads off and shouting each other down for the glory of reason and the truth. Those great talkers no more thought about their digestion at dinner than the heroes of the Iliad or the Song of Roland felt their own pulses and took their own temperatures in the thick of the battle. It is true that I did not confine myself to complaining of meals being spoiled by music. I also complained of music being spoiled by meals. I was so impertinent as to suggest that if we want to listen to good music we should listen to it, and honour it with our undivided attention. A fine musician might surely resent a man treating fine music as a mere background to his lunch. But a fine musician might well murder a man who treated fine music as an aid to his digestion.

But what interests me is this swift, unconscious substitution of the subject of digestion, which I had never mentioned, for the subject of human intercourse, which I had. It has hidden in it somewhere a sort of secret of our social and spiritual abnormality. It is a sort of silent signal of all that has gone wrong with our brains and tempers and memories and hearts—and also, doubtless, digestions. It is so significant that it is worth while to attempt to resolve it into the elements that make it the monstrous and ominous thing it is. Before this evil and elusive creature escapes me once more, I will attempt to dissect it and make a sort of diagram of its deformities.

First, there is that stink of stale and sham science which is one of the curses of our times. The stupidest or the wickedest action is supposed to become reasonable or respectable, not by having found a reason in scientific fact, but merely by having found any sort of excuse in scientific language. This highly grotesque and rather gross topic is supposed to take on a sort of solemnity because it is physiological. Some people even talk about proteids, vitamins—but let us draw a veil over the whole horrid scene. It is enough to note that one element in the hideous compound is a love of talking about the body as a scientific thing—that is, talking about it as if it were a serious thing.

Next, there is a morbidity and a monstrous solitude. Each man is alone with his digestion as with a familiar demon. He is not to allow either the wine or the music to melt his soul into any sociable spirit of the company. Wine is bad for his digestion and music is good for his digestion. He therefore abstains from the one and absorbs the other in the same inhuman isolation. Diogenes retired into a tub and St. Jerome into a cave; but this hermit uses his own inside as his cavern—every man is his own cask, and it is not even a wine cask.

Third, there is materialism or the very muddiest sort of atheism. It has the obscure assumption that everything begins with the digestion, and not with the divine reason; that we must always start at the material end if we wish to work from the origins of things. In their hapless topsy-turvy philosophy, digestion is the creator and divinity the creature. They have at the back of their minds, in short, the idea that there is really nothing at the back of their minds except the brute thing called the body. To them, therefore, there is nothing comic or incongruous about saying that a violin solo should be a servant of the body or of the brute; for there is no other god for it to serve.

There also hides in the heart of this philosopher the thing we call hypochondria and a paralysing panic. I have said that it serves the body; but many men in many ages have served their bodies. I doubt if any men in any ages were ever so much afraid of their bodies. We might represent in some symbolic drama a man running down the street pursued by his own body. It is inadequate to say of this sort of thing that it is atheism; it would be nearer the truth to say it is devil-worship. But they are not even the red devils of passion and enjoyment. They are really only the blue devils of fear.

Then there is what there always is in such philosophy, the setting of the cart to draw the horse. They do not see that digestion exists for health, and health exists for life, and life exists for the love of music or beautiful things. They reverse the process and say that the love of music is good for the process of digestion. What the process of digestion is ultimately good for they have really no idea. I think it was a great medieval philosopher who said that all evil comes from enjoying what we ought to use and using what we ought to enjoy. A great many modern philosophers never do anything else. Thus they will sacrifice what they admit to be happiness to what they claim to be progress; though it could have no rational meaning except progress to greater happiness. Or they will subordinate goodness to efficiency; though the very name of good implies an end, and the very name of efficiency implies only a means to an end. Progress and efficiency by their very titles are only tools. Goodness and happiness by their very titles are a fruition; the fruits that are to be produced by the tools. Yet how often the fruits are treated as fancies of sentimentalism and only the tools as facts of sense. It is as if a starving man were to give away the turnip in order to eat the spade; or as if men said that there need not be any fish, so long as there were plenty of fishing rods. There is all that queer inversion of values in talking about music as an aid not only to dinner, but even to the digestion of dinner.

There is more generally a flat, unlifted, unlaughing spirit, that can accept this topsy-turveydom without even seeing that it is topsy-turvy. It does not even rise high enough to be cynical. It does not utter its materialistic maxim even as a pessimist's paradox. It does not see the joke of saying that the Passion Music can assist a gentleman to absorb a veal cutlet, or that a mass of Palestrina might counteract the effects of toasted cheese. What is said on this subject is said quite seriously. That seriousness is perhaps the most frivolous thing in the whole of this frivolous society. It is a spirit that cannot even rouse itself enough to laugh.

In short, it is the magic of that one trivial phrase, about music and digestion, that it calls up suddenly in the mind the image of a certain sort of man, sitting at a table in a grand restaurant, and wearing a serious and somewhat sullen expression. He is manifestly a man of considerable wealth; and beyond that he can only be described by a series of negatives. He has no traditions, and therefore knows nothing of the great traditional talking that has enriched our literature with the nights and feasts of the gods. He has no real friends, and therefore his interests are turned inwards, but more to the state of his body than of his soul. He has no religion, and therefore it comes natural to him to think that everything springs from a material source. He has no philosophy, and therefore does not know the difference between the means and the end. And, above all, there is buried deep in him a profound and stubborn repugnance to the trouble of following anybody else's argument; so that if somebody elaborately explains to him that it is often a mistake to combine two pleasures, because pleasures, like pains, can act as counter-irritants to each other, he receives only the vague impression that somebody is saying that music is bad for his digestion.

GENERALLY SPEAKING (1929)

ROBERT BURTON

The Secret Power of Musick

MANY and sundry are the means which philosophers and physicians have prescribed to exhilarate a sorrowful heart, to divert those fixed and intent cares and meditations, which in this malady so much offend; but, in my judgement, none so present, none so powerfull, none so apposite, as a cup of strong drink, mirth, musick, and merry company. . . . Musick is a roaring-meg against melancholy, to rear and revive the languishing soul; *affecting not only the ears, but the very arteries, the vital and animal spirits, it erects the mind and makes it nimble.* This it will effect in the most dull, severe, and sorrowfull souls, expell grief with mirth; *and, if there bee any cloudes, dust, or dreggs of cares yet lurking in our thoughts, most powerfully it wipes them all away,* and that which is more, it will perform all this in an instant—*chear up the countenance, expell austerity, bring in hilarity, informe our manners, mitigate anger.* Many other properties Cassiodorus reckons up of this our divine musick, not only to expell the greatest griefs, but it *doth extenuate fears and furies, appease cruelty, abateth heaviness; and, to such as are watchfull, it causeth quiet rest; it takes away spleen and hatred,* bee it instrumentall, vocall, with strings, winde; it cures all irksomness and heaviness of the soul. Labouring men that sing to their work, can tell as much; and so can souldiers when they go to fight, whom terror of death cannot so much affright, as the sound of trumpet, drum, fife, and such like musick, animates. *It makes a childe quiet,* the nurses song; and many times the sound of a trumpet on a sudden, bells ringing, a carremans whistle, a boy singing some ballad tune early in the street, alters, revives, recreates a restless patient that cannot sleep in the night, etc. In a word, it is so powerfull a thing that it ravisheth the soul, *regina sensuum,*[1] the queen of the senses, by sweet pleasure (which is an happy cure); and corporall tunes pacifie our incorporeall soul: *sine ore loquens, dominatum in animam exercet,* and carries it beyond it self, helps, elevates, extends it. Scaliger gives a

---

[1] This phrase and others in this passage are translated by Burton in the words immediately preceding or following the Latin.

reason of these effects, *because the spirits about the heart take in that trembling and dancing air into the body, are moved together, and stirred up with it*, or else the minde, as some suppose, harmonically composed, is roused up at the tunes of musick. And 'tis not onely men that are so affected, but almost all other creatures. You know the tale of Hercules, Gallus, Orpheus, and Amphion (*felices animas* Ovid cals them) that could *saxa movere sono testudinis*, etc. make stocks and stones, as well as beasts, and other animals, dance after their pipes: the dog and hare, wolf and lamb, as Philostratus describes it in his images, stood all gaping upon Orpheus; and trees, pulled up by the roots, came to hear him.

Arion made fish follow him, which, as common experience evinceth,[1] are much affected with musick. All singing birds are much pleased with it, especially nightingales, if we may believe Calcagninus; and bees amongst the rest, though they be flying away, when they hear any tingling sound, will tarry behinde. *Harts, hindes, horses, dogs, bears, are exceedingly delighted with it.* Elephants, Agrippa addes, and in Lydia in the midst of a lake there be certain floating ilands, (if ye will beleeve it) that, after musick, will dance.

But to leave declamatory speeches in praise of divine musick, I will confine my self to my proper subject: besides that excellent power it hath to expell many other diseases, it is a soveraigne remedy against despair and melancholy, and will drive away the divel himself. Canus, a Rhodian fidler in Philostratus, when Apollonius was inquisitive to know what he could do with his pipe, told him, *that he would make a melancholy man merry, and him that was merry much merrier than before, a lover more inamoured, a religious man more devout.* Ismenias the Theban, Chiron the Centaure, is said to have cured this and many other diseases by musick alone: as now they do those, saith Bodine, that are troubled with S. Vitus Bedlam dance. Timotheus the musician compelled Alexander to skip up and down, and leave his dinner (like the tale of the frier and the boy); whom Austin[2] so much commends for it. Who hath not heard how Davids harmony drove away the evill spirits from king Saul? (I Sam. 16) and Elisha, when he was much troubled by importunate kings, called for a minstrel; *and,*

---

[1] Carew of Anthony in his Description of Cornwall saith of whales that they will come and shew themselves dancing at the sound of a trumpet. [Burton's note.]

[2] St. Augustine, *City of God*, Bk. XVII, chap. 14.

when he played, the hand of the Lord came upon him (II Kings 3).
Censorinus reportes how Asclepiades the physician helped many fran-
tike persons by this means, *phreneticorum mentes morbo turbatas.*—Jason
Pratensis hath many examples, how Clinias and Empedocles cured
some desperately melancholy, and some mad, by this our musick;
which because it hath such excellent vertues, belike, Homer brings in
Phemius playing, and the Muses singing at the banquet of the gods.
Aristotle, Plato,[1] highly approve it, and so do all politicians. The
Greekes, Romanes, have graced musick, and made it one of the liberall
sciences, though it be now become mercenary. All civill common-
wealths allow it: Cneius Manlius (as Livius relates) brought first out
of Asia to Rome singing wenches, players, jesters, and all kinde of
musick to their feasts. Your princes, emperours, and persons of any
quality, maintain it in their courts: no mirth without musick. Sir
Thomas Moore, in his absolute Utopian common-wealth, allowes
musick as an appendix to every meal, and thoughout, to all sorts.
Epictetus cals *mensam mutam praesepe*, a table without musick a manger;
for *the concent of musicians at a banquet is a carbuncle set in gold; and as the
signet of an emerald well trimmed with gold, so is the melody of musick in a
pleasant banquet.* Lewes the eleventh, when he invited Edward the
fourth to come the Paris, told him, that, as a principall part of his entertainment, he should hear sweet voices of children, Ionicke and Lydian
tunes, exquisite musick, he should have a . . . . . ., and the Cardinal
of Burbon to be his confessor; which he used as a most plausible
argument, as to a sensuall man indeed it is. Lucian is not ashamed to
confess that he took infinite delight in singing, dancing, musick,
womens company, and such like pleasures; *and if thou* (saith he) *didst
but hear them play and dance, I know thou wouldst be so well pleased with
the object, that thou wouldst dance for company thy self: without doubt thou
wilt bee taken with it:* So Scaliger ingenuously confesseth, *I am beyond
all measure affected with musick; I do most willingly behold them dance; I am
mightily detained and allured with that grace and comeliness of fair women;
I am well pleased to bee idle amongst them.* And what young man is not?
As it is acceptable and conducing to most, so especially to a melancholy
man; provided alwaies, his disease proceed not originally from it, that
he bee not some light *inamorato*, some idle phantastick, who capers in
conceit all the day long, and thinks of nothing else, but how to make
jigs, sonnets, madrigals, in commendation of his mistress. In such

[1] Respectively: *Politics*, Bk. VIII, chap. 5; *Laws*, II.

cases, musick is most pernicious, as a spur to a free horse will make him run himself blinde, or break his wind; for musick enchants, as Menander holds; it will make such melancholy persons mad; and the sound of those jigs and hornpipes will not bee removed out of the ears a week after. Plato, for this reason, forbids musick and wine to all young men, because they are most part amorous *ne ignis addatur igni*, lest one fire increase another. Many men are melancholy by hearing musick; but it is a pleasing melancholy that it causeth, and therefore, to such as are discontent, in wo, fear, sorrow, or dejected, it is a most present remedy: it expells cares, alters their grieved minds, and easeth in an instant. Otherwise, saith Plutarch, *musica magis dementat quam vinum*; musick makes some men mad as a tygre; like Astolphos horn in Ariosto, or Mercuries golden wand in Homer, that made some wake, others sleep, it hath divers effects: and Theophrastus right well prophesied, that diseases were either procured by musick, or mitigated.

ANATOMY OF MELANCHOLY (1621)

CONSTANT LAMBERT

The Spirit of Jazz

Constant Lambert (1905–51) is considered by many to have written the best book on modern music, brief extracts from which appear in these pages. But his main musical activity was as composer and conductor, particularly in his connection with the Sadler's Wells opera and ballet companies.

JAZZ is naturally dependent for its progress on the progress of the sophisticated material used as a basis for its rhythmic virtuosity. The sudden post-war efflorescence of jazz was due largely to the adoption as raw material of the harmonic richness and orchestral subtlety of the Debussy-Delius period of highbrow music. Orchestral colour of course is not a thing that can really be appreciated in itself; it is largely dependent for its colour on the underlying harmonies. The harmonic background drawn from the Impressionist school opened up a new world of sound to the jazz composer, and although the more grotesque orchestral timbres, the brute complaints of the saxophone, the vicious spurts from the muted brass, may seem to belie the rich sentimentality of their background, they are only thorns protecting a fleshy cactus—a sauce piquante poured over a nice juicy steak.

Jazz, or to be pedantically accurate, 'ragtime,' from having a purely functional value—a mere accompaniment to the tapping of toe and heel, the quick linking of bodies and the slow unburdening of minds —has suddenly achieved the status of a 'school,' a potent influence that can meet the highbrow composer on his own terms. Though popularly regarded as being a barbaric art, it is to its sophistication that jazz owes its real force. It is the first dance music to bridge the gap between highbrow and lowbrow successfully. The valse has received august patronage from Beethoven onward, it is true, but the valses of the nineteenth-century composers are either definite examples of unbending or definite examples of sophistication—sometimes both. Chabrier's *Fête Polonaise* has an harmonic and orchestral elaboration far beyond anything imagined by the popular valse writers of his time, but the modern highbrow composer who writes a foxtrot can hardly hope to go one better than Duke Ellington, if indeed he can be considered as being in the same class at all. In the nineteenth century the split between the classical and popular came between a follower of Liszt, let us say, and a follower of Gungl. Today the split occurs between a composer like Kurt Weill and a composer like Jarnach—both of them pupils of Busoni.

The same rapprochement between highbrow and lowbrow—both meeting in an emotional *terrain vague*—can be seen in literature. Though Byron wrote a poem about the valse there is little in common between his poems and the popular songs of the period; Rossetti kept his limericks and his sonnets severely apart; and though Dowson frequented the breezy music halls of his day there is no touch of Dolly Gray about Cynara. In the poetry of T. S. Eliot, however—particularly in 'Sweeney Agonistes'—we find the romantic pessimism of the nineteenth century expressed in the music-hall technique of the twentieth-century lyric writer, not ironically but quite genuinely. 'This is the way the world ends, this is the way the world ends, this is the way the world ends, not with a bang but a whimper' echoes not only the jingle of the jazz song but its sentiment. Whimpering has indeed become recognized as one of the higher pleasures.

MUSIC HO! (1934)

SIDNEY LANIER

Music is Infinite

Flutist, composer, and poet, author of the Centennial Cantata of 1876, Lanier was a born and trained musician who has left a volume of excellent essays on music. The following is from a manuscript fragment first printed in his collected works.

ALL shades in an American audience; from those who cry give us a tune, something quick and devilish, to those who find in music a religion of the emotions and a comfort and triumph in the darkest hour of the soul. Composers must not be characterized. We must not take Beethoven and Mozart and stick a pin through each one like so many bugs and butterflies in a glass case, and say this one Beethoven belongs to the class of the big beetles (*Coleoptera gigans*) and Mozart to the class of the butterflies (——!). If we do, the composers will become as dry and dusty as an entomologist's collection.

In the same way we must not assign too definite *ideas* to musical compositions: this means longing, etc., this means etc. etc. (Bayard Taylor's experience with Wagner's music: one of the party said it meant moonlight, another sea, another so and so, etc. etc.: on the other hand, that burlesque orchestra piece where the sun was represented rising over Pike County, Arkansas, (piccolo and drum) etc.) Cf. Thos. Hood's *Musical Party*. Music is vague: purposely so. This is no objection. If it is, the Bible must fall. The Bible furnishes a text for every creed. The Mormon allows you to have twenty wives, and furnishes you good authority from the Bible, while the old George Raff and his Harmonists (and the Catholic Priest) allow you no wife, and give you good authority from the Bible: the slaveholder draws his warrant from the Bible, the abolitionist draws *his* warrant from the Bible: the Unitarian proves from the Bible that there is but one person in the Godhead, the Trinitarian that there are three. Arnold reads the plain and lucid statements of St. Matthew and Paul and arrives at Rationalism, while from the more mystical writings of St. John a thousand mystagogues construct a thousand forms of belief. This is because the Bible is so great; and it is purely because music is so great that it yields aid and comfort to so many theories.

NOTES AND FRAGMENTS (Undated)

FERRUCCIO BUSONI[1]

The Unity of Music

Iᴛ is time to recognize that all the manifestations of music constitute a *unity*. It is time to say farewell to the subdividing of music based on its purpose, its forms, or the means it employs—as is still done today. It is time to be persuaded that the sole differences consist in its *contents* and *quality*.

By *purpose* I have in mind the three fields of opera, church, and concert music; by *form*, such things as lyric, dance, fugue, or sonata; by *means employed*, the use of the human voice or of instruments, and, among these, the orchestra, the quartet, the piano, and their multiple combinations.

Music, in whatever shape and place and however paired, remains music and nothing else. It may enter into and become part of a given genre, but only through the imagination, by means of a title or motto, or of a text, or by reason of the situation in which it is placed. But there is no such thing as music that bears the indelible imprint of *church music* and is recognizable as such. I am convinced that no one hearing a fragment of Mozart's *Requiem* or Beethoven's *Missa Solemnis* can detect and define it as ecclesiastical unless he knows the text or title.

The Gregorian chant, which is univocal and bare, entirely devoid of harmony, is strictly bound up in our imagination with the idea of the church, and we hear it as church music in the same way as the style of Palestrina. Yet the love songs of Palestrina's time are identically similar to an offertory—the text and the occasion alone differentiate the two. When Pope Gregory set the rules for the liturgy, there was no other style of music, and we are bound to admit that a romance of that time was not very different from that which today we think we distinguish as originating in music of the church.

Our sensibility responds in just the same way to 'operatic music' in so far as—by a slavish habit—a given attitude has been as if

[1] See head note p. 223.

naturalized there, and now *seems* operatic because we have learned to know it at the theatre. Yet the operatic attitude proper is but a formula in which music has the smallest part. Usually what it amounts to is a sort of give and take that the opera-makers closely ape one from the other; also a concession to the singing and often a device to make up for the lack of a more elevated expression, or else to fashion some clever passage work.

In 'concert music'—beginning with Haydn, and wherever it exists as a living art—we continually find theatrical reminiscences, especially in Beethoven's minor mood: long stretches in his allegro movements follow the pace and expression of *opera buffa*. Such a remark in no way lessens the value of the music. Art is the interpretation of life, and the theatre is such in ever-greater measure than the other arts. For which reason it is natural that living music should bear an affinity with the music of the theatre.

SKETCH FOR A PREFACE TO *DR. FAUSTUS* (1921)

JULES RENARD & MAURICE RAVEL

Music and Nature

*Jules Renard (1864–1910) was a novelist and playwright of the naturalistic
school who specialized in the minute recording of human and animal life.*

January 12. M. Ravel, the composer of *Histoires Naturelles*,[1] swarthy,
rich, and subtle, insists that I go tonight to hear his melodies.

I tell him how ignorant I am of music, and ask what he has added
to the *Histoires*.

'My aim is not to add anything,' he says, 'but to interpret.'

'What does that mean?'

'Why, to say in music what you say in words when you look at
a tree, for example. I think and feel in sounds, and I should like to
think and feel the same things as you. One kind of music is instinctive,
made of feelings—that is my kind. Of course one must first learn the
craft. Then there is the intellectual kind—d'Indy's music.[2] Tonight
there will be hardly anybody there who is not a d'Indy. They reject
feeling, which they refuse to go into. My mode of thought is the
opposite, but they find my work interesting since they are willing to
play it. It is a trial of considerable importance to me. But of one
thing I am sure: the performer is absolutely first-rate.'

RENARD'S *JOURNAL* (1907)

[1] A volume of sketches published by Renard in 1896, illustrated by Toulouse-
Lautrec in 1899.

[2] Vincent d'Indy (1851–1931); see p. 105.

THOMAS DE QUINCEY

How Music Imitates

THE first elementary idea of a Greek tragedy is to be sought in a serious Italian opera. The Greek dialogue is represented by the recitative, and the tumultuous lyrical parts assigned chiefly, though not exclusively, to the chorus on the Greek stage, are represented by the impassioned airs, duos, trios, choruses, etc., on the Italian. And here, at the very outset, occurs a question which lies at the threshold of a Fine Art—that is, of *any* Fine Art: for had the views of Addison upon the Italian opera had the least foundation in truth, there could have been no room or opening for any mode of imitation except such as belongs to a *mechanic* art.

The reason for at all connecting Addison with this case is, that *he* chiefly was the person occupied in assailing the Italian opera; and this hostility arose, probably, in his want of sensibility to good (that is, to Italian) music. But whatever might be his motive for the hostility, the single argument by which he supported it was this—that a hero ought not to sing upon the stage, because no hero known to history ever summoned a garrison in a song, or charged a battery in a semichorus. In this argument lies an ignorance of the very first principle concerned in *every* Fine Art. In all alike, more or less directly, the object is to reproduce in the mind some great effect, through the agency of *idem in alio*. The *idem*, the same impression, is to be restored; but *in alio*, in a different material—by means of some different instrument. For instance, on the Roman stage there was an art, now entirely lost, of narrating, and in part of dramatically representing, an impassioned tale, by means of dancing, of musical accompaniment in the orchestra, and of elaborate pantomime in the performer. *Saltavit Hypermnestram*, he danced (that is, he represented by dancing and pantomime the story of) Hypermnestra. Now, suppose a man to object, that young ladies, when saving their youthful husbands at midnight from assassination, could not be capable of waltzing or quadrilling, how wide is this of the whole problem! This is still seeking for the *mechanic* imitation, some imitation founded in the very fact;

whereas the object is to seek the imitation in the sameness of the impression drawn from a different, or even from an impossible fact. If a man, taking a hint from the Roman 'Saltatio' (*saltavit Andromachen*),[1] should say that he would 'whistle Waterloo,' that is, by whistling connected with pantomine, would express the passion and the charges of Waterloo, it would be monstrous to refuse him his postulate on the pretence that 'people did not whistle at Waterloo.' Precisely so: neither are most people made of marble, but of a material as different as can well be imagined, viz., of elastic flesh, with warm blood coursing along its tubes; and yet, for all that, a sculptor will draw tears from you, by exhibiting, in pure statuary marble, on a sepulchral monument, two young children with their little heads on a pillow, sleeping in each other's arms; whereas, if he had presented them in waxwork, which yet is far more like to flesh, you would have felt little more pathos in the scene than if they had been shown baked in gilt gingerbread. He has expressed the *idem*, the identical thing expressed in the real children; the sleep that masks death, the rest, the peace, the purity, the innocence; but *in alio*, in a substance the most different; rigid, non-elastic, and as unlike to flesh, if tried by touch, or eye, or by experience of life, as can well be imagined. So of the whistling. It is the very worst objection in the world to say, that the strife of Waterloo did not reveal itself through whistling: undoubtedly it did not; but that is the very ground of the man's art. He will reproduce the fury and the movement as to the only point which concerns you, viz., the effect upon your own sympathies, through a language that seems without any relation to it: he will set before you what *was* at Waterloo through that which was *not* at Waterloo. Whereas any direct factual imitation, resting upon painted figures drest up in regimentals, and worked by watchwork through the whole movements of the battle, would have been no art whatsoever in the sense of a Fine Art, but a base *mechanic* mimicry.

This principle of the *idem in alio*, so widely diffused through all the higher revelations of art, it is peculiarly requisite to bear in mind when looking at Grecian tragedy, because no form of human composition employs it in so much complexity.

THE *ANTIGONE* OF SOPHOCLES (1846)

---

[1] He (the actor) danced (the role of) Andromache.

MARTIN LUTHER

In Praise of Music

Luther played both the flute and the guitar, sang and composed hymns, as well as indited thoughts and essays on his favourite art.

MUSIC is one of the greatest gifts that God has given us: it is divine and therefore Satan is its enemy. For with its aid many dire temptations are overcome; the devil does not stay where music is.

Music is among the highest of the arts: its sounds bring the words of a text to life. It puts to flight all sad thoughts, as we see happened to Saul.[1]

Many of our courtiers would boast of saving our overlord the three thousand florins a year that he spends on music; but they squander in other ways three times as much. Music must be supported by the king and the princes, for the maintenance of the arts is their duty no less than the maintenance of the laws. Private citizens, however much they may love art, cannot afford to support it. Duke George, landgrave of Hesse, and John Frederic, elector of Saxony, have had a full complement of musicians, vocal and instrumental; and now the Duke of Bavaria, the Emperor Ferdinand, and the Emperor Charles are doing the same.[2]

After a concert in his own house, December 17, 1538

If God gives us such boons in this life, which is but a vale of trials and tears, what will it be like hereafter!

Singing is a noble art and a good exercise. It has nothing to do with worldly affairs, with the strife of the market place and the rivalries of the court. The singer fears no evil; he forgets all worry and is happy. . . .

I have always been very fond of music. I would not change my little knowledge of music for a great deal. Whoever is proficient in

[1] Allusion to I Samuel 16: 23.
[2] Ferdinand, Charles V's brother, colleague and successor to the Empire.

this art is a good man, fit for all other things. Hence it is absolutely necessary to have it taught in the schools. A schoolmaster must know how to sing or I shan't tolerate him. Nor must one ordain young fellows into the priesthood unless they have learned and practised the art during their schooling.

In fact, I want all the arts, but especially music, dedicated to the service of Him who has created and given them to us. The Christian religion is a religion of joyousness, for God has through his Son made our hearts joyful. Anyone who truly believes this cannot help saying it and singing it with gladness. . . . Anyone who won't say it and sing it shows that he doesn't really believe it.

To a harpist:
Friend, play me an air, as David did. Indeed, I think that if the Psalmist were to return among us, he would be surprised to find how many have skill in his art.

How is it that we have so many and such excellent examples of secular music, while our sacred music is frigid and dull? [To illustrate his meaning he sang, first, one or two German folk-songs, and then one or two of the commonest hymns.] As for those who despise music, the dreamers and the mystics, I despise them. I shall ask the prince, out of all this money we have, to establish a good band.

To Ludwig Senfl,[1] *Court musician of Bavaria, asking for a musical setting:*
My love of music has made me overcome any fear I might have of being rebuffed by you on your seeing at the bottom of this request a name which is doubtless odious to you. The same devotion and faith in music makes me hope at the same time that correspondence with me will not involve you in trouble or vexations. The Grand Turk himself could not make the request of a letter on this subject a matter of discredit to you. Except for theology, there is no art that can be placed in comparison with music.

TABLE TALK AND *LETTERS* (1530-41)

---

[1] (? –1555); composer of a famous imitative piece, '*Kling-Klang.*'

P. E. VERNON

The Ear is Not Enough

At the time of writing, the author was research fellow in both psychology and sacred music at Cambridge University. He is now Professor of Educational Psychology at the University of London and specializes in the measurement of abilities, but he has by no means given up his interest in music.

MUSIC is generally regarded as essentially something that is heard, and though, admittedly, various factors may occasionally affect appreciation, yet these are thought of as irrelevant and having little bearing on the music itself. I wish to show how many and how important are such factors, music without them being an impossibility. Only when they are taken into account and their musical significance is considered does it become possible to point the way to an adequate theory as to the nature of aesthetic appreciation.

I have been investigating the subject of the appreciation of music and its psychology at Cambridge, using ordinary discussions, questions, introspections, and observations, certain psychological tests, and also two experimental concerts at which members of the audiences (each numbering about fifty people of all degrees of musicianship) tried to write down what they had actually thought about and felt while listening. Previous investigators in this sphere seem to have depended almost entirely on gramophone music, and often appear only to have played bad music to more or less unmusical people; neither the title nor the composer of the music were told to the subjects of such experiments, and an extremely artificial and abnormal situation resulted. To demonstrate this effect my first concert was as normal as possible, ordinary chamber music, such as a Mozart trio, sixteenth-century and Brahms songs, Bach and contemporary pianoforte music, being performed under usual concert conditions by members of the Cambridge University Musical Club. At a second concert the conditions were abnormal, the performers being behind a curtain and the programme announced only in outline, e.g., violin suite, two songs, etc. It consisted of music almost wholly unknown to the audience, especially chosen to throw light on certain points.

Now it would obviously be difficult to write out very complete introspections while listening, hence the following method was developed and proved to be fairly satisfactory, not disturbing appreciation of the music unduly. The introspective records (which were treated confidentially) were on the whole quite good and clear. After each item of music the audience were asked to indicate, individually, how much they had attended to, thought about, or felt certain general categories or headings by giving each 0, 1, 2, or 3 marks according to its relative importance for them in that item. These headings were given in printed directions and explained in a preliminary talk. The audience were required to use only those which seemed to them necessary to summarize all their thoughts and feelings while listening —for example: anything irrelevant to the music—visual images (mental pictures); bodily movements and rhythmic responses; thoughts as to the identity of the music, composers, performers; interest in other technical aspects of the music; the goodness or badness of the music; feelings aroused; aesthetic appeal.

During the rest of each interval (five to ten minutes), or, if it did not distract them, during the music, they amplified their marks by describing as fully as possible any details of their experiences.

The audience were quite serious and interested throughout; at the first concert only 18 per cent complained at all of the situation; at the second 47 per cent, including all the most musical, admitted to being somewhat distracted, but the majority rather enjoyed being free from performers' mannerisms and the noise of applause. The main difficulty in working out the results was that no two people mean the same thing by aesthetic appeal or value, nor do they estimate their wandering of attention and the like by the same standards. But both the marks, the remarks, and the data obtained by other methods supplemented one another, and it was possible to obtain a good deal of evidence by noting what characteristics were prominent in the more musical subjects of the investigation, what in the less musical. Certain questions with regard to their musical education and other factors were answered at the time, and my personal knowledge of more than three-quarters of them was of the greatest use.

The first and most obvious non-musical factor is wandering of attention from the music to various associations (recollections of previous performances, and so on) and often to quite irrelevant affairs. To many this free play of the imagination is a source of considerable pleasure, and some people, with but little knowledge of or interest in music, are definitely stimulated to think about extraneous matters by having music going on when not attending. (Tolstoy and Stendhal were presumably of this type.) Analogous is the use of music to help factory workers engaged on monotonous and rhythmic jobs; sailors and savages also often work much better when they sing.

At the concerts the marks for this first category varied with the length of the items, and with their lack of emotional and intellectual interest. I found quite definitely that the more musical, on the average, attend better than the unmusical, for the musician develops a musical sentiment or conscience which debars him from enjoying such lapses, and helps him to concentrate.

The more representational the music the more easily are associations aroused, so that many listeners like to weave emotional dramas into what they hear; any work that attains much popularity is inevitably supplied with a programme, whether the composer intended it or no. In about one-third of the audience either the emotional flux aroused by the music or its physical characteristics may lead on into sporadic visual images, while up to 10 per cent may enjoy the music because it evokes a continuous kind of dream which they watch as if at a theatre. This phenomenon of visualization only appears in people with a low degree of mental control, and so increases in frequency with fatigue; it requires a passive, almost hypnotic, state without any critical or objective attitude toward the music. The visual imagery of savages and primitive peoples is very vivid, so that this is probably one of the main effects of music on them; hence the magical powers ascribed to music in the many legends like that of Orpheus. That music is not capable of suggesting specific scenes has often been proved. However, there is some consistency in its effect. For example, in a polka from Casella's *Puppazetti*,[1] played as a pianoforte duet, about one-fifth of the audience saw either wooden or foreign soldiers, or a war dance of Red Indian or African natives, and the like (thus combining symbolically the martial, rhythmic, and strange characteristics of the music). Though visualization is not absent in some people in the most abstract music, yet, together with emotional interpretations, it is naturally most com-

[1] Alfredo Casella (born 1883), Italian pianist, composer, and critic. The *Puppazetti* is an orchestral suite (1917).

mon in songs, opera, and avowed programme music. The more
musical, however, often say that when listening to music such as
L'Après-midi d'un Faune they may at first visualize scenes or incidents;
when they get to know it better they forget the programme and listen
to it more abstractly. Some never make use of such associations or
interpretations at all. I find that the more musical also have, on the
average, a considerable preference for orchestral and chamber music
concerts over choral concerts and operas, and show little appreciation
of any vocal music. When they do listen to songs they pay but little
attention to the words; in fact, at the second concert it was demonstrated that an audience of average musical level takes remarkably
little notice of the text, for to a song by Campion[1] the following words
were sung:

> Now that the sun hath sunk and risen,
> And she the world hath all forgiven,
> Though youth is wanting far and nigh,
> Yet from the embers falls the sky.

> Do not like others when-the time
> Seeking their passion from the rhyme,
> Though without e'er full straightly given
> Fast with a step too slow for heaven.

Actually only 6 per cent noticed that these words were nonsense;
16 per cent found them uninteresting, or in some way suspected that
they were unusual, or thought them badly enunciated (as a matter of
fact they were sung very clearly, but this is a natural psychological
reaction to nonsense words); 15 per cent thought they had attended to
the words but noticed nothing wrong; and the remaining 63 per cent
took no notice of the sense of the words at all.

Now though the abstract type of listeners combine in condemning
the representational effects of music, yet too much technical interest
may be equally distracting from full appreciation. Thinking about the
cleverness of the composer, or of oneself for elucidating his cleverness,
may easily become an end in itself, presumably gratifying some self-
assertive or constructive instinct; but such pleasure is hardly aesthetic.
Yet the attitude is to a large extent inevitable, even when (as in the

[1] Thomas Campion (1567–1620), English poet, composer, and theorist about
the art of each.

second experimental concert) an attempt is made to eliminate it by dispensing with programmes, in the hope that the music may be appreciated solely for itself. Although the audience were particularly requested not to regard the concert as a guessing competition, all but the most unmusical 12 per cent speculated as to the composers, their period, the performers, etc., in most of the items; the more musical half got about two-fifths of their guesses right, the less musical about one-quarter. The latter made fewer technical allusions, but criticized the performers more than the musical. The first item was a violin suite consisting of four movements, none of them originally written for the violin, by Purcell, Berlioz (Fugue on Brander's song from *Faust*), Rameau, and Mozart. Only about the most musical 20 per cent noticed any heterogeneity of styles, and not more than a third of these suspected it to be a hoax. Incidentally this shows that the supposed necessity for coherence and continuity in a sonata or suite, and the objection to music being transcribed, have little weight for the great majority of listeners. In another item, a Purcell 'Ground in Gamut,' only 16 per cent (again the most musical) noticed the ground bass; most of the rest, not knowing what it was about, were rather bored. Finally an original improvisation in the modern style was played, introducing the tune of 'God Save the King'; only one person noticed this theme, two guessed that it was an improvisation, while most of the others ascribed it to some such composer as Debussy, Stravinsky, Scriabin, or Goossens.

It appears, therefore, that abnormal conditions merely distort technical interest and make it more prominent; they are, in fact, most unsound. We inevitably interpret what we hear in the light of our past musical or non-musical experience; we build up special knowledge and means of perception so as to put ourselves into the appropriate period and style of the composer or of the title of the piece. We try to appreciate Beethoven's music not as a poor edition of Bach's, nor a funeral march as a gigue, but each for its own qualities. Completely abstract (that is, purely auditory) music is unattainable; and as music was primarily connected with words or other non-musical meaning, so-called absolute music being a later specialization, the representational attitude is almost equally unavoidable. Most musicians attach some significance to words such as *allegro* and *scherzo*, or even more suggestive ones such as *agitato*, *maestoso*, and *perdendosi*, so that they have no right to condemn fancy titles, analytic programmes, and the like; all help in the comprehension of the composer's intention. Nor is music generally of itself abstract or programme, but is largely what different listeners make of it. One person on hearing, say, a Handel gigue may visualize people dancing round a maypole; another will concentrate solely on the composer's technical devices. All that one can safely assert is that, among musicians with most experience, on the one hand the emotions tend to be controlled, integrated, and to lose their concrete reference, and on the other hand technical interests tend to be regarded as means to an end, to be used for getting the most out of music; but that, for fullest appreciation, they should become largely automatic and subconscious.

We must now return to visualization. In certain cases it assumes more musical forms. For instance, at the second concert many of the audience mentally saw the performers behind the screen; naturally this must be an almost constant element among a large number of people who listen in to broadcast music. The innumerable portraits in the *Radio Times* probably help in this process, and increase the so-called human element. Visual or other non-auditory means are also used in the actual perception and recall of music by most of the ordinary listeners, and even by about 10 per cent or more trained musicians. Some visualize the notes that are being played on the score or on the instruments, or else their names, or the name of the key; others respond to music not in terms of sound but by a subconscious tendency to hum it. Many also hear or think of music muscularly. They raise their heads or contract some other muscle when the music rises, or they perceive it in terms of their hands at the pianoforte or other instruments. Thus several of my audience noticed that their fingers tried to follow those of the pianists, others felt that they wanted to dance, especially in strongly rhythmic music. In slow movements any audience obviously sinks down with relaxed muscles; but it seems that, for most people, full perception of music requires that the body should be in good muscular tone and well braced; standards of taste are often lowered when one is reclining in a comfortable chair; possibly this is partly responsible for the high level of the tastes of a Promenade concert audience, many of whom have to stand up and are correspondingly capable of appreciating 'strong' music. Rhythm is an aspect of music that is more of a bodily than an auditory nature; over three-quarters of my audience acknowledged making considerable or moderate bodily responses to it, though often only feeling tendencies to move their legs, hands, etc., rather than actually swaying them to and fro. Again, the more musical seem to respond less overtly, more mentally or implicitly. We see, therefore, that much that is non-auditory may be quite efficient and helpful in appreciation, and far from being non-musical.

A phenomenon rather similar to visualization of scenes is 'coloured hearing,' or synaesthesia; out of about a hundred people with whom I dealt there were half-a-dozen genuine cases. As an example, one man, when he hears the chord of A major, sees the colour green and then remembers that green is A, so that he has absolute pitch through colour. For him the colours are essentially tonal, so that those corresponding to related keys are similar. They are only seen when a piece is characteristically in one key; in this case the notes of the music were seen mentally superimposed on a background of the prevailing key colour. Many other people have associations: for example, the trumpet reminding them of scarlet, the flute of blue, etc.; but real synaesthetic colours seem to be inextricably bound up with the actual perception and recollection of the notes. Synaesthetic persons always regard their colours as quite natural, and, until they inquire into the matter, imagine that everyone is like themselves in this respect, while actually no two synaesthetics are likely to agree in their colour schemes. Scriabin was a synaesthetic who very strongly associated odours as well as colours with music.

About half-a-dozen more subjects saw moving or stationary patterns when listening to music; such phenomena may appear ridiculous or incredible, yet of musicians with absolute pitch (say 30 to 40 per cent) the majority often have precisely analogous associations of keys, not with colours but with various emotional characteristics. They often state, for example, that the overture to *Die Meistersinger* could be in no other key but C major, and that E major is typical of such music as Mendelssohn so often wrote, and, as a corollary, that the overture to *Tannhäuser* is weakened by being largely written in E. Naturally such opinions may seem quite illogical to those who do not generalize in this way, which presumably results from associating this key, so often used by Mendelssohn, with one's emotional attitude toward him and his works, and then projecting this attitude, often unconsciously, on to the works of other composers in the same key. But again, even those without absolute pitch may associate specific chords or progressions with the style of, say, Vaughan Williams, or Franck, so that in general these are not, I think, non-musical phenomena. There is no essential difference between coloured hearing, seeing patterns, giving keys special characteristics, and mere generalizations about the style of well-known composers. Like the translation of heard music into terms of sight or muscles, they are merely modes of thinking, analogous to different languages; they are found at all musical levels, and there is no reason why everyone should not have individual peculiarities of this type without finding them to be irrelevant or distracting from the highest appreciation.

So far we have been considering some of the apparently non-musical responses or effects produced by music. We may now pass on to non-musical influences or stimuli that affect music.

The first of these are visual sensations; a few people listen with their eyes closed, but the great majority receive and react to a very large number of visual impressions while they are supposed to be listening. But this does not mean that all this side of their mental activity is wasted from a musical point of view. The amateur musician may attain to a fuller perception and appreciation of music by following the score, thus aiding hearing with vision; or by watching performers he may keep his attention more closely on the music and may follow the inner parts by seeing the appropriate instruments playing. Again, there is the important factor of intuition, a kind of subconscious perception by one member of a group of the bodily expressions of the thoughts and feelings of the rest, and hence an automatic realization of the 'atmosphere' or significance of these aggregate thoughts and feelings. A performer or a lecturer does not necessarily take conscious note of the stillness or fidgeting of his audience, but always knows by intuition if he is holding them or no. And on the listener's side, if a soloist, or a conductor and orchestra, are working up to a furious climax, or playing a very rhythmic piece, the audience tends to follow them and intuit their mental and bodily state by becoming similarly moved. Watching the performers also helps by intuition in the apprehension of their personalities which they express in the music, and so of their contribution to the total experience, for most people would allow, for example, that a Beethoven sonata played by Busoni was a far more valuable experience than the same sonata played note-perfectly by an average pianist. Any intuition or attitude in one member of the performers or audience is reciprocally reinforced by all the rest if they are sympathetically inclined toward one another and similarly interested in the music. Hence it is (as Brent-Smith points out) that Kreisler cannot attempt to play good music at an ordinary 'celebrity' concert, since he realizes that the audience are not in sympathy with him toward it. Several of my subjects find that they can only obtain full musical enjoyment if they are among sympathetic companions. Again, few would not admit that pleasant or suitable surroundings, even if not specifically attended to, enhance their appreciation. Thus an organ recital in a cathedral is aesthetically more valuable than the same recital in an ugly concert hall, though the latter may be acoustically superior.

However, among the musically more advanced the whole process of musical perception is so integrated that surroundings, performers, score, etc., are often regarded as distracting, and are seldom considered in deciding whether to go to concerts. They are often able to listen 'ideally,' that is, to value the music they hear largely by their own ideas as to how it should be played rather than by how it actually is played.

Personality and the like are only too apt to become objects of interest *per se;* a Pachmann, for example, is more often distracting and non-musical than relevant and helpful to appreciation, in that he tends to overbalance the music. I find an interesting division between people who like singers because their personality 'gets across' and the more musical people who, conversely, dislike most singers, especially female ones, because they are tying to 'make an effect.'

This brings us at once to the role of gregarious factors in musical appreciation. Frank Howes has dealt with them very fully in his 'Borderland of Music and Psychology,' but has, I think, as regards musical people, considerably over-emphasized them. His thesis is, roughly, that aesthetic appreciation is impossible without the gregarious satisfaction obtained by listening to music together with a large number of other people who are similarly moved; the amount of applause is determined not by the depth of feeling or the intensity of pleasure experienced, but by the homogeneity of feeling evoked in the whole audience. He regards applause as a necessity, since the audience feels, often subconsciously, after sitting still and listening for a long time, that it must do something, hence it is psychologically unjustifiable to discourage applause between the movements of a symphony or quartet. He also states, in support of this, that true musical enjoyment can never be obtained in solitude from the gramophone or broadcast music, or from playing the pianoforte to oneself. Now it must be acknowledged that the gregarious or fellowship feeling of seeing and hearing a large orchestra, or applauding in unison with a huge audience, are highly pleasurable to most people of the more or less unmusical type. But I find that as a rule the more musical people prefer string quartets and chamber music to orchestral music; they also object to being carried away, as a large group of people so often is, or to descending with the group to a lower level in the scale of civilization and self-control. Similarly, the desire to applaud, especially between movements, obviously becomes controlled and tends to disappear in really musical audiences, so that almost the only reasons why we do applaud, it seems to me, are convention, politeness to the performers, or the hope of getting an encore. Most of my audience, at the second concert, were glad to be relieved from it, and in general at Cambridge chamber music concerts it seldom lasts more than twenty seconds as compared with the one or two minutes that are so familiar at Promenade concerts and the like. In fact, one theory of aesthetics that contains a good deal of truth states that the essential features of the aesthetic experience are a complete equilibrium and harmony whereby there is no tendency to action at all; after it one should be as ready to do any action as willingly as any other, since all one's instincts and impulses have been satisfied, and it is only in so far as the experience is incomplete that there is a disposition toward any one action such as applause. Again, a large proportion of musical people seem to prefer to listen to broadcast or gramophone music when it is sufficiently well reproduced, and they like to play the pianoforte to themselves so as to escape these gregarious factors. However, people vary considerably in the strength of their gregarious and social tendencies, and for some this gregarious satisfaction is an essential element in their musical appreciation, and not necessarily to be condemned.

Many other non-auditory stimuli obviously affect musical appreciation, e.g., one's general comfort, recent emotional experiences, one's relative familiarity with different instruments, and various outside interests; the connection between mathematics or science and the higher appreciation of music is very marked. Hence the formalist's assumption that the artistic faculty is quite unconnected with ordinary life cannot be upheld. Temperament, personal and racial prejudices are of great importance; Parry, in his *Art of Music*, gives several examples of the influence of environment on music. The connection is, however, obscured by the factor of compensation, as, for instance, when very submissive people seem to like very vigorous music, or very aggressive ones like sentimental stuff. The unpopularity of German music among English audiences during the war is an illustration of the effect of non-musical prejudices, though here again the more musical were less influenced in their opinions. Similarly, I attempted to show the influence of a composer's name in my second concert by having played a nocturne by Field. Most of the audience were unable to guess the composer, or knew it already, but, as I had hoped, the remaining 18 per cent thought it was by Chopin, and their remarks indicate all their usual prejudices for, or usually against, Chopin, e.g., 'the Victorian drawing-room atmosphere' (the piece really having been composed in about 1814).

We largely adopt our tastes from the musical minority whose opinions we respect, and reject those of the unmusical majority. But this subjective nature of musical standards is a commonplace of musical criticism which I need not emphasize.

The conclusion of the discussion may now be pointed out. As a psychologist I have no intention of entering into the controversy as to the ethics of various factors, emotion, intellect, etc., in music. I have merely tried to show that a great many apparently non-musical factors always occur in the appreciation of various people to various degrees, depending on their individual mental and temperamental peculiarities and musical training, and that they may almost all of them help in the perception of music or add to the enjoyment or value obtained. On examining the part played by such factors at the lowest and highest musical levels and in the poorest and fullest appreciation, it seems that some of them tend to disappear or to become subconscious or controlled and integrated; so that it is only attention to any one aspect (be it intellectual, emotional, gregarious, or anything else), to the detriment of or distraction from the whole, that is really non-musical. The average marks given to different categories by individual members and by the whole of my audiences demonstrate the truth; the average marks for aesthetic appeal or value of different items did not run parallel either with the marks for intellectual interest or with those for emotion, but were almost exactly parallel with the sum of these two headings. From another approach, namely, genetic studies or case histories of several of my subjects, one finds that people usually seem to possess initially either, (*a*) a mainly objective, critical, or analytic attitude toward music, or, (*b*) a mainly subjective and emotional one. As their musical experience has developed each attitude has become more tinged with the other till they fuse in the fullest appreciation. Each person should be able to synthesize all his various dispositions, tendencies, instincts, impulses, etc., as many elements as possible being included. Thus we are justified in concluding that aesthetic appreciation, which we are now led up to via our examination of non-musical effects and influences, consists not so much in an absolute and definite experience that only a few highly cultured people attain to, but in this ideal organization and synthesis.

MUSICAL TIMES (1929

SIR THOMAS BROWNE

Music and the Deity

IT is my temper, and I like it the better, to affect all harmony; and
sure there is musick even in the beauty, and the silent note which
Cupid strikes, far sweeter than the sound of an instrument. For
there is a musick where ever there is a harmony, order or proportion;
and thus far we may maintain the musick of the Sphears: for those
well-ordered motions, and regular paces, though they give no sound
unto the ear, yet to the understanding they strike a note most full of
harmony. Whosoever is harmonically composed, delights in harmony;
which makes me much distrust the symmetry of those heads which
declaim against all Church-Musick. For my self, not only from my
obedience, but my particular Genius, I do embrace it: for even that
vulgar and Tavern-Musick, which makes one man merry, another
mad, strikes in me a deep fit of devotion, and a profound contemplation
of the first Composer. There is something in it of Divinity more than
the ear discovers: it is an Hieroglyphical and shadowed lesson of the
whole World, and creatures of God; such a melody to the ear, as the
whole World well understood, would afford the understanding. In
brief, it is a sensible fit of that harmony, which intellectually sounds in
the ears of God. I will not say with *Plato*, the soul is an harmony, but
harmonical, and hath its nearest sympathy unto Musick: thus some
whose temper of body agrees, and humours the constitution of their
souls, are born Poets, though indeed all are naturally inclined unto
Rhythme. This made *Tacitus* in the very first line of his Story, fall
upon a verse, and *Cicero* the worst of Poets, but declaiming for a Poet,
falls in the very first sentence upon a perfect Hexameter. I feel not in
me those sordid and unchristian desires of my profession; I do not
secretly implore and wish for Plagues, rejoyce at Famines, revolve
Ephemerides and Almanacks, in expectation of malignant Aspects,
fatal Conjunctions, and Eclipses: I rejoyce not at unwholesome Springs,
nor unseasonable Winters; my Prayer goes with the Husbandman's;
I desire everything in its proper season, that neither men nor the times
be put out of temper.   *RELIGIO MEDICI* (1642)

PHILIP HESELTINE

The Idea of a Song

Known as a composer under the pseudonym Peter Warlock, Heseltine (1894–1930) managed in his short life to endow English music with some magnificent songs, to write two scholarly works, and to edit a lively periodical, The Sackbut, to which the following was the Foreword.

AMONG the Chippewa Indians of North America, we are told, 'there is no musical notation; a picture of the idea of a song is drawn on a bark strip, from which another person who has never heard it can sing it accurately.'

This, like so much in the art of so-called primitive races, puts us all to shame. We cannot draw a picture of the idea of a piece of music from which another person who has never heard the music can get an accurate impression of what it is about. Yet if musical criticism has any purpose in it, that purpose is surely to convey, by words perhaps rather than by pictures, 'the idea of a song' to others who have never heard it.

Our chief enemy is Time. We can hold the score of a symphony in our hand complete and whole and all at once: but to hold the music signified by that score, the idea of the song, in the mind in a like completeness and wholeness is a very different and vastly more difficult proposition. When listening to music we are subject to all the limitations that time imposes: but when we reflect upon what we have heard, when we try to sum it all up, to distil its quintessence, we have to pit ourselves against time in an effort to transcend its restrictions on the mind.

To see a piece of music whole, like a picture, to grasp the rhythm and design not merely of particular sections but of the entire work— and, as the result of this process, to be able to comprehend and share with its composer the complex synthesis of mental and emotional states the work expresses—such is the task of the writer on music.

This being admitted, it becomes painfully apparent that when we speak or write about music—and here the professional critic is in much the same case as the man who tries to record the impressions of his first concert—we embark upon a well-nigh impossible task.

Music, for us, begins where words end: how then should we adequately translate music into words? Only the simplest music yields to our attempts to draw a satisfactory verbal picture of the idea underlying it. We have lost the art of the old magicians who could compass the universe in a pentacle.

Music, one may say, is the outward and audible signification of inward and spiritual realities: implying, it would seem, that there is something else behind or beyond the music itself, that is not the music. And yet, some will reply, are we justified in assuming the separateness of the two things? Is it not, in a sense, the expression that makes the thought, the symbol that makes the reality, that *is*—as far as we can ever know it—the reality?

The fact is that when we come to the fundamental question of what music really is, we are all—composers, critics, and public alike—very much in the dark. Music's a rum go. Composers cannot really tell you how or why they write this or that kind of music, and professional critics are inclined to avoid the simpler and profounder problems of the art, taking refuge in technicalities which the ordinary music lover— who is always more interested in music's relation to life than in its relation to other music—finds more bewildering than the most abstruse specimen of actual composition. Thus the simplest and most natural questions of the non-musician are apt to prove the most embarrassing to the theorist or the critic who has so long taken these elementary problems for granted as already solved, that he has no answer but gibberish or evasion. The plain man is kept perpetually in the position of the child who is 'not old enough' for the intelligence he demands. Nevertheless the general public has frequently welcomed and understood the man of original creative genius long before his fellow-composers and critics have ceased chattering their protests against his drunken and disorderly conduct.

[Hence] it is to be hoped that something may be done to break down the barrier of unnecessary modesty which so frequently prevents the non-professional music lover from contributing to discussions on musical subjects, by showing him that music is not the esoteric mystery that many of its professors and pseudo-critical jargon-mongers would have him believe, and that the only honourable ideal of the musical critic is so to educate and enlighten his public that he himself, as a professional institution, will in the end become unnecessary.

FOREWORD TO *THE SACKBUT* (1920)

MUSIC AND DRAMA

JEAN-JACQUES ROUSSEAU

The Paris Opera in 1760

A musician all his life, Rousseau not only composed and copied music, but contributed voluminously to its theory. In his influential novel, The New Héloïse, *he inserted the following bit of satire in the form of a letter addressed by the hero, Saint-Preux, to his country cousin, Mme d'Orbe.*

IMAGINE a crate about fifteen feet long and proportionately wide: that is the stage. On each side are placed a row of screens on which the settings of the acts to be played are crudely painted. The backdrop is a big curtain, similarly daubed and almost always torn, which may represent caverns on earth or holes in the sky, depending on the perspective. Everyone who walks across the stage behind this curtain produces a sort of tremor in it which is rather attractive. The sky is represented by some bluish rags that hang from rods or ropes like laundry on a line. The sun, which is occasionally to be seen, is a torch inside a lantern. The chariot for the gods and goddesses is made of two-by-fours hung like a swing within a frame, the god sitting on a transverse board in front of which is bunched some tinted cloth—the cloud appropriate to the god's magnificence. Near the bottom of the machine stand two or three stinking candles, which, while the illuminated personage waves and shrieks in his little swing, smoke him up to his heart's content—incense worthy of the god.

Since chariots form the most important part of the Opera's equipment, you can from these infer the rest. The troubled sea consists of long structures of blue cloth or cardboard mounted on parallel rods and turned by urchins. Thunder is a heavy cart drawn across the beams—by no means the least touching instrument of this delightful band. Lightning is achieved by throwing handfuls of resinous pitch on a lighted torch; but a real bolt calls for a fuse and rocket.

The stage is provided with little square trap-doors which on being opened signify that demons are coming up from the cellar. Should they need to rise into the air, they are cleverly replaced by straw demons of brown buckram, or sometimes by actual chimney sweeps who majestically vanish into the aforementioned blue rags. But what is really tragic is when the ropes jam or break, for then the infernal spirits or immortal gods fall and break their legs and are sometimes killed. To all this you must add the monsters used to lend excitement to certain scenes (such as dragons, lizards, tortoises, crocodiles, or large toads), which, by perambulating the stage in a menacing way, permit us to witness the Temptations of Saint Anthony. Each of these characters is animated by a lout of a Savoyard who actually hasn't sense enough to act the dumb beast.

But what you cannot imagine is the frightful cries, the prolonged bellowings, which fill the theatre during the performance. You see actresses virtually in convulsions as they rend from their lungs the most violent ululations; both fists clenched against the breast, the head thrown back, cheeks aflame, veins bursting, and diaphragm heaving. It is impossible to say which is the more unpleasantly assailed, the eye or the ear; these motions cause as much pain to those who look as the singing to those who listen, but what is still more astonishing is that the howls and cries are almost the only thing applauded by the audience. From the handclapping you might suppose a company of deaf-mutes in a frenzy of delight at catching here and there a few piercing sounds, and eager to encourage their repetition. For my part, I am convinced that people applaud a prima donna as they do the feats of the strong man at a fair. The sensations are painfully disagreeable, hard to endure, but one is so glad when it is all over that one cannot help rejoicing. Remember, besides, that this style of singing at the Opera is used to express the tenderest, most courtly thoughts of Quinault;[1] think of the Muses, the Graces, the Cherubs—Venus herself—uttering their souls with such delicacy, and you can judge!

THE NEW HÉLOÏSE (1761)

---

[1] Librettist of Lulli's operas (1635–88); see p. 94.

ROGER NORTH

Semi-Operas

Attorney-General under James II, historian, and biographer, Roger North (1653–1734) also left sizable manuscripts about music, which until the middle of the last century were known only through extracts in Dr. Burney's History.

IT had bin strange if the gentlemen of the theatres had sate still all this while, seeing as they say a pudding creep, that is, a violent inclination in the towne to follow musick, and they not serve themselves of it. Therefore Mr. Betterton who was the chief ingineer of the stage, contrived a sort of plays, which were called Operas, but had been more properly styled Semi-Operas, for they consisted of half musick, and half drama. The chief of these were *Circe*[1], *The Fayery Queen*,[2] *Dioclesian*,[3] and *King Arthur*;[4] which later was composed by Purcell, and is unhappyly lost. These were followed at first, but by an error of mixing two capitall entertainments, could not stand long. For some that would come to the play hated the musick, and others that were very desirous of the musick, would not bear the interruption that so much rehearsal gave; so that it is best to have either by it self intire.

MEMOIRS OF MUSICK (1728)

[1] By Charles Davenant, music by Banister (1676).
[2] Adapted from *A Midsummer Night's Dream*, music by Purcell (1692).
[3] Adapted from Beaumont and Fletcher's *Prophetess*, music by Purcell (1690).
[4] Text by Dryden (1691). The score as we have it lacks five of the original numbers.

STENDHAL

Banish the Libretto

P LEASE note that I speak throughout of the music, not of the words, which I never know. I always recast for myself the words of an opera. I catch the poet's situation and take from him a single word, just one, to designate the sentiment. For example, I find in Mustafa[1] a man who is bored with his greatness and his mistress, and yet is a prince not without vanity. The full complement of words might well spoil this notion for me. Too bad! No doubt it would have been better had Voltaire or Beaumarchais written the libretto. It would then be as delightful as the music. One could read it without the least disenchantment. But since Voltaires are scarce, it is fortunate that the charming art which concerns us can manage so well without the aid of a great poet. Only, one must not be so rash as to read the libretto. At Vicenza I noticed that people perused it the first night in order to get an idea of the action. At each successive number one read the first verse, which names the passion or the nuance of the sentiment depicted by the music. Never during the next forty performances did it occur to anyone to open that little book covered with gold paper.

In Venice, Mme. B——, who also feared the disagreeable effect of the libretto, would not allow it in her box even on the first night. Someone summarized the plot for her very briefly, and then by means of numbers gave her in four of five words the subject of each air, duet, or ensemble—for example, jealousy of Ser Taddeo, passionate declaration of Lindor, coquetting of Isabella with the Bey.[1] This résumé was followed by the first verse of the air or duet. I saw that everyone found this idea most convenient, and that is the way they should edit librettos for amateurs who—really I don't know how to avoid sounding conceited—for amateurs who love music as they love it in Venice.

LIFE OF ROSSINI (1824)

---

[1] In Rossini's *L'Italiana in Algeri* (1813)

CLAUDIO MONTEVERDI

The Passionate Style

REFLECTION shows the principal emotions of mankind to be three: anger, equanimity, and supplication or humility. This truth is corroborated by what the great philosophers say, as well as by the character of the human voice with its high, low, and middle pitch. It is further manifested clearly in the art of sound through its threefold expressions—passionate, soft, and calm. But though I have carefully searched the works of earlier composers, I have not been able to find any examples of the passionate style—only of the calm and soft. Yet Plato speaks of the agitated style in the third book of his *Republic* when he describes 'that kind of harmony which fittingly imitates the voice and accents of a brave man going into battle.'

Now I am aware that contrasts are what stir our souls, and that such stirring is the aim of all good music. As Boethius puts it: 'Music was given us either to purify or to degrade our conduct.' Accordingly, I set about by study and effort to rediscover this style of expression, and finding that all the best philosophers declare that a Pyrrhic, that is to say, a rapid, tempo should be used for all war-like or agitated dances, and on the contrary a slow tempo for the opposite situations, I pondered the repeated crotchet, which seemed to me to correspond to a spondee when performed by an instrument. And when I reduced this note to semiquavers, and matched these one-to-one with a speech connoting anger and disdain, I could hear in this simple example the likeness of the effect I was seeking—and this even though the voice could not keep pace with the speed of the instrument.

In order to test the device still further, I had recourse to the divine Tasso, as being the poet who expresses most aptly and most naturally in words the passions he wishes to describe. I turned to the account he gives of the combat between Tancred and Clorinda[1] and there I found as subject for my music the two contrary passions of battle and prayer on the point of death.

---

[1] In the twelfth canto of *Jerusalem Delivered*.

In the year 1624 I offered my work[1] for a hearing by the noblest citizens of Venice at the house of the Honourable Gerolamo Mozzenigo, knight and notable of the Venetian Republic, who is my special patron and protector. I was heard, much applauded, and praised.

My principles having met with success in the imitation of anger, I pursued my investigations by further diligent study and produced divers compositions, both sacred music and chamber works, which were so successful in point of style that other composers praised them not only in words but also in their writings, by imitating my technique in their own works, to my great honour and joy.

PREFACE TO *MADRIGALS OF WAR AND LOVE* (1638)

[1] The famous *Combattimento*, in which among other innovations are to be found effective tremolos and pizzicati.

THOMAS LOVE PEACOCK

Mangled Operas and the Star System

*Between 1815 and 1835, Peacock was known among London men of letters
as a critic of plays and operas no less than as an essayist and book reviewer
attached to several magazines. The occasion of the long review essay from
which the following is taken was the appearance of the fourth, enlarged edition
of Lord Mount Edgcumbe's* Musical Reminiscences. *The noble lord, second
earl of the name, was an amateur composer who lived between 1764 and 1839,
and whose reminiscences span the years 1773–1834.*

THE object proposed by the Italian Opera is to present the
musical drama in the most perfect possible form. To this end
there must be, in the first place, a good drama: an interesting
story, intelligibly told in good poetry, and affording ample scope for
strong and diversified expression: good music, adapting the sound to
the sense, and expressing all the changes and trains of feeling that
belong to the ideas and images of the drama: good performers—
persons of good figures and features—picturesque in action, and
expressive in countenance—with voices of fine tone and great power,
having true intonation, scientific execution, and above all, or rather as
the crown of all, expression—expression—expression: the one all-
pervading and paramount quality, without which dramatic music is
but as a tinkling cymbal: elegant and appropriate dresses—beautiful
scenery—a chorus, each of whom should seem as if he knew that he
had some business of his own in the scene, and not as if he were a
mere unit among thirty or forty automata, all going like clockwork
by the vibrations of the conductor's pendulum: a full orchestra of
accomplished musicians, with a good leader—and especially without
a conductor keeping up, in the very centre of observation, a gesticulation and a *tapage* that make him at once the most conspicuous and
most noisy personage in the assembly, distracting attention from the
sights and sounds that ought exclusively to occupy it—an affliction to
the eye, and a most pestilent nuisance to the ear. But, with all this,
there should be (as there used to be) an audience regulating its costume

and its conduct by the common conventional courtesies of evening society; not with men wearing hats among well-dressed women, and rubbing dirty boots against white petticoats; nor with an influx of late-comers, squeezing themselves between the crowded benches, and sitting down in the laps of their precursors, as we have both seen and suffered. We are aware that some advocates for universal liberty think that the morning liberty of the streets should be carried into all evening assemblies; but, looking back to the Athenians, we cannot consider that cleanliness and courtesy are incompatible with the progress of freedom and intelligence.

Now, by following out the principal points which we have enumerated a little in detail, we shall see what we have had, and what we have wanted—what we are likely to have, and what we are likely to continue to want—for the bringing together of the constituent portions of a perfect musical drama. Lord Mount Edgcumbe touches all these points. We shall content ourselves, on the present occasion, with citing a few of his observations, and expressing our own opinions in a subsequent commentary:

The opera in England, for the period of ten years after the departure of Catalani,[1] will afford much less room for observation than any of the preceding, as far as the singers are concerned; for, with one or two exceptions, there were not any of whom I feel inclined to say much, because there is not much to be said in their praise. But so great a change has taken place in the character of the dramas, in the style of the music, and in its performance, that I cannot help enlarging a little on that subject before I proceed farther.

One of the most material alterations is, that the grand distinction between serious and comic operas is nearly at an end, the separation of the singers for their performance entirely so. Not only do the same sing in both, but a new species of drama has arisen, a kind of mongrel between them, called *semi-seria*, which bears the same analogy to the other two that that nondescript the melodrama does to the legitimate tragedy and comedy of the English stage. . . .

He adds:

The consequence of this is that all the new dramas written for Rossini's music are most execrably bad, and contain scarcely one line that can be called poetry, or even one of common sense.

[1] Angelica Catalani (1780–1849), one of the most accomplished sopranos of the nineteenth century. She left England in 1813 after seven years during which she was the most tyrannical and most highly paid of prima donnas.

This sweeping condemnation is by no means merited. Some of Rossini's libretti are detestable enough; but there is much good dramatic poetry in some of them, *Tancredi* and *Semiramide*[1] especially. It is true that in these dramas the Italian poet had only to condense the essence of Voltaire's tragedies, but the task is well executed. The libretto of Donizetti's *Anna Bolena*[2] is an excellent dramatic poem.

It is seldom that we are enabled to judge fairly either of an Italian libretto, or of the music of an opera as a whole. For example, in 1832 Mr. Monck Mason professed to bring forward Pacini's *Gli Arabi nelle Gallie*.[3] He first cut it into halves, and put the second half aside, or into the fire. He then cut away the beginning and substituted that of Rossini's *Zelmira*.[4] He then tacked a strange air, we forget from whence, to the middle, by way of an end, and thus presented to the public both author and composer literally without head or tail. The critics discovered that the drama was nonsense, and that much of the music was stolen; and Pacini and his poet bore the blame which belonged to the manager. This mode of murdering reputations ought to subject the offender to an action for damages. 'I was induced, unfortunately,' says Lord Mount Edgcumbe, 'to go one night to see *Gli Arabi nelle Gallie*, a very poor opera by Pacini.' What he saw was poor enough, but it was not Pacini's opera. In the same season Bellini's *La Straniera*,[5] which has much beautiful melody, and an interesting and intelligible story, founded on the Vicomte d'Arlincourt's *L'Etrangère*,[6] was presented in such a chaotic fashion that the intentions of both poet and composer remained an unfathomable mystery.

These liberties are taken more or less with the works of all masters, from the greatest to the least. Mozart himself does not escape them. Interpolation indeed he does escape. The audiences of the King's Theatre are justly strict in this one point only, that they will not permit the sewing on of an extraneous purple shred to any of his great and sacred textures. But garbled and mutilated his works are abominably, to fit the Procrustean bed of an inadequate company, or to quadrate with the manager's notions of the bad taste of the public. A striking instance of this is in the invariable performance of *Il Don*

---

[1] 1813 and 1823 respectively.   [2] I.e., Anne Boleyn, 1830.
[3] *The Arabs in Gaul*, 1827.   [4] 1821.
[5] *The Foreign Woman*, 1829.
[6] Victor Prévost, Vicomte d'Arlincourt (1789–1856) wrote a number of semi-successful works, foreshadowing the preciosity of the Decadents.

Giovanni without its concluding sestetto. Don Juan's first introduction to a modern English audience was in a pantomime (at Drury Lane, we believe), which ended with the infernal regions, a shower of fire, and a dance of devils.[1] Mozart's opera has, properly, no such conclusion. Flames arise—a subterranean chorus is heard—Don Juan sinks into the abyss—the ground closes above him—Leporello remains on the stage: a strongly marked modulation leads from the key of D minor into that of G major, with a change from common time andante to triple time allegro assai; and the other characters, ignorant of the catastrophe, rush in to seek their revenge:

> *Ah! dov' è il perfido,*
> *Dov' è l'indegno?*[2]

Leporello explains the adventure, and after a general exclamation, a solemn pause, and an exceedingly sweet larghetto movement, in which the dramatis personae dispose of themselves, '*Or che tutti, o mio tesoro,*' the opera is wound up by a fugue in D major—'*Questo è il fin di chi fa mal*':[3] one of the very finest things in dramatic music, and the most appropriate possible termination of the subject; and yet is this most noble composition, this most fitting and genuine conclusion, sacrificed to a dance of devils flashing torches of rosin, for no earthly reason but that so ended the Drury Lane pantomime.

Le Nozze de Figaro and *Il Flauto Magico*[4] both require a better and more numerous company than is ever assembled in this country. If we have in the former an Almaviva, a Figaro, a Contessa, and a Susanna, it is the usual extent of our good fortune. We have seldom an endurable Cherubino; Marcellina is generally a nonentity: Barbarina always so; Bartolo, Basilio, and Antonio take their chance, which is seldom good for any of them, and never for all; and Don Curzio is for the most part abrogated.

Il Don Giovanni and *Le Nozze di Figaro* are both specimens of excellently written libretti, separating most effectively the action and passion from the ratiocination of the originals; but we have seen the

[1] This seems to have been 'traditional' since the second Viennese production of 1791.

[2] 'Ah, where is the faithless, the worthless Don . . .'

[3] 'Now that all have gone, my darling . . . ,' and 'Such is the end of all evil doers. . . .'

[4] *The Marriage of Figaro* and *The Magic Flute.*

latter especially performed in such a manner, that if we had known nothing of it but from the representation, we should have found it incomprehensible; and this sort of experiment on things which we know well should make us cautious of pronouncing summary judgment on things of which we know nothing but from the showing of the King's Theatre.

Il Flauto Magico is a well-written libretto, but the subject is too mystical to be interesting, or even generally intelligible; and this is a great drawback on its theatrical popularity, which has never approached that of the *Giovanni* and *Figaro*, though the music exhausts all the fascinations of both melody and harmony, and may be unhesitatingly cited as the absolute perfection of both. It requires more good singers than either of the others, and it requires them the more imperatively, as it depends more exclusively on the music. It requires seventeen voices besides the chorus. The music which is assigned to the three nymphs and the other genii is almost supernaturally beautiful: for this alone there should be six good voices, and there are, without these, six principal and five secondary parts. We may therefore despair of ever hearing this opera performed as it ought to be.

The works of Italian composers do not require, in any instance that we remember, so many performers. Those of the most modern composer of any name—Bellini—are singularly restricted in their principal parts. He seems to endeavour to defend himself against the caprices and jealousies of the performers by giving them nothing to quarrel about. A prima soprano, a primo tenore, a primo basso, and the ordinary components of a chorus, can perform his *Pirata*.[1] There can be no dispute here about pre-eminence, but the general effect is necessarily meagre. But the progress of self-conceit among singers has made this result inevitable. A prima soprano is now to be found everywhere, and a seconda nowhere; and though many who assume to be first are scarcely fit to be second, they will not be content with what they are fit for, but will be first or nothing. There appears to be this great difference between a German and an Italian company—that the Germans will co-operate to the production of general effect, and the Italians will look to nothing but their own individual display. We have seen, in a German opera, the same person taking a principal part one night, and singing in the chorus the next. We have seen the

[1] 1827.

same with the French; but with the Italians this never occurs. A German author and composer may therefore give fair scope to their subject; but the Italians must sacrifice everything to their company, and all in vain, except for the first production—for to the whims and inefficiency of every new company the unfortunate opera must be refitted and garbled. Bellini's is the true plan for his own reputation. A soprano, a tenor, a bass, and a chorus there must be in every company, and they can have nothing to quarrel for; but the musical drama must be ruined if this were to become the rule of its construction. And the scheme, after all, is not always successful: for in 1830 the prima donna transposed the middle and end of *Il Pirata*, in order that she might finish it herself instead of the tenor.

'*Ma femme, et cinq ou six poupets*,' will not make a company in the opinion of any one but Catalani's husband.[1] No one, indeed, who has seen and heard Catalani, or Pasta, or Malibran, or Giulietta Grisi,[2] would willingly dispense with one such prima donna; but the single star should not be worshipped exclusively to the sacrifice of the general effect. She can be but a component, however important, part of it; and if the general effect fails, the star will fall.

But with us, though the star cannot shine if the general effect be bad, no general effect, however otherwise excellent, will produce attraction without a star. In 1832, though the star of the French opera of *Robert le Diable* (Madame Cinti)[3] was but one of the fourth magnitude, yet with her eclipse the opera fell. The manager has collected stars, but not a company: there is a soprano too much, and a contralto too little—a tenor wanting, and a basso to spare: they patch up a performance as they may—altering, garbling, omitting, interpolating —and the result is a bad concert instead of a good opera. A good opera is a whole, as much in the music as in the poetry, and cannot be dislocated and disfigured by omissions and interpolations, without destruction to its general effect.

Lord Mount Edgcumbe justly observes that

a mean economy prevails in all the inferior departments, with regard to

---

[1] A soldier and gambler in the French diplomatic service, named Valabrègue. His remark was: 'My wife and five or six dolls (*poupées*)—that's all you need [for an opera].'

[2] All famous prima donnas. See pp. 83 and 184.

[3] Laure Cinthie Damoreau (1801–63), French soprano who sang under the name of Cinti. For *Robert le Diable*, see pp. 121, 123 and ff.

secondary singers, the chorus, and orchestra: the scenery, decorations, and wardrobe are in every respect unworthy of the largest theatre in the country.

But the enormous expense of the principal singers and dancers would not alone render this mean economy necessary, if it were not for the enormous rent exacted for the house. By a rough calculation which we made the other day, it appeared to us that the Italian Opera has been carried on in England for about a century and a quarter, at an average net loss of £5,000 a year; but of late years the Opera has yielded what would have been a liberal profit to the proprietors of the theatre, if it had been carried on by the proprietors, and not by a lessee, saddled with a disproportionate rent.

Lord Mount Edgcumbe reprobates the novel introduction of a conductor into the orchestra, not playing himself but beating time with a noisy baton. Assuredly our Italian opera conductor verifies the remark of Dr. Burney:[1]

Rousseau says, that the more time is beaten the less it is kept; and it is certain that when the measure is broken, the fury of the musical general, or director, increasing with the disorder and confusion of his troops, he becomes more violent, and his strokes and gesticulations more ridiculous in proportion to their disorder.

Lord Mount Edgcumbe makes some observations on the change which has taken place in the appearance and conduct of the audience of the King's Theatre, which we fully agree with him is a change altogether for the worse. We confess we have a prejudice in favour of sitting at our ease among well-mannered company, and we have been elbowed and annoyed out of all endurance of the pit at the Opera. Amongst the principal causes of this change is the profuse admission of orders; and on what ground these are given we saw the other day some curious evidence in a case in the Court of Requests. One of the former managers of the Opera had set up a paper called the *Theatrical Critic*, which did not succeed, and had left off in debt to the editor two guineas, for which important amount he was summoned; and it appeared that, in postponing the payment, he had told the editor a box was always at his service. After this we need not wonder at the heterogeneous composition of the audience in the pit. Assuredly those who pay have a right to complain, if they find all the places preoccupied by those who do not. They do not complain,

[1] See p. 146.

however, but they exercise another right more fatal to the management, and more just to its misconduct—the right of staying away. In short, as Lord Mount Edgcumbe justly observes:

The whole system is radically bad; and nothing can restore the Opera in this country to its former respectable and agreeable footing, or the performances to that excellence which a public paying so dearly has a right to expect, but a total reformation, an entire change of proprietors, of managers, of all parties connected with the theatre, I had almost said, hampered and embarrassed as it is, of the theatre itself.

We should be sorry to change the theatre, because it is the finest vehicle for sound in Europe; but we wish to see it thoroughly reformed in all the points to which we have adverted, and in another very important matter—that of its exits and its entrances. It was not intended for a crowd, but it is now often crowded, legitimately or artificially; and the occurrence of a fire on a crowded night would ensure the destruction of the audience. It is surrounded, or rather built in, by shops and taverns, and even the alarm of fire in any one of these would occasion incalculable mischief.

But it is vain to anticipate any reform of this theatre while it is in the hands of the assignees of a bankrupt estate, who think only of exacting the utmost possible rent within the year—(a double rent, in short: first, a fair return on the capital; and, second, a most unfair and unjustifiable tax on the monopoly of the license)—from an impresario who is only an annual tenant, who can, therefore, make no prospective arrangements—who is always taken unprovided at the beginning of the season—who thinks of nothing but how to make both ends meet at the end of it—who trusts to his skill in the 'detection of a star' to redeem himself by a temporary attraction in the course of it—and who, if he can fill the theatre by a fiddler or a dancer, is content to let the opera take its chance.

COLLECTED ESSAYS (1835)

BEAUMARCHAIS

A New Kind of Opera

During his high-spirited career, the author of the Figaro comedies tried his hand at many things, including the fomenting of American Independence. Reforming opera was no doubt a more difficult enterprise, whence the need for a diplomatic preparation of the public, as shown below.

Ast ego barbarus sum[1]

To the Opera Subscribers who would like to like Opera

Not the art of singing, not that of modulation, nor the combining of sounds—not music in itself—is my present theme. My theme is the action of poetry on music and the reaction of music on dramatic poetry in works where the two arts are conjoined. I want to analyse not so much a new opera as a new means of making opera interesting.

To predispose you to listen to me with some favour, let me say, dear contemporaries, that I know of no century in which I should prefer to have been born, no nation to which I would rather belong. Apart from the charms of French society, I find that for the last thirty or forty years there has been among us a lively sense of enterprise —a general desire to enlarge thought by intelligent research and to increase the happiness of all by the use of reason.

The last century is often cited as an age of great literature. But what is literature among man's many useful endeavours? A noble exercise of the mind. Our century will be instanced as one of deep science and philosophy, rich in discoveries, full of energy and reason. The mind of the nation seems to be in a happy kind of crisis: a bright light over all things makes each one feel that everything could be better. People are concerned, agitated, resourceful; they innovate and reform; and from the profound science of government to the frivolous art of

[1] But then I'm a barbarian.

making melodies; from the heights of genius upon which we behold Voltaire and Buffon, down to the easy and lucrative trade of criticizing that which one cannot do, I see throughout all classes of society a desire for accomplishment and right opinion, for the extension of one's ideas, knowledge, pleasures, and the increase of one's contributions to the common good. Thus it is that everything grows, prospers, and improves. Let us, if possible, see if we can improve a great type of entertainment.

The mind needs relaxation. After the compulsory strain of business one must follow one's hobby—one man hunts, the other drinks; this one gambles, another intrigues. For my part, lacking as I do all these diversions, I have fashioned a modest opera. To forestall argument, I will readily agree that of all literary frivolities the most frivolous is to write a poem of this kind. I agree also that if the author of such a work were going to complain of the little esteem he gains by it, he would be ridiculously unhappy and unhappily ridiculous—the silliest man among all his enemies.

But whence this contempt for the poem of an opera? When all is said and done, the making is not so easy as it seems. Can it be that the French nation is fonder of songs than of music and prefers vaudeville and its epigrams to music and its madrigals? Someone has said that the French really like ditties but only pretend (from vanity) to like music. I would not press the point for fear of confirming it. I would incline rather to believe that our indifference to operatic poems is due to the fact that in opera the poor jointing of the constituent arts creates confusion in the mind as to their respective ranks, and as to the pleasure to be expected from each.

Their true ranking, it seems to me, is as follows: first, the plot or invention of the subject which sustains the interest; then the beauty of the poem, including narrative skill; next the charm of music, which is but a new expressiveness added to the charms of verse; finally, the ornament of the dance, whose gaiety or loveliness relieves certain static situations.

Yet by a reversal peculiar to opera, it would seem that the play counts as nothing but a vulgar excuse for displaying every other merit. The accessories have usurped the first place, while the fundamental subject has become a trifling accessory. It is a mere canvas on which everybody else embroiders. How has this come about? Why is it that the most zealous followers of opera (myself among them) are always bored at a performance? This is the ancient problem which I shall now try to explain in my own way.

I start from the conviction that the public cannot err. Led by pleasure, it will follow wherever pleasure is to be found. If one kind of satisfaction eludes the spectator, he turns to something else. Bored at the opera because he cannot hear the words, he recoups himself with music. But this art, deprived of the dramatic interest which the poem might give, merely tickles the ear and must soon yield to the dance, which, moreover, holds the eye. As regards this undermining of true theatrical art, obviously, the spectator is right and the spectacle wrong.

Boileau once wrote to Racine: 'There will never be such a thing as a good opera, for music cannot tell a story.' In his day he was right. He might even have added: 'Music cannot carry on a dialogue.' No one suspected then that this development was possible. Again, in a letter of that great man who thought of everything and wrote of everything—I mean Voltaire—one reads these remarkable words: 'The opera is but a social meeting place where one goes on certain days, without quite knowing why. It is a house where everybody goes, even though one cares nothing for the host and finds him utterly dull.' Before Voltaire, La Bruyère had said: 'Clearly, opera is a sketch for a grand spectacle; I can form a notion of it; but I cannot tell how such perfect music and such regal expense have so perfectly and regally bored me.'

Speaking for myself, who am sensitive to the pleasure of good music and who delight in many a piece at the keyboard, I find the same piece burdensome when it is restored to the operatic setting from which it came. And I think I know why. There is too much music in dramatic music. To adopt the crude maxim of the justly celebrated Chevalier Gluck, our opera *puzza di musica*: it stinks of music. I conclude that music in an opera should be like poetry—only another means of embellishing speech and one which must not be used to excess.

Our dramatic poets long ago noticed that the splendour of words and the poetical lavishness which are proper to the ode were too exalted for the stage. They knew that in order to hold attention they must tone down this poetic bedazzlement and bring verse closer to nature. A play requires the simple and native truth. This reform accomplished in drama remains to be carried out in music.

But here the vain musician, lacking taste or genius, may want to lord it over the poet or make of his music an independent work. The play had then better look out for itself. The spectator sees only incoherence, divided interest, disconnected effects, and want of unity. For two purposes cannot produce a single result and must necessarily spoil the show. Therefore, just as a French author says to his translator, 'Since you are Italian, turn this into Italian, but without adding extraneous matter,' so I, as dramatic poet, will say to my collaborator, 'Since you are a musician, translate this poem into music, but do not, like Pindar, wander off into irrelevancy and sing of Castor and Pollux apropos of an athletic victory: they have nothing to do with the case.'

I cannot repeat often enough that musical excess is the vice of our grand opera. Music is what makes it so slow. As soon as the actor sings, the action stops—that is, if he sings merely to sing—and when the action stops the spectators' minds wander. 'But,' you will say, 'what else can the poor actor do but sing? It is his only idiom.' 'True, but he should try to make us forget it.' The composer's art ought to accomplish precisely this. Let the subject be sung for the same reason that it is couched in verse—as an ornament. I want an added charm, not a cause for distraction. I who have faithfully cherished music, at all times and places, find myself saying to it with an ungracious shove of the shoulder, 'Out of my way, Music! Why repeat yourself so much? Why so slow? Instead of lively narration, you give us twice-told tales. Instead of depicting passion, you cling to empty words!'[1] What is the upshot? While the poet makes every effort to save words and tighten his style, the musician contrariwise dilutes his, doles out syllables, dissolves them in repeats, saps their strength, and kills their meaning. The one pulls this way, the other that. In between I yawn and leave the hall.

To bring me back, and pleasure with me, let us try to re-establish the several arts of opera in their natural order. Does not the very word 'opera' signify their union? Carrying forward the efforts made by Chevalier Gluck in his *Iphigénie* and *Alceste*, let us add a few remarks on librettos and their employment.

In the first place, an opera must be neither a tragedy nor a comedy, though it has connections with each and may embrace both. I should

[1] Beaumarchais quotes these three lines from his Preface to *The Barber of Seville* (1775).

therefore not choose a wholly tragical subject. The tone would be so austere that entertainments would seem dropped incongruously from on high. Let us equally avoid a pure comedy plot. Passion and grandiose moments are alike incompatible with it, and hence the corresponding music would be too lacking in nobility. I rather think that for an opera historical subjects are less successful than imaginary ones. Must we then treat the impossible wonders of fairyland, which strike us as shocking or absurd? Experience has shown that the intervention of the gods and the unravelling of the plot by magical means invariably leave us cold. Now, mythological subjects usually exhibit these defects, and in my system I can only afford to ration music if I am lavish with dramatic excitement. Again, since the slow pace of musical discourse forbids amplification in words, the interest must be concentrated on the groupings, the masses, which must be strong and clear. Situations are paramount in the theatre, but they are indispensable in lyric drama, for sheer movement has to replace the other kind of eloquence.

I infer from all this that one should strike a happy medium between legendary and historical drama. I also think that civilized manners are too regular for the theatre. Oriental manners, being less orderly and familiar, leave the imagination freer and seem best suited to opera. Wherever despotism reigns, contrasts are marked—slavery is close to power, love next to ferocity. The passions of the great rage unchecked. One may behold in a single person the most abysmal ignorance and the most unlimited power, an unworthy cowardice and a contemptuous pride of place. In such climes, I see the abuse of power trifling with the lives of men and the modesty of women. Rebellion and tyranny go hand in hand, for the despot makes everyone tremble, and he trembles himself, simultaneously. This chaos is very much to the point. It spurs the poet's imagination and disturbs his mind so as to produce *strangenesses*—to use Montaigne's expression. These, in short, are the circumstances most favourable to opera; they allow every kind of atmosphere, just as the seraglio permits every kind of situation. Within them, one can be by turns lively, solemn, gay, playful, menacing, or jocose. The very religions of the Orient have something wondrous about them which compels attention and promotes suspense.

And now suppose it possible to crown the whole with a great philosophical idea—indeed make the subject arise from the idea— then the resulting entertainment would not be idle. All right-thinking men would in fact be grateful for such an opera. Though partisanship might set the dogs of ignorance and envy howling, the public would still recognize that a work of this sort was not to be despised. The response might even encourage men of greater genius to repeat the attempt and offer to the greatest nation in the world a new genre for their delectation.

Whatever others may do, such has been my aim. *Tarare* is the title of my opera, but it is not the subject. The subject is that of the following maxim, which is at once severe and comforting:

> Man! Thy merit on the earth,
> Does not depend upon thy birth:
> It springs from character alone.

Now music, the invincible obstacle to character portrayal, forbade my making known my dramatis personae in their remote setting, essential though this knowledge is for any enjoyment. I therefore devised a new kind of prologue, in which is presented all that has to be known about the persons of the drama and its plot. The spectator thus begins *in medias res*, without effort, and in possession of the facts: the prologue is my exposition. Made up of aerial beings, shades and spirits, it constitutes the miraculous part of the poem. Operatic tradition suggested this device, of which I saw no reason to deprive the genre: magical wonders are excellent when used in moderation.

After I had finished my poem I came across an Arabian tale which resembles it and which reminded me that long ago I had heard it read to me in the country. The reader of this preface can look up Volume III of *The Genii*[1] and discover what I owe to the Arabian, as well as note how the confused recollection of a striking thing can work in the memory and fertilize the mind without one's being aware of it.

But what belongs far more to another hand is the beautiful music of my friend Salieri.[2] This great composer, who is the glory of the Gluckist school, possesses the style of the master together with a natural sense of taste, of judgment, of drama and, what is more, a wealth of ideas. To comply with my views he has had the courage to give up a quantity of musical splendours; they adorned his score but made the play too long and retarded *the action*. Surely the vigour,

---

[1] I.e., the *Arabian Nights*.
[2] Antonio Salieri (1750–1825).

the speed, the proud and energetic tone of the work will indemnify him for his many sacrifices. And his score will refute the likely objection that my poem lacks lyricism: it was never our aim to be lyrical, but only to make music dramatic. 'My dear friend,' I would say to Salieri, 'the trouble with opera is that it is effeminate in word and thought, out of subservience to music. Let us dare to raise the art to the level of sinewy verse and powerful situations, then we may recapture those vaunted effects attained in the drama of the ancient Greeks.' Our conversations would, I believe, have made an excellent Poetics for the makers of opera, for M. Salieri is a born poet and I am something of a musician. Without this concurrence I doubt whether success would have been possible.

During rehearsals our work aimed at reducing the recitative to the level of speech without destroying musical harmony, and I must praise the singers for their efforts in this direction. Short of speaking altogether, no musician could have done better, and the spoken voice would have deprived the work of the orchestral reinforcement which our able composer employed whenever appropriate.

Two other precepts, both very short, comprised the rest of my doctrine for the rehearsals. To our most willing actors I said, 'Enunciate clearly'; and to the best orchestra in the world I said, 'Control your ardour. Rightly understood and applied, this counsel will make us deserving of attention.' For I had discovered another secret worth imparting. I found that the reason people cannot hear at the Opera is that they have lost the habit of listening. No doubt boredom is the ultimate cause, yet I have noticed that in several modern works, which are full of good things, certain passages absolutely compel the public to hear. Accordingly, whether I deserve it or not, I beg the fullest attention for the première of *Tarare*. If I do not deserve it, let the public avenge itself afterward with the most infernal noise.[1]

PREFACE TO *TARARE* (1787)

---

[1] Precisely what happened at the public dress rehearsal. But the first night was successful and the opera enjoyed a run of several months.

FRIEDRICH NIETZSCHE

The Greatness of Wagner[1]

O N that dismal cloudy day of May 1872, when the foundation
stone had been laid on the heights of Bayreuth amid torrents
of rain, and Wagner was driving back to the town with a
small party of us, he was exceptionally silent, and there was that
indescribable look in his eye as of one who has turned his gaze deeply
inwards. That day happened to be the first of his sixtieth year, and his
whole past now appeared as but a long preparation for this great
moment. What went through Wagner's mind on that day, how he
became what he is, and what he is yet to be—we who are nearest to
him can imagine up to a certain point: we can follow him in his
self-examination. But to understand his great achievement we must
try to see through his eyes, and then, having understood, we can
vouch for that achievement's fruitfulness.

. . . It is typical that a modern man gifted with exceptional talents
should as a child and youth so seldom be blessed with ingenuousness
and simple originality that he is hardly able to have these qualities
at all. As a matter of fact, men of rare talent, such as Goethe and
Wagner, more often achieve ingenuousness in manhood than during
their tender years of childhood and youth. This is especially true of
the artist, who, being born with a more than usual capacity for
imitating, falls a prey to the morbid multiplicity of modern life as to
an infectious childhood disease. As a child he will more nearly resemble
an old man. The amazingly sincere picture of a representative of youth
that Wagner gives us in the Siegfried of the *Nibelungen Ring* could
only have been conceived by a grown man, and by one who had found
his youth but late in life. Wagner's maturity, like his adolescence,
came late and he is, in this respect at least, the very reverse of the
precocious type.
. . . The characters an artist creates are not himself, but the series
of creations to whom it is clear that he is deeply attached must some-

[1] See head note, p. 131.

how reveal something of his nature. If you recall Rienzi, the Flying Dutchman and Senta, Tannhäuser and Elizabeth, Lohengrin and Elsa, Tristan and Marke, Hans Sachs, Wotan and Brunhilde—all these characters are linked together by a hidden current of strong moral feeling, which as it flows through them becomes ever purer and clearer. Here we respectfully and diffidently come into the presence of the innermost secret of Wagner's soul and its development. In what other artist do we find this same quality to the same degree? Schiller's characters, from the Robbers to Wallenstein and William Tell, do indeed pursue an ennobling course, and also reveal something of their author's progression; but in Wagner the plane is higher and the scope much greater. I find, for example, in the *Ring of the Nibelungen*, when Brunhilde is awakened by Siegfried, a passage of the most moral music that I have ever heard. Wagner attains here to such a height of saintly feeling that our mind unconsciously seeks a likeness among the glistening peaks of ice and snow in the Alps—so pure, inaccessible, solitary and chaste, yet so bathed in love beams, does Nature show herself in these forms that clouds and tempests—and even the sublime itself—seem to lie below.

Now looking down from such a height upon Tannhäuser and the Flying Dutchman, one begins to understand how Wagner as a human being developed, how restlessly and darkly he began; how he stormed to satisfy his lusts, to seize power, and taste those raptures of delight from which he often fled in disgust; how he wanted to throw off discipline, to forget, negate, and renounce everything; hurling himself like a flood, now into this valley, now into that, leaving no remote or hidden corners uncovered.

In the night of these half-subterranean convulsions a star appeared and glowed high above him with a sad brilliancy: as soon as he recognized it, he named it Fidelity, unselfish faith. But why did this star strike him as the brightest and purest of all? What special meaning did the word 'fidelity' carry for him as a conscious being? The bare fact is that it has etched itself upon all his thoughts, all his deeds. His works contain an almost complete series of the finest and most beautiful examples of fidelity: that of brother to sister, of friend to friend, of servant to master; of Elizabeth to Tannhäuser, of Senta to the Dutchman, of Elsa to Lohengrin, of Isolde, Kurvenal, and Marke to Tristan, of Brunhilde to the most mystic vows of Wotan—and these are but a few. It is Wagner's most personal and characteristic experience, which he reveres like a religious mystery. He names it Fidelity and never tires of imparting it to hundreds of different characters, of endowing it with his sublimest thought, so overflowing is his gratitude. In a word, it spells his awareness that the two sides of his nature have remained faithful each to each, that the creative, ingenuous, and brilliant elements arising out of free and unselfish love have kept pace with the dark, the intractable, and the tyrannical side.

Examined in detail and without prejudice, Wagner's life may be said—to borrow an expression of Schopenhauer's—to consist largely of comedy, indeed of burlesque. What the feelings must have been that accompanied his awareness of living, for long stretches of time, a paradoxically undignified life, how they must have acted upon an artist who more than anyone else, perhaps, breathed freely only in elevated spheres—all this only a philosopher can imagine. In the midst of such confusion, which should be described in detail in order to inspire the amount of pity, awe, and admiration that it deserves, Wagner developed a talent for acquiring knowledge, which even in a German —a son of the nation most bent upon learning—was really extra-ordinary. Moreover, this talent was threatened by another danger, more overwhelming than that of leading an existence without apparent rule or discipline, carried hither and thither by distracting illusions: from a tyro testing his strength, Wagner became a thorough master of music and the theatre, as well as an inventive technician in the realm of the practical prerequisites of his art. No one can any longer deny him the glory of having given us the supreme models for the large-scale execution of lofty conceptions.

But Wagner came to be something more than this, and in order to this accomplishment he had to reach the highest degree of culture by sheer study. How wonderfully he achieved this end! It is a delight to follow his progress. All was grist to his mill; the materials drawn from all sides became a part of him, and the larger and heavier the resulting structure became, the stouter was the arch of the organizing thought that sustained it.

And yet access to the arts and sciences has seldom been more difficult for any man than for Wagner; he often had to break his way through to reach them. The restorer of primitive drama, the discoverer of the place of art in the true human society, and poetic interpreter of ancient philosophies, the thinker, the historian, the critic and aesthetician, the master of language, the mythologist and the myth-maker, the man, in short, who first closed the circle around these wonderful and beautiful products of an eternal spirit in a single *Ring*, and who engraved upon this solid piece of work the runic characters of his thought —what a wealth of knowledge Wagner had to store up and master, in order to be and to do all this! And at the same time this mass of material was just as powerless to arrest the motion of his will as a single detail—however attractive—was to divert his purpose from its goal.

Wagner concentrated upon all of life, past and present, the light of an intelligence strong enough to take in the most remote regions within its scope. That is why he is a simplifier of the universe. The simplification of the universe is possible only to him whose eye has been able to master the vastness and wildness of an apparent chaos, and to relate and unite things which before had lain helplessly apart. Wagner did this by discovering a connection between two objects that seemed to dwell apart as though in separate spheres—that between music and life, and likewise that between music and drama. Not that he invented nor was the first to create this relationship: they have always existed; they lie, as it were, at everybody's feet. But as is so often true of a great problem, this was like a precious stone which thousands kick underfoot before one man finally picks it up. Wagner asked himself why an art such as music should have become so very important a feature of modern life.

One need not think meanly of life in order to suspect a riddle behind this question. On the contrary, it is only when the great forces of existence are accounted for, and the living energies regarded as striving toward conscious freedom and independence of thought, that music appears as a riddle of the present. Surely one must admit that music could hardly have been born in our own day. What then is the meaning of its presence among us? An accident? A single great artist might certainly be an accident, but the appearance of a whole group of artists, such as the history of modern music shows—a group only once before equalled on earth, that is to say, in the time of the Greeks—a fact so striking as this leads one to think that perhaps necessity rather than accident is at the root of the phenomenon. The meaning of this necessity is the riddle Wagner answers.

For he was the first to recognize an evil as widespread as civilization itself: language is everywhere diseased, and the curse of this dread disease weighs heavily upon the whole of man's development. Language having more and more abandoned its true function—the expression of strong feelings, which it was once able to convey in all their simplicity; and having been forced to strain after the virtually impossible achievement of communicating the reverse of feeling—that is to say thought—its strength has become so exhausted by this excessive enlargement of its duties during the relatively short span of modern civilization that it is no longer able to perform the function which alone justifies its existence, namely, helping those who suffer to communicate about the sorrows of existence. Man can no longer make his misery known to others by means of language, hence cannot really express himself any longer.

. . . If now the music of our German masters burst upon mankind when it was sick to this degree, what is the real meaning of this music? Only this: genuine feeling—the enemy of all convention, of artificial estrangements and misunderstandings between man and man. This music signifies a return to Nature, and at the same time a purification and refashioning of Nature. For the need of such a return took shape in the souls of the most loving of men; and *through their art, Nature transformed into love made its voice heard.*

Let us regard this as *one* of Wagner's answers to the question, 'What does music mean in our time?' He has a second. The relation between music and life is not merely that which exists between one kind of language and another; it is also the relation between the perfect world of sound and that of sight. Regarded merely as a spectacle, and compared with other and earlier forms, modern life is characterized by an indescribable barrenness and enfeeblement, despite the unspeakable garishness that rejoices the superficial observer. If one looks a little closer at the impression made on oneself by this vehement and kaleidoscopic play of colours, does not the brilliant, blazing whole seem to consist of the shimmer and sparkle of innumerable little stones borrowed from former civilizations? Is not everything one sees merely a compound of clumsy bombast, apish gesticulations, arrogant superficiality? a ragged suit of motley for the naked and the shivering? a deceptive dance of joy enjoined upon an invalid? airs of overbearing pride put on by one who is sick unto death? And moving all about with such speed and confusion that they are thereby disguised and hidden: sordid impotence, devouring dissension, solicitous ennui, dishonest misery! The appearance of humanity these days is mere appearance, and nothing more: in what he now puts forth, man has himself become invisible. He is masked off, blotted out.

In fact, the remnants of the creative faculty in art, still surviving in such countries as France and Italy, are all concentrated upon this one task of concealing. Wherever the demands of form are still made, in society, conversation, literary style, or the relations among states, men have unconsciously come to believe that they are adequately met by a kind of agreeable simulation, quite the opposite of genuine form conceived as a necessary relation among the parts of a figure—a relation which has nothing to do with the 'agreeable' or the 'disagreeable,' since it is necessary and not optional. . . . How far this simulation is agreeable at times, and why it pleases everybody to see modern man doing his best to dissemble, everyone can judge in the exact degree to which he himself happens to be modern, 'Only galley slaves can recognize one another,' says Tasso, 'and if we make a mistake of identity, it is only out of courtesy, and with the hope that others in turn will mistake us.'

Now, in this world of forms and intentional misunderstandings, what purpose is served by the occurrence of beings overflowing with music? With noble candour and impersonal passion they pursue their course to a grand and unrestrained rhythm; they glow with the mighty and peaceful fire of music, which breaks forth into the light of day from their inexhaustible depths—and all this to what end? To the end of helping music express the longing that it feels for the company of its natural ally, gymnastics, through which it takes on its necessary *form* in the order of visible phenomena. In its search and longing for this ally, music becomes the arbiter of the whole visible world and of the world of deceptive, topical phenomena. And this is Wagner's second answer to the question, 'What is the meaning of music in our times?' 'Help me,' he cries to all who have ears to hear, 'help me to discover that culture of which my music, being the rediscovered language of genuine feeling, seems to foretell the existence. Remember that the soul of music now seeks a body, and that with your aid it wants to become visible in movement, deeds, institutions, and customs!'

THOUGHTS OUT OF SEASON (1876)

HECTOR BERLIOZ

The Limits of Music

*All his life as theorist and composer, Berlioz fought against the musical
literalism inherited from the eighteenth century, while seeking at the same
time to define the true relation of music, drama, and words.*

I

LET us begin by discussing *imitation* in music, not in the technical
sense which refers to fugue and the fugal style, but in the sense
of producing certain noises which describe or depict by musical
means objects whose existence we are aware of only through our
eyes. This notable element of art, which not a single great composer
of any school has neglected to use, whether or not his attempts were
successful, and which admittedly has seduced more than one into
ridiculous and deplorable errors, has seldom been treated with any
fullness or examined with judgment. I shall therefore try to throw
some light on the darker side of its theory, while seeking the criterion
by which to determine when its application ceases to be art and falls
into absurdity after exhibiting the silly and the grotesque.

M. Joseph Carpani, the excellent Italian critic to whom we owe,
among other things, a volume of letters on the life and works of
Haydn,[1] will help us in our search. His views on the matter seem
those of a man gifted with musical good sense and a proper feeling
about the true limits of the art of music. Yet he appears to me not
to have sufficiently brought out the main features of the subject.
Hence the present attempt to fill in the gaps left by his discussion,
which I mean to follow step by step.

In one of his letters about the famous oratorio *The Creation*,[2] in
which Haydn makes frequent use of the descriptive style, M. Carpani
remarks that long before Haydn composers had been making use
of the imitative means open to the musician; of these the critic

[1] *Le Haydine* (Milan, 1812) by Giuseppe Carpani (1763-1825).
[2] (1798).

distinguishes two kinds—the physical and the emotional. The first he calls direct, the second indirect.

By direct imitation [says M. Carpani], I mean the imitation of sounds as they occur in the throats of animals, or as they are made by the air vibrating in different ways around solid bodies. The air soughs through foliage, bellows in caverns, murmurs along uneven places, etc., all of which it is proper for music to imitate, even though it be not its highest prerogative. Such imitations are difficult and deserve credit. It is said that a Greek was once asked to go and hear a man whistle like a nightingale. 'Not I,' replied the Greek, 'I have heard the actual bird.' The reply has been wrongly lauded. 'My dear logician,' I should have said to him, 'it is precisely because the song is not made by a bird that it is worth hearing and admiring. If some one told you to look at a battle painted by Giulio Romano and you replied, "I have seen a real battle," what sense would there be in the rejoinder? It is exactly because you have witnessed real battles that you must find pleasure in seeing art reproduce the likeness with a little coloured earth.'

Here M. Carpani seems to me to go seriously astray by borrowing an argument from a comparison with painting. That art may not indeed have any other object than to reproduce with fidelity, to give a beautiful imitation of Nature; whereas music is in most cases an art *sui generis*. It is sufficient unto itself, and possesses the power to charm without having recourse to any kind of imitation. Painting, moreover, cannot encroach on the domain of music; but music can by its own means act upon the imagination in such a way as to engender sensations analogous to those produced by graphic art. This point, however, belongs to the second part of our subject, that which M. Carpani calls indirect or emotional imitation. As to the first, the direct or physical imitation of the sounds and noises of Nature, here is what I would say about it, and what our author fails to bring out:

If we are to accept imitation among musical devices without detracting from music's independent power of nobleness, the first condition is that imitation shall virtually never be an *end* but only a *means*; that it shall never be considered (except very rarely) the main musical idea, but only the complement of that idea, joined to the main idea in a logical and natural manner.

The second condition to making imitation acceptable is that it shall concern something worthy of holding the listener's attention, and that it shall not (at least in serious works) be used to render sounds, motions, or objects that belong outside the sphere which art cannot desert without self-degradation.

The third condition is that the imitation, without aping reality as by an exact substitution of Nature for art, shall nonetheless be close enough for the composer's intent to avoid misconception in the minds of an attentive audience.

The fourth and last condition is that this physical imitation shall never occur in the very spot where *emotional* imitation (expressiveness) is called for, and thus encroach with descriptive futilities when the drama is proceeding apace and passion alone deserves a voice.

To illustrate and support the foregoing distinctions, I shall take examples from the great masters of music and poetry (for in this matter music and poetry have a common stake), and I shall begin with Beethoven. It might seem as if the 'Storm' in the Pastoral Symphony were a magnificent exception to our first rule, which allows imitation only as a means and not as an end. For this symphonic movement is wholly given over to the reproduction of the divers noises heard during a violent storm which breaks suddenly over some village festivities. First a few drops of rain, then the rising wind, the thunder grumbling dully in the distance, the birds seeking shelter; finally the approaching gale, the boughs that split, men and animals scattering with cries of dismay, the shattering bolts of lightning, the floodgates of heaven opening, the elements let loose—chaos.

And yet this sublime depiction, which outstrips anything that had ever been attempted in the genre, actually falls within the category of *contrasts* and *dramatic effects*, which are required by the scope of the work. For it is preceded and followed by gentle and smiling scenes to which it acts as a foil. That this is so may be tested by imagining this storm transplanted into another composition in which its presence would not be motivated: it would unquestionably lose a great deal of its effectiveness. Hence this piece of imitation is strictly speaking a means of achieving contrasts, devised and managed with the incalculable power of genius.

In *Fidelio*, on the other hand, a work by the same composer, we find another piece of musical imitation of very different purport from the one just reviewed. It occurs in the famous duet at the grave: the jailer and Fidelio dig the place where Florestan is to be buried. Halfway through their toil the pair unearth a large rock and roll it with difficulty to one side. At that point the double basses of the orchestra play a strange and very brief figure—not to be confused with the ostinato phrase of the basses which runs through the whole piece—by which it is said Beethoven wished to imitate *the dull sound of the rolling stone*.

Now this imitation, being in no way necessary either to the drama or to the effectiveness of the music, is really an end in itself for the composer: he imitates in order to imitate—and at once he falls into error, for there is in such imitation no poetry, no drama, no truth. It is a sad piece of childishness, which one is equally grieved and surprised to have to complain of in a great master. The same could be said of Handel, if it be true—as is commonly said—that in his oratorio *Israel in Egypt* he tried to reproduce the flight of locusts, and this to the point of shaping accordingly the rhythmic figure of the vocal parts. Surely that is a regrettable imitation of a subject even more regrettable—unworthy of music in general and of the noble and elevated style of the oratorio.

Haydn, on the contrary, in his essentially descriptive works *The Creation* and *The Seasons*, does not seem to have lowered his style appreciably when, in order to follow the poem, he applied imitation to such agreeable noises as the warbling of turtledoves—an imitation that is, moreover, quite exact.

This brings us back to Beethoven and the Pastoral. There has been frequent criticism of the song of the three birds toward the end of the 'Scene by the Brook.' As regards the suitability of this imitation, it seems obvious enough. Most of the quiet voices of the waters, earth, and sky naturally find a place here and contribute easily to the serene magnificence of the landscape, but they are not all equally capable of faithful rendering. Beethoven wanted to make the quail, the cuckoo, and the nightingale heard in his orchestra. Now, the first two are unmistakable from the very outset, whereas it is clear that no listener would ever recognize the nightingale in its pretended imitation without being told. The reason is that the fixed sounds of the quail and cuckoo are available in our scale and our instruments, but the voice of the nightingale, sometimes plaintive, sometimes brilliant, and ever irregular, is not imitable. It is odd that this fact of observation has escaped the many composers who have similarly tried and failed to ape the elusive vocalizations of the warbler of dusk.

One may mention other imitations which reason does not exactly reprove but which have been so long in the public domain that they have become vulgar; so that the musician who uses them must show rare tact or strong inspiration to ennoble them or give them the appearance of freshness. In one of the duets of *William Tell*, for example, under Arnold's words 'I seek the field of glory,' there is a prolonged rhythmic pedal point for trumpets. Its effect seems to me commonplace, or at any rate open to criticism of a kind that a man of judgment such as M. Rossini should not make himself liable to. On the other hand, in Gluck's *Armide* the clamour of war with which the composer accompanies Dunois' exclamation 'Our general summons you!' makes the most phlegmatic listener thrill with enthusiasm; it will remain, regardless of the revolutions of taste, as one of the most dazzling strokes of genius.

When, finally, physical imitation is used as a means, there is a pitfall into which some of the greatest poets have fallen, and to which I shall draw the attention of musicians. When Talma, playing Orestes, used to hiss the *s*'s as he exclaimed, '*Pour qui sont ces serpents qui sifflent sur vos têtes?*'[1] far from being terrifying he always made me want to laugh. For it seemed to me clear, then as now, that this solicitude of Orestes to imitate the hissing of serpents when his soul is filled with terror, his heart with despair, and his head with ghostly visions, was directly opposed to any idea we may form of what is dramatically natural and likely. Obviously Orestes is not *describing* the Furies; he imagines that he is actually seeing them. He hails them, pleads with them, defies them; and one must be a very docile spectator not to find comic a piece of imitation ascribed to such a sufferer at such a juncture.

As against this, Virgil's many imitative passages strike me as most felicitous, for he has taken care to put them in the narratives made by his characters or in the descriptions for which the poet himself is responsible, e.g. '*Ruit alto a culmine Troia; Nox atra cava circumvolat umbra; Quadrupedante putrem sonitu quatit ungula campum,*' etc.[2]

II

The kind of imitation that M. Carpani calls *emotional* is designed to arouse in us by means of sound the notion of the several passions of the heart, and to awaken solely through the sense of hearing the impressions that human beings experience only through the other senses. Such is

---

[1] 'For whom these snakes that hiss atop your heads?'—from Racine's *Andromaque*, Act IV, scene 5.   [2] From the *Aeneid*.

the goal of *expression, depiction,* or *musical metaphors.* As regards expressive power, I doubt whether the arts of drawing and even of poetry can equal music. It is only the infatuation of a certain celebrated composer's followers, joined to their total lack of musical feeling and education, that has enabled them to defend their idol on the ground that all musical accents were interchangeable, whence it followed that the composer of *Otello*[1] was not guilty of nonsense or absurdity, since no music could be *true.* He himself refuted them in masterly fashion by his score of *William Tell.*[2] But it would be tedious to dwell on the point.

Musical *depiction,* as I shall show in a moment, is not quite the same thing as a musical *metaphor* and does not seem to me to be nearly so genuine a possibility. The famous naturalist Lacépède,[3] who among his scientific colleagues passed for a very fine composer, says somewhere that 'since music has only sounds at its disposal, it can act only through sound. Hence in order to produce the signs of our perceptions these signs must themselves be sounds.' But how can one express musically things that make no sound whatever, such as the denseness of a forest, the coolness of a meadow, the progress of the moon? Lacépède answers, 'By retracing the feelings these things inspire in us.' And our Italian critic finds this sort of imitation worthy, admirable, enchanting. He deems it the musical sublime. I am far from sharing that opinion, and I incline rather to think him mistaken—deceived, like many other writers, by a play on words or, if you prefer, by the lack of precision noticeable in the terms that define the subject.

Is there, for example, any single, fixed manner in which we are affected by the sight of a forest, a meadow, or the moon in the sky? Assuredly not. The woods whose shade and coolness will draw a reminiscent sigh from the happy lover will make the jealous or jilted man gnash his teeth, and will fill his heart with gall at the thought of his happy rival. Meanwhile the hunter will approach it full of eagerness and expansive joy, whereas the maiden will look upon it with secret fears. Now music will easily express blissful love, jealousy, carefree gaiety, anxious modesty, violent threats, suffering and fear, but whether these feelings have been caused by the sight of a forest or anything else, music is forever incapable of telling us. And the preten-

---

[1] Rossini (1816).   [2] Rossini (1829).
[3] Count Bernard de Lacépède (1756–1825), known chiefly as a botanist, wrote operas as well as a widely read treatise, *The Poetics of Music* (1785).

sion to extend the prerogatives of musical expression beyond these already spacious limits strikes me as wholly untenable. Hence there are hardly any composers of real merit who have wasted their time in pursuit of such an illusion. Their business was quite other, and their achievement far superior to these so-called imitations. If some few have occasionally given up music in favour of something which, after all, is neither music nor painting—and thus given up substance for shadow— I am inclined to think that art as a whole has not lost much thereby, and that in their case substance and shadow equally lacked merit.

Handel, it is true, tried in one of his works to depict a natural phenomenon which has nothing to do with sound or even with silent rhythm, and which affects no one, I should imagine, in any determinate manner—the phenomenon of falling snow. I find it quite impossible to understand how he hoped to get a grip on such a subject once he had made up his mind to imitate it in music.

I shall be told, perhaps, that there exist admirable examples of musical depiction which must be taken account of, if only as exceptions. But on looking closer it becomes clear that these poetical beauties in no way overstep the vast circle, within which our art is circumscribed by its very nature. For these imitations are not in fact offered us as pictures of objects but only as images or analogues. They help to reawaken comparable sensations by means which music undoubtedly possesses. Yet even so, before the original of these images can be recognized, it is strictly required that the hearer be notified of the composer's intent by some indirect means, and that the point of the comparison be patent. Thus Rossini is thought to have depicted in *William Tell* the movement of men rowing. In point of fact all he has done is to mark in the orchestra a *rinforzando* accented at regular intervals—an *image* of the rhythmic straining of the oarsmen, whose arrival has been announced by the other characters.

Again, Weber is credited with having painted the moonlight in the accompaniment to Agatha's aria in the second act of *Der Freischütz*; this is because the calm, veiled, and melancholy colouring of the harmonies and the chiaroscuro of the instrumental timbre form a faithful metaphor or *image* of the pale light of the moon, and, moreover, admirably express the dreaminess of lovers beneath the moon, whose assistance Agatha just then invokes.

Of certain other compositions one may say that they represent a broad expanse or infinity itself, because the composer has been able to suggest to the ear, through the breadth of his melodies, the grandeur and clarity of the harmony and the majesty of the rhythm—all of these being set off by contrary effects—impressions analogous to those a climber might feel on the summit of a mountain when beholding in space the splendid panorama suddenly unrolled *before his eyes*. And here, too, the truth of the *image* will appear only if the listener has taken the pains to inform himself ahead of time about the subject treated by the musician.

It is evident that the possibility of *arousing emotions by images* that only words sung or spoken can identify, is very far from sustaining the ambitious and vain design of positively denoting by musical means objects that are inaudible or rhythmless.

There is to be sure another kind of *image* that fastens on the words of vocal music, but it succeeds only in shackling expression at large by dwelling on accessory details regardless of meaning. This sort of image is almost invariably childish or petty. How many asininities of this sort could be pointed out in the works of more or less renowned composers! Some cannot come to the word 'Heaven' without leaping to a high note: another would think it a disgrace not to speak of Hell in the lowest vocal register. One makes the dawn rise and another makes the night fall. Nothing is so unbearable as this mania for continually playing on words—a mania which, it must be said, is gradually being cured. For to judge from J.-J. Rousseau's assault upon his contemporaries, it was never more prevalent nor more acute than among the French musicians of the last century.

III

It is already more than twenty years since I first analysed[1] in some detail Gluck's system of dramatic composition and the exposition of it which he gives in the dedicatory epistle prefixed to his Italian score of *Alceste*. Perhaps I may be allowed to recur to it and to add a few fresh observations on the subject.

'When I undertook,' says Gluck, 'to write music for the opera *Alceste*, I made it my aim to avoid all the abuses which the ill-considered vanity of the singers and the weak compliance of composers had brought into Italian opera, and which had made of the most beautiful and pompous

---

[1] That is, in 1834. This third part of the present composite essay was written some twenty-five years later than the first two sections.

of all spectacles the most boring and ridiculous. I sought to bring back music to its true function, that of seconding poetry by strengthening the expression of the feelings and the purport of the situations without interrupting action or paralysing it through superfluous ornaments. I felt that music should add to poetry what is added to correct draughtsmanship by lively colour and the adroit use of light and shade, which help to give figures life without distorting their true contours.

'I carefully avoided interrupting an actor in the heat of speech merely so that he could wait for the end of a refrain. Nor did I make him hold a convenient vowel in the midst of his remarks on the pretext of exhibiting at length the agility of his voice or of giving him a chance to breathe before the orchestra provided him with a cadence. I did not hurry over the second part of an aria, passionate and significant though it might be, that I might finish the piece despite the continuation of the sense, and so help the singer to show off his ability to vary an air indefinitely. In short, I tried to prevent those abuses which reason and common sense have long since rebelled against.

'I conceived the idea that the overture should prepare the spectators for the character of the action about to be shown them, and should indicate its subject: that the several instruments should be called into play only in proportion to the intensity of the mood or passion depicted, and that there should not be too great a discrepancy in dialogue between the recitatives and the arias. Throughout, the meaning should not be broken up, nor the forward movement or excitement of a scene checked without reason. Again, I conceived that my task was to attain a beautiful simplicity rather than to show off intricacy at the expense of clarity. I set no value on the discovery of novelty unless it was suggested by the situation or linked in some way with expressiveness. Finally, there was no rule that I did not feel I should readily sacrifice for the sake of the right effect.'

This credo seems to me in the main worthy of all praise for its straightforwardness and good sense. Its underlying principles, however absurdly and monstrously perverted of late years, rest upon judicious arguments and a true feeling for dramatic music. Apart from the few reservations to which we shall turn in a moment, these principles are of such excellence that the majority of great composers of all nations have for the most part followed them. But it may be asked whether in promulgating this theory, which the slightest feeling for art in his day —or indeed ordinary common sense—would have shown to be called for, Gluck did not overstate its results in practice. This conclusion seems hard to avoid after one has impartially studied Gluck's own works. For he himself did not rigorously apply his principles throughout. Thus in the Italian version of *Alceste* there are recitatives accompanied by a figured bass, very likely for chords on the cembalo (harpsichord), as was the custom in Italian theatres at the time. The result is that there is a *very marked discrepancy* between recitative and aria.

Again, several of the arias are preceded by a long instrumental solo; hence the singer must keep silent *until the end of the refrain*. Moreover, Gluck makes frequent use of a form of air which his theory of dramatic music should exclude. I mean the *aria da capo*, of which each section is sung twice, without any reason assigned for the repeat, but rather as if the public had shouted 'Encore!' Such is Alceste's air:

> Never did I cherish life
> But as showing thee my love;
> Oh, a thousand deaths befall me,
> If they but prolong thy days!

Why, when the melody has come to a cadence on the dominant, should the song start all over again without any change in the vocal or orchestral part: 'Never did I cherish life,' etc.? Surely the dramatic sense is spoiled by such a repetition, and if anyone should have avoided this offence against plausibility and naturalness it is Gluck. Yet he commits the fault in nearly every one of his works. The composers who followed him have proved much stricter than he in this regard, and no comparable example is to be found in modern music.

As for his saying that music in a lyric drama has no other end but to add to poetry what colour adds to drawing, I think he is guilty of a fundamental error. The musician's task in an opera, it seems to me, is of far greater importance. His work includes both drawing and colour; and to carry on Gluck's simile, the words are the *subject* of the painting, hardly anything more. Expression is by no means the sole aim of dramatic music; it would be foolish and pedantic to disdain the purely sensual pleasure that we find in certain aspects of melody, harmony, rhythm, or instrumentation, independently of their relation to the depicting of sentiments and passions in a drama.

And even if one should want to deprive the hearer of these pleasures, and not let him refresh his attentiveness by withdrawing it for a moment from the main object, there would still be numerous occasions when the composer must alone sustain the interest of the lyric drama. In dances, for example, in pantomimes and marches, and in all the pieces where instrumental music is the only fare, what, given the absence of words, becomes of the poet's supremacy? There, surely, music must contain both drawing and colour.

If one excepts a few of those brilliant sonatas for orchestra in which the genius of Rossini disported itself so gracefully, it is a fact that up to thirty years ago most of the instrumental compilations which the Italians honoured with the name of overtures were grotesque absurdities—and how much more absurd a hundred years since. Gluck himself, under the influence of bad example, and being, as one must admit, not so great a musician, strictly so called, as he was a composer of scene music, permitted himself to put forth that incredible inanity, the *Orpheus* overture. He did better for *Alceste* and still better for *Iphigénie en Aulide*. His theory of expressive overtures gave the momentum that led to the creation of symphonic masterpieces which, despite the failure and the oblivion that overtook the operas they were written to introduce, have remained standing, like superb gateways to fallen temples.

Yet here again, by overdoing a sound idea, Gluck fell into error; not this time by limiting the power of music, but by ascribing to music a power it will never possess. For he says that the overture must indicate the *subject* of the drama. Musical expressiveness cannot go so far. It may well enough render joy, sadness, gravity, playfulness; it will show a striking difference between the joy of a pastoral people and that of a warlike nation, between the grief of a queen and the sorrow of a village girl, between calm, serious meditation and the ardent reveries which precede the bursting forth of the passions. Or again, by using the characteristic musical styles of different peoples, it will be able to distinguish the serenade of an Abruzzi brigand from that of a Tyrolese or Scottish huntsman, the evening march of religious pilgrims mystically inclined from that of a troop of cattlemen coming home from the fair. Music will be able to contrast extreme brutality, vulgarity, and the grotesque with angelic purity, nobility, and innocence. But if it wishes to go beyond this immense circle, music will have to have recourse to speech, whether sung, recited, or read. Thus the overture to *Alceste* will foretell scenes of desolation and tenderness, but it will never impart either the object of this tenderness or the cause of this desolation.

It will never inform the spectator that Alceste's husband is a king of Thessaly whom the gods have condemned to death unless he can find someone who will sacrifice himself in his place. Yet that is the true *subject* of the play. Some readers may possibly be astonished to find the writer of the present essay vindicating such principles, since some persons believe, or affect to believe, that his opinion on the expressive power of music goes as far beyond the truth as theirs falls short of it. They have accordingly ascribed to him in all generosity their whole share of foolishness—be it said in passing, with no hard feelings.

The third proposition of Gluck's whose fitness I shall take the liberty of questioning is that in which he professes to attach no importance to 'the discovery of new effects.' Composers had already blackened a good deal of score paper by the time Gluck wrote, and any musical discovery whatever, though it were but indirectly connected with dramatic expression, was not to be despised.

For the rest, I believe that no one could successfully attack their cogency, even including the last assertion, which proclaims Gluck's indifference to the rules, and which many professors will find a blasphemous impiety. Though Gluck was not, I repeat, equal as a musician, strictly so called, with some of those who came after him, he was certainly enough of a musician to have the right of answering his critics as Beethoven once did: 'Who forbids this harmony?' 'Why, Fux, Albrechtsberger, and a dozen other theorists.' 'Well, I allow it.' Such superb assurance better becomes the musician than the poet; he has better grounds for believing in the acceptability of his neologisms, for his language is not of a conventional sort.

We now know what Gluck's theory about dramatic music was. Without question, his *Alceste* is one of the most magnificent applications of it he ever made. One would have to be a great writer, a poet with a soul on fire, worthily to describe such a masterpiece of grace touched with grief, such a model of antique beauty, so striking an exemplar of musical philosophy united to so much sensibility and elevation. And would the greatest of poets, after all, be equal to the task? Music like this is indescribable; it must be heard and felt. What can one say of those who do not feel it, or feel it dully? They are unfortunate, and surely to be pitied.

ON IMITATION IN MUSIC (1837)
THE *ALCESTIS* OF EURIPIDES (1862)

CAMILLE SAINT-SAËNS

The Composer as Psychologist

NOTHING is more difficult than to speak about music. The attempt is very arduous for musicians themselves and nearly impossible for others. The strongest, subtlest minds can lose their bearings. Recently a 'prince of critics,' tempted by the allurements of the Wagner question, addressed his luminous mind to it and was soaring on powerful pinions, was spiralling upward to the heights—the while I admired his daring yet confident flight across the azure sky—when suddenly, like ancient Icarus, he sank heavily to the ground by declaring that musical drama 'may exploit the realm of philosophy but cannot enter into psychology.' I rubbed my eyes, only to read further that music is an art that has no insight into the soul and cannot enter into its inmost recesses. Its hold on human passions is 'strictly limited to the grand passions in their fullest and healthiest manifestations.'

I must be permitted to differ with the illustrious and justly admired writer just quoted. It will perhaps be conceded that I have some claims to understanding the hidden resources of an art in the midst of which I have lived, since childhood, like a fish in water.[1] Well, I have invariably found this art by nature unable to convey purely abstract ideas—and what else is the domain of philosophy if not abstract ideas?—whereas, on the contrary, music is all-powerful when it comes to expressing the several degrees of passion, the infinite nuances of feeling. Insight into the soul, the exploration of its inmost recesses, is precisely its most congenial task, the scene of its triumphant success. Music takes up where speech leaves off, it utters the ineffable, makes us discover in ourselves depths we had not suspected, conveys impressions and states of being that no words can render. That is, incidentally, why dramatic music has so often been able to get along with mediocre words—to say no worse of them; for at times music is the original Logos; it is music that creates the whole; words take second place or become actually needless.

[1] Saint-Saëns was a child prodigy on the piano, who gave his first public concert at the age of ten.

With his ingenious system of leitmotives (ugly word!) Richard Wagner has extended still farther the reach of musical expressiveness by making clear the secret thoughts of his characters beneath and beyond the words they speak. This device had been forecast and sketched out before him, but few paid attention to it before the appearance of the works in which it was fully developed. Take a very simple example, chosen from among a thousand: Tristan asks, 'Where are we?' Isolde replies, 'Near the goal,' but the music is that which previously accompanied the words 'Head destined for death,' which she whispered while gazing at Tristan. The listener understands at once what 'goal' she has in mind. Now tell me, is that philosophy or is it psychology?

Unfortunately, like all delicate and complex agencies, this particular one is frail; it acts on the spectator only if he can distinctly hear the words and if he possesses a first-rate musical memory. Still, that is not my main point and the reader will kindly excuse this digression.

So long as commentators stick to describing the beauties contained in Wagner's works there is nothing—apart from a tendency to partiality and hyperbole, which is not surprising—that one can object to. But as soon as they come to the heart of the question, as soon as they try to explain how music drama differs from lyric drama and either from opera; as soon as they tell us why music drama must of necessity be symbolic and mythical, how it must be 'thought musically' and must reside not in the voices but in the orchestra, how impossible it is to employ for music drama the same kind of music as for opera; as soon as they define the 'essence of the leitmotive' and so on ad infinitum—in short, as soon as they seek to indoctrinate us about all these beautiful things, a thick fog overspreads the discourse, strange words crop up, and incoherent sentences multiply like genii out of a bottle: to put it politely, what is said defies human understanding. Nor am I thinking back to the fabulous and short-lived *Revue Wagnérienne*,[1] which announced one fine day to its stupefied readers that henceforth it would be written in intelligible prose. The wisest and coolest writers of today have not escaped the contagion.

Being myself endowed by nature with a stock of naïveté that the passing years have not exhausted, I have repeatedly tried to understand. I said to myself, 'Light is not wanting, hence it is my sight which

---

[1] Edited by Edouard Dujardin from 1885 to 1888 and numbering among its contributors most of the French Symbolist poets and Naturalistic novelists.

is at fault.' I blamed my native stupidity and made genuine efforts to catch the meaning of those learned dissertations; so much so that on one occasion, finding these same impenetrable arguments over the signature of a critic who is usually crystal clear, I wrote to him asking whether he could not favour my deficient eyes with a little more light. He was gracious enough to publish my letter with his reply below— a reply that answered nothing, threw no light, and left things as they were. Since then I have given up the struggle and have started to look rather for the causes of this amazing phenomenon.

No doubt there is more than one cause. Possibly the original theory itself, from which the whole discussion springs, is somewhat lacking in clarity. 'When I re-read my theoretical works,' Richard Wagner once said to Villot,[1] 'I can no longer understand them.' It is therefore hardly surprising that others should experience difficulties.

We are told that it is a new idea, or rather one revived from the ancient Greeks—like the noble *Jeu de l'Oie*[2]—to want to make a perfect whole of music, drama, pantomime, and scenic display. I am sorry, but this is not true. The idea has ever been the basis of opera for as long as opera has existed. The way of going about it may have been faulty, to be sure, but the intention was there; and the way of going about it was not invariably so faulty as some would like to think. When Mlle Falcon sang in the *Huguenots*, when Mme Malibran played in *Otello*, when Mme Viardot appeared in *Le Prophète*,[3] the public's emotions were roused to the highest pitch. People were horror-stricken at the blood-strewn scenes of the Saint Bartholomew; they shuddered at the fate of Desdemona; or thrilled with Fides, the mother finding her son as a Prophet surrounded by the pomp of the Church when she had thought him dead. The spectator was thoroughly satisfied.

Now Richard Wagner has in his turn put the stamp of his own personality on his art. His system has achieved a new, close, and powerful union of the several arts comprised in lyric drama. Very good. But is this system definitive, is it The Truth? No, it is not, because it cannot be: no system can be definitive. If it were possible, art would then have reached perfection, which we know to be out of the reach of man. If it were possible, subsequent art would only be a hodgepodge of

[1] Frédéric Villot (1809–75), patron and bibiliographer of the arts.
[2] A game on the principle of parcheesi.
[3] Rossini's *Otello* (1816), Meyerbeer's *Huguenots* (1836) and *Prophète* (1849). For the singers, see p. 184 and note.

imitations whose being such would make them as worthless as they would be superfluous. The different elements of lyric drama will always tend toward perfect equilibrium without ever finding it, no matter what the attempts at solving the problem.

Formerly, people willingly forgot the drama in order to listen to the voices, and if the orchestra took it upon itself to be too engrossing there was complaint that it distracted attention.

Nowadays, the public heeds the orchestra, trying to follow the myriad interwoven lines and the iridescent play of tone-colour. In so doing they forget to hear and see what is said or done upon the stage. The new system almost completely annihilates the art of singing, and boasts of this. Thus the sole *living* instrument, *the* instrument *par excellence*, is no longer entrusted with the rendering of melodic phrases. Other instruments, made by our hands in feeble imitation of the human voice, sing in its place. Is this not a handicap?

Never mind, let us go on. The new art, by its complexity, imposes on the performer, and even on the listener, a considerable strain, an effort that is sometimes superhuman. Again, the special sensuous delights that result from the unheard-of employment of harmonic and orchestral combinations give rise to a nervous excitement, an extravagant exaltation, which go beyond the legitimate aims of art. The brain is overtaxed to the point of becoming unsettled. I am not criticizing, I am only describing: the ocean may drown you and the lightning kill, but they are no less sublime for that.

Go one step farther. It seems contrary to good sense to put the drama in the orchestra when it obviously belongs on the stage. Yet I freely admit that in the present instance all argument leaves me indifferent. Genius has its reasons which Reason knows nothing of. But I think the facts sufficiently prove that the new art has defects like everything else in the world. It is by no means the perfect, definitive art, after which one can safely pull up the ladder. The ladder is always there, and, as Victor Hugo says, the top rung is ever unoccupied.

By now,[1] the demand that lyric drama be based on legend has been given up. Else it would be necessary to condemn the most celebrated Russian operas, and that wouldn't do. But 'method' is still invoked,

---

[1] Some dozen years later than the preceding section.

and at once the discussion becomes snarled, for one method seems to be approved at the expense of others, which creates not a few perplexities.

At this point I shall have to argue somewhat on my own behalf, in connection with my *Henry VIII*,[1] which has been said not to follow 'the right method.' My intention is not, of course, to defend my music as such, nor to protest the judgments it has brought forth; that is not done. But I may be permitted to speak of the drama and of the manner in which the music is adapted to it. I am told that the work is superficial in every part, lacking in depth, a mere façade; that the minds of the characters are never exhibited; that the king, who is all sweetness and light at first, turns suddenly to ferocity without pretext or preparation, and so on and so forth. I am referred to *Boris Godunov* and told, 'There is historical drama of the right sort for music.'

I have seen this famous *Boris* and heard it with the liveliest interest. I noticed impressive as well as delightful pieces in it, and others that were less so. I noticed in one scene an insignificant little monk who in the next scene suddenly became tsar; I saw a whole act filled with processions, bell-ringing, popular songs, and dazzling costumes. In another was a nurse in charge of some little children, to whom she told fairy tales. Then there was a love duet for which nothing had prepared us and which led to no sequel; also some incomprehensible festivities at night, played in total darkness, and, finally, some funereal scenes in which M. Chaliapin was magnificent. In all this, I cannot help it if I failed to find the inner life, the psychology, the preparation and the motivation of which my critics deplore the absence in *Henry VIII*.

'To Henry nothing is sacred,' says the book at the outset, 'friendship, love, pledged word, or human law—he tramples all as passion moves him.' When a little later the smiling king offers holy water to the ambassador whom he is receiving, the orchestra takes up as he speaks the music of that earlier scene and thus casts light into the interior of his mind. Such is the way in which the work has from beginning to end been 'superficially' composed.

Of course, I should add that no effort has been made to indoctrinate the public by means of disquisitions upon these details. There has been no singling out of the 'theme of treachery,' the 'theme of cruelty,' the 'theme of duplicity,' the theme of such-and-such, and the theme of

[1] Produced in Paris in 1883.

what-you-will. Lacking this fashionable aid, my critics can be excused for having missed the point.

Not a word, we are told, not a scene lets us see the workings of Henry's mind. Come, now! What about the big scene with its horrible piling up of one piece of hypocrisy on another? Is there in all this no passion at work? What more do the Russian librettos offer? Or subjects taken from legend?

To sum up: myth or legend affords one advantage to lyric drama and one only—the miraculous. For the rest myth rather entails a disadvantage. How can characters who never existed, or in whose existence no one any longer believes, excite interest by themselves? They do not prop up the music and poetry, as is erroneously thought; it is the music and the poetry that prop them up and give them life. Who would endure the interminable harangues of the woeful Wotan without the superb music that goes with them? Would Orpheus weeping the loss of Eurydice move us as deeply if Gluck had not from the first few notes gripped our hearts? And without Mozart's music what should we think of the puppets in *The Magic Flute*?

Let us then allow musicians to choose their opera librettos—no less than the form of their operas—in accordance with their temperaments. How many young talents are wasted today because they feel obligated to follow the word of command! The truth is that all great artists, and the illustrious Richard more than any other, paid not the slightest attention to criticism. Like the miller in the fable, they followed their own bent and they were right.

PORTRAITS ET SOUVENIRS (1903)
ECOLE BUISSONNIERE (1913)

W. J. TURNER

Bury the Programme

*By vocation a poet, Turner (1889–1946) was professionally a music critic for
the* New Statesman *and other periodicals. He gave permanent form to some
of his ideas in his biographies of Mozart, Beethoven, Wagner, and Berlioz,
from the last of which the following is taken.*

I ASK any musician who reads these pages to consider the following
facts. I would not venture to assert that my instinct for music was
secondary to my instinct for words, yet what talent I have is entirely
literary. But I do not need any programme—and never did need a
programme—to understand Berlioz's *Symphonie fantastique*, my
pleasure in hearing it being purely musical and precisely of the same
nature as my pleasure in hearing any one of Beethoven's quartets.
Further, I find the greatest difficulty in even reading the 'programmes'
or literary explanations of pieces of music, and am never helped or in
any way enlightened as to the music by them.[1]

I carry this so far that I have never even read and rarely understood
the texts of the majority of operas I have heard. For me music always
speaks adequately without any words, and I judge it (rightly or
wrongly) without reference to words. Even in the case of a modern
opera like *Wozzeck*[2] I have never read Büchner's play, and on the sole
occasion on which I heard *Wozzeck* I did not understand one word in
a hundred of the German text. But this did not prevent me from
enjoying Berg's music or from having very definite opinions about it.
In short, I am of the opinion that the whole ancient controversy about
programme music was the result of a misconception and is a controversy about an illusion. The text of an opera, the words of a song, the
programme of a symphony or tone poem, or whatever name in the
future may be given to any musical composition is of *no importance or
significance whatever*. I know this will be going too far for the majority

---

[1] One reason for this may be my literary sense, for all these texts and 'programmes' bore or irritate me by their (for me) unreadableness. [Turner's note.]

[2] *Wozzeck*, an opera by Alban Berg. [Turner's note.]

of musicians; nevertheless I am convinced that it is true, literally and strictly true.

In order, however, to help make my meaning clearer, I will offer an analogy. If a painter like Cézanne were to make two pictures, two 'still lifes,' one a picture of an apple and one a picture of a pear; and suppose in the catalogue by a mistake 'The Pear' was numbered as 'The Apple,' and vice versa. Now the fact that one picture had as its subject an apple and the other a pear would have no bearing on the pictorial or artistic merit of the paintings. In fact, when looking at them you wouldn't bother about the subjects 'apple' or 'pear' at all. But if you looked at the catalogue and saw the apple picture labelled as 'The Pear,' you would be worried at once. Why 'The Pear'? you would ask. And unless you noticed that the pear picture was labelled 'The Apple' and so surmised immediately that it was a simple mistake in cataloguing, you would be so fretted by this incongruity that you would no longer be able to look at the picture as a picture, a work of pictorial art, at all.

Now this is what happens with programme music and opera. Those whose innate sense of music is weak fasten on the label and cannot hear the music for seeing the label. Take the label off, bury it, and let them forget it utterly (if they can); and only then will they be able to listen to the music and hear what it is. But even then they may hear nothing at all, just as anyone whose pictorial sense is weak is incapable of seeing a picture but sees only a likeness to something. If the likeness to the label is for him invisible he declares it to be a bad picture, but he really doesn't know what a picture *is*, good or bad. So those who say Berlioz's music is not music are simply saying they can't see its likeness to the label. To them I say, tear off the label, forget all about it, and listen again. If they have ears they will find it is music, pure music. Indeed, what else can it be, being merely a succession of sounds? The merit of this succession of sounds, its virtue, must be judged, can only be judged, by listening to it and ignoring all words, labels, descriptions, analyses, and explanations.

Now, I am perfectly aware that a deeper question is involved here, namely, the relation of the artist to his nominal subject. But people in general are not discussing this problem when they are discussing 'programme' music, abstract or representative art, or 'pure' poetry; and I do not propose to discuss it either, for this is not the place for it. I will only say that in any case what is primarily important is the *relationship* between the artist and his subject. One can no more estimate the value of the *subject in itself* in a work of art than one can estimate the relative value of a sparrow or an eagle, a vegetable or a man, in the love of God. It is the love that gives value, and I do not propose, I repeat, to attempt to explain why God loves a sparrow or why Berlioz loves Harriet Smithson and composes a *Symphonie fantastique* rather than a string quartet. The value of the *Symphonie fantastique*—as of the C Sharp Minor Quartet (Beethoven's Opus 131)—depends equally upon what Berlioz and Beethoven respectively *give* in their work. If Van Gogh chooses to paint a sunflower and Rembrandt an old woman, the virtue of their pictures depends entirely upon Van Gogh and on Rembrandt, and not upon the sunflower or the woman—which have both been the subjects of many lifeless and valueless but recognizable paintings. And if any humanist says there is more life in an old woman than in a sunflower, I reply, 'How do you know?' It may be so, but to choose an old woman rather than a sunflower as a subject of a picture does not ensure a better picture.

I therefore dismiss all this loose talk of 'pure' music in the abstract as leading nowhere. We can only judge music as music, and its value is entirely independent of its programme or label. If anyone says to me that Beethoven's Pastoral Symphony is inferior to his Second Symphony because the former has a 'programme' and the latter has none, I simply do not understand him; his words seem to me to have no more meaning than if he were to say that the Sixth Symphony was inferior to the Second because six is an inferior number to two, or vice versa.

BERLIOZ, THE MAN AND HIS WORK (1934)

COMPOSERS AND PERFORMERS

CHARLES GOUNOD

Palestrina

THIS music—severe, ascetic, horizontal, and calm, like the boundary of the ocean; monotonous by dint of serenity; anti-sensual and yet so intense in its contemplativeness that it sometimes attains to the ecstatic—made at first a strange, almost disagreeable impression upon me. Was it because of the very style of these works, which was entirely new to me? Was it the particular sonority of these special voices which my ear heard for the first time? Or was it the strong attack, strong to the point of roughness, emphatic like hammer strokes, which gives such high relief to the performance by stressing the entrances of each voice into the rich, close-spun web of the polyphony? I could not say. The fact remains that this impression, bizarre though it was, did not repel me. I went back for more, and then more, and in the end could not do without it.

There are works which must be seen or heard in the spot for which they were designed. The Sistine Chapel is one of these exceptional places—a unique monument. The colossal genius who decorated its ceiling and altar walls with his incomparable visions of Genesis and Judgment Day, the artist who painted the Prophets as if he were their equal, will never again find his peer, any more than will Homer or Phidias. Men of that calibre do not return a second time. They are summations: they embrace a universe, they exhaust it and finish it off. They have spoken, and after them none dare repeat. But Palestrina's music seems like a sung translation of Michelangelo's great poem, and I am inclined to think that the two masters throw light one upon the other for the common understanding. The beholder teaches the hearer and vice versa; and to such a degree that after a time one begins to wonder whether the Sistine Chapel, considered as paint and music, is not the product of one and the same inspiration. Music and painting interpenetrate in perfect and sublime unity, so that it seems the double utterance of a single thought, the double voice of a single hymn. What one hears is like the echo of what one sees.

There are indeed so many analogies between Michelangelo's work and that of Palestrina, such a family likeness, that it is hard not to infer an identical set of qualities—I almost said, of virtues—in these two extraordinary intellects. In both we find the same simplicity, the same humility in the use of materials, the same absence of concern with effect, the same disdain for what might appeal. One feels that the physical skill, the handling, is no longer of any moment, and that only the soul, with its gaze unshakably bent upon the higher spheres, is intent on imparting through forms at once submissive and wholly mastered the full sublimity of its contemplation. Even the general uniformity of shading that characterizes this music and these paintings contributes to the impression of a voluntary rejection of all shades. The art of these two men is as it were a sacrament, in which the tangible symbol is little more than a veil cast over the living reality of the divine. And that is why neither the one nor the other of these two great masters makes an immediate appeal. In all things we are caught first by the outer brilliancy of surface. Here, nothing of the kind: one must penetrate beyond the visible and the tangible.

On hearing a work by Palestrina, one feels something like the effect produced by reading one of Bossuet's great pages. One finds nothing striking along the way; but by the end one has been carried to the heights. Faithful and docile servant of the thought, the word has neither arrested nor diverted the reader for its own sake, and thus you have scaled the peak without shock or error, led by a mysterious guide who has hidden his own traces and kept his secret. It is this absence of visible devices, of worldly artifices, of vain sophistication, which makes the really great works altogether inimitable. In order to reach their level nothing less is required than the mind that conceived them and the bliss that inspired them.

MEMOIRS (1896)

ROMAIN ROLLAND

Johann Sebastian Bach

HE could hear the thunders of Johann Sebastian Bach's oceanic soul: the winds and storms, the gusts and scudding clouds, the peoples intoxicated with joy, fury, or pain; he could hear Christ, the Prince of Peace, soaring above them, his heart full of pity; the cities awakened by the watchman's cry, rushing with joyful clamour toward the divine Bridegroom, whose steps shake the world; he could hear the roaring fountainhead of thoughts, passions, and musical forms; of heroic life, Shakespearean hallucinations, and Savonarola-like prophecies; of visions—pastoral, epic, or apocalyptic— that were contained within the narrow frame of the small-statured cantor from Thuringia, with his bright eyes and double chin, his upturning brows and wrinkled lids. He could readily see him—sombre, jovial, a trifle ridiculous; at once Gothic and rococo, quick to anger, stubborn, serene, gripped by a passion for life and a nostalgia for death. He could see him in the schoolroom, acting the pedant with genius amid blowsy and lousy boys who were gross and beggarly besides, whose screechy voices jarred, with whom he occasionally fought like a carter, and one of whom once beat him black and blue. He could see him at home among his twenty-one children, thirteen of whom died before him and one of whom was born an idiot. The others, good musicians, would play for him. Illnesses, burials, sordid quarrels, want of money, unrecognized genius—and above it all his music and his faith, liberation and light, the glimpse of long-awaited and finally captured Bliss, which was God and God's burning Word almost consuming, horrifying, destroying him. . . . Oh, Power! Power! Blessed thunderbolt of Power!

JEAN-CHRISTOPHE IN PARIS (1908)

VOLTAIRE

Lulli and Rameau

ITHERTO French music—or at least French vocal music—has
not satisfied the taste of any other nation. It could hardly do
so, because French prosody differs from that of all other
European languages: we always stress the last syllable, whereas everybody else leans on the penultimate or, like the Italians, on the syllable
before. Our tongue is the only one that ends words with mute *e*'s,
which are not pronounced in ordinary utterance but must be sounded
in singing, and are so sounded with complete uniformity—*gloir-uh*,
victoir-uh, *barbari-uh*, *furi-uh*. That is enough to make our airs and
recitatives unbearable to anyone not accustomed to them.

Then again the climate denies to our voices the lightness afforded to
the Italian. We have never acquired the habit, long in use at the papal
and other Italian courts, of depriving men of their virility in order to
endow them with voices more beautiful than women's. All this,
added to the slow pace of our songs, which is in sharp contrast with
our national vivacity, will always make French music the property of
the French alone.

Yet, in spite of these causes, foreigners who have resided in France a
long time will agree that our musicians have composed masterpieces
by suiting melodies to our speech, and that this musical declamation
is often admirably expressive. But it seems so only to accustomed ears,
and it requires perfect execution. We need actors: in Italy singers are
enough.

Our instrumental music has somewhat suffered from this same
monotony and sluggishness which is objected to vocal works; but not
a few of our symphonies, and especially our dance tunes and ballets,
have won greater approval among foreign nations. They are often
played as additions to many Italian operas. Indeed, scarcely any other
kind is to be heard at the court of a king who maintains the best opera
house in Europe, and who among many unusual talents has cultivated
music especially.[1]

[1] Frederick the Great of Prussia.

Jean-Baptiste Lulli, who was born in Florence in 1633 and was brought to France in his fourteenth year, as yet knowing only the violin, was the true father of music in France. He accommodated his art to the genius of the language. This was his only hope of success, though it should be noted that at the time Italian music had not yet abandoned the gravity and noble simplicity that we still find admirable in Lulli's recitatives. Nothing can be closer to these than the famous motet 'Sunt breves mundi rosae,'[1] which used to be sung all over Italy in the seventeenth century.

It is important to remark that in such purely declamatory music as this, which is like the melopoeia of the ancients, it is chiefly the natural beauty of the words that produces the beauty of the song. One can declaim with art only what deserves to be said. This was quite misunderstood in the time of Lulli and Quinault. The other poets were jealous of Quinault but not of the musician. Hence Boileau attacked him for

> . . . his cold immoral platitude
> Which even warmed by Lulli still is lewd.

But the tender passions that Quinault expressed so well were a faithful account of the human heart rather than any lewdness. Quinault's diction gave warmth to Lulli's music a good deal more than the other way round. Quinault was in fact much Lulli's superior, for one reads him still, whereas Lulli's recitative can no longer be sung. In their day it was believed that the poet owed his reputation to Lulli, but time sets everything in its place. Quinault had a share in the rewards given by Louis XIV to the notables of his reign, but only a slight share—all the great gifts went to Lulli.

It took these two men and some actors to make of a few great scenes from *Atys*, *Armide*, and *Roland* a spectacle of a kind that neither antiquity nor any contemporary people ever possessed. As for the separate arias, large and small, they were not in keeping with the perfection of those great scenes. These airs were in the style of our noëls, or akin to the Venetian barcarolles. No one in those days asked for anything better. The feebler these melodies were, the more easily they stayed in the memory. But the recitatives were so superb that not even Rameau could equal them. 'I need singers,' he would say, 'and Lulli wants actors.' Rameau has cast a spell upon our ears, Lulli cast

---

[1] 'The roses of this world last but a day.'

his spell upon the listener's soul. It was one of the happy advantages of the age of Louis XIV that Lulli found a Quinault.

After Lulli, all other musicians, such as Colasse, Campra, Destouches, and the rest, simply imitated him until Rameau came, when, by the depth of his harmony, he surpassed them and made of music a new art.

THE AGE OF LOUIS XIV (1752–56)

RICHARD WAGNER

Beethoven's Day

Ｆ we wish to form a picture of a day in the life of our sacred
genius, we can do no better than to derive it from one of his own
marvellous compositions. But we must not deceive ourselves. We
must hark back to what was said earlier, when referring the genesis of
music as an art to the phenomenon of dreaming, and use simple
analogy—not identify one thing with another. To illustrate such a
typical day from Beethoven's inner life, I will choose the great C-Sharp-
Minor Quartet, and what can hardly be done while listening to it—for
then we are forced to forgo all mechanical comparisons and give
ourselves entirely to the direct revelation of another world—we can
in a measure achieve by simply calling up this tone poem in our memory. Yet, even so, the reader's fancy must add the living details of the
picture to the bare outline I here offer.

The long opening adagio, surely the saddest utterance ever made in
notes, I should call the awakening on the dawn of a day which 'in its
whole long course shall not fulfil a single wish, not one.'[1] It is at the
same time a penitential prayer, a communing with God out of a firm
belief in the Eternal Good. The mind's eye then perceives the con-
soling vision (allegro $^6/_8$), which it alone can descry, wherein the
longing becomes a sweet and playful though plaintive daydream. The
image of the dream takes waking form as the loveliest of memories.
Then, with the short transitional passage (allegro moderato), it is as if
the master, recalling his art, were settling down to practise its magic.
Its power he summons afresh (andante $^2/_4$) in order to conjure up one
graceful figure, the blessed embodiment of native innocence, and he
finds unending rapture in that figure's ceaseless, unheard-of trans-
formations under the prismatic lights which his immortal genius casts
upon it.

Then we seem to see him, profoundly happy by virtue of his own
effort, direct his glowing vision upon the outer world (presto $^2/_2$).
Once more nature stands before him as in the Pastoral Symphony,

---

[1] From Goethe's *Faust*.

96

radiant with his inner joy. It is as if he heard the native accents of the apparitions that dance before him in a rhythm now gay, now gross. He looks on life and seems to ponder (brief adagio $3/4$) how to fashion the tune for life itself to dance to—a short but gloomy spell of brooding, as if the master were sunk in the lowest depths of his dream. One look has shown him the essence of the world: he wakes anew and strikes the strings to sound a dance the like of which the world had never before heard (allegro finale). It is the whole world dancing: frenzied joy, the cry of pain, the transports of love, the acme of bliss, fury, riot, agony, infatuation, suffering. The lightning flickers and thunder growls, and above it the stupendous Performer who rules and moves it all, who leads it masterfully from whirlwind to cataract, to the edge of the abyss, smiles to himself, for to him the magic is child's play. And now night beckons; his day is done.

BEETHOVEN, A CENTENARY ESSAY (1870)

CLAUDE DEBUSSY

The Conductor

THE Société des Grandes Auditions de France did not give me admittance to its performance of *Parsifal*, which was recently given at the Nouveau-Théâtre under the direction of M. Alfred Cortot.[1] M. Cortot is the French musician who has profited most from the customary pantomime of the German conductors. He has the same lock of hair as Nikisch[2] (who, by the way, is a Hungarian), and this lock proves to be in the highest degree arresting because of its agitation in conformity with each nuance. See how it droops, weary and sad, in the softer passages, a barrier to all communication between M. Cortot and the orchestra. Then see it rear itself proudly for the music's martial strains. At such moments M. Cortot lunges at the orchestra, pointing his stick menacingly, like the *banderilleros* when they mean to irritate a bull. But the players are as cool as Eskimos—they've been through much worse than this. Then, like Weingartner,[3] the conductor leans affectionately toward the first violins, whispering intimate secrets into their ears. Next he turns upon the trombones and galvanizes them with a gesture which seems to say, 'Come on, boys, put some punch into it! See if you can't manage to be trombones out of this world!'— and the obedient trombones conscientiously start swallowing down their tubes.

It is only fair to add that M. Cortot knows his Wagner to the last detail and that he is a thorough musician. He is young and his love of music is disinterested. These are reasons enough not to hold it against him that his gestures are less useful than ornamental.

M. CROCHE, ANTI-DILETTANTE (1911)

---

[1] Born 1877; better known as pianist.

[2] Arthur Nikisch (1855–1922), one-time leader of the Boston Symphony.

[3] Felix Weingartner (1863–1942), Austrian conductor, composer, and critic, of international repute.

SAMUEL BUTLER

Handel

Handel fulfilled Butler's ideal of the good man and great artist. Handelian
chords are quoted in Erewhon, *Butler took composition lessons from Handel's*
biographer, William Rockstro (1823–95), and he fashioned the words and
music of Handel-like cantatas that combine pastiche and parody.

I

As a boy, from twelve years old or so, I always worshipped
Handel. Beethoven was a *terra incognita* to me till I went up to
Cambridge; I knew and liked a few of his waltzes but did not
so much as know that he had written any sonatas or symphonies. At
Cambridge Sykes tried to teach me Beethoven but I disliked his music
and would go away as soon as Sykes began with any of his sonatas.
After a long while I began to like some of the slow movements and
then some entire sonatas, several of which I could play once fairly well
without notes. I used also to play Bach, and Mendelssohn's 'Songs
without Words,' and thought them lovely, but I always liked Handel
best. Little by little, however, I was talked over into placing Bach and
Beethoven on a par as the greatest, and I said I did not know which
was the best man. I cannot tell now whether I really liked Beethoven
or found myself carried away by the strength of the Beethoven current
which surrounded me; at any rate I spent a great deal of time on him,
for some ten or a dozen years.

One night, when I was about thirty, I was at an evening party at
Mrs. Longden's and met an old West End clergyman of the name of
Smalley (Rector, I think, of Bayswater). I said I did not know which
was the greatest—Handel, Bach, or Beethoven.

He said, 'I am surprised at that; I should have thought you would
have known.'

'Which,' said I, 'is the greatest?'

'Handel.'

I knew he was right and have never wavered since. I suppose I was
really of this opinion already, but it was not till I got a little touch from

outside that I knew it. From that moment Beethoven began to go back, and now I feel towards him much as I did when I first heard his work, except, of course, that I see a *gnosis* in him of which as a young man I knew nothing. But I do not greatly care about *gnosis*, I want *agape*; and Beethoven's *agape* is not the healthy robust tenderness of Handel, it is a sickly maudlin thing in comparison. Anyhow I do not like him. I like Mozart and Haydn better, but not so much better as I should like to like them.

Handel and Domenico Scarlatti were contemporaries almost to a year, both as regards birth and death. They knew each other very well in Italy, and Scarlatti never mentioned Handel's name without crossing himself, but I have not heard that Handel crossed himself at the mention of Scarlatti's name. I know very little of Scarlatti's music and have not even that little well enough in my head to write about it; I retain only a residuary impression that it is often very charming and links Haydn with Bach; moreover, that it is distinctly un-Handelian.

Handel must have known and comprehended Scarlatti's tendencies perfectly well: his rejection, therefore, of the principles that lead to them must have been deliberate. Scarlatti leads to Haydn, Haydn to Mozart, and hence, through Beethoven, to modern music. That Handel foresaw this I do not doubt, nor yet that he felt, as I do myself, that modern music means something, I know not what, which is not what I mean by music. It is playing another game and has set itself aims which, no doubt, are excellent but which are not mine.

Of course I know that this may be all wrong: I know how very limited and superficial my own acquaintance with music is. Still I have a strong feeling as though from John Dunstable, or whoever it may have been, to Handel the tide of music was rising, intermittently no doubt, but still rising, and that since Handel's time it has been falling. Or, rather, perhaps I should say that music bifurcated with Handel and Bach—Handel dying musically as well as physically childless, while Bach was as prolific in respect of musical disciples as he was in that of children.

What, then, was it, supposing I am right at all, that Handel distrusted in the principles of Scarlatti as deduced from those of Bach? I imagine that he distrusted chiefly the abuse of the appoggiatura, the abuse of the unlimited power of modulation, which equal temperament placed at the musician's disposition, and departure from well-marked rhythm, beat, or measured tread. At any rate I believe the music I like best myself to be sparing of the appoggiatura, to keep pretty close to tonic and dominant and to have a well-marked beat, measure, and rhythm.

Handel was a greater man than Homer (I mean the author of the Iliad); but the very people who are most angry with me for (as they incorrectly suppose) sneering at Homer are generally the ones who never miss an opportunity of cheapening and belittling Handel, and, which is very painful to myself, they say I was laughing at him in *Narcissus*.[1] Perhaps—but surely one can laugh at a person and adore him at the same time.

II

If you tie Handel's hands by debarring him from the rendering of human emotion, and if you set Bach's free by giving him no human emotion to render—if, in fact, you rob Handel of his opportunities and Bach of his difficulties—the two men can fight after a fashion, but Handel will even so come off victorious. Otherwise it is absurd to let Bach compete at all. Nevertheless the cultured vulgar have at all times preferred gymnastics and display to reticence and the healthy, graceful, normal movements of a man of birth and education, and Bach is esteemed a more profound musician than Handel in virtue of his frequent and more involved complexity of construction. In reality Handel was profound enough to eschew such wildernesses of counter-point as Bach instinctively resorted to, but he knew also that public opinion would be sure to place Bach on a level with himself, if not above him, and this probably made him look askance at Bach. At any rate he twice went to Germany without being at any pains to meet him, and once, if not twice, refused Bach's invitation.

Rockstro says that Handel keeps much more closely to the old Palestrina rules of counterpoint than Bach does, and that when Handel takes a license it is a good bold one taken rarely, whereas Bach is niggling away with small licenses from first to last.

People say the generous British public supported Handel. It did

[1] A Handelian cantata, words and music by Samuel Butler and H. F. Jones (1888).

nothing of the kind. On the contrary, for some thirty years it did its best to ruin him, twice drove him to bankruptcy, badgered him till in 1737 he had a paralytic seizure which was as near as might be the death of him, and, if he had died then, we should have no *Israel*, nor *Messiah*, nor *Samson*, nor any of his greatest oratorios. The British public only relented when he had become old and presently blind. Handel, by the way, is a rare instance of a man doing his greatest work subsequently to an attack of paralysis. What kept Handel up was not the public but the court. It was the pensions given him by George I and George II that enabled him to carry on at all. So that, in point of fact, it is to these two very prosaic kings that we owe the finest musical poems the world knows anything about.

Rockstro told me that Sir Michael Costa,[1] after his severe paralytic stroke, had to conduct at some great performance—I cannot be sure, but I think he said a Birmingham Festival—at any rate he came in looking very white and feeble and sat down in front of the orchestra to conduct a morning rehearsal. Madame Patey was there, went up to the poor old gentleman and kissed his forehead.

It is a curious thing about this great singer that not only should she have been (as she has always seemed to me) strikingly like Handel in the face, and not only should she have been such an incomparable renderer of Handel's music—I cannot think that I shall ever again hear anyone who seemed to have the spirit of Handel's music so thoroughly penetrating his or her whole being—but that she should have been struck with paralysis at, so far as I can remember, the same age that Handel was. Handel was struck in 1737 when he was fifty-three years old, but happily recovered. I forget Madame Patey's exact age, but it was somewhere about this.

It cost me a great deal to make Ernest [in *The Way of All Flesh*] play Beethoven and Mendelssohn; I did it simply *ad captandum*. As a matter of fact he played only the music of Handel and of the early Italian and old English composers—but Handel most of all.

<hr />

[1] Impresario and orchestra conductor in England (1808–84).

It takes as great a composer as Handel—or rather it would take as great a composer if he could be found—to be able to be as easily and triumphantly commonplace as Handel often is, just as it takes—or rather would take—as great a composer as Handel to write another Hallelujah chorus. It is only the man who can do the latter who can do the former as Handel has done it. Handel is so great and so simple that no one but a professional musician is unable to understand him.

After all, Dr. Morell[1] suited Handel exactly well—far better than Tennyson would have done. I don't believe even Handel could have set Tennyson to music comfortably. What a mercy it is that he did not live in Handel's time! Even though Handel had set him ever so well he would have spoiled the music, and this Dr. Morell does not in the least do.

Handel and Shakespeare have left us the best that any have left us; yet, in spite of this, how much of their lives was wasted. Fancy Handel expending himself upon the Moabites and Ammonites, or even the Jews themselves, year after year, as he did in the fullness of his power; and fancy what we might have had from Shakespeare if he had gossiped to us about himself and his times and the people he met in London and at Stratford-on-Avon instead of writing some of what he did write. Nevertheless we have the men, seen through their work notwithstanding their subjects, who stand and live to us. It is the figure of Handel as a man, and of Shakespeare as a man, which we value even more than their work. I feel the presence of Handel behind every note of his music. Neither was self-conscious in production, but when the thing has come out Shakespeare looks at it and wonders, whereas Handel takes it as a matter of course.

Handel left no school because he was a protest. There were men in

---

[1] Thomas Morell (1701–84), English theologian and lexicographer who wrote the text of Handel's *Judas Maccabaeus*.

his time, whose music he perfectly well knew, who are far more modern than Handel. He was opposed to the musically radical tendencies of his age and, as a musician, was a decided conservative in all essential respects—though ready, of course, to go any length in any direction if he had a fancy at the moment for doing so.

NOTE-BOOKS (*c.* 1890)

VINCENT D'INDY

César Franck is Inspired

*Pupil of Franck, composer, and co-founder of the famous Paris music school,
the Schola Cantorum, d'Indy was the master's chief confidant and solicitous
biographer.*

'FATHER FRANCK' was one of those who—like many others—need
stimulants in order to find ideas, but it was not by artificial
means that he tried to spur his inspiration: he had recourse to
music itself.

How many a time have we not seen him in a scrimmage with his
piano, pounding out in a jerky yet constant fortissimo the overture to
Meistersinger, or some other piece by Beethoven, Bach, or Schumann!
After a shorter or a longer time, the deafening racket would dwindle
into a murmur, then nothing—the master had found his idea.

All his life, whenever he could, Franck used this method of enticing
inspiration by means of musical noise. One day, when Franck was
composing one of his last works, a pupil came upon him during one
of these struggles with some piano piece which he was remorselessly
butchering. The pupil expressed surprise at the choice of such music,
to which the old master rejoined, 'Oh that's only for a work-out; when
I want to find something really good, I play over my *Beatitudes*;[1] in
the long run that's what serves me best.'

CÉSAR FRANCK (1912)

---

[1] The composer's own piano arrangement of his oratorio for soloists, chorus,
and orchestra (1879).

BERNARD SHAW

Sir George Grove and Beethoven

To Sir George I must have been a positively obnoxious person, not in the least because I was on the extreme left in politics and other matters, but because I openly declared that the finale of Schubert's Symphony in C could have been done at half the length and with twice the effect by Rossini. But I knew Beethoven's symphonies from the opening bar of the First to the final chord of the Ninth, and yet made new discoveries about them at every fresh performance. And I am convinced that 'G' regarded this as evidence of a fundamental rectitude in me which would bear any quantity of superficial aberrations. Which is quite my own opinion too.

It may be asked why I have just permitted myself to write of so eminent a man as Sir George Grove by his initial. That question would not have been asked thirty years ago, when 'G,' the rhapsodist who wrote the Crystal Palace programmes, was one of the best-ridiculed men in London. At that time the average programists would unblushingly write, 'Here the composer, by one of those licenses which are, perhaps, permissible under exceptional circumstances to men of genius, but which cannot be too carefully avoided by students desirous of forming a legitimate style, has abruptly introduced the dominant seventh of the key of C major into the key of A flat, in order to recover, by forced modulation, the key relationship proper to the second subject of a movement in F: an awkward device which he might have spared himself by simply introducing his second subject in its true key of C.' 'G,' who was 'no musician,' cultivated this style in vain. His most conscientious attempts at it never brought him any nearer than 'The lovely melody then passes, by a transition of remarkable beauty, into the key of C major, in which it seems to go straight up to heaven.' Naturally the average Englishman was profoundly impressed by the inscrutable learning of the first style (which I could teach to a poodle in two hours), and thought 'G's' obvious sentimentality idiotic. It did not occur to the average Englishman that perhaps Beethoven's symphonies were an affair of sentiment and nothing else. This, of course, was the whole secret of them. Beethoven was the first man who used music with absolute integrity as the expression of his own emotional life. Others had shown how it could be done—had done it themselves as a curiosity of their art in rare, self-indulgent, *unprofessional* moments—but Beethoven made this, and nothing else, his business. Stupendous as the resultant difference was between his music and any other ever heard in the world before his time, the distinction is not clearly apprehended to this day, because there was nothing new in the musical expression of emotion: every progression in Bach is sanctified by emotion; and Mozart's subtlety, delicacy, and exquisite tender touch and noble feeling were the despair of all the musical world. But Bach's theme was not himself, but his religion; and Mozart was always the dramatist and storyteller, making the men and women of his imagination speak, and dramatizing even the instruments in his orchestra, so that you know their very sex the moment their voices reach you. Haydn really came nearer to Beethoven, for he is neither the praiser of God nor the dramatist, but, always within the limits of good manners and of his primary function as a purveyor of formal decorative music, a man of moods. This is how he created the symphony and put it ready-made into Beethoven's hand. The revolutionary giant at once seized it, and, throwing supernatural religion, conventional good manners, dramatic fiction, and all external standards and objects into the lumber room, took his own humanity as the material of his music, and expressed it all without compromise, from his roughest jocularity to his holiest aspiration after that purely human reign of intense life—of *Freude*—when

> *Alle Menschen werden Brüder*
> *Wo dein sanfter Flügel weilt.*[1]

In thus fearlessly expressing himself, he has, by his common humanity, expressed us as well, and shown us how beautifully, how strongly, how trustworthily we can build with our own real selves. This is what is proved by the immense superiority of the Beethoven symphony to any oratorio or opera.

In this light all Beethoven's work becomes clear and simple; and the old nonsense about his obscurity and eccentricity and stage

---

[1] All men shall brothers be
Where thy gentle pinion hovers.

sublimity and so on explains itself as pure misunderstanding. His criticisms, too, become quite consistent and inevitable: for instance, one is no longer tempted to resent his declaration that Mozart wrote nothing worth considering but parts of *Die Zauberflöte* (those parts, perhaps, in which the beat of *'dein sanfter Flügel'* is heard), and to retort upon him by silly comparisons of his tunes with *'Non piu andrai'* and *'Deh vieni alla finestra.'* The man who wrote the Eighth Symphony has a right to rebuke the man who put his raptures of elation, tenderness, and nobility into the mouths of a drunken libertine, a silly peasant girl, and a conventional fine lady, instead of confessing them to himself, glorying in them, and uttering them without motley as the universal inheritance.

I must not make 'G' responsible for my own opinions; but I leave it to his old readers whether his huge success as a programme writer was not due to the perfect simplicity with which he seized and followed up this clue to the intention of Beethoven's symphonies. He seeks always for the mood, and is not only delighted at every step by the result of his search, but escapes quite easily and unconsciously from the boggling and blundering of the men who are always wondering why Beethoven did not do what any professor would have done. He is always joyous, always successful, always busy and interesting, never tedious even when he is superfluous (not that the adepts ever found him so), and always as pleased as Punch when he is not too deeply touched. Sometimes, of course, I do not agree with him. Where he detects anger in the Eighth Symphony, I find nothing but boundless, thundering elation. In his right insistence on the jocular element in the symphonies, I think he is occasionally led by his personal sense that octave skips on the bassoon and drum are funny to conclude too hastily that Beethoven was always joking when he used them. And I will fight with him to the death on the trio of the Eighth Symphony, maintaining passionately against him and against all creation that those 'cello arpeggios which steal on tiptoe round the theme so as not to disturb its beauty are only 'fidgety' when they are played 'à la Mendelssohn,' and that they are perfectly tender and inevitable when they are played 'à la Wagner.' The passage on this point in Wagner's essay on Conducting is really not half strong enough; and when 'G' puts it down to 'personal bias' and Wagner's 'poor opinion of Mendelssohn,' it is almost as if someone had accounted in the same way for Beethoven's opinion of Mozart. Wagner was

almost as fond of Mendelssohn's music as 'G' is; but he had suffered
unbearably, as we all have, from the tradition established by
Mendelssohn's conducting of Beethoven's symphonies. Mendelssohn's
music is all *nervous music*: his allegros, expressing only excitement
and impetuosity without any ground, have fire and motion without
substance. Therefore the conductor must, above all things, *keep them
going*; if he breaks their lambent flight to dwell on any moment of
them, he is lost. With Beethoven the longer you dwell on any moment
the more you will find in it. Provided only you do not sacrifice his
splendid energetic rhythm and masterly self-possessed emphasis to a
maudlin preoccupation with his feeling, you cannot possibly play
him too sentimentally; for Beethoven is no reserved gentleman, but
a man proclaiming the realities of life. Consequently, when for generations they played Beethoven's allegros exactly as it is necessary to
play the overture to *Ruy Blas*, or stone him to death—a practice which
went on until Wagner's righteous ragings stopped it—our performances
of the symphonies simply spoiled the tempers of those who really
understood them. For the sake of redeeming that lovely trio from
'fidgetiness,' 'G' must let us face this fact even at the cost of admitting
that Wagner was right where Mendelssohn was wrong.

PEN PORTRAITS AND REVIEWS (1896)

FRANZ LISZT

Chopin a National Poet

*Prolific in all things, Liszt wrote much upon music and at one time planned
a series of volumes on his great contemporaries. The volume on Chopin was
the only one completed and published, originally in French.*

SINCE nowadays the native folk-songs of all countries are eagerly
—and quite rightly—being noted down and collected, it would
seem to us of even greater interest to give some attention to the
characteristics of those artists who are especially inspired by the genius
of the nation to which they belong. So far only a few can be found
whose chief works do not originate in either of the two great divisions
of Italian and German music. But it is likely that given the tremendous
expansion which our art seems destined to attain—thus making our
age a glorious era akin to that of the cinquecento in painting—composers will arise whose works will be marked by an originality due to
the differences of climate, race, and national temperament. In music,
presumably, as in the other arts, it will be possible to recognize the
influence of native soil upon the greatest masters, and to discern in
their works the influence of the popular mind. It will appear therein
more fully, more poetically, and more worthy of study than in the
crude and sketchy, or incorrect and clumsy, efforts of popular music
itself.

Chopin will have to be classed among the first musicians who
have thus individualized in their own work the poetical feeling of a
whole nation—and not simply because he borrowed the rhythms of
polonaises, mazurkas, and cracowiennes, nor because he gave those
names to many of his works. Had he merely multiplied those patterns,
reproducing the same outline and the same reminiscences of a single
experience, it would have soon become a tedious kind of imitation,
and would only have been the proliferation of a monotonous form.
It is on the contrary because he used these forms in order to express
ways of feeling which are more usual in his country than elsewhere,
that his name will remain as that of an essentially Polish tone poet;

and also because these feelings may be found in all the forms that he employed. His preludes, études, scherzos, concertos, and especially his nocturnes—the short works as well as the largest—all exhibit the same sensibility in varying degrees of explicitness. It occurs modified and transformed in a hundred ways, yet always one and the same.

Pre-eminently a subjective composer, Chopin has given to all his creations the same life, and it is his own life which animates all his works. They are bound together in a unity which determines at once their beauties and their defects: both are the consequence of a single order of emotion, of an exclusive way of feeling—which indeed is essential if a poet is to cause the hearts of all his compatriots to beat as one.

F. *CHOPIN* (1852)

EUGENE DELACROIX

Mozart and Modernism

Between the years 1853 and 1856, Delacroix's Journal dwells repeatedly on the theme embodied in the caption above, so that a little essay can be made by piecing together the entries made in the diary after each soirée that Delacroix attended.

DELIGHTFUL music at Princess Marcelline's.[1] My recollection of the Mozart 'Fantasia'—a sombre piece which occasionally reaches the terrible, and whose title is lighter than the character of the music suggests. Then a Beethoven sonata, well known but admirable. This unquestionably gave me pleasure, particularly through the sad regions of the imagination. That man is always sad. Mozart is modern too, that is, he is not afraid to touch on the melancholy side of things, but, like the men of his time—French gaiety, the being compelled to deal only with attractive things and to banish from art and conversation whatever is gloomy and serves to recall our human condition—Mozart combines just enough of this touch of pleasurable sadness with the easy cheerfulness and elegance of a mind lucky enough to take in what is agreeable.

I argued with their good friend R——, who dislikes Cimarosa, who 'sees nothing in him,' as he says with a certain self-satisfied air. How different is Chopin! Just see, I said to them, how much he is a man of his own time, how he makes use of the advances that others have contributed to his art, how he loves Mozart without being like him. His friend Kiatkowski often used to chide him for the echoes of Italian music in his works, suggestions of Bellini and other moderns. That does not bother me much. What charm! And novelty besides!

In the evening, listening to the Mozart trio for viola, piano, and clarinet, I responded with delight to certain passages. The rest seemed to me monotonous. If I say that such works afford but a few pleasurable moments, I do not mean that it is the fault of the work. As regards Mozart, I am sure the fault was mine. In the first place, certain forms

[1] Princess Czartoriska.

have become dated; they have been rehashed and ruined by all the later-comers, and this is enough to spoil the freshness of the work. It is in fact a matter for surprise that other parts have kept their charm for so long a time—time rushes by so fast in the matter of fashion and fine art, and after so much good and bad music patterned on this enchanting model.

Another reason why a creation by Mozart is less remarkable for that abrupt novelty which we find today in Beethoven and Weber is that *they* belong to our time. And then again, they lack the perfection of their predecessor. It is exactly the same effect as that produced by a sketch as compared with a finished monument, by a ruin or an incomplete structure as compared with the final form. Mozart outtops them all by his accomplished form.

The Spectator speaks of what it calls 'the greatest geniuses,'[1] such as Pindar, Homer, the Bible, Shakespeare, etc., whose works are a confusion of things sublime and unpolished. Then it mentions those in which it discerns greater art, such as Plato, Virgil, and others. A mighty question! . . . What would be the use of a fine style and polish applied to crude or common ideas? Perhaps the men of the first rank are like those prodigals to whom much is forgiven because of their occasional good deeds. It's the old story of the sketch and the finished work, of the monument which exhibits only the main structural features until the completion and co-ordination of all the parts enable it to convey the sense of fixed limits. These necessarily lessen its effect on the imagination, which prefers vagueness, expands readily, and embraces great matters on a slight hint.

Even so, in the sketch for the monument as compared with its finished state, the imagination can hardly conceive things too unlike the ultimate form, whereas in the works of genius in Pindar's manner are found monstrosities side by side with the grand and the beautiful. Corneille is full of such discrepancies, and so is Shakespeare. But Mozart is not so, nor are Racine, Virgil, and Ariosto. The mind feels pleasure throughout. . . .

If geniuses like Homer and Shakespeare present such disagreeable features, what shall we say of the imitators of this genre, the careless

---

[1] This is Addison's *Spectator*, No. 160.

and abandoned? The *Spectator* scolds them quite justly, for nothing is more detestable: of all conceivable forms of imitation it is the worst and most foolish. Nor have I said that *original genius* is the warrant for the *Spectator's* admiration of the Homers and Shakespeares. That subject calls for another discussion and a comparison with the Mozarts and the Ariostos, who seem to me nowise lacking in originality, for all the symmetry of their works.

I should add that the perfected works of a Racine or a Mozart do not at first make as deep an impression as those of geniuses who are less correct or more negligent. The salient parts of these last seem all the more striking because other parts nearby are more neutral, or downright bad.

In gazing at that beautiful tree (the oak at Antin) whose proportions are so fine, my ideas find fresh confirmation. If I stand far enough away to see all its parts at once, it seems of average size. But if I step underneath it, my impression is altogether different. Seeing only the trunk, which I can almost touch, and the rise of those mighty boughs stretching over my head like the arms of a forest giant, I am astonished by the scale of the parts; in short, I find it enormous and almost frightening by its size.

Could disproportion be a prerequisite to admiring? If, on the one hand, Mozart, Cimarosa, and Racine are less than striking because of the wonderful proportions of their works, may not Shakespeare, Michelangelo, and Beethoven move us by reason of the opposite cause? I am inclined to think so.

Concert by the Saint-Cecilia Society. I really listened only to the *Eroica* symphony. I found the first movement splendid. The andante[1] is perhaps Beethoven's most tragic and sublime composition, but only halfway through. Then came Cherubini's 'Consecration March,' which I heard with pleasure. As for *Preciosa*[2] whether it was the heat or the brioche I had eaten beforehand, at any rate my immortal soul was paralysed and I slept all the way through.

While listening to the first work I was thinking of the devices by which musicians try to establish unity in their compositions. The

[1] The funeral march, actually an adagio.
[2] Opera by Weber. Here, probably, only the overture is meant.

recurrence of motives is what they generally seem to consider the
most effective way, but it is also the one which is most accessible to
mediocre talent. Though this recurrence is in some cases very satisfying
to the mind and the ear, when overdone it seems like a second-rate
device, or indeed a mere trick. Is our memory so inadequate that it is
impossible to establish relations among the several parts of a piece
without relentlessly driving the main idea into our minds by continual
repetition? A letter, a poem, or a piece of prose can show a deductive
order, a unity which derives from the development of the ideas one
from the other, and not from the repetition of the sentence which
may be the chief point of the composition. In this regard musicians
resemble the preachers who reiterate *ad nauseam*, in every connection,
the text of their sermon.

I can think right now of several airs by Mozart whose logic and
coherence are admirable yet free of repetitions: the aria '*Quì l'odio non
facunda*,'[1] the chorus of priests in *The Magic Flute*, the trio and quintet
in *Don Giovanni*, etc. These last are good-sized pieces, which only
increases their worth. In his symphonies, of course, he sometimes
repeats his main theme to the point of satiation. Perhaps he is following
an established custom. The art of music seems to be more subject than
the rest to the pedantic habits of the trade, which may give pleasure
to people who are exclusively musicians but which always bore
the hearer who is not versed in the technicalities of the craft, such as
re-entries in learned fugues, etc.

However agreeable at times, as I just said, repetitions do not give
the feeling of unity so much as of weariness. Unity must come naturally
out of the right elements, which is a secret of genius. The mind is so
imperfect, so fugitive, that the man most sensitive to art will nonetheless
invariably feel a kind of unease in the presence of a masterpiece, a
hindrance to complete enjoyment, which is not to be dispelled by the
lesser devices for creating a fictitious unity: repetition in music or the
concentration of effects in painting. These are petty and trivial ingenui-
ties, which the common run of artists seize upon and apply in that
same spirit. . . .

Masterpieces would never grow old if they were wholly pervaded
by true feeling. The language of passion and the impulses of the heart
are ever the same. What inescapably marks with age—and may at

[1] Italian version of '*In diesen heil'gen Hallen*,' from the second act of *The
Magic Flute*.

times obscure—the greatest beauties is these 'effective' devices which anyone can master. They are in vogue at the time the work was composed; they seem to be necessary ornaments for the idea. Fashion approves them, and they are generally responsible for the success of the work. Those artists who by a rare feat have done without these accessories are understood later in life and with great difficulty—or else by subsequent generations for whom the charm of the fashionable ornaments no longer exists.

There seems to be an ordained *mould*, into which everybody casts his thoughts, good or bad, and the most gifted, most original minds show the marks of it. What music can possibly withstand, after the passage of years, the taint of out-of-dateness imparted by the cadences and embroidery which made it popular when new? . . . We should deplore the sad condition into which certain inventions of original talents fall. The new sonorities and harmonies of Beethoven have already become the legacy, indeed the spoils, of the rawest beginner.

The public in its stupidity is now deserting Rossini for Gluck, just as it formerly deserted Gluck for Rossini. A ditty of the year 1500 is suddenly exalted above all that Cimarosa has written. Grant that the stupid herd must absolutely change from fad to fad for the good reason that it possesses no taste or discernment about anything whatever. But that men of the craft, that artists—or nearly—who are called 'superior minds,' should weakly lend themselves to all these vagaries passes understanding.

I thought yesterday while going to Saint-Sulpice[1] of writing something on the regular progression of the arts: they keep refining and refining. The source of my ideas was the impression made upon me by hearing at the Princess's the compositions of Mozart that Gounod played through for us. This evening at the Countess d'Haussonville's my impression was confirmed by hearing Mme Viardot[2] sing the aria from *The Marriage of Figaro*. Bertin[3] was telling me that he thought this kind of music far too delicate and too subtly expressive ever to

[1] Paris church where Delacroix was painting murals (1855–61).

[2] Pauline García-Viardot; see pp. 83 and 184 note.

[3] Childhood friend of Delacroix, newspaper owner, painter, and patron of the arts.

appeal to the public. But that is not what one ought to say, for in times like ours the public comes to love detail for itself, as a result of hearing works that have taught it to refine on everything. In our time, on the contrary, one must not paint in broad strokes if one is aiming at the public; indeed, breadth would only reach some few extremely rare minds who rise above the common requirements and who still feed on beautiful things of the best periods—in short, those who love the kind of beauty that is also simplicity.

Let us therefore paint in broad strokes. In primitive times works of art are not otherwise. The upshot of my thought is the need of belonging to one's own time. Voltaire in his Huron[1] makes the hero say that 'Greek tragedies are good only for the Greeks,' and he is right. It is absurd to go against the current and attempt archaism. Racine seems over-refined when compared with Corneille, and how much farther the moderns have gone along that path! Walter Scott and Rousseau, among the first, have delved and delved into vague impressions and feelings of melancholy which the ancients hardly suspected. And the moderns do not merely depict feelings, they also describe external facts, they take everything apart.

In music, the perfecting of the instruments or the invention of new ones tempts composers to go farther into certain sorts of imitation. The time will come when the real noise of the wind, the sea, or a waterfall will be physically imitated. . . . In the theatre, it is imperative to improve scenery and costumes, and it is clear that this is not altogether in bad taste. Everything must be refined upon: all the senses must be satisfied, and there will in time be performances of symphonies accompanied by beautiful pictures, to complete the impression.

It is said that Zeuxis or some other painter of antiquity was showing a painting representing a great warrior or the horrors of war and had trumpeters play behind the picture to encourage the admiring spectators. It soon won't be possible to do a battle in paint without burning a little powder nearby, to edify the feelings thoroughly, or indeed to arouse them.

Already some twenty years ago, on the stage of the Opera, the scenery and props were made real in order to enhance the lifelikeness; for instance in the operas La Juive and Gustave III.[2] In the former one could see real statues and other accessories, which are usually painted

---

[1] A novel entitled L'Ingénu whose hero is a Huron (1767).

[2] By Halévy and Auber respectively (1835 and 1833), both librettos by Scribe.

in. In *Gustave*, there were real rocks—imitations, to be sure, but cut out of solid blocks. Thus from love of illusion no illusion was left.

I dined at Princess Marcelline's: duets for piano and bass by Mozart and Beethoven. . . . What a life mine is! I was thinking of this while listening to this superb music, especially Mozart's, which suggests the calm of an orderly epoch. I have come to the time of life when the tumult of passion no longer intrudes upon the delightful emotions aroused by objects of beauty. I have no knowledge of the paper work and drudgery that form the occupation of most men. Instead of thinking about business, I think only of Rubens or Mozart: my chief concern for a week at a time is a melody or a picture. . . .

JOURNAL (1853–56)

JOSEPH MAZZINI

Meyerbeer's Achievement

The Italian liberator was another of the nineteenth-century publicists who wrote about everything, convinced as they were that the world must be made anew. The following is taken from an essay that appeared in an Italian journal in 1836.

O NE cannot be too thoroughly persuaded of the fact that if music is to flourish anew, it must be *spiritualized*; that if it is to rearise and exert power, it must be reconsecrated to a mission; that if we are not to see it sink into the useless and eccentric, we must join that mission to the general mission of the arts in our epoch, and seek in the epoch the true character of the art; in other words, we must make music *social* and identify it with the progressive movement of humanity. And we should be persuaded, too, that our business today is not to perpetuate or make over an *Italian school*, but rather *from Italy* to lay the foundations of a *European* school of music.

Now a European school of music can only be one which will take account of all the musical elements developed by the previous partial schools, and without suppressing any of them will harmonize and direct them toward a single end. When, therefore, I say that we must emancipate ourselves today from the Rossini school, I have in mind only the *exclusive* spirit of that school—the exclusive predominance of melody and the exclusive attention to individuality which animates it, which makes it fragmentary, uneven, incoherent, and which limits it to materialism, that plague of any art, doctrine, or enterprise. Again I have in mind the divorce which that school has brought about between music and the march of society; the degradation which reduces art to the pastime of a small minority; the frivolous and venal habits with which it has tainted the sanctity of art. I do not propose an emancipation from individuality itself, which must ever remain the starting point of any music, and the lack of which in German music deprives it of half its energy.

Other improvements, of a technical sort, will also be required in a

time of science: on these and others I shall not dwell. But choosing at
random from the many that naturally suggest themselves to all who
do not follow present-day musical drama with their ears alone, I may
ask why accompanied recitative—once a principal part of opera and
now so rare, perhaps because more difficult to sing than is generally
supposed—should not assume in the music of the future a far greater
importance and realize the full measure of its inherent power. Why
should a mode of musical development capable (as Tartini's examples
show) of the highest dramatic effect play so small a part in our musical
drama? By this type of recitative the listener can be carried along at
the composer's will through infinite gradations of feeling quite beyond
the reach of the aria, and thus explore a particular sentiment or passion
to the very depths, revealing the slightest movements of the heart
without violating its secrets; it is a device which can anatomize inner
conflicts, whereas the aria can only with difficulty express anything
but their result. Recitative, moreover, does not distract the listener's
attention from the meaning of the music to the mechanism of its
execution, and thereby leaves its power over the soul undivided.
Must such a mode of expression remain forever relegated to one
corner of the drama instead of being enlarged and perfected—even at
the expense of the often needless cavatina and inevitable da capo?

One might also get rid of the monotony engendered by the vulgar
and tedious cadences, which we have come to regard as fated from
eternity. Likewise, the arbitrary ornaments, the embellishments and
additions that singers indulge in should be prohibited—at least until
singers become a little more philosophical than they are now. Though
war has been waged against these irrelevancies, they still occur often
enough to break in upon true feeling, which they transform into a
heartless and misplaced admiration. What a saving of time spent in
these futilities could be effected and applied to the enhancement of the
historical basis and aesthetic working out of the drama itself!

I know that most spectators already consider our operas too long,
and it cannot be otherwise as long as the work lacks all spiritual
intention. I speak for a time when public and drama will have reciprocally improved each other; for a time when the dramas of the divine
Schiller, being felt and understood, will be produced without profane
rehandlings, without the indignity of mutilation, and will be listened
to in a reverent mood; for a time when musical drama will be offered
to a people neither materialist, nor idle, nor frivolous, but, on the

contrary, regenerated by the consciousness of a Truth which must be won by struggle and which yields the highest moral teachings. I speak for a time in which music will have added to its own power all the powers combined in a dramatic spectacle.

I know that for the artist to educate his public is slower work, and harder for us, than for Nature to fashion a genius as initiator of an epoch; but I know also that just for this reason the work of education should begin. The genius will do the rest.

And the power of genius itself will be multiplied a thousandfold when Poetry, today the servant, will once again be as she should, the sister of Music, and will harmonize with her as does the particular instance to the general statement, the number to the algebraic formula. In that epoch poets will write lyric dramas, not make verses or worse than verses. Poets and musicians, instead of degrading and tormenting themselves in their joint work, will faithfully devote themselves to their task as to a sacred office, calling one upon the other and uniting their inspiration as well as the powers of music and of poetry in a common social purpose. Then, then, genius will be magnified by the awareness of the goal and the greatness of the means, by faith in an immortality which none today dare hope for. It will rise to heights yet unattempted, and will draw from art secrets still unsuspected. Its Raphael-like melodies and unbroken harmonies will adumbrate that infinity to which our souls aspire, and of which we have a thousand intimations in woman, in the starry heavens, in beauty and greatness, in love and piety, in the memory of the dead and our hope of seeing them hereafter.

Genius will resolve the problems and conflicts which for a thousand years have agitated mankind—the struggle of good and evil, mind and matter, Heaven and Hell, the struggle symbolized by Meyerbeer, with touches worthy of Michelangelo, in an opera which will long repay study by artists—*Robert le Diable*.[1] For the mission that music must serve is to raise cold and casual belief to the height of enthusiastic faith in the potency of SACRIFICE, which is true virtue.

And genius will reward sacrifice, will aid and comfort the spirit which trusts itself to its guidance by leading it, from circle to circle, through the musical expression of all the passions, in a rising scale of sublime harmonies, in which every instrument will represent a feeling, every melody a true deed, every chord an assuagement of the soul;

[1] First performed in Paris in 1831, five years before Mazzini wrote.

by which the soul will be raised above the mire of sensation and the tumult of the instincts to the angelic heavens beheld in vision by Weber, Mozart, and Beethoven—the heaven of pure rest, of moral serenity, wherein the soul is revigorated by love, where virtue is not faltering but secure, where martyrdom becomes immortal life, where mothers' tears are transmuted into gems with which God adorns the brow of their sons, and where the sigh of the beloved becomes the kiss of holy and eternal love.

Neither to me who write these words, nor to our generation, born in a time destined only to foresee this genius and the art reborn through him, will that heaven be opened. We have the bitterness, not the solace of the Ideal. But to have had a glimpse of what will be for those who come after is enough to make it a duty that we should work toward the goal with all the means and talents at our command.

Perhaps if genius sufficed, instead of presentiment and distant hope, we might have the reality; that is, if reconstituting music required only genius and not the indefatigable, super-human energy to fight the desperate fight against prejudice, against the tyranny of commercial managers and the mob of careerists and the indifference of the age, then we might perhaps find one among the living who, if he would, could become founder of an Italian-European school, and hence be the reformer—as he is the leader—of those who fight under the banner of the purely Italian school of Rossini. I refer to Donizetti, the only one whose eminently progressive talents show tendencies toward renovation, the only one, it seems to me, in whom one can have any hope today when one is thoroughly nauseated by the vulgar tribe of musical imitators who swarm over our Italian soil.[1]

Whether by Donizetti or by others, the reform of music must and will take place. Whenever a school or movement or epoch is exhausted, whenever a course has been run through and there is nothing to do but run through it again in the same footsteps, reform is imminent, inevitable, certain; for humanity cannot go backward. Let our young composers, then, prepare, dedicate themselves, as to a

[1] Bellini, whose premature death we all deplore, was not, it seems to me, a progressive mind; nor would he, had he lived, ever have gone beyond the limits which his music now occupies. The most beautiful of his inspirations are to be found in *Pirata* and *Norma*. The duets 'Tu sciagurato' and 'Tu m'apristi,' which are so rarely sung in Italy, together with the last act of *Norma*, so like Raphael in form and conception, sum up all there is to Bellini. [Mazzini's note.] For the operas and composers mentioned in this article, see pp. 52, 83, and 334.

religious rite, to the inauguration of the new musical school. This is their time of knightly vigil, so let them remember how those who were about to receive knighthood prepared themselves by silence, solitude, and meditation upon the duties they were to assume, for the fulfilment of the mission to which they were dedicated the day after, in the generous hope of a new dawn.

Let our young artists enlarge their minds by the study of our national songs, of history and the mysteries of poetry and Nature, so as to enlarge their scope and take in wider horizons than those of academic textbooks and the ancient rules of art. Music is the fragrance of the universe, and to capture it for his works the artist must, by loving and faithful study of the harmonies that float on earth and in heaven, identify himself with the mind of the universe.

Let them also study the masterpieces of music, the works of genius not of a single country, time, or school, but of all of these; and study not merely to dissect according to the dry and frigid methods of the professors, but rather to make their own the creative and unifying spirit which lives and moves in these works; and again, not to imitate it in narrow and servile fashion, but to emulate it as free men eager to link the new work to the great tradition.

Since the foregoing article was written,[1] an immense step has been taken in advance. The problem, which may be said to have been musically stated by Meyerbeer in *Robert the Devil*, is not solved in the *Huguenots*; but its solution is at least suggested. That opera stands alone, a beacon to indicate to future composers the course through which Music may be directed toward a high social aim.

In his conception of *Robert the Devil*, the author has symbolized in Alice and Bertram the principles of Good and Evil, and the struggle between them for mastery over the human soul; but Robert himself is little more than passive in their hands, and throughout the course of the opera their forces appear equally balanced. The antagonistic principles oppose each other, something after the manner in which

[1] This supplement, dated 1867, does not occur in the National Edition of Mazzini's works, but only in the six-volume English selection from the writings. It is therefore given in the English of the translator of that edition, who presumably was the only one to see the Italian original.

the Homeric gods fight *for* and *against*, rather than *through*, the individuals whose interests they defend or attack; the moral effect of the representation of the contest within a human breast is lost, and the final triumph of the good principle assumes the appearance of an accident or fatality, in which we rather contemplate a *fact* than confess a Providence. Moreover, the image of duty presented to us by the human agent is somewhat cold and rigid; faith triumphs over superstition, but it is faith unwarmed by enthusiasm, unsanctified by suffering.

In the *Huguenots*, on the contrary, while the interest of the struggle is increased by its revelation through human suffering and passion, the sense of a guiding Providence pervades the whole work. The sublime inspiration of faith and duty is the soul of the magnificent chorale with which the opera opens, and which throughout the piece re-echoes from time to time upon our hearts, holy as the chant of angels, yet stern and solemn as a passing bell; it finds its human expression in the austere, insistent, severe yet loving musical individuality of Marcel, in whom the rugged invincible earnestness of the *believer* ever rises above and dominates alike the lightest and most brilliant, or gloomiest and most bigoted, scenes of the Catholic world by which he is surrounded; so that his very presence on the stage arouses in the heart of the spectator the sense of a providential influence at work to bring about the triumph of good through human suffering, sacrifice, and love.

Nor is it only in the ruling conception that informs this opera that Meyerbeer has surpassed his predecessors and his own previous works. The hand of the master is revealed in the exquisite blending of the Italian and German elements of melody and harmony, which the music of the future is destined to combine. In *Robert*, the two elements are each represented by turns; rarely do we find them conjoined; but in the *Huguenots* they are inseparably united and fused into an harmonious whole. In a period of transition like our own, we may not expect the high priest of the music of the future to appear amongst us; but Meyerbeer is the precursor spirit sent to announce his coming.

While he has sketched for us the outlines of the musical drama of the future, and created musical individualities which remind one of the personages of Shakespeare, Meyerbeer has inherited from Weber, to whom he owes much, the power of reproducing in music the characteristics of local scenery and manners—witness the truly Breton

Pardon de Ploërmel, the vision of Paris in the Middle Ages represented to us by the scene in the Pré aux Clercs at curfew time in the *Huguenots*, etc. etc. Moreover, he has, as I said, *moralized* the musical drama by making it the echo of our world and its eternal problem. He is no disciple of the atheistic school of *l'art pour l'art*; he is the prophet of the music to come, of that music whose high and holy mission will place it but one step below religion itself.

I lack time and space to do justice to Meyerbeer; nor can I do more than allude to the *Etoile du Nord*, the *Prophète*, and the *Africaine*, each of which is worthy of a separate essay; but the little I have said may, I hope, suffice to convince the musical reader of the necessity of an earnest and diligent study of the works of this great master.

Of German descent, though born in Italian Istria, one might almost fancy this combination of the two elements in his own person, significant, symbolic, and prophetic. The figure of Giacomo Meyerbeer appears before us as the first link between the two worlds, the complete union of which will constitute the highest music of the future.

THE PHILOSOPHY OF MUSIC (1836; 1867)

The Paris of Berlioz and Liszt

From 1830 until his death in 1856, Heine kept German periodicals supplied with Parisian news of all kinds. The need to entertain his readers often led him to exaggerate or to make 'good stories' out of scant materials. In this extract, the 'facts' about his friend Berlioz are, to say the least, fanciful.

N
ow, what is music? This question occupied me for hours before I fell asleep last night. Music is a strange thing. I would almost say it is a miracle. For it stands halfway between thought and phenomenon, between spirit and matter, a sort of nebulous mediator, like and unlike each of the things it mediates—spirit that requires manifestation in time, and matter that can do without space.

We do not know what music is. But what good music is we know well enough; and even better, we know what music is bad. For of the latter our ears receive a larger quantity. Musical criticism must accordingly base itself on experience, not on *a priori* judgments; it must classify musical compositions only by their similarities, and take as standard only the impression that they create upon the majority.

Nothing is more futile than theorizing about music. No doubt there are laws, mathematically strict laws, but these laws are not music; they are only its conditions—just as the art of drawing and the theory of colours, or even the brush and palette, are not painting, but only its necessary means. The essence of music is revelation; it does not admit of exact reckoning, and the true criticism of music remains an empirical art.

Apart from Meyerbeer, the Parisian Académie Royale de Musique[1] boasts few composers of whom it would be worth the trouble to speak at length. Nonetheless the French Opera is most flourishing or, to speak more precisely, its box office greatly flourishes day by day. This state of prosperity began some six years ago with the directorship of the famous Dr. Véron, whose principles have since been adopted,

[1] The Paris Opera; see pp. 287–89.

with the same success, by the new director, M. Duponchel. I say 'principles' because Dr. Véron did in fact have principles, born of meditation upon the world of art and science; and just as in his capacity as druggist he invented an admirably musical expectorant, so as an opera director he discovered a cure for music.[1]

Having noticed that a show at Franconi's gave him more pleasure than the best opera, he became convinced that the greater part of the public received the same impression; that most people went to the Opera out of habit, and enjoyed themselves there only when the beauty of the scenery, the dances, and the costumes gripped their attention so strongly that they could quite overlook—or overhear—the fateful, inescapable music. The great man thereupon had the stroke of genius by which he decided to satisfy the people's lust for spectacle so completely that the music scarcely annoyed them at all; and so well indeed that they could enjoy at the Opera the very same delights they found at Franconi's.

From these considerations you will have grasped the significance of French Grand Opera at the present time. It has made its peace with the enemies of music; and the well-to-do bourgeoisie crowds the Académie de Musique just as it does the Tuileries.[2] Meanwhile the best society has quitted the field. The true aristocracy, the elite distinguished by rank, birth, breeding, fashion, and leisure, has fled to the Italian opera, that musical oasis where the great nightingales of music forever trill, while round about the level sands stretch away, a Sahara of music.

Still, a few good concerts spring up now and again amid this waste and afford to the friends of music uncommon relief. This winter the Sundays at the Conservatoire were of this kind; again, a few private soirées in the rue de Bondy,[3] and especially the concerts of Berlioz and Liszt.

These last named are indeed the two most remarkable phenomena in the contemporary musical world; I say the most remarkable, not the most beautiful or the most rejoicing. From Berlioz we shall soon have an opera. Its subject is an episode from the life of Benvenuto Cellini, the casting of the 'Perseus.' Something extraordinary is

[1] Véron's fortune came from a patent medicine.
[2] Where Louis-Philippe held court.
[3] In the hall of the Ambigu-Comique theatre, otherwise devoted to melodrama.

expected, for this composer has already accomplished the extraordinary; his inclination is toward the fantastic, not so much linked with soul as with sentiment. He has a close affinity with Callot, Gozzi, and Hoffmann. Even his outward appearance suggests this. It's a pity that he has had his monstrous, antediluvian head of hair cut off; it used to bristle upon his brow like a forest upon a craggy cliff. That was how he looked when I saw him for the first time six years ago, and thus he will remain in my memory. It was at the Conservatoire, where a great symphony of his was being played—a bizarre nightpiece, lighted up only at times in a sentimental way by the flitting about of a woman's dress, or else by the sulphurous gleam of irony.[1]

The best part of it is a Witches' Sabbath in which the Devil reads the mass and the liturgy is parodied with the most horrifying, bloodiest grotesqueries. It is a farce which gaily releases in us all the hidden snakes that we carry in our hearts. My neighbour in the next seat, a talkative young man, showed me the composer, who stood at the far end of the hall, in a corner of the orchestra, playing the kettledrums —for the drum is his instrument. 'Do you see,' said my neighbour, 'a plump Englishwoman in one of the forward boxes? That is Miss Smithson. For three years M. Berlioz has been madly in love with her, and it is to this passion that we owe the symphony we shall hear today.' And indeed there sat, in a forward box, the famous actress from Covent Garden. Berlioz looked unswervingly in her direction, and whenever her glance met his, he beat upon his drum like a man in a fury. Miss Smithson has since become Mme Berlioz and her husband has since let his hair be cut. As I heard his symphony again this winter at the Conservatoire, he sat once more behind the drums in the orchestra, the plump Englishwoman sat once more in a forward box, her glances once more met his—but he no longer struck the drums so furiously.

Liszt bears the closest relation to Berlioz and is the best performer of his works. I need not speak to you of Liszt's talent: his fame is European. He is without doubt the artist who finds in Paris the most unreserved enthusiasm, as well as the keenest opposition. It is significant that no one speaks of him with indifference. A man who lacks positive stature cannot in this world arouse either favourable or antagonistic passions. It takes fire to enkindle men, whether to hate or to love. What speaks most for Liszt is the respect with which even his

[1] The *Symphonie fantastique*, Op. 4 (1830).

enemies recognize his personal merits. He is a man of unruly but noble character, unself-seeking and without falseness.

Most noteworthy are his intellectual tendencies. He has a bent toward philosophizing. Even more than in his art, he is interested in the speculations of the several schools that attempt to solve the great all-embracing problems of heaven and earth. For quite a while he glowed with enthusiasm for the Saint-Simonian ideal; later he was wrapped up in the spiritualist, or, rather, the vaporistic ideas of Ballanche; now he is fervent about the Catholic republicanism of Lamennais, who has put the Jacobin's cap upon the cross. God only knows in what spiritual stall Liszt will next find his hobby horse. But his untiring search for divine light and leading remains praiseworthy; it testifies to his sense of holiness and religion.

That so restless a head, driven hither and thither by all the demands and doctrines of the day, a heart that feels the need to care for all the ills of humanity, and to stick his nose into every pot in which God cooks up the future, makes Franz Liszt anything but a peaceful pianist for settled citizens and complacent bourgeois—that goes without saying. When he sits at the piano and, having repeatedly pushed his hair back over his brow, begins to improvise, then he often rages all too madly upon the ivory keys and lets loose a deluge of heaven-storming ideas, with here and there a few sweet flowers to shed fragrance upon the whole. One feels both blessedness and anxiety, but rather more anxiety.

I freely confess that, much as I love Liszt, his music does not affect me agreeably. This is all the more so that I am a Sunday child and can also see ghosts where other people only hear them—that is to say, as you know, in each note struck by the master's hand, in each corresponding melodic phrase—in short, music is visible to my inner eye. . . .

It was in the concert for the benefit of the unfortunate Italians[1] that I last heard Liszt play this past winter. I forget what he played but I would swear it was variations upon themes from the Apocalypse. At first I could scarcely make them out, those four mystical beasts; I only heard their voices, especially the roaring of the lion and the croaking of the eagle. But the ox with a book in its mouth was very plain to see. What he played best was the Valley of Jehoshaphat. There were lists as in a tournament, and like spectators around the

[1] Exiles after unsuccessful uprisings.

huge space were crowded the resurrected peoples, coffin-pale and trembling. First came Satan galloping in the lists, black-besaddled on a milk-white charger; and, riding slowly behind, Death on her pale horse. Last came Christ in golden armour, on a black steed. With his holy lance he first thrust Satan down, then Death—and the beholders rejoiced loudly. Stormy applause greeted Liszt's playing. He left the piano exhausted, bowed to the ladies, and upon the lips of the beauties there was that melancholy-sweet smile.

It would be wrong of me to miss this occasion to mention another pianist who next to Liszt is most honoured. I refer to Chopin, whose accomplishment is great not solely as a virtuoso of brilliant technical mastery but also as a composer. He is a man of the first rank, the darling of the elite which seeks in music the highest spiritual pleasure. Chopin's fame is aristocratic, it is perfumed with the approval of good society, it is as distinguished as his person.

. . . Yes, one must grant Chopin genius in the fullest sense of the word; he is not simply a technician, he is a poet and can express for us the poetry that lives in his soul; he is a poet in sound, and nothing is quite like the delights he lavishes on us when he sits at the keyboard and improvises. At such times he is neither Pole, Frenchman, nor German; he betrays a far higher origin, and seems to come from the land of Mozart, Raphael, and Goethe: his true native shores seem to be the dreamland of poetry.

LETTERS ON THE FRENCH STAGE (1837)

FRIEDRICH NIETZSCHE

Wagner as Actor

Contrary to common belief, Nietzsche felt and wrote down his chief strictures against Wagner's mind and work before publishing his initial eulogy (see p. 63). But in that first essay, being a very young enthusiast, he palliated his doubts with hopes and arguments. Later on, he did not so much 'turn' against Wagner as reveal in violent language the substance of his first objections.

M Y objections to Wagner's music are physiological—why disguise them as usual behind aesthetic formulas? Aesthetics is nothing else than applied physiology. I base myself upon fact—indeed it is my 'small, real fact'[1] when I say that I breathe with difficulty as soon as Wagner's music begins to act upon me. I say that my *foot* gets annoyed and rebels against the music; my foot wants rhythm, dancing, marching. The rhythm of Wagner's '*Kaisermarsch*' keeps even the young emperor[2] from marching in time with it. My foot asks of music, above all, the pleasure of *good* pacing, stepping, dancing, capering.

And then is not my stomach in revolt as well? my heart and the circulation of my blood? It seems as if my bowels were saddened too, and my throat made hoarse by imperceptible degrees: in order to listen to Wagner I need medicated lozenges. And so I ask myself the question: What, in the last analysis, does *my body as a whole* require of music? For there is no such thing as the soul. Well, I think my body needs lift, lightening, it needs all the animal functions accelerated by light, bold, heedless, and proud rhythms; so that our leaden life, our cast-iron existence shall lose its gravity under the influence of golden melodies, delicate, fluent as oil. My melancholy wants to find surcease in the crannies and abysses of *perfection*.

But Wagner makes one ail! What matters to me the theatre? Of what value to me the cramps of its 'moral' ecstasies which satisfy the crowd—and do not belong to the crowd? What do I care about the

[1] An allusion to Stendhal on novel writing: *de petits faits vrais.*
[2] William II, aged twenty-nine at his accession in 1888.

grimaces of the comedian? It is easy to see that my nature is essentially anti-theatrical. In the depths of my being I feel for the theatre—*the art for the masses par excellence*—the infinite contempt that today every true artist feels. Mention *success* in the theatre, and my regard hits bottom; *lack* of success, I prick up my ears and begin to pay attention.

Wagner, on the contrary—side by side with the Wagner who wrote the most solitary music there is—was essentially a comedian and man of the theatre. He was the most enthusiastic mime-lover there has ever been, *even as a musician*. I may add in passing that if Wagner's theory declared the drama to be the goal and music only a means, his *practice* throughout has invariably been: 'Attitudes are the goal; drama just as much as music is but a means.' Music serves him to accentuate, to reinforce, to *in*ternalize the outward dramatic gesture of the comedian. Wagnerian drama is only a pretext for a number of interesting attitudes.

For beside all his other instincts, Wagner had the commanding instincts of a great actor—always and everywhere; and as I have said, he had these instincts as musician too. I managed to demonstrate this once to a fanatical Wagnerian with complete clarity—clarity and Wagnerism! I need say no more. But I had reason then for adding: 'Why not be a little more honest with yourself? We're not in Bayreuth!' In Bayreuth one can be honest only in the mass; as an individual, one is a liar—a liar to oneself. One leaves oneself at home by going to Bayreuth; one gives up the right to choose and speak out; gives up one's taste and even one's courage, in other words, one's normal strength for facing God and men.

No one can bring to the theatre the finest feeling for art, least of all the artist who works for the theatre. There is no solitude there, and all perfection requires an absence of witnesses. At the theatre one becomes people, woman, Pharisee, voter, founding-patron, nitwit—Wagnerite. In the theatre the most individual mind succumbs to the levelling spell of the mass. In the theatre the neighbour is king, and one becomes a neighbour.

NIETZSCHE CONTRA WAGNER (1877-88)

STENDHAL

Rossini's 'Barber of Seville'

The only works by Stendhal to achieve any circulation during his own life were his writings on Haydn and Mozart and especially his Life of Rossini. The conversational style, which deserts logic in favour of 'jottings,' is a part of Stendhal's method and should not deceive or disconcert the unaccustomed reader.

I F one ever wants to become intimately acquainted—for pleasure or out of mere curiosity—with Rossini's style, it is in *The Barber of Seville* that one must study it. For the composer's chief characteristic is undoubtedly writ large over that opera. It is this: Rossini, who is so adept at finales, ensembles, and duets, is feeble and pretty-pretty in the airs which should depict passion with simplicity. The *canto spianato*[1] is his downfall.

The Romans think that if Cimarosa[2] had composed the music of *The Barber*, it would have been a little less lively but more comic and infinitely more expressive. I wonder. Have you ever been a soldier? Have you trotted all over the globe? Has it happened to you to find suddenly once again at the waters of Baden a charming mistress whom you had worshipped ten years before at Dresden or Bayreuth?[3] The first moment of recognition is delightful, but the third or fourth day, you begin to feel too much delight, too much adoration, too much sweetness. The boundless devotion of this good dear German girl makes you regret, even if you will not admit it to yourself, the capricious piquancy of a haughty Italian who is both beautiful and mad— exactly the same impression that has just been made upon me by the admirable music of [Cimarosa's] *Matrimonio segreto*,[4] which has been revived in Paris for Mlle de Meri.

[1] Song in smooth style.
[2] Opera composer (1749–1801) who died after imprisonment for his part in the attempted liberation of Italy from Bonaparte's troops.
[3] Stendhal is not knowingly prophetic. Bayreuth was then a sleepy little town where, in his army days, he may have spent some time.
[4] *The Secret Marriage* (1792).

The first day, on leaving the theatre, I could see Rossini only as a pygmy. I remember saying to myself, 'One must not be too quick about passing judgment; I am under the spell.' Yesterday (August 19, 1823), on leaving the fourth performance of the *Matrimonio*, I had a glimpse of the towering monument which is Rossini's glory. The absence of dissonance makes itself cruelly felt in the second act of the *Matrimonio*. I find despair and misery expressed there with a flavour of rose water. We have progressed as regards misery since 1793.[1] The great quartet of the first act—

> What sorrowful silence!

seems long. In a word, Cimarosa has more ideas than Rossini, and indeed better ideas, but Rossini has the better style.

A connoisseur to whom I submitted this chapter on the *Barber* so that he could correct the errors of fact into which I so often fall— like the astrologer into a well, from looking at the heavens—said to me, 'Is that what you mean to give as an analysis of an opera? Why, it's just whipped cream. I can't stand those frothy sentences! Come, get down to work seriously. Open the score; I'll play you the principal arias, and you will make a tight and reasoned analysis.'

It is obvious in the chorus of serenaders which opens the *Barber* that Rossini is competing with Paisiello.[2] It is all sweetness and grace but there is no simplicity. Count Almaviva is weak and common; he is a French lover of the 1770s. By contrast, Rossini's full fire bursts out in the chorus—

> A thousand thanks, my lord!

and this vivacity rises quickly to real verve and brilliance, which is not always true of Rossini. Here his soul seems to have been brought to incandescence by the very force of his wit. The Count withdraws as he hears Figaro coming, and as he goes he remarks—

> Yes, the dawn is hardly here,
> But love is—if not modesty.

How like an Italian! A lover, says the Count, permits himself every-

<hr />

[1] Allusion to the Terror and Napoleonic wars.

[2] Composer of over a hundred operas (1741–1816), rival of Cimarosa and Napoleon's favourite musician.

thing. Everyone should feel that love is an excuse that covers everything in the eyes of those not concerned. But in northern climes, on the contrary, love is timid and fearful even before the unconcerned.

Figaro's cavatina—

> Make way for the steward!

as sung by Pellegrini, is and will long remain the masterpiece of French music. What fire, lightness, and wit in the line—

> By a barber of quality!

What expressiveness in—

> With the little wench . . .
> With the gentleman. . . .

This pleased the Parisians, though it could easily have been hissed because of the risqué meaning of the words.

The balcony scene of *The Barber* is divine for music; it is pure grace and tender naïveté. But Rossini slights it in order to reach the superb buffoonery of the duet—

> At the thought of clinking coin!

The first measures express to perfection the omnipotence of gold in the eyes of Figaro. Whereas the Count's exhortation—

> Come! let's see that clinking coin!

is that of a young nobleman who is not so much in love that he can't in passing make fun of Figaro's plebeian greed for money. I have spoken elsewhere of the marvellous rapidity of—

> Today there comes a regiment—
> Yes, but the colonel is my friend.

This passage seems to me Rossini's masterpiece in that particular genre, which makes it the high point of musical art. I only regret a touch of vulgarity in—

> What an excellent invention!

That duet is what will kill French grand opera. No heavier enemy, you will admit, could fall under a lighter assailant. It availed nothing that French opera used to bore people of taste in the time of La Bruyère,[1] a mere hundred and fifty years ago. That kind of opera has

---

[1] French satirist (1645–96) who scorned Lulli's operas as absurdities.

survived sixty different ministries. To kill it, there had to appear a genuine French music. The greatest criminals in the affair, after Rossini, are MM. Massimino, Choron, and Castil-Blaze.[1]

Now let me brave again the charge of paradox. The air upon Calumny seems to me only an extract from Mozart, made by an extremely clever man who is himself capable of composing excellently well. The air is too long for dramatic effect; yet it makes an admirable contrast with the lightness of all the preceding songs. It was wonderfully sung at La Scala in Milan by M. Levasseur, who was much applauded. In Paris he sings too timidly and gives the impression of being afraid to make a mistake. Voltaire used to say that in order to succeed in the arts, the theatre especially, one must be possessed by a demon.

MM. Meyerbeer, Morlacchi, Pacini, Mercadante, Mosca, Mayer, Spontini, and others who are contemporary with Rossini are glad enough doubtless to copy Mozart; but they have never yet found in the scores of the great man an air like that upon Calumny. Without pretending to make Rossini the equal of Raphael, I may say that it is thus Raphael used to copy Michelangelo in the beautiful fresco of Isaiah, in the church of St. Augustine, near the Piazza Navone in Rome.

Not on purpose, but just because of the susceptibility to feeling which makes for genius in the arts, Rossini has depicted in his music the women who loved him and whom, perhaps, he loved a little bit in return. Without knowing it, he took as arbiters of the melodies which he wrote at three in the morning the ladies with whom he had just passed the evening, and in whose eyes any tender or timid sentiment would have looked like the silliness of a college boy. Rossini owed his incredible success with women to a self-possession and disinterestedness out of the common. The Barber and several of the operas he has written since make me apprehend the effect of such success upon his art. Does he not owe his good fortune in love to the absence of any sense of distinction among women? I am inclined to fear that his luck with the Roman ladies has made him insensible to feminine grace. In The Barber, as soon as he has to be gentle he becomes

[1] Respectively, voice teacher and composer; choral conductor; and adapter of operas in Paris.

elegant and affected, he never drops the temperate style. He is like Fontenelle the philosopher speaking of love.[1] This way of life is all very well in day-to-day affairs, but it will not do for real fame. I find a great deal more energy and abandon in Rossini's earliest works.

I should willingly conclude that if Rossini had been born with fifty thousand francs' income, like his colleague M. Meyerbeer, his genius would have fixed him in *opera buffa*. But he had to live. He knew that Mlle Colbran, who sings only *opera seria*, was all-powerful in Naples; so, in the rest of Italy, is the police, which is as ridiculous in small things as it is impotent in great. It is the basic ideas of that same police, invented forty years ago by Leopold, Grand Duke of Tuscany, that have deprived Italy of that beautiful genre of native literature, the *commedia dell'arte*, or comedy played impromptu, which Goldoni thought he was displacing by his flat dialogue.

Here I can no longer set forth my meaning, even between the lines. I must appeal to the travellers who have spent a winter in Rome, or who know, for example, the stories about the elevation of the popes Pius VI and Pius VII. Those are the people which it is feared the words of an opera libretto will corrupt. Good Lord! Raise four more companies of police, hang the twenty crookedest judges each year, and you'll be doing rather more for good morals. Putting aside theft, bribery-at-law, and other trifles of that sort, just think of what the morals must be in a country where all the employees of the state are celibate and live under such a climate with such opportunities! Why, two centuries of Napoleon's despotism would not succeed in establishing in Rome the decent and pure habits of a small English town—of Norwich or Nottingham.

But to return to *The Barber*—a long distance it may seem. Not so long as you suppose: a source of limpid water, full of taste and salubrity, springs from the foot of a mountain. Do you know how it came to be in the heart of the rock? Until we are given the demonstration of the *how*, I shall maintain that every condition of the mountain, the form of its valleys, the slope of its woods—everything has contributed to produce this delicious spring, at which the hunter slakes his thirst and recovers strength as by a miracle. All the governments of Europe

[1] Fontenelle (1657–1757) acknowledged that there were three things he had never understood—women, gambling, and music. One recalls his remark: 'Sonata, what do you want with me?'

establish conservatories; several princes really love music and sacrifice their budget to it; but do they manage to produce beings like Rossini and Davide, that is to say, great composers and great singers? No. There must consequently be some circumstance which is unknown but necessary in the life of beauteous Italy and Germany. It is less cold in the rue Le Peletier[1] than in Dresden or Darmstadt. Why then are the people of rue Le Peletier more barbaric? Why does the orchestra of Dresden or Reggio perform divinely a crescendo of Rossini's which is found impossible in Paris?

I hear that in Vienna, where they had the bliss to hear simultaneously Davide, Mme Fodor, and Lablache (1823), they always repeat the end of the trio—

Quiet, quiet, gently, gently . . .

I have the highest respect for the musical taste of the Viennese. They have had the honour of forming Haydn and Mozart. Metastasio,[2] who lived among them for forty years, carried the taste for art into high society. Finally the great lords, the richest in Europe, do not disdain being opera directors.

I certainly hope that if this book of mine still exists in 1840, it will be infallibly thrown into the fire. Just see what is done today with the essays on political theory written in 1789. Everything I have just been saying for an hour will seem feeble and commonplace in the salon of Merilde, that pretty young girl, aged ten, who so loves Rossini but prefers Cimarosa. The revolution that is beginning in music will totally eclipse the good old French taste. What a pity! . . . In fact, what seems obscure and risky in this book will be feeble and commonplace by 1833. The party committed to the good old things has only one recourse, and that is to drive out the Italians or mate them with Frenchwomen. Superb voices that did not know how to sing would soon destroy music.

Before I finish I should say a word about the peculiarities of Rossini's style; that seems to be a necessity connected with my subject. To speak of paintings in a book, to praise pictures, is an appalling task;

---

[1] Site of the Paris opera house.
[2] Librettist, poet, and musician (1698–1782).

but pictures at least leave a distinct impression, even on fools. What then must writing about music be like! Into what queer and absurd nonsense will not one fall! The reader may guess he won't have to go far to find examples.

Good music is only *our emotion*. It would seem that music gives us pleasure by compelling our imagination to feed for the moment on illusions of a certain kind. These illusions are not calm and sublime like those of sculpture, nor tender and dreamy like those of Correggio's paintings.

The first characteristic of Rossini's music is speed—a speed which removes from the soul all the sombre emotions that are so powerfully evoked within us by the slow strains of Mozart. I find also in Rossini a cool freshness, which, measure by measure, makes us smile with delight. Any score seems heavy and tedious after one of Rossini's. If Mozart were a newcomer today, that is the judgment we should pass upon his music. We would have to hear him for two weeks on end before we could find pleasure in his work; he would be hissed the first night. If Mozart has survived Rossini's fame, if we often prefer him to Rossini, it is because he has the aid of our old admiration and the memory of the past pleasures he has afforded us. In general, it is people strong enough to resist ridicule who greatly prefer Mozart. The vulgar amateurs speak of him as vulgar men of letters speak of Fénelon. They praise him but would be in despair if suspected of writing like him.

Though Rossini's music is never heavy, it palls quite soon. The most distinguished judges in Italy who have heard his works for a dozen years want something new. What will the consensus be twenty years hence, when *The Barber of Seville* will be as old as the *Matrimonio segreto* or *Don Giovanni*? Rossini is rarely sad; but what is music without a touch of pensive sadness in it? 'I am never merry when I hear sweet music' is said (in *The Merchant of Venice*) by the modern poet who best knows the secrets of the human heart—the author of *Cymbeline* and *Othello*.

Still, in our expeditious century, Rossini has one advantage: he can dispense with attentiveness.

In a drama where music seeks to express the shade or degree of the feeling indicated by the words, one must pay attention in order to be moved, which is to say, in order to find pleasure. There is an even more exacting requirement: one must have a heart in order to be moved.

In a score by Rossini, on the contrary, each air or duet is usually but a brilliant concert piece—especially so in the operas written at Naples for Mlle Colbran. And with these only the slightest degree of attention will procure pleasure; most of the time there is no need whatever to possess what people of feeling call heart.

I am aware that I must justify so provocative an assertion. Kindly open your piano and remind yourself of the first scene of the *Matrimonio segreto*, where Carolina enjoys the blissful presence of her lover. She makes a sweet remark on the happiness they could share—

> If love could but run smooth . . .

These extremely simple words have given rise to one of the most beautiful musical phrases ever penned. Now Rosine, in *The Barber of Seville*, discovers that her lover is faithful after she has thought him a monster of ingratitude and baseness—a man who was selling her to Count Almaviva. In this instant of transport, the most heavenly that can be conceived, our thankless Rosine manages only to sing us some *fioriture*, which apparently suited the graceful voice of the first Rosine, Mme Giorgi. These *fioriture*, fit for a pleasant concert, are sublime for nobody, but Rossini wanted to make them entertaining—and succeeded. He is without excuse. The happiness of the scene in question is far too great to be mere joyousness. Such is the principal fault of Rossini's second manner; he composes his scores by writing ornaments of the kind his singers were in the habit of adding ad lib to the songs of other masters. What used to be a more or less agreeable accessory, he often makes into the main dish.

Rossini, like all the other masters, writes operas in the confident belief that his two acts will be separated by an hour and a half of ballet or interlude. In France, where genuineness is hardly what is uppermost in the pursuit of pleasure, people would think themselves lukewarm about Rossini if they did not listen to him steadily for three hours on end. This musical glut, presented with so much wit to the European audience that has the least patience and the best dancers, is unbearable when *Don Giovanni* is being given, or any other *passionate* work of the kind. No one can hear the four acts of *The Marriage of Figaro* without a headache and a feeling of mortal lassitude. One thinks to forgo music for at least a week. But one feels entirely different after hearing uninterruptedly the two acts of *Tancred* or *Elizabeth*: Rossini's music, which at all points condescends to be nothing more than a concert piece, does very well under the theatrical habits of Paris, and emerges triumphant from the test. In all possible senses of the term, his is music ideally designed for the French, yet by working upon us daily it helps to make us worthy of more passionate accents.

LIFE OF ROSSINI (1824)

HUGO WOLF

The Russian School

'EVERYTHING in moderation.' This touted maxim of the wise proves true in art no less than throughout ordinary life. It applies equally to the excessive partaking of pigs' knuckles (as Mörike's poem 'Everything in Moderation' points out) as to an excessive partaking of music, as Anton Rubinstein's[1] piano recitals in no little measure demonstrate. We certainly do not belong to the apostles of moderation. Abstinence, self-laceration, and mortification of the flesh are things we have never preached. We are not musical Trappists. But listening to a whole evening of Russia's hopeful music of the future would put even the most nihilistic patriots of the Czar's empire out of humour. 'Out of tune' is the right word.[2] I would just as soon be turned by magic into an old woodwind as go through another such evening. I was so out of tune that even the most harmless triad could not allay my distrust for 'The Power of Music.'

Now the Poles, wherever and however they come face to face with the Russians, always get the worst of it in the end; but this time it went badly for the Russians, in spite of their numerical superiority. Yes indeed! Chopin played them a nasty trick. Eleven études by Chopin opened the manual affray at the last Rubinstein evening. It was a hot fight—eleven études: yet there were no broken bones. Melodious strains fell upon the ear; the ghosts of exotic flowers danced now their dithyrambic and wild, now their sweetly languishing rounds, to rhythms both emphatic and original. Music such as this may narcotize, but it will cause no aches and pains.

How different the Russians! And first of all the wild Balakirev.[3] What a glutton for notes! He gobbles everything down to the hair and hide! There's a Jacobin for you! Poor abused and slandered Berlioz! How innocent you are compared to this body-snatcher Balakirev. Not content with murdering music, this bloodthirsty villain also mocks at

[1] (1830–94).
[2] The author plays on the word *verstimmt*.
[3] Mili Balakirev (1836–1910).

her corpse and jokes over the thousand wounds which in his fits of frenzy (composer's whims) he inflicts upon her. Fortunate Russia that produces such men of progress.

Only Tchaikovsky, among all these Cuis, Liadovs, Rimsky-Korsakovs,[1] and so forth, stands out as an honourable exception. Tchaikovsky really strives to create not merely Russian national music, but music first and foremost. His 'Song without Words,' his waltzes and romances, are charming inventions and finished compositions. His 'Scherzo à la Russe' is also to my taste, even though the Russian-national element in that work overlays with a rough hand the lines of beauty, to the point of making them unrecognizable.

The most favourable impression, after that made by Chopin's études, came unquestionably from the compositions of Michael Glinka.[2] Glinka is the classicist as opposed to the new hyper-Romanticist direction of the modern Russian school. His operas, A Life for the Czar and Ruslan and Ludmilla[3] are also known in Germany and admired there. His piano pieces are melodious, delicately felt, and not without ingenious touches. The evening concluded with compositions by the two brothers Rubinstein.[4] The celebrated virtuoso revealed no especial talent in his choice of works to perform on this occasion. He could have done himself a better turn. Waltzes and Album Leaves by Nicholas Rubinstein constitute a fixture in the Rubinstein programmes —and are known accordingly.

With this performance Anton Rubinstein has put a good piece of work behind him. To have carried through an undertaking of this magnitude is something unique in the annals of concert-giving. It deserves to be called a superhuman feat if one thinks of what the thing involves. How it was done is of course a question of genius. Now Rubinstein managed like a genius the task that he set himself. And in another respect he supplied an example which showed the humane and generous quality of his convictions in the finest light. For apart from the proverbial largesse of Franz Liszt, hardly any instance compares with this, of giving seven piano recitals gratis for the benefit of indigent musicians and music lovers. This noble trait in Rubinstein's character

[1] César Cui (1835–1918); Liadov (1855–1914); Nicholas Rimsky-Korsakov (1844–1908).
[2] Michael Glinka (1803–57).
[3] 1836 and 1842 respectively.
[4] Anton and his brother Nicholas (1835–81).

is no less an ornament to the man than his genius is to the artist. And as the great public presents the laurel wreath to the celebrated man, so will the small community of Bösendorfer Hall[1] dedicate in heartfelt gratitude a modest leaf of evergreen in faithful memory of true humanity.

COLLECTED CRITIQUES (1886)

---

[1] Named after Ignaz Bösendorfer, piano manufacturer (1796–1859).

IGNAZ MOSCHELES

Johann Strauss in London

'Almack's' was a fashionable place of resort established by a Scotsman named Macall. It was later renamed Willis's Rooms, and young Thomas Hardy used to dance quadrilles there before the days of romps and gallops.

BY a recent and sudden change in taste, however, we saw the rise to popularity of Johann Strauss. Where he fiddles, all dance—dance they must. In the concerts which he gives with his small orchestra, people dance as they sit; at Almack's, the most fashionable of all subscription ballrooms, aristocratic little feet tap in time with his tunes. And we too, the other night, had the good fortune to dance to his playing. Old married people as we are, we felt as if young again. He himself dances, body and soul, while he plays—not with his feet but with his violin, which keeps bobbing up and down while the whole man marks the accent of every bar. He is a good-natured Viennese, none of your sophisticated worldlings, but lively and always cheerful—a pleasant change from the many melancholy specimens we have had.

JOURNAL (1838)

CHARLES BURNEY

The First Handel Festival

The friend of Dr. Johnson and the father of the author of Evelina, *Dr. Charles
Burney was the founder of musicology in England. His History and his
Travels are still read for pleasure and instruction. The present description
of the first Handel commemoration was written for the Royal Family.*

PREFACE

A PUBLIC and national tribute of gratitude to deceased mortals,
whose labours and talents have benefited, or innocently amused
mankind, has, at all times, been one of the earliest marks of
civilization in every country emerged from ignorance and barbarism.
And there seemed no more rational solution of the mysteries of ancient
Greek mythology, than to imagine that men, whose virtue and abilities
surpassed the common standard of human excellence, had excited that
degree of veneration in posterior times, which gave rise to their
deification and apotheosis.

Such a gigantic idea of commemoration as the present, for the
completion of which it was necessary that so many minds should be
concentrated, must have been long fostering ere it took a practicable
form, and was matured into reality. But from the conception of this
plan to its full growth, there was such a concurrence of favourable
circumstances as the records of no art or science can parallel: the Royal
Patronage with which it was honoured; the high rank, unanimity, and
active zeal of the directors; the leisure, as well as ardour and skill of the
conductor; the disinterested docility of individuals; and liberal contributions of the public; all conspired to render this event memor-
able, and worthy of a place, not only in the annals of Music, but of
mankind.

And indeed it was hardly possible for a Musical Historian not to
imagine that an enterprise honoured with the patronage and presence
of their Majesties; planned and personally directed by noblemen and
gentlemen of the first rank; attended by the most numerous and
polite audience that was ever assembled on a similar occasion, in any

country; among whom, not only the King, Queen, Royal Family, nobility, and great officers of state appeared, but the archbishops, bishops, and other dignified clergy, with the heads of the law, would form an aera in Music, as honourable to the art and to national gratitude, as to the great artist himself who has given occasion to the Festival.

Handel, whose genius and abilities have lately been so nobly commemorated, though not a native of England, spent the greatest part of his life in the service of its inhabitants: improving our taste, delighting us in the church, the theatre, and the chamber; and introducing among us so many species of musical excellence, that, during more than half a century, while sentiment, not fashion, guided our applause, we neither wanted nor wished for any other standard. He arrived among us at a barbarous period for almost every kind of music, except that of the church. But, besides his oratorio choruses, which are so well intitled to immortality, his organ-pieces, and manner of playing, are still such models of perfection as no master in Europe has surpassed; and his operas were composed in a style so new and excellent, that no Music has since, with all its refinements of melody and symmetry of air, in performance, had such effects on the audience.

Indeed his works were so long the models of perfection in this country, that they may be said to have formed our national taste. For though many in the capital have been partial, of late years, to the compositions of Italy, Germany, and France; yet the nation at large has rather tolerated than adopted these novelties.

The English, a manly, military race, were instantly captivated by the grave, bold, and nervous style of Handel, which is congenial with their manners and sentiments. And though the productions of men of great genius and abilities have, since his time, had a transient share of attention and favour; yet, whenever any of the works of Handel are revived by a performer of superior talents, they are always heard with a degree of general satisfaction and delight, which other compositions seldom obtain. Indeed, the exquisite manner in which his productions are executed at the concert established for the preservation and performance of old masters, stimulates a desire in all who hear them to have a more general acquaintance with his works. And it was, perhaps, at the late performance in Westminster Abbey, that the compositions of this great master were first supplied with a band, capable of displaying all the wonderful powers of his harmony.

I

Early in the morning, the weather being very favourable, persons of all ranks quitted their carriages with impatience and apprehension, lest they should not obtain seats, and presented themselves at the several doors of Westminster Abbey, which were advertised to be opened at Nine o'clock; but the door-keepers not having taken their posts, and the Orchestra not being wholly finished, or, perhaps, the rest of the Abbey quite ready for the reception of the audience, till near Ten o'clock; such a croud of ladies and gentlemen were assembled together as became very formidable and terrific to each other, particularly the female part of the expectants; for some of these being in full dress, and every instant more and more incommoded and alarmed, by the violence of those who pressed forward, in order to get near the door, screamed; others fainted; and all were dismayed and apprehensive of fatal consequences: as many of the most violent, among the gentlemen, threatened to break open the doors; a measure, which if adopted, would, probably, have cost many of the most feeble and helpless their lives; as they must, infallibly, have been thrown down, and trampled on, by the robust and impatient part of the croud.

It was a considerable time after a small door at the west end was opened, before this press abated: as tickets could not be examined, and cheques given in return, fast enough, to diminish the candidates for admission, or their impatience.

However, except dishevelled hair, and torn garments, no real mischief seems to have happened. In less than an hour after the doors were opened, the whole area and galleries of the Abbey seemed too full for the admission of more company; and a considerable time before the performance began, the doors were all shut to every one but their Majesties, and their suite, who arrived soon after Twelve; and on entering the box, prepared for their reception, pleasure and astonishment, at the sight of the company and disposition of the Orchestra and Performers, were painted so strongly in their countenances, as to be visible to all their delighted subjects present. Eagerness and expectation for the *premier coup d'archet*[1] were now wound up to the highest pitch of impatience; when a silence, the most profound and solemn, was gently interrupted by the processional symphony of the

[1] The first attack of the bow. See p. 359.

CORONATION ANTHEM

And from the time that the first sound of this celebrated, and well-known composition, was heard, to the final close, every hearer seemed afraid of breathing, lest it should obstruct the stream of harmony in its passage to the ear.

From the progress which practical Music has made in this country, since Handel's time, it might, perhaps, be safely pronounced, that this Anthem was never so well performed, under his own direction. As I heard it myself at the Coronation of his present Majesty, when a numerous band was assembled under the direction of the late Doctor Boyce, I can, at least, venture to say that, in recollection, the perform-ance then will bear no comparison with that now, in the same place, in honour of the composer.[1]

OVERTURE IN ESTHER

The first movement of this grave and majestic Overture has always astonished me, by the simplicity of its modulation; which, though almost rigorously confined to the diatonic intervals, and harmony of the key, is never monotonous in its effects. And the first bar of the melody, though so often repeated by the two violins, is so grateful and pleasing, as to be always welcome to the ear.

All the movements of this admirable Overture first appeared in Handel's *Trios*, as did many of those he introduced afterwards in his Organ Concertos. This overture, almost ever since it was composed, has been so constantly played at Saint Paul's, at the Feast of the Sons of the Clergy, that it now seems in a peculiar manner dedicated to the service of the Church.

[1] There was, doubtless, the greatest propriety in saluting their Majesties, at their entrance, with the *Coronation Anthem*; and yet, I could not help wishing, that this performance, so different from all others, had opened with some piece in which every voice and every instrument might have been heard at the same instant; as such an effect might then have been produced, as can never be obtained by gradation: the difference between *nothing* and *something* being greater, than between any two degrees of excellence. Indeed, the most sudden and *surprising* effect of this stupendous band, was, perhaps, produced by simul-taneous tuning: as all the stringed-instruments performed this task, *à double corde*, and these strings being all *open*, their force was more than equal to that of two stopt-strings, upon two different instruments. [Burney's note.]

THE DETTINGEN TE DEUM

This splendid production has been so frequently performed at Saint Paul's and elsewhere, that nothing could be added to its celebrity by my feeble praise. I shall only observe, that as it was composed for a military triumph, the fourteen trumpets, two pair of common kettle-drums, two pair of double drums from the Tower, and a pair of double-base drums, made expressly for this Commemoration, were introduced with great propriety; indeed, these last drums, except the destruction, had all the effect of the most powerful artillery.

There is some reason to suspect that Handel, in setting his grand *Te Deum* for the peace of Utrecht, as well as this, confined the meaning of the word *cry* to a sorrowful sense: as both the movements to the words—

> '*To thee all angels* cry *aloud,*'

are not only in a minor-key, but slow, and plaintive. It contrasts well, however, with the preceding and subsequent movements. Indeed, the latter glows with all the fire and vehemence of Handel's genius for polyphonic combinations and contrivances.

The grave and solemn praise of the *Apostles*, *Prophets*, and *Martyrs*, measured by the constant majestic motion of the base, is well symbolized.

> '*Thou sittest at the right hand of God,*' etc.,

is expressed in a strain that is remarkably pleasing, and which, in spite of forty years, still retains all the bloom and freshness of novelty: and

> '*We therefore pray thee help thy servants, who thou hast redeemed with thy precious blood,*'

is admirable, in fugue, modulation, and counterpoint, *à Capella*; as is the next movement, to the three verses:

> '*Make them to be numbered*'—
> '*O Lord save thy people*'—and
> '*Govern them and lift them up for ever,*'

with the additional merit of a happy verbal expression.

> '*Day by day we magnify thee,*'

is grand and well accented, though some of the trumpet passages are a little *vieillis*. The art of fugue, both in that, and the next verse:

> '*And we worship thy name ever world without end,*'

is treated with Handel's usual clearness and felicity.

As he was sure of a great and varied band, when he composed this *Te Deum*, he has made as judicious a use of the several instruments of his Orchestra, as a painter could do of the colours on his palette: now exhibiting them in their full lustre, singly; then augmenting or diminishing their force, by light and shade, and often by combination with others, making them subservient to different purposes of expression and effect.

> '*Vouchsafe, O Lord, to keep us this day without sin,*'

is set to an exquisite strain, in which the modulation is no less surprising, learned, and curious, than pathetic and pleasing.

The last movement:

> '*O Lord, in thee have I trusted,*' etc.,

is what the Italians would allow to be *ben tirato*. Indeed, it is an excellent display of Handel's resources in discovering and availing himself of the most latent advantages which every simple as well as artificial subject affords him. The symphony of this Chorus, which is chiefly constructed upon a *ground-base*, beginning by two trumpets, that are afterwards joined by the other instruments, is stately and interesting, though in the measure of a common minuet. The long solo part, after the symphony, for a contralto voice, with soft and sparing accompaniments, renders the subsequent sudden burst of all the voices and instruments the more striking. And the latter part, in fugue, with an alternate use of the ground-base, seems to wind up this magnificent production by

> 'Untwisting all the chains that tie
> The hidden soul of harmony.'

II

OVERTURE IN SAUL

The first movement of this admirable composition, so different from the common style of Overture, which Lulli had established, and to which all the composers in Europe, for more than fifty years, implicitly conformed, is extremely pleasing; and when it was first heard, must have surprised, by the grace and novelty of its conduct and passages.

Though the rest of this Overture was superseded, in favour of the *Dead March*, yet it is but justice to the author to say, that the second movement, with solo parts for the principal hautbois and violin, is so *chantant*, as perpetually to remind the hearer of a vocal duet, richly accompanied. The fugue, indeed with solo parts for the organ, was, perhaps, very judiciously omitted; as the passages have been long in such favour with the imitators of Handel as to be rendered trite and vulgar. The *Minuet* will, however, always preserve its grace and dignity; being one of the few final movements of an Overture, which neither age, nor fashion, can deform.

THE DEAD MARCH IN SAUL

This most happy and affecting movement, which has retained its favour near half a century, and which is so simple, solemn, and sorrowful, that it can never be heard, even upon a single instrument, without exciting melancholy sensations, received here all the dignity and grandeur which it could possibly derive from the various tones of the most powerful, as well as best disciplined, band, that was ever assembled.

PART OF THE ANTHEM

WHICH WAS PERFORMED IN WESTMINSTER ABBEY AT THE FUNERAL OF HER SACRED MAJESTY QUEEN CAROLINE, 1737

'*When the ear heard her, then it blessed her; and when the eye saw her, it gave witness of her.*' Job 29: 11.

This elegant, mild, and sorrowing strain, after all the riotous clangour of jubilation in the *Te Deum*, and powerful percussion of drums, and tuneful blasts of trumpets and sacbuts, in the *Dead March*, was soothing and comforting to the ear. Contrast is the great source of our musical pleasure; for however delighted we may be with *quick, slow, loud, or soft*, for a certain time, variety is so necessary to stimulate attention, that the performance which is in want of the one, is never sure of the other. This charming movement is still so new, that it would do honour to the taste, as well as knowledge in harmony, of any composer now living. Handel had a versatile genius; and, if he had continued to write for the Opera, instead of the Church, there was no elegance or refinement which Hasse, Vinci, Pergolesi,[1] and their successors, ever attained, that was out of his reach.

'*She delivered the poor that cried, the fatherless, and him that had none to help him*'—Job 29: 12. '*Kindness, meekness, and comfort were in her tongue*'—Eccles. 36: 23. '*If there was any virtue, and if there was any praise, she thought on those things*'—Phil. 4: 8.

The trebles singing alone, and only accompanied in unison, by treble instruments, at the words—'*kindness, meekness, and comfort were in her tongue*,' had an admirable effect, in point of contrast, with the full harmony of the rest of this charming Chorus. Indeed, this *Naenia* contains all the requisites of good Music, in plain counterpoint: as good harmony, melody, rhythm, accent, and expression. The beauties of this strain are of every age and country; no change of fashion can efface them or prevent their being felt by persons of sensibility.

'*Their bodies are buried in peace*'—Eccles. 44: 14.

This admirable fragment of solemn and sorrowful harmony, in the Church style, almost wholly without instruments, is an excellent introduction to the less plaintive strain which follows:

'*But their name liveth evermore*'—Ibid.

which is one of the most singular and agreeable Choruses I know, and was performed with an accuracy, power, and spirit, which neither that, nor, perhaps, any Music of the kind ever received before. Each of the three movements from the *Funeral Anthem*, seemed to excite such lively sensations of grief, as reminded all present of the ravages which death had made among their particular families and friends, and moved many even to tears.

GLORIA PATRI. From the Jubilate, 1713.

'*Glory be to the Father,*' etc.

This Chorus, from the *Jubilate*, which Handel set at the same time as the grand *Te Deum*, for the peace at Utrecht, and the only *Jubilate*

[1] See, respectively, pp. 302, 222, and 213.

he ever composed, being in his grandest and most magnificent style, received every possible advantage in the performance, from a correct and powerful band, and the most mute and eager attention in the audience.

III

ANTHEM. Composed about the Year 1719.

AIR AND CHORUS

'*O sing unto the Lord a new song; O sing unto the Lord all the whole earth.*' Ps. 96: 1.

Madame Mara's voice and manner of singing in this plain and solemn air, so admirably accompanied on the hautbois by Fisher, had a sudden effect on myself, which I never before experienced, even from her performance of more pathetic Music. I have long admired her voice, and abilities in various styles of singing; but never imagined tenderness the peculiar characteristic of her performance: however, here, though she had but a few simple notes to deliver, they made me shiver, and I found it extremely difficult to avoid bursting into tears on hearing them. Indeed, she had not only the power of conveying to the remotest corner of this immense building, the softest and most artificial inflexions of her sweet and brilliant voice, but articulated every syllable of the words with such neatness, precision, and purity, that it was rendered as audible, and intelligible, as it could possibly have been, in a small theatre, by meer declamation.

CHORUS

'*Declare his honour unto the Heathen, and his wonders unto all people— For the Lord is great, and cannot worthily be praised.*' Ps. 96: 3, 4.

This Chorus is in a truly grand style, and produced great effects though there are only three vocal parts. The subject is reversed, at the latter end, in a most ingenious manner.

'*He is more to be feared than all gods*'—Ps. 96: 3, 4.

Here the modulation is sublime, and truly ecclesiastic.

'*The waves of the sea rage horribly; but yet the Lord who dwells on high is mightier*'—Ps. 93: 5.

Handel, in the accompaniments of this boisterous air, has tried, not unsuccessfully, to express the turbulence of a tempestuous sea; the style of this kind of Music is not meant to be amiable; but it contrasts well with other movements, and this has a spirit, and even roughness, peculiar to our author.

DUET

'O worship the Lord in the beauty of holiness.' Ps. 96: 9.

The solemnity of this movement may, perhaps, seem as much too languid to the admirers of the preceding air, as that may be too turbulent for the nerves of those who are partial to this. The truth is, that both verge a little on the extreme; but a composer, of such extensive powers of invention as Handel, dares every thing, for the sake of variety: and this Duet is much in the admired style of Steffani.

CHORUS

'Let all the whole earth stand in awe of him.' Ibid. 'Let the heavens rejoice, and let the earth be glad; let the sea make a noise and all that therein is.' Ibid., 11.

In the last movement of this Chorus, when all the instruments are busied, such a commotion is raised, as constitutes one of Handel's most formidable hurricanes.

CHORUS IN ISRAEL IN EGYPT

'The Lord shall reign for ever and ever.' Exod. 15: 18.

This most admirable composition which is written *a due cori*, begins by the tenors and counter-tenors, in unison, accompanied only by a ground-base.

RECITATIVE

'For the horse of Pharaoh with his chariots,' etc. Exod. 15.

Mr. Norris pronounced this and the following Recitative with the true energy of an Englishman, who perfectly comprehended and articulated the words.

CHORUS

'The Lord shall reign for ever and ever.'

The return to this short strain of Chorus, after each fragment of Recitative, has a fine effect.

RECITATIVE

'*And Miriam the prophetess, the sister of Aaron, took a timbrel in her hand: and all the women went out after her with timbrels and with dances.*' Exod. 15: 19.

CHORUS

'*Sing ye to the Lord, for he hath triumphed gloriously.*[1] *The Lord shall reign for ever and ever. The horse and his rider he hath thrown into the sea.*' Exod. 15: 21.

The effects of this composition are at once pleasing, grand, and sublime! The aggregate of voices and instruments had here its full effect. And such is the excellence of this production, that if Handel had composed no other piece, this alone would have rendered his name immortal, among true lovers and judges of harmony.[2]

· Upon the whole, the success of this day's performance may, with the utmost truth, be pronounced entire; as its effects surpassed the most sanguine expectations of the greatest enthusiasts for the honour of Handel, the glory of the profession, and prosperity of this grand enterprise. And, indeed, he must have been not only a fastidious, but a very ignorant and insensible hearer, who did not receive new and exquisite pleasure from the composition and execution of the pieces which were this day performed.

But, in justice to the audience, it may be said, that though the frequency of hearing good Music in this capital, of late years, has so far blunted the edge of curiosity and appetite, that the best Operas and Concerts are accompanied with a buz and murmur of conversation, equal to that of a tumultuous croud, or the din of high 'Change; yet

---

[1] Handel's uncertainty in whatever concerned the accent and pronunciation of our language appears very remarkably in his manner of setting this last Chorus; where he accents the words, '*For he hath triumphed gloriously,*' thus: '*Fŏr hĕ hāth trĭūmphed gloriously.*' But in the year 1738, when he composed the Oratorio of *Israel in Egypt*, our language was not very familiar to him; and he had then but little experience in setting it to Music. [Burney's note.]

[2] The art with which Handel, in the midst of all the fire of imagination and ebullition of genius, introduces a sober, *chanting* kind of *counter-subject*, while the other is carried on with uninterrupted spirit, is marvellous! [Burney's note.]

now, such a stillness reigned, as, perhaps, never happened before in so large an assembly. The midnight hour was never founded in more perfect tranquillity, than every note of these compositions. I have long been watching the operations of good Music on the sensibility of mankind; but never remember, in any part of Europe, where I attended Musical exhibitions, in the Church, Theatre, or Chamber, to have observed so much curiosity excited, attention bestowed, or satisfaction glow in the countenances of those present, as on this occasion. The effects, indeed, upon many were such as modern times have never before experienced. The *Choral power* of harmonical combinations affected some to tears, and fainting; while others were melted and enrapt, by the exquisite sweetness of *single sounds*. I had little leisure to contemplate the countenances of those around me; but, when I happened to turn my eyes from the performers, I saw nothing but tears of extacy, and looks of wonder and delight. Nothing, however, discovered the admirable discipline of the band, and unwearied and determined attention of the audience, so much as the *pauses*, which are so frequent in Handel's Music: for these were so unanimously calculated, and measured, that no platoon, or single cannon, was ever fired with more exact precision or unity of effect, than that with which the whole phalanx of this multitudinous band resumed its work, after all the sudden, and usually, unlimited cessations of sound, commonly called *pauses*, which, in general, catch loquacity in the fact; but now, at all these unexpected moments, the silence was found as awful and entire, as if none but the tombs of departed mortals had been present.

COMMEMORATION OF HANDEL (1785)

VARIOUS HANDS

Beethoven's 'Third' and 'Fifth'

Announcement of the first public playing of the Eroica:

A GRAND Sinfonie in D Sharp Minor by Herr Ludwig von Beethoven and dedicated to His Highness Prince von Lobkowitz will be played on Sunday, April 7, 1805, at the Theatre an der Wien. The composer will have the pleasure of conducting it himself.

The Vienna correspondent of the Allgemeine musikalische Zeitung:

I have heard a new sinfonie by Beethoven in E flat (erroneously announced as being in D sharp major)[1] under the composer's own direction. It was performed by a quite complete orchestra, but even this time I found no reason to change my earlier opinion.[2] Truly this new work of Beethoven's contains some grand and daring ideas, as one might expect from the powerful genius of the composer, and shows great expressive strength as well. But the sinfonie would be all the better—it lasts a whole hour—if Beethoven could reconcile himself to making some cuts in it and to bringing into the score more light, clarity, and unity—virtues that were never absent from the Sinfonies in G Minor and C Minor of Mozart, those in C and D of Beethoven, and those in E Flat and D of Eberl.[3] Here in place of the andante there is a funeral march in C minor, which is developed fugally, but this fugue is completely lost and confused in the way it is handled. Even after several hearings it eludes the most sustained attention, so that the unprepared connoisseur is really shocked. As a result this sinfonie was anything but enjoyed by the greater part of the audience.

[1] *Sic*: these several discrepancies of key are a telling part of the story. The Eroica is in E flat, the Fifth in C minor.

[2] At a private performance with incomplete instrumental forces, in December 1804.

[3] Anton Eberl (1766–1807), pianist and composer, friend of Mozart's.

Two and half years later:

This reviewer remains, in spite of all that has been written on this work, of his original opinion, namely, that this symphony undoubtedly contains many beautiful and sublime things, but that these elements are mixed with many harsh things and longueurs, and that it will be able to acquire the purity of form of a work of art only by a thorough revision.

About the same time, a Berlin reviewer:

The symphony is full of originality; it is abundant and even excessive in its harmony, but also full of bizarre ideas. . . . On the whole, this symphony by no means made an impression comparable to that made by Mozart's and Haydn's. The applause of those who know went to the performers, for their skilful overcoming of great difficulties for about three-quarters of an hour.

After Beethoven's concert of December 1808, intended by him as a farewell to the Viennese, and containing for the first time the Symphony in C Minor, No. 5, the composer wrote to his publishers:

To begin with, the musicians had lost their place and made a mistake in the simplest passage imaginable. So I stopped them sharply and cried out loud, 'Begin again!' It had never happened to them, and the public signified its satisfaction thereat.

The correspondent of the Allgemeine musikalische Zeitung:

The first movement in C minor is a fiery allegro, a little obscure, noble in feeling and in working out, firmly and evenly developed. It is a worthy piece, which will afford real pleasure even to those who are attached to the older way of composing large symphonies. The andante is very original and attractive, composed as it is of the most heterogeneous ideas—gentle reverie and warlike fierceness. Its handling from beginning to end is *sui generis*. Under its appearance of arbitrariness it is possible to find in this remarkable piece much thought, a firm grasp of the whole, and a very careful elaboration. As for the ensuing scherzando (which is hardly playable by a large orchestra), we must confess ourselves unable to enjoy it, owing to its far too insistent whims. But humour in art—if I may be permitted the comparison—is not just

like fine cooking: however elaborate it may be one must try and try
again in order to ascertain what might prove pleasing. The finale is a
tempestuous explosion, born of a powerful fancy, and such as one
would hardly find in any other symphony.

E. T. A. Hoffmann, the following year:

Beethoven's instrumental music opens to us the realm of the vast
and the mighty. Burning shafts of light pierce the gloom of that
empire, where we discern giant shadows rising and falling, entwining
themselves more and more closely about us, destroying everything
within us and not merely the pain of an infinite desire. All pleasure
springing forth in joyful notes sinks and disappears, yet it is in this
distress of consuming love, joy, and oppression—as if our heart would
burst in a single great chord uniting all our passions—that we continue
to live and find ourselves made into enchanted seers.

Nothing could be simpler than the motif on which the master bases
his whole allegro, but it will be noticed with amazement how he has
arranged all the secondary motives, all the episodes, so that by means
of their rhythmic connection with the first, they enhance the character
of the entire movement. Of all this the first motif was only the bare
hint. All the phrases are short; they consist of only two or three
measures and are usually divided among themselves by the constant
opposition of the strings and wind instruments. One might suppose
this would produce nothing but a broken-up, incoherent effect; on the
contrary, it is just that disposition of the whole, just that succession of
short phrases and single chords, which raises to the highest pitch our
feeling of unspeakably ardent desire.

Beethoven has kept to the ordinary sequence of movements in his
symphony, but they seem fantastically linked together and the whole
work resounds like a rhapsody of genius. Yet the mind of any sensitive
listener will undoubtedly be struck deeply, intimately, by one *single*
and lasting impression—that of desire, infinite, unappeasable—stretching to the very last chord. Even after the end, he will be unable to
escape from that marvellous realm of spirit in which pain and pleasure
envelop him in the guise of musical energies.

Twenty years later, F.-J. Fétis[1] writes of the Paris première:

Such a creation as the finale is above and beyond music. It is no

[1] See p. 323.

longer flutes, horns, violins, and basses that one hears, it is the world which totters, the universe. . . . Unfortunately Beethoven never knows when to stop. Nearly all his most beautiful movements keep on beyond the bounds of their necessary development and spoil the impression they create by passages of more or less bizarre workmanship. That is because in spite of the immense capacity of his genius Beethoven lacks that good taste which was the mark of Haydn's and Mozart's work. If these two great artists had found the sublime idea of the march I have just spoken of, and the admirable way of linking it with the preceding scherzo, they would carefully have avoided falling into the extravagance which follows and which quickly cools the listener's enthusiasm for Beethoven's symphony.

The next month, also in Paris, young Berlioz:

Lesueur[1] consented to let me take him to the Conservatoire for one of the performances of the Symphony in C Minor. He wanted to listen to it conscientiously and without distractions of any kind, and so took a seat among strangers in the last row of a first-tier box, sending me elsewhere. When the symphony was over, I came down from the upper tier in order to find out what Lesueur had felt and what he thought of this extraordinary work. I met him in one of the corridors. He was very red in the face and taking long strides.

'Well, master?' said I.

'Whew! I'm going out, I want some air, it's incredible, it's marvellous! It moved me so, it disturbed me and upset me so much that, on leaving the box and trying to put on my hat, I thought I should never find my head again. Leave me to myself. Come tomorrow.'

I was exultant. The next day I was promptly at his house. The conversation turned at once to the masterpiece that had so deeply affected us both. Lesueur allowed me to speak a little while, nodding with a somewhat constrained air at my admiring exclamations. But it was easy to see that I had no longer before me the same man as yesterday, and that the subject was now painful to him. I kept on nevertheless until Lesueur, from whom I had once again extorted an admission of the deep emotion he had felt on hearing the symphony, shook his head with a strange smile and said, 'All the same, one ought not to write music like that.'

[1] Composer of operas and oratorios, famous teacher of Berlioz, Gounod, etc.

To which I replied, 'Never fear, my dear master, there won't be much written *like that*.'

Poor human nature, poor dear master! His remark, so often echoed by other men in similar circumstances, is a compound of stubbornness, regret, terror before the unknown, jealousy, and an implicit admission of impotence. For to say 'one ought not to write music like that' when one has experienced its power and recognized its beauty is to declare that one will not compose in that manner because one feels that one could not even if one would.

LOUIS SPOHR

First Baton in London

Spohr's fame as the composer of a Faust *opera and many symphonies has greatly dimmed since the last century (though his name is embalmed in a verse of* The Mikado*). But his* Autobiography *is still full of interest, if only for its revelation of the author as a true and energetic artist. His span is 1784–1859 and the time of this narrative is the early spring of 1820.*

THE time for my trip to London had now come. Since I had agreed to buy for my wife in London a new Erard[1] harp with the improved 'double action' mechanism, we left her old instrument in Herr Vogel's care. The Vogel family were delighted with this plan, for now they were sure of seeing us again on our return journey.

Having arrived in Calais, I went at once to the packet-boat office to secure our berths. Then I took a walk to the port to see the ship on which we were to sail in the afternoon. But as I saw that even inside the harbour the sea was very rough and ran so high outside that the waves broke high over the pier, I lost all heart for the journey and hurried back to the shipping office in order to exchange our reservations for others on the following day.

In the afternoon, while taking a tour of the city with my wife, I took good care not to bring her within sight of the sea, so that, dreading the passage as she did already, she might not see the raging waters. The thought of having to cross at so stormy a time of year with my delicate and nervous wife kept me from resting throughout the night, and as soon as dawn broke I hurried again to the harbour to see whether the storm had abated. It seemed to me that it had; I therefore hurried Dorette on board and advised her to lie down at once in the cabin. A good-natured German who shipped as seaman on this English packet promised me to look after her and bring her whatever she might

[1] Famous firm of inventors and manufacturers of pianos and harps, established in both Paris and London.

require. This allowed me to go up on deck, where in the open air I hoped to be able to withstand seasickness.

Meanwhile preparations had been made for casting off, and the vessel was being towed with long ropes close upon the left side of the pier by some sixty to eighty men. Hardly had we reached the end of the pier when we were caught up by a colossal wave and in a twinkling hurled to the other side of the harbour; we nearly hit the point of the right-hand jetty. At once the waves broke over the deck so that the ports and hatches and cabin doors had to be made fast. I alone of all the passengers remained on deck and sat on a bench near the main mast, around which stood various high coils of cable. Here I hoped to be protected from the flood that swept the deck. But soon the waves broke so high that in order to avoid being entirely swamped I had to climb upon the bench. I had not done this many times before seasickness overcame me and I found my strength ebbing. Nor was it long before I was wet through to the skin, in spite of my thick overcoat. This made my earlier discomfort even more unbearable. On top of this I was seized by violent cramps, especially after my stomach had nothing more to yield, and I hardly thought I would survive.

Fortunately the trip was uncommonly rapid—thanks to the storm. Nevertheless the three hours it lasted seemed to me an eternity. At last we arrived in Dover, but here a new misfortune awaited us; it proved impossible to make the harbour owing to the ebb tide, and the passengers had to disembark in the offing. As soon as we had anchored, boats were lowered and the passengers summoned to trans-ship. I now saw my fellow-sufferers rise pale and shaky, like ghosts from the grave, and it was evident that they had not fared better down below than I had up on deck.

At length my poor wife also appeared, supported by the kind sailor, and seeming to suffer greatly. Just as I was about to hurry toward her, a young and beautiful girl, whom I had already noticed when we came on board, but who then had not deigned to look at me, suddenly threw her arms around my neck and without speaking a word held me close. I easily guessed the motive of this extraordinary behaviour. The poor frightened creature had seen the way in which the first passengers had been expedited into the boats, which tossed high upon the still raging waves and then sank into an abyss, and again rose as high as the deck of our vessel—at which moments the sailors would throw in another passenger or piece of luggage. This

procedure had so frightened the girl that she left the arm of her duenna
and fastened on to me, who doubtless looked to her like the sturdiest
man among the passengers. There was no time for explanations; I
carried her into the boat, then hurried back to my wife to do the
same for her. No sooner had I managed this as well than the still
anxious beauty clung to me again, to Dorette's considerable surprise.
But the dangers of the trip did not permit any remarks. After landing,
the girl scarcely touched terra firma before she broke loose from me
without a word of thanks, rejoined her companion, and walked away.
That she was some young lady of quality accompanied by her governess
can be readily inferred from this truly English behaviour.

Having changed my dripping clothes at the inn, and quelled our
reawakened appetites at the table d'hôte, and generally restored our
strength for travel, we took our seats in the coach for London. We
made most of the trip by night, and when we and our baggage were
set down the next morning in London, I found myself in a real
predicament. In spite of all my attempts I could find no one at the
coach office or outside to whom I could make myself understood. I
spoke not a word of English and no one there understood either
German or French. I had no other recourse but to roam the streets
and, while my wife watched the luggage, to hunt up an interpreter.

But it was still early morning and I met only people of the lower
classes from whom I could not expect knowledge of a foreign tongue.
There came at last a well-dressed man whom I addressed first in
German, then as he shook his head, in French, telling him my plight.
But he shrugged and walked away. A second person, however, who
had witnessed the scene, approached me and asked in excellent French
what it was I wanted. He was a courier on hire, and at my request
he immediately hailed a cab for us to drive over to Mr. Ries,[1] whose
address I fortunately remembered. We were now taken to the lodgings
that had been reserved for us, where we could at last rest after the
strain of the crossing and the night journey.

The next morning I was to be presented by Mr. Ries at the meeting
of directors of the Philharmonic Society. I therefore took especial care
about my toilet, and put on for this purpose one of the prize pieces
in my wardrobe—a bright red waistcoat made of Turkish shawl
material. On the Continent it was the latest fashion. But I had hardly

[1] Ferdinand Ries (1784–1838), Beethoven's pupil, an active member of the
London Philharmonic, and famed as piano virtuoso and composer. See p. 312.

appeared in the street when I found myself the target of public notice. The adult passers-by contented themselves with an amazed stare and went on their way, but the dear little urchins were loud in their comments, which I unfortunately missed, for I could not conceive what displeased them so. They gradually formed a procession in my wake, which became more and more vocal and unruly. A passer-by spoke to me and doubtless explained the cause, but his English was of no use to me.

Fortunately, Ries's house was not far from mine and I soon arrived. His wife, a charming young Englishwoman who spoke fluent French, gave me the clue to my adventure. George III had but recently died and national mourning had been decreed. By custom no one was to appear in public except in black. The rest of my costume, to be sure, was entirely black and therefore proper, but that unlucky red waistcoat only shone the more brilliantly by contrast. Mme Ries told me that I could certainly thank my imposing stature and earnest expression for saving me from physical insults at the hands of the street urchins, namely, pelting with mud. To avoid all further offence, Ries drove with me first to my rooms and I exchanged my red waistcoat for a black one.

After I had been kindly welcomed by the directors of the Philharmonic, some of whom spoke German and others French, we discussed the programme of my first concert. I was requested to play two solos and to lead the orchestra from the first-violin desk. I replied that I was ready to do the former, but must beg that I be allowed to lead at a later concert, for my solos would appear to less advantage if I was obliged to perform in two capacities on the same evening. Obvious as this was to those of the directors who were soloists, it gave rise to a long and lively argument before the point, which was contrary to custom, could be admitted.

Still greater offence was caused by my request to present at this first concert only compositions of my own. The Philharmonic Society had made it a rule—designed to exclude the usual virtuoso's worthless, empty concertos—to permit no such pieces to be played except Mozart's and Beethoven's piano concertos, and to choose, themselves, what soloists were to perform. When Ries had assured them in English —hence, to me unintelligibly—that in Germany my violin concertos would be put side by side with the works excepted from their prohibition, my point was finally conceded. I therefore appeared on the first Philharmonic programme with my *Scena cantante*[1] and, in the second half, with my Solo-quartet in E Major, and met with general applause. It gave me special pleasure as a composer that the directors now all shared Mr. Ries's opinion. And as a violinist I was made happy by the fact that old Viotti,[2] who had always been my model and who was to have been my teacher in youth, heard me and told me many things in praise of my playing.

Having successfully weathered my first appearance in London, I devoted the next day to delivering my letters of recommendation. For me who knew not a word of English this was a gruelling task and I often got into difficulties. No one had told me that in London one must knock at the street door, the gentlemen being supposed to announce themselves by loud, rapid, and reiterated knocks. I followed rather the German custom of modestly ringing the bell, which in London is only for tradesmen having business with the kitchen. Therefore I could not understand why the servants who opened to me stared in surprise and could hardly believe that I wanted to be announced to their masters.

Moreover, since the persons I visited occasionally knew as little German or French as their servants, there ensued some embarrassing moments. An amusing one occurred at Rothschild's, to whom I brought a letter of introduction from his brother in Frankfort and a letter of credit from Speyer. When Rothschild had taken and read my two letters, he said in a condescending tone, 'I see here'—pointing to *The Times*—'that you've managed your business pretty well. Now I know nothing about music. My music is this'—striking his change pocket. 'They hearken to it on the Exchange.' And he laughed loudly at his own joke. Then, calling a clerk, without even asking me to sit down, he gave him the letter of credit and said, 'Pay the gentleman his money.' He gave me a nod and the audience was at an end. But as I reached the door he called out to me, 'Perhaps some day you'll come and dine with me at my country place!' A few days later Mme Rothschild did write to ask me to dinner, but I did not go although she repeated her invitation. Nevertheless my letter of introduction was not wholly useless, for when I gave my benefit concert he took a whole box.

[1] The full title of this, Spohr's eighth violin concerto, is: *Scene in Vocal Style and in Dramatic Mood*.

[2] Founder of the modern school of violin playing (1753–1824).

At Mr. Ries's house I had also met M. Erard, the head of the London branch of Erard, Frères, and together with my wife visited their show-rooms to look at the improved harps. But we could not immediately make up our minds to choose one, because Dorette wanted first to try out which size of instrument suited her best, and whether she would get used to the new mechanism. M. Erard put an end to this hestitation by offering to lend her a harp of her choice for the duration of our stay in London. If it did not suit, she could exchange or return it. She accepted with thanks and began at once to practise; but at first could make no headway. The new harp, though of the smallest size, was nonetheless a good deal larger and more tightly strung than her own, and therefore required far more strength to play. It was also difficult for her to become accustomed to the new double action after having been used to the single from childhood. She soon discovered that it would take her several months before she could play in public on this harp. I decided accordingly to let her appear only once, at my benefit concert, to which it would give an added attraction.[1]

Meanwhile my turn had come to direct one of the Philharmonic concerts, and I managed to create no less a sensation than I had with my violin playing. It was still the custom at that time, when sym-phonies and overtures were played, for the pianist to have the score before him, not in order to conduct, but to read along and join in at will—which, when it was heard, produced a deplorable effect. The real conductor was the first violin, who gave the tempi and who, when the orchestra began to falter, gave the beat with his bow. Now an orchestra of the size of the Philharmonic, with its members sitting so far one from another, could hardly play exactly together under such conducting, and in spite of the excellence of the individual players the ensemble was a good deal poorer than one is accustomed to in Germany. I had therefore resolved that when my turn cáme to direct I would try to remedy the situation.

Fortunately, on the day when I was to direct, Mr. Ries was at the piano and he readily agreed to give up the score to me and to hold aloof from the proceedings. I took my stand at a special desk in front of the orchestra, drew my baton from my pocket, and gave the signal to begin. Quite shocked at this innovation, some of the directors wanted to protest, but as I begged them to grant me at least one trial,

[1] Mme Spohr finally gave up the harp as unhealthful, and performed only as piano accompanist to her husband.

they calmed down. I knew thoroughly the symphonies and overtures, which we rehearsed, having often played them in Germany.[1] I therefore could not only give the tempi in decisive fashion but also give the wind and brass the cues for all their entrances. This imparted a confidence they had never had before. I also took the liberty, whenever the execution was not satisfactory, to stop and offer polite but earnest comments on the performance, Ries translating my remarks to the gentlemen of the orchestra.

Stimulated by all this to an uncommon degree of attention, and led with complete certainty by the *visible* beat, everyone played with a fire and precision such as no one had ever heard before. The result surprised and inspired the orchestra, and at the end of the first movement they expressed aloud their collective approval of the new manner of conducting, and thereby overruled all further opposition on the part of the directors.

In the vocal pieces, which I also took over at Mr. Ries's request, and especially in the recitatives, giving the beat with the baton (after I had explained the meaning of my movements) was completely successful, and the singers reiterated their satisfaction at the precision with which the orchestra now accompanied them.

The success of the evening was even greater than I had hoped. To be sure, at the beginning the audience was startled by the novelty and laid their heads together to whisper. But after the music had begun and the orchestra played the well-known symphony with unusual power and precision, the listeners gave their general approbation by their long sustained applause at the end of the first movement. The triumph of the baton was decisive, and no one was ever seen again at the piano during the performance of symphonies and overtures.

AUTOBIOGRAPHY (1861)

---

[1] One of them was Spohr's new Symphony in D Minor, No. 2. The date was April 10, 1820.

GIUSEPPE VERDI & LOUIS ENGEL

'La Traviata' in Venice

Intimate with many of the great composers of his century, Louis Engel showed himself in his criticism and reminiscences at once an intelligent and an amiable man. He was Shaw's predecessor on the London World.

IN 1851, at the Fenice at Venice, Verdi produced *Rigoletto*, which created one of those furores which carry the name of a composer with electric power to the top of the column of glory. He himself had great hopes for his score, but he was afraid for the famous air, 'La donna è mobile.'[1] Being very easily retained, it might from the rehearsal get into the streets and be sung all over the town before the first performance, and he would then appear to have copied instead of having created the work. In order to prevent this possibility he did not let the tenor have his air. At last Mirate [Merelli?],[2] fancying that Verdi had not written it, pressed him, and Verdi always said, 'Time enough—you shall have it.' And at last, at the general rehearsal, he brought it. The air and the quartet above mentioned and the whole opera were soon the property of the whole world.

In Paris a most amusing quarrel began between two papers—one, *La France Musicale*, which praised every note of Verdi to the sky, unreservedly, stupidly, with open partiality, so as even to make him enemies through this puffing injustice; the other, the *Gazette Musicale*, which with nearly equal violence and injustice attacked him, so much so, that they said there was not a melody, not a *morceau d'ensemble* in *Rigoletto*, which nevertheless contained some of the most popular airs the world has known, and the most admirable quartet. The *hinc illae lachrymae* was that both papers were owned by publishers, *La France* by the publisher of Verdi's works, the *Gazette* by the publisher of Meyerbeer's works. Their fighting only advertised the opera immensely and thereby increased its fame.

Not two years after this eventful performance Verdi produced (in the first week of the year 1853) *Il Trovatore*. To say that *Il Trovatore*

---

[1] 'Woman is fickle.'   [2] Opera manager.

conquered the world is not saying too much, because there is scarcely a village in Europe or America where those instruments of torture against which fortunately an Act of Parliament does protect us [Englishmen], the barrel organs, don't grind the '*Miserere*' or '*Il balen*' or some piece of that score.[1] Let those who pretend that the first necessity for a successful opera is a good libretto read the idiotic exposé of this *Trovatore*, the first idea of which comes from an extremely interesting Spanish sketch of the same name, by a gifted youth only seventeen years old. Antonio García Gutíerez is the author of a book so excellent that one cannot imagine how it was possible for Piave to convert it into such rubbish, which, nevertheless, inspired Verdi with that treasure of sparkling melodies his score is studded with.

Paris, London, Rome, St. Petersburg, brought it out with the greatest artists the lyric stage has known. It is one of the most remarkable events of musical publication that this opera, which in single airs, in arrangements for all kinds of instruments, bands, quadrilles, waltzes, etc., yielded untold sums, brought not one penny of English money to its composer. No copyright! Just as it happens to us all in America.

While the *Trovatore* was being rehearsed at Rome, Verdi had nearly finished another opera, *La Traviata*, which was performed at Venice in March 1855. The *Traviata* is certainly his most melodious, most original, least exaggerated work; it possesses at the same time the greatest of his qualities and the fewest of his faults. Yet *La Traviata* made a complete fiasco. Here again, *embonpoint* rendered the situation ridiculous. Mlle. Donatelli, an immensely stout woman, yet a good singer, played the '*Traviata*.' When in the last act the doctor came to see the poor consumptive, she, falling on the floor in a fit, raised such a cloud of dust that the doctor became invisible, and the Venetians roared outright. Moreover, the tenor was so hoarse that he could barely be heard, and the baritone, imagining that his was only a secondary part, took no trouble with it, and the work was sacrificed.

The next morning and again two days later, Verdi wrote as follows:

[1] See p. 241 for the situation forty years earlier. '*Il balen*'—'the lightning of her glance,' aria from *Il Trovatore*.

To Emanuele Muzio,[1] Venice, March 7, 1853.

Dear Emanuel: *La Traviata*, last night, a fiasco. The fault? Was it mine or the singers? Time will tell!

To Vincenzo Luccardi[2]

Dearest Luccardi: I did not write to you after the première of *Traviata*; I write to you after the second night. It is a fiasco, a decided fiasco! I don't know who is to blame. Better not speak of it. I shan't tell you anything about the music, and you will permit me to tell you just as much about the way it was sung.

To Giulio Ricordi [3]

Dear Ricordi: I am sorry to have to send you bad news, but I cannot conceal the fact: *La Traviata* was a fiasco. Don't try to fathom the reason why; that's the way it is. Farewell, farewell!

LOUIS ENGEL, *FROM MOZART TO MARIO* (1886)
VERDI, *LETTERS* (1853)

[1] Friend, pupil, and defender of Verdi.
[2] Verdi's scene designer and friend.
[3] Verdi's publisher; see pp. 335–36.

VLADIMIR STASSOV

'Boris Godunov'

To the Editor of 'Novoye Vremya':

OUR operas resemble chickens that can't defend themselves against a powerful cook. At any day and hour of his choice some Terenti or Pakhom has the right to catch the most talented Russian opera by the wings, chop off its legs or tail, cut its throat and cook a fricassee of his own invention. When Moussorgsky's *Boris* was being considered, I remember hearing some profound connoisseurs saying with an important mien and with their customary aplomb that the entire fifth act was quite superfluous, that it simply had to be cut off, or, at least, that it should be transposed, and played before the fourth act. O God, it was just like being in the kitchen! . . . Poor Glinka paid bitterly all his life for the famous 'experience' of those who surrounded him. 'Count Vielgorsky,' says Glinka in his *Memoirs*, 'made merciless cuts in *Ruslan* (after its first performances) and often in its best parts, saying with a self-satisfied air, "Am I not a master at making *coupures*!" ' This self-satisfied air and merciless barbarity continue to this day. . . . The other day all Petersburg saw with amazement that the entire fifth act of *Boris* had been discarded, and this without consulting or notifying anybody. One goes to hear an opera as it has been conceived and created by its author, and not as some manager thinks it should be! It may be objected, 'Yes, but we have the author's consent!' While you hold the author in your claws, he'll consent to anything. He can't defend himself or protest, and when his entire opera may be removed from the calendar he has no alternative but to consent. Not everyone has the fortitude of a Beethoven or a Schubert, not everyone is big enough to withdraw his work rather than have it mutilated. . . .

OCTOBER 27, 1876

Bizet's 'L'Arlésienne'

ONE of the greatest of recent theatrical successes in Paris is the lyrical drama entitled *L'Arlésienne*—the joint creation of Alphonse Daudet and of his lamented friend Bizet, the author of *Carmen*. As the work will doubtless be widely appreciated in this country, our readers may be interested in the history of the composition —a history at once romantic and pathetic, and curiously illustrative of the fickleness of public favour. Several foreign journals have narrated the story, but none so prettily as *Le XIXe Siècle* in its issue of May 6.

The history of *L'Arlésienne* carries us back thirteen years to the period of depression immediately following the tremendous shock of the Franco-Prussian war, and the convulsions of the Commune. The world of artists and writers had suffered severely in those great struggles; some of the most celebrated names in the French literature of the century found place upon the endless roll-call of the dead; many a mighty painter and sculptor had been swept away by the wind of battles, and the surviving members of the grand companionship of art and belles-lettres mostly found themselves ruined. Among these were Alphonse Daudet, the novelist; and César Bizet (who always signed himself Georges), the musician—both already illustrious. Bizet at the age of *eleven years* had taken the solfeggio prize at the Conservatory; had in his nineteenth year won the great prize of Rome; and had subsequently given to the theatre two audaciously original and exquisite compositions, *Les Pêcheurs de Perles* and *La Jolie Fille de Perth*. Daudet had published a number of dainty and delightful little things, *Les Amoureuses*, *Le Petit Chose* (said to be partly autobiographical), the uniquely humorous *Tartarin de Tarascon*, and the *Lettres de mon Moulin*—charming sketches which have found translators in almost all European countries. It was in the latter work that first appeared the story entitled *L'Arlésienne*—the story of a young Provençal who dies for love.

Both the novelist and the musician, whose last pecuniary resources had been wrested from them by the hard necessities of the war, began to look about them anxiously for a chance to repair their losses by good work. Both had families to care for, and the situation was desperate. Publishers refused to risk their capital in any undertaking; the newspapers, seriously affected in their finances, could not or would not pay a respectable price for fiction; and the bookstores had little patronage to encourage them. Only one way to success seemed still open—the theatre; and Daudet proposed to his friend Bizet an opera based on the story of *L'Arlésienne*. Bizet readily acceded; and produced in a short time one of the most delicately beautiful musical creations ever composed—full of passionate southern melody, of strangely delightful variations upon quaint Provençal themes.

Everything seemed propitious. Great critics believed the music would enthuse Paris. Admirable actresses had been found for the leading parts—many of whom have since become famous. The directors were hopeful; the support of the press seemed assured. . . . *L'Arlésienne* was performed for the first time at the Vaudeville Théâtre, on October 1, 1892.

It was a momentous evening for both Daudet and his friend; the first had everything to gain, the latter much to lose. As the French journalist who describes the events of that evening remarks, nothing is so utterly a failure as the failure of a theatrical piece. There is often some hope for an unpopular book; if it contains aught of real talent, it may work its way slowly but steadily into public notice; it may be suddenly resurrected from dusty oblivion by some timely sensation, some great excitement about the very theme upon which it treats. But the theatrical failure is apparently irremediable, and the petty whim, malice, or mere indifference of critics, or of audiences, may bring about such a failure. Even literary giants have been driven from the stage for ever, and masterpieces hopelessly damned by nothing more than popular ill-humour. To Daudet a failure meant the closure of all theatrical doors against him for long years, and the destruction of a hundred projects—among which was a drama in preparation founded on the theme which afterwards was to form the plot of that admirable novel, *Fromont Jeune et Risler Aîné*.

There was a large audience, but a strange one—an assembly made sombre of aspect by the multitude of mourning robes—an assembly wearied to nervousness by the long strain of the war, saddened by memories of death, anticipating in a visit to the theatre rather the consolation of social distraction than the pleasure of studying a rare and charming art. The music was admirably performed, but no one seemed to hear it; the text was faultlessly declaimed, yet no one appeared to listen. People with programmes upon their knees were discussing politics in whispers; others, who had met as if by chance, thought and spoke only of their bereavements. The vast gloom of the war seemed to fill all the theatre; and the ghosts of a thousand haunting sorrows drew away the gaze of the spectators from the stage. The audience seemed to have forgotten the mock drama, and to remember only the terribly real drama in which all had taken part; they stared without seeing, as in dream; they felt no passing emotion; they uttered no applause. L'Arlésienne was concluded in a great buzz of indifference; and its close was marked only by a moment of icy silence, as though all present had suddenly awakened to the knowledge of the fact that a lyrical drama had just been performed of which they had not heard a word.

Daudet went home in despair, destroyed the manuscript of his unfinished play, and after a while bravely sat down to write the novels which were destined to make his fortune. It was slow work but sure success. Bizet wrote Carmen; but the public waited for his death to admire it.

. . . Thirteen years passed by; and Daudet's name had become familiar to the whole civilized world. Fame smiled upon him, and wealth; translations of his novels appeared simultaneously in England, Germany, Spain, Italy, Russia, and America; his Sapho reached a sale of eighty thousand copies within a few months of its appearance. Bizet was long dead; but his marvellous music had conquered indifference, had mastered criticism, had compelled the enthusiasm of a thousand audiences. And suddenly the fickle and forgetful public, moved by some strange souvenir, remembered L'Arlésienne while remembering Bizet. So it happened that on the fifth of May, 1885, a great concourse of people found themselves in the Odéon, madly applauding the music they had refused to hear thirteen years before, weeping at the spectacle that had left them unmoved in 1872. There were new decorations, new costumes, and other actors; but the words and the music were the same, and L'Arlésienne was a triumph! . . . Daudet, sitting alone, watched the tumultuous pleasure of the crowd but never smiled; doubtless he saw beside him the shadow of the dead musician, the beloved friend, gazing as one that seeks to speak in vain, yearning for the utterance denied to those who dwell for ever in the Place of Silence. *EDITORIAL* (New Orleans, 1885)

EDUARD HANSLICK

Brahms' Second Symphony

Long the butt of the Wagnerians, Hanslick (1825–1904) has only recently been reappraised with fairness. Though he recanted his early 'modernism' somewhat unpleasantly, he is a good representative of the neo-classic school which accelerated Brahms' recognition.

THE new work was a great, a universal success. Seldom has public enjoyment been so sincerely and warmly expressed. Brahms' First Symphony, which was presented a year ago, was a work for serious connoisseurs capable of following with a magnifying glass its minutest ramifications. This Second Symphony is like the sun shedding its warmth over connoisseurs and laymen alike. It belongs to all who yearn for good music, whether capable of grasping difficulties or not.

Among Brahms' works, the nearest to it in style and mood is the Sextet in B Flat, the most popular of his instrumental works—so popular, indeed, that the later, more complicated quartets have ridden on its popularity. The new symphony glows with a healthy freshness and clarity. It is easy to understand throughout, even though it offers much to listen to and ponder. Much in it is new, yet there is none of that unfortunate modern tendency to insist on novelty in the sense of the unprecedented. Nor are there coy glances at extraneous realms of art—no hidden or overt borrowings from poetry or painting. It is all purely musical in conception and form, and purely musical in effect. It affords incontrovertible proof that one can still write symphonies after Beethoven—not *everyone*, of course—in the old forms and on the old foundations.

Richard Wagner and his adherents deny not only the possibility of writing symphonies after Beethoven's, but also the *raison d'être* of pure instrumental music as such. The symphony is said to have become superfluous since its transplantation into opera by Wagner. The farthest concession is to admit the compatibility of modern musical philosophy with Liszt's *Symphonic Poems* in one movement, based on definite poetic programmes. This idiotic, fatuous theory has been cooked up for the domestic requirements of the Wagner-Liszt ménage, and if any further refutation of it were needed, none could be more brilliant than the long succession of Brahms' instrumental works—particularly this Second Symphony.

Its chief characteristic can be best defined as cheerful serenity, at once gentle and manly. It is lively and serious, good natured and reflective by turns. The first movement opens with a tenderly over-cast horn theme and resembles a serenade in mood, which becomes more pronounced in the scherzo and finale. This first movement, an allegro moderato in three-four time, envelopes us as in a melodic wave on which we gaily sport, undisturbed by two lightly intruding Mendelssohnian reminiscences. After the reserved and melodious beauty of its last fifty measures, the movement is followed by a broad, singing adagio in B major. Here the thoughtful development of the themes strikes me as more meaningful than the themes proper; on which account it has less success with the public than the other three movements.

The charming scherzo with its delicate motives, in tempo a minuet, is twice interrupted by a presto in two-four time which brightens its surroundings like an evanescent spark. The finale is still more lively, yet cosy in its glowing good cheer. How unlike the stormy finales of the modern school! Mozartian blood flows in its veins.

This D major symphony is to the C minor rather an antithesis than a companion piece. Possibly the effect of the First Symphony on the public is like that of reading a work of erudition, full of deep philoso-phic ideas and hidden intimations. Brahms' tendency to cloak or stifle anything that might have the appearance of 'effect' is evident in the C minor to an excessive degree. The listener cannot possibly take in all the motives and fragments of motives, which at times seem like flowerets hibernating beneath the snow and at other times resemble remote specks beyond the clouds. The Second Symphony has nothing to compare with the grandiose pathos of the finale in the First Symphony. But by way of compensation it surpasses the latter by a uniform shading and a sunny clarity that are not to be underestima-ted. Brahms has managed to control the imposing but dangerous skill by which he hides his ideas within the polyphonic texture or subjects them to contrapuntal crucifixion. If the thematic working out is less amazing, the themes themselves are fresher and more flowing, their development is more natural and perspicuous—hence more effective. I cannot say enough to express my delight at the fact that Brahms, having given such a forceful rendering of Faustian striving in his First Symphony, should have turned back to the blossoms of the earth in spring in his Second.

CONCERT REVIEWS (1878)

The Musical
Life

GEORGE SAND

Art and Revolution

*Moved like many other artists of her time by the teachings of Saint-Simon,
George Sand wrote about socialism in both fictional and essay form. The
friend addressed below was Michel de Bourges (1789–1853), an independent
and very courageous thinker, who throughout the century led the fight for
republicanism in France. At the time of this open letter he was George Sand's
lover, which perhaps increases the merit of her resistance to his Spartan views.*

FRIEND, you rebuke me for 'social unbelief'; you tell me that
whatever exists outside the rules of Utility can never become
either truly great or truly good. You say that my indifference is a
crime and a bad example, and that I must overcome it or accept moral
suicide—as it were cut off my right hand and lose the power to communicate with my fellow man. You are hard on me, but that is the
way I like you. From you the call to Virtue deserves my admiration
and respect.

You say again that any doctrine of non-participation is an excuse
for cowardice or selfishness, because no human act can avoid being
either helpful or harmful to mankind. Whatever my ambition is,
according to you, whether it is to be admired or to be loved, I must
become serviceable—and with discrimination; I must serve thoughtfully, doctrinally, scientifically—that is to say, I must be a professional
Friend of Man. I usually answer those who talk to me like this by
being facetious or sophistical. But here it is different. I recognize your
right to preach to me the Virtuous Word, to which I am indeed so
resistant that I find it hard even to repeat it after you. For my trouble
has been that others have always tried to baptize me into their creed
with impure hands. . . . What has convinced and touched me is the
simplicity and purity of all your words and deeds.

I do not know whether the day will ever come when men will be
able to tell infallibly and with finality what is useful for Man. I am not

going into details now about the system you have adopted, though the other day I was making fun of it. But if you put it to me so that I must reason it out (no small victory of your mind over mine), I will freely admit that the great law of equality and fair sharing, for all its present inapplicability in the eyes of those who fear it, and for all the uncertainty of its coming, looks to me, from my retired cell, as the first and only invariable law of ethics that I have ever been able steadily to conceive.

Yet what I feel bound to add, my dear Everard, is that your virtue does not seem to me required of everyone, but of a few only. What is required of all is honesty. Do you be virtuous and I'll try to be honest. . . . Let the governed be honest, temperate, straightforward—in short, let them be *moral beings*, and the governors will be able to build on them a stable edifice. . . . O Republic, dawn of justice and equality, divine Utopia, sun of a conceivable Eden of the future, hail! Shine in the sky and be desired on earth. If thy reign come here below sooner than seems probable, thou shalt find me ready to accept it and already clothed according to the laws of thy austerity!

Yes, I am yours, whatever the colour of your flag, provided your cohorts be on the road to the Republic of the Future; in the name of Jesus, who has but one true apostle now on earth; in the name of Washington and Franklin, who did not go far enough and who have left us a task to do; in the name of Saint-Simon,[1] whose disciples are marching straight toward the sublime and terrible goal of the redistribution of wealth (God protect them!). Provided that good may prevail and that those who believe in it prove it good, I am a trooper in your ranks.

But on your side, friend, you might tell me what you are really after when you declaim against artists. Abuse them all you want, but respect Art. Vandal! I like your impudence—to want to put sackcloth and wooden shoes on Taglioni[2] and use the hands of Liszt to turn a wine press, you who dissolve in tears at the song of any warbler and cause riots in the theatre to prevent Otello's choking Malibran![3] Our austere citizen wants to banish artists as superfluous drones in the

---

[1] Count Henri de Saint-Simon (1760–1825) social reformer on Christian and 'technocratic' lines.

[2] Famous ballerina (1804?–84).

[3] Famous singer (1808–36), daughter of Manuel García and sister of Pauline Viardot. *Otello* is Rossini's opera.

good society, but Monsieur loves vocal music and grants a reprieve to singers. I trust that painters will find among you a good fellow who knows about painting and will keep you from walling up the windows of the studios!

As for the poets, they are your first cousins; when you are trying to influence the crowd from the top of your soapbox, you dare not disdain the poets' forms of speech and the machinery of their eloquence. Go to the poets and learn metaphor and how to use it! Besides, the genius of the poet is an elastic substance, easy to handle. No conqueror has ever lacked a bard. Praising is a profession like any other, and when the poets say just what you wish, you may let them say what *they* wish. For all they want is to sing and make themselves heard. And yet, O venerable Dante, thy Muse, with its tones of ringing bronze, could surely never have been swayed to perjury.

But tell me again what you complain of in artists. The other day you blamed them for all the evils of society; you called them 'dissolving elements'; you accused them of dispersing energy, of corrupting morals, of weakening the mainsprings of the will. Your denunciation did not quite come to an end, and your charges remained vague because I yielded to a foolish impulse and argued with you. I should have listened, and you might then have found better reasons. As it is, you really gave me nothing to think about, pleasant or unpleasant, and that was the first time this has ever happened between us.

Is it art itself you are putting on trial? As if *it* cared what you and your friends and all the systems in the world thought about it! You're trying to snuff out a sunbeam. You can't mean that. If I had to refute you I should simply bring out the old commonplaces: flowers smell good; summer warmth is grateful; birds have feathers—and asses have much longer ears than horses.

If it isn't art you want to kill, then it can hardly be artists either, for as long as mortals believe in Jesus there must be priests, and no power on earth will keep a man from taking in his heart a vow of humility pity, and chastity. So there must be some accidental misunderstanding here, between the sons of the new republic of Rome and those of the old Babylon. What caused it? I am in the dark. The other day one of your friends, which is to say one of ours, a true republican, declared with some seriousness that I deserved death. The devil take me if I know what he meant by it, but I am nonetheless pleased. I glory in it for all I am worth, and since that time I never fail to tell all my friends

in confidence that I am a literary and political figure of the first importance, one able to disturb the leaders of his own party by his superior
intellect and influence on society. This surprises my friends a little but
they are kind enough to share my satisfaction.

Now let us examine the case against my colleagues in art. Not that
I want to defend them; I should be afraid of being let off as innocent
and thus miss the honours of martyrdom. . . . But as regards the
others—what have they done, the poor dears? Apart from Lord Byron
and myself, there is not one capable of encompassing the death even
of a fly. Of course, I readily confess that we all deserve the name of
Sophists. The new teaching has spread everywhere, as far as the legs
of the ballet at the Opera. Berlioz has even made it into a fantastic
symphony. Unfortunately for the ancient wisdom, when you will
hear Berlioz's March to Execution, you will feel a certain tremor in
your nervous system, untamed lion though you may be; and it is
possible that you will start to roar exactly as when you are trying to
save Desdemona from Otello. It will be hard on me as your companion, for I have a reputation to maintain as a sober subscriber to the
Conservatoire concerts. So the least you can do is to confess that
this new music is rather better than that which we used to have in
Sparta under Lycurgus. . . .

You're going to say that I am not being serious. I *am* serious. Berlioz
is a great composer, a man of genius, a true artist. And since his name
comes apropos, let me say I am delighted to have the chance of telling
you that he is a real artist, for I see you have no notion of it. When we
argued the other day you mentioned several pseudo-artists and railed
at them. There was a leather man, a dealer in furs, a peer of the realm,
an apothecary. There were others (more famous, according to you) of
whom I had never heard. I can see that you take shadows for real men,
stockbrokers for true artists, and our garrets for pleasure domes.

Now Berlioz *is* an artist. He is poor, proud, and courageous. Maybe
he is scoundrel enough to think to himself that all the peoples of the
universe are not as important as a chromatic scale used in the right
place—just as I happen to prefer a white hyacinth to the crown jewels.
But bear in mind that a man can hold such crazy ideas and yet not be
the enemy of the human race. You are all for regimentation, as Berlioz
is for semiquavers and I am for flower gardens—each to his taste.

When the time comes to build the Great City of the Mind, you
may be sure everyone will help build it according to his powers:

Berlioz with pick and shovel, I with my golden toothpick, the rest with their two arms and their will. But the New Jerusalem will, I trust, have days of rest and joy, and it will be permitted to some to go back to their pianos, and to others to cultivate their gardens—each innocently following his capacities and tastes.

What are you yourself guilty of, pray tell, when you contemplate the heavens at midnight, poeticizing to the rest of us about the galaxy? What if I should interrupt you in your sublimities with the stupid and brutal question, 'What use is it? Why waste your brain cells on conjecture? Will it feed and clothe anybody?' You would answer that it feeds noble emotions and renews mystical enthusiasm in those who painfully toil for the good of mankind. It helps them to hope, to dream of the Deity, and to rise courageously above the petty miseries of human affairs by fixing their thoughts on the future Utopia. What made you what you are, Everard, if not the habit of dreaming at night? What gave you the strength to continue so long amid trouble and thankless toil, if not the religious enthusiasm of the artist? And it is you, the most candid, lovable, and unworldly among men of genius, who wage war on the singing priests of your own God! You are Saul and you want to kill David because he plays the harp so well that in listening to him you are transported.

LETTERS FROM A TRAVELLER (1835)

SERGEI PROKOFIEV

Statement to the Soviet

ECAUSE the condition of my health deprives me of the opportunity to attend and to participate in the general meeting of composers, I wish to express in this letter, which I ask you to read at the meeting, my thought concerning the decision of the Central Committee of the Party of February 10, 1948.

The decision of the Central Committee of February 10, 1948, has separated the rotten threads from the healthy ones in the creative work of composers. No matter how painful it is for many composers, myself included, I agree to the resolution of the Central Committee, which establishes the condition for making the whole organism of Soviet music healthy. The resolution is especially valuable because it exposes a formalistic direction foreign to the Soviet people, a direction leading to the impoverishment and downfall of music, and with great clarity shows us the goals which we must reach for the best interests of the Soviet people.

I shall talk of myself. Elements of formalism were already peculiar to my music fifteen or twenty years ago.

The contagion appeared evidently from contact with a number of Western friends. After the exposure by *Pravda* of formalistic mistakes in the Shostakovich opera, I thought a great deal about the creative manner of my music and came to the conclusion that such a direction was incorrect. As a result, there followed a search for clear and more expressive language. In a number of my following works, *Alexander Nevsky, Zdravitza, Romeo and Juliet*, the Fourth Symphony, I attempted to liberate my work from the element of formalism, and I consider I have succeeded to a certain extent. The existence of formalism in several of my compositions is probably explained by a certain complacency and by insufficiently clear recognition that it is totally unwanted by our people. However, after the resolution which has shaken to the depths our whole society of composers it became apparent exactly what specific music is needed by our people, and the ways of curing the formalistic ailment have become clear.

I have never doubted the importance of melody. I like melody very much, and I consider it the most important element in music, and I labour many years on the improvement of its quality in my compositions. The most difficult task for a composer is to find a melody comprehensible even to the uninitiated audience. Here he is confronted with many dangers. He can fall into trivial or mundane paths, or into rewriting that which has already been composed. For this reason, the composing of more complicated melodies is considerably easier. It sometimes happens that the composer works over his melody and corrects it for so long that, without noticing it, he makes it extremely complicated and loses its simplicity. In the process of work, I fell into this trap.

When composing, there must be special vigilance that the melody remain simple but, at the same time, does not become cheap, sweet, or imitative. This is easier to say than to achieve. And all my efforts will be directed to making these words more than a mere formula, enabling me to apply them in my future works.

I am also guilty of atonality, which is often related to formalism, although I must confess with happiness that I began to yearn for tonal music long ago. Then I felt that the construction of musical composition 'in tone' is construction of the building on a solid base, but construction 'without tone' is construction on the sand. Besides, the greater range of opportunity in tonal and distonal music than in atonal and chromatic music is especially well demonstrated by that impasse in which Schönberg and his followers find themselves. In some of my compositions of recent years individual atonal moments can be found. Without feeling any special sympathy for this device, I still use it, particularly for contrast, and to accent tonal passages. In the future I hope to overcome this device.

In my operatic creations I am often reproached when using a recitative rather than a singing line. I like the stage as such very much. I consider that a man having come to the opera has a right to demand impressions not only for the ear but also for the eye. (Otherwise he would not have gone to an opera but to a concert.) But movement on the stage can be better adapted to recitative, whereas singing to a certain degree demands immobility on the stage. I remember how painful it was to look at the stage during some Wagnerian operas, when for the duration of a whole act of about an hour in length not a single person moved. This very fear of immobility has prevented my concentration on singing for a long time. In connection with the resolution, I meticulously considered this question and came to the conclusion that in each opera libretto there exist passages absolutely demanding recitative, and passages absolutely demanding singing. But there are also certain passages, and these passages require an enormous place, sometimes as much as half of the whole opera, which the composer may interpret according to his own wish, either by recitative or by aria. Let us take, for example, Tatyana's letter from *Eugene Onegin;* it would have been very easy to write a large part in recitative, but Tchaikovsky has used his musical language in the direction of singing and has presented the whole letter as a great aria, which has the advantage that it is performed with some simultaneous action on the stage. In this manner it gives food not only for the ear but also for the eye. It is in this direction that I wish to place my work on my new opera on a contemporary Soviet subject, *The Story of a Real Man* by Polevoy.

I was greatly pleased by the instruction in the resolution on the desirability of polyphony, especially in choir and ensemble singing. This is a really interesting problem for a composer, and a real pleasure for the listener. In the above-mentioned opera I intend to introduce trios, duets, and counterpoint development of choir, for which I make use of the extremely interesting notes of northern Russian folk-songs. The clear melodies and as much as possible simple harmonic language, such are other elements which I will try to obtain in this opera.

In conclusion, I should like to express my gratitude to our Party for the clear decisions of the resolution, which help me to find a musical language comprehensible to our people, worthy of our people and of our great country.

ON SOVIET MUSIC: DOCUMENTS (1948)

HECTOR BERLIOZ

An Interview with the Police

WE had hardly finished paying our musicians, copyists, printers, instrument makers, masons, roofers, joiners, carpenters, upholsterers, ushers, and guards when the Prefect of Police, who had charged us the modest sum of 1,238 francs for his men—at the Opera the charge is but 80 francs—summoned us urgently before him.

'What is it about?' I asked my colleague Strauss.[1] 'Have you any idea?'

'Not the least.'

'Perhaps M. Delessert is conscience-stricken at having made us pay so dear for his useless minions. Could he be thinking of a refund?'

'Not likely!'

We come before the Prefect, who addresses me. 'Sir! It grieves me to say that you have committed a very serious offence!'

'Pray, what is that?' I rejoined in astonishment.

'You have surreptitiously added to the programme of your Festival Concert a selection calculated to arouse political passions of a sort the government wants to allay and indeed suppress. I refer to the chorus from *Charles VI*, which was not listed in the first announcements of the concert.[2] The Minister of Interior has cause to be gravely annoyed by the demonstrations which that chorus provoked, and I am entirely on his side in the matter.'

'Your Honour,' I replied as coolly as I could, 'your supposition is altogether wrong. It is indeed true that the selection from *Charles VI* did not appear on the very first announcements, but I learned that M. Halévy felt aggrieved at not being represented on an occasion

[1] A French impresario unrelated to the Viennese Strausses.

[2] The chorus occurs in Act III, scene 2, of the opera by C. and G. Delavigne, music by Halévy, first performed on March 17, 1843. The provocative lines are: 'Down with tyrants! Never, never in France will the English rule.' The greater part of the audience at Berlioz' concert, several thousand strong, sang the words in unison with the performers, presumably in protest against the government's pro-English policy.

when nearly all the great composers of our time were being played. I therefore consented to his publisher's suggestion and added the chorus, on account of its suitability for a large body of singers such as I had. That was the sole reason for the choice. Personally I have not the slightest sympathy with the outbursts of nationalism that may occur in 1844 about a scene that goes back to the days of Charles VI.[1] As for the "surreptitious addition" of that scene to my programme, the charge is so little founded that the incriminated piece has figured on all the placards in Paris for more than eight days. It was posted during all that time on the very walls of your Prefecture. Be good enough to entertain no doubt whatever of this fact and to disabuse the Minister of Interior accordingly.'

M. Delessert, a trifle abashed, declared himself satisfied, and even excused himself for the unmerited rebuke he had inflicted upon me. But from that day forth a censorship of concert programmes has been established. One may not now sing in public a parlour song by Bérat or by Mlle Puget without an authorization from the Minister of Interior countersigned by a Police Commissioner.

MEMOIRS (1844)

[1] That is, the days of Agincourt (1415), when Henry V of England made himself king of France.

MOLIÈRE

Patron and Professional

ACT I

*T*HE *overture is played by a large number of instruments, and in the centre of the stage the Music Student is seen seated at a table, composing a melody which M. Jourdain has ordered for a musical* entertainment.

MUSIC TEACHER, *speaking to his musicians:* Come here, go into that room and rest while we wait for him to show up.

DANCING MASTER, *speaking to the dancers:* And you, too, over on this side.

MUSIC TEACHER, *to the Music Student:* Is it finished?

STUDENT: Yes.

MUSIC TEACHER: Let's see. . . . Yes, that's fine.

DANCING MASTER: Is it something new?

MUSIC TEACHER: Yes, it's a melody for a serenade which I've had him compose while we're waiting for our man to wake up.

DANCING MASTER: May I see what it's like?

MUSIC TEACHER: You'll hear it, with dialogue, when he comes down. He won't be long.

DANCING MASTER: Our duties, yours and mine, are nothing to sneeze at any more.

MUSIC TEACHER: You're right. We have found just the man for us. This Jourdain, with his notions of nobility and fashion, means a neat little income for both of us. I wish the world were full of people like him.

DANCING MASTER: Not altogether. For my part, I could wish that he knew a little more than he does about the things we do for him.

MUSIC TEACHER: It's true he knows little but he pays much, and right now that's what our two arts of music and dancing need more than anything else.

DANCING MASTER: Well, I must say that I feed pretty well on praise. Applause goes to my heart, and I insist that in all the arts it's torture to perform for fools and to receive nothing but stupid philistinism for the pains of creation. You cannot deny that it's more fun to work for people who have some appreciation of art, people who can see the fine points and know how to applaud them, and so make a man enjoy his work by flattering compliments. Yes indeed, the most agreeable reward is to have an intelligent audience recognize and like what we do; nothing better than enlightened praise! Nothing, in my opinion, repays us better for all our effort.

MUSIC TEACHER: Granted. I enjoy praise too. But incense isn't food. Pure praise never paid the rent. You have to mix it with something more solid, and the best manner of praising I know is to do it in the palm of my hand. You are, of course, absolutely right about Jourdain. His notions are shallow, he says the wrong thing about everything and applauds at the wrong time, but his money is a great corrective, in excellent taste; his approval makes a clinking noise, and as you can see for yourself, this ignorant business man counts for more in our lives than the cultivated lord who introduced us here.

DANCING MASTER: There's something in which you say, but I think you put a little too much stress on money. Self-interest is so low a thing that a well-bred man must not betray a passion for it.

MUSIC TEACHER: Still you readily take the cash when our good man hands it out.

DANCING MASTER: Of course. But I don't make it my sole blessedness. And I wish that he had good taste as well as cash.

MUSIC TEACHER: So would I. That's what you and I are trying to impart just as hard as we can. He gives us a chance to make ourselves known and he pays to have us produce what others will praise and enjoy—a fair exchange.

DANCING MASTER: Here he comes.

Enter Jourdain, in his dressing gown and nightcap, two valets, some musicians and dancers.

JOURDAIN: Well, gentlemen! What about it? Will you show me your little trifle?

DANCING MASTER: I *beg* your pardon, what little trifle?

JOURDAIN: You know: your prologue or dialogue of song and dance.

DANCING MASTER: Well, well!

MUSIC TEACHER: We're quite ready, M. Jourdain.

JOURDAIN: I kept you waiting a little, because I was being fitted out like people of quality, and my tailor had sent me silk stockings which I thought I never could pull on.

MUSIC TEACHER: We are here, M. Jourdain, to await your pleasure.

JOURDAIN: Well, don't either of you go until they bring me my suit so you can see me in it.

DANCING MASTER: Whatever you say.

JOURDAIN: You will see me properly attired from head to foot.

MUSIC TEACHER: We do not doubt it in the least, sir.

JOURDAIN: I had this Indian print made up. . . .

DANCING MASTER: It's lovely indeed.

JOURDAIN: My tailor told me that people of quality dress this way in the morning.

MUSIC TEACHER: It's most becoming.

JOURDAIN: Hey there! Valet! Both valets!

FIRST VALET: What is it, sir?

JOURDAIN: Nothing. I just wanted to see if you could hear me. *Turning to the two teachers:* What do you think of their liveries?

DANCING MASTER: Magnificent, magnificent.

JOURDAIN, *half opening his gown to show his red velvet breeches and green velvet waistcoat:* I had this informal suit made for my morning devotions.

MUSIC TEACHER: It's very elegant, very.

JOURDAIN: Valet!

VALET: Yes, sir.

JOURDAIN: The other valet.

SECOND VALET: Yes, sir.

JOURDAIN: Hold my gown. *To the two artists:* How do you think I look?

DANCING MASTER: Very well, M. Jourdain; you couldn't look better.

JOURDAIN: Now about this little trifle of yours.

MUSIC TEACHER: First I'd like to play for you an air which he (*pointing to the music student*) has just composed for the serenade you have ordered. He is one of my students, and he is particularly talented at this sort of thing.

JOURDAIN: Good enough, but you shouldn't have a *student* compose the music I order. You yourself were by no means too talented to do it yourself.

MUSIC TEACHER: Oh, but you must not deceive yourself. Student in this case doesn't mean what student usually means. This scholar is of the kind that know as much as the great masters. What he has written is as beautiful as can be. Just listen!

JOURDAIN: Give me my gown, so I can listen better. Wait! I think I'd hear better without it. No! Bring it back and put it on. It will be more suitable.

GIRL MUSICIAN, *singing:*

> Day and night, I languish and pine from distress
> Since your eyes, O Iris! have pierced me of late;
> But if someone who loves you these rigours oppress,
> Pray what would you do to a person you hate?

JOURDAIN: A depressing sort of song. It puts me to sleep. Can't you liven it up here and there?

MUSIC TEACHER: But, sir, the music must fit the words.

JOURDAIN: Not long ago I learned a very pretty one. Let's see—how did it go?

DANCING MASTER: I'm sure I don't know.

JOURDAIN: It had sheep in it—

DANCING MASTER: Sheep?

JOURDAIN: Yes. I have it! *He sings:*

> I thought Jenny as dear,
> I thought Jenny as sweet
> As the lambs that do bleat.
> But she's proven, I fear,
> Her heartless deceit:
> She's more cruel to me
> Than a tigress could be!

There! Isn't it pretty?

MUSIC TEACHER: Oh, very pretty.

DANCING MASTER: And you sing it so well!

JOURDAIN: Never had a music lesson in my life.

MUSIC TEACHER: You should study music, M. Jourdain; you've taken up dancing and there's a very close connection between the two—

DANCING MASTER: They broaden the mind for the appreciation of beauty.

JOURDAIN: Do society people study music?

MUSIC TEACHER: It goes without saying.

JOURDAIN: Then I will. But I don't know how I'll find time, because, besides the Fencing Teacher, I've also hired a Master of Philosophy who is to start with me this morning.

MUSIC TEACHER: Philosophy is something, no doubt, M. Jourdain, but music, music!

DANCING MASTER: Music and dancing . . . music and dancing, that's all you need to know!

MUSIC TEACHER: There is nothing so useful to the State as music.

DANCING MASTER: And nothing is so necessary to man as dancing.

MUSIC TEACHER: Without music a State cannot survive.

DANCING MASTER: Without dancing man cannot act.

MUSIC TEACHER: All the political upheavals, all that goes wrong with the world, occur only from a failure to learn music.

DANCING MASTER: All the miseries of man, all the disasters recorded in history—the mistakes of statesmen, the blunders of great generals—all came to pass only from not knowing how to dance.

JOURDAIN: How so?

MUSIC TEACHER: Well, doesn't war result from discord among men?

JOURDAIN: True.

MUSIC TEACHER: Then if all men learned music, would this not remove discord, and bring about concord, or universal peace?

JOURDAIN: You are right.

DANCING MASTER: When a man commits a fault, either in the conduct of his affairs, or in the governing of a State, or in the commanding of an army, does not one say, 'That was the wrong step to take'?

JOURDAIN: Yes, that's what people say.

DANCING MASTER: Now, can taking the wrong step result from anything except ignorance of dancing?

JOURDAIN: True! You are both absolutely right.

DANCING MASTER: We only meant to show you the virtue and usefulness of music and dancing.

JOURDAIN: I quite understand.

MUSIC TEACHER: Would you now care to see our productions?

JOURDAIN: Yes.

MUSIC TEACHER: You will remember, mine is just a little attempt I once made to show how many different feelings music can express.

JOURDAIN: Very good.

MUSIC TEACHER, *to the musicians:* Come forward. *To Jourdain:* You must imagine them dressed as shepherds—

JOURDAIN: Why always shepherds? That's all one sees everywhere one goes.

MUSIC TEACHER: It's indispensable when you want to make people talk through the medium of music. Verisimilitude calls for shepherds. They have sung and piped from time immemorial, whereas it's hardly likely that princes or merchants should converse to music or express their sentiments in song. Shepherds play on pipes, you know, and sing to themselves when they're alone.

JOURDAIN: Never mind, never mind, let's get on. *Here follows a pastoral trio executed by one female and two male voices.* Finished? Is that the end?

MUSIC TEACHER: Yes.

JOURDAIN: Not badly put together; there were one or two very good lines.

DANCING MASTER: And now may I present my attempt to bring together the most varied steps and the most graceful movements of which dancing is capable?

JOURDAIN: Is it still shepherds?

DANCING MASTER: Whatever you fancy. *To dancers:* Let's begin. *Here follows a ballet.*

ACT II

JOURDAIN: Very clever, I must say. Those people certainly know how to get about.

MUSIC TEACHER: And when we combine the dancing with the music, you will find the effect still finer. This ballet we have fashioned for you will strike you as something really delightful.

JOURDAIN: It's for this afternoon, don't forget. The person for whom all this is intended will do me the honour of coming here to dine this evening.

DANCING MASTER: Everything is ready, M. Jourdain.

MUSIC TEACHER: But I might add that even this is not nearly enough! A man like you, who is interested in magnificence and who has a bent toward the beautiful, ought to give musicales every Wednesday—or every Thursday.

JOURDAIN: Is that what society people do?

MUSIC TEACHER: Why, of course.

JOURDAIN: Then I will too. Is it nice?

MUSIC TEACHER: Unquestionably. You'll need at least three voices—soprano, contralto, and bass, accompanied by a bass viol, a theorbo, and a harpsichord to play the continuo, and two violins for the refrains.

JOURDAIN: And a marine trumpet.[1] That's my favourite instrument, it's so smooth.

[1] Not a brass instrument, as might be supposed, but a single-stringed 'nun's violin,' the prototype of all bowed instruments.

MUSIC TEACHER: You had better leave it to us.

JOURDAIN: Anyhow, don't forget to send me some men this afternoon to sing while we're at table.

MUSIC TEACHER: Rest assured that you will have everything you need.

JOURDAIN: Above all, let the ballet be grand.

MUSIC TEACHER: You will be satisfied, I promise you. Among other things, they will dance some minuets—you'll see—

JOURDAIN: Ah! The minuet's my dance. I want you to see me do it. Come, dancing master!

DANCING MASTER: Your hat, sir, if you please. *Jourdain reaches for his valet's hat and puts it over his own nightcap. The teacher takes his hands and sings a minuet:* La, la, la, la, la, la . . . try to keep in step. La, la, la, la, la, your right foot!—La, la, la . . . don't move your shoulders so much, la, la, la . . . your arms look as though amputated, la, la, la . . . your head up! Turn the toes out, straighten up the whole body!

JOURDAIN: Oh!

MUSIC TEACHER: That couldn't have been better.

JOURDAIN: By the way, show me how to bow to a Marquise. I'll have to know how this afternoon.

DANCING MASTER: The proper bow to make to a Marquise?

JOURDAIN: Yes, a Marquise named Dorimène.

DANCING MASTER: Give me your hand.

JOURDAIN: No, just do it and I'll remember.

DANCING MASTER: Very well. If you wish to bow with the utmost respect, you must first make a backward bow, then walk toward her with three bows forward, and at the third go down about the level of her knees.

JOURDAIN: Show me a little. *The dancing master makes three bows.* Right. *Enter Valet.*

VALET: Sir, the Fencing Master is here.

JOURDAIN: Tell him to come in for my lesson. I want you two to watch me.

Enter Fencing Master, followed by valet holding two foils. The Master puts one in Jourdain's hand.

FENCING MASTER: Now, sir, first we bow. Your body straight. Lean just a little on the left thigh. Your legs not so far apart. Your feet on a line. Your wrist opposite your hip. The tip of the foil level with your shoulder. The arm not quite so extended. The left hand at the height of the eye. The left shoulder less hunched. The head straight and the glance assured. Now, advance! Keep the body steady. Now, a thrust in quarte . . . and follow through. One, two. . . . Steady! Once again, full strength. Jump back! When you thrust, M. Jourdain, thrust with the foil, and flatten out the body! One, two . . . now thrust in tierce and follow through. Forward . . . body firm . . . forward . . . thrust from where you are. One, two, take position again. Once more . . . leap back . . . en garde, M. Jourdain, en garde! *The Fencing Master lunges at him two or three times, all the while shouting,* 'En garde, en garde.'

JOURDAIN: Oh!

MUSIC TEACHER: You are marvellous, M. Jourdain.

FENCING MASTER: As I told you before, the whole secret of fencing lies in two things—giving and not receiving—and, as I demonstrated to you the other day, it is impossible that you should receive if you know how to turn your enemy's foil away from the line of your body; and this, in turn, depends altogether upon a little movement of the wrist, either inward or outward.

JOURDAIN: So that, according to you, one is sure to kill his man, and not be killed, even though one has no heart for the business?

FENCING MASTER: Precisely. Didn't you watch the demonstration?

JOURDAIN: I did.

FENCING MASTER: And hence the high regard in which we fencers must be held in the State. The art of fencing is thereby shown superior to all the useless arts, such as dancing or music or—

DANCING MASTER: Just a moment, master swordsman. Kindly speak of dancing with more respect.

MUSIC TEACHER: And remember the proper way to treat the excellence of music.

FENCING MASTER: Well, I must say you are an amusing pair to pretend to compare your arts to mine.

MUSIC TEACHER: My, what self-complacency!

DANCING MASTER: A regular baboon with his chest protector!

FENCING MASTER: Why, you little jumping jack, I'll teach you how to dance! *To Music Teacher:* As for you, musicaster, I'll soon show you how to sing.

DANCING MASTER: Ironmonger, I can beat you at your trade.

JOURDAIN, *to the Dancing Master:* You must be mad to quarrel with a man who knows tierce from quarte and kills a man according to demonstration.

DANCING MASTER: A fig for his demonstrations, and his tierces and his quartes!

JOURDAIN: Gently I tell you.

FENCING MASTER, *to the Dancing Master:* What was that, you whipper-snapper?

JOURDAIN: Here! Here! Master Fencer!

DANCING MASTER: What was that, old cart horse?

JOURDAIN: Dancing Master, please!

FENCING MASTER: If I ever get my hands on you—

JOURDAIN: Not so loud!

DANCING MASTER: If my hands find their way—

JOURDAIN: Easy, easy.

FENCING MASTER: I'll give you a polishing—

JOURDAIN: For pity's sake!

DANCING MASTER: When you get from me the drubbing that—

JOURDAIN: I *beg* of you!

MUSIC TEACHER: Please, M. Jourdain, allow us to teach him manners.

JOURDAIN: Good God! Why don't you stop!

Enter Teacher of Philosophy.

JOURDAIN: Welcome, welcome, Philosopher. You are just in time with your philosophy. Come and pacify these three.

TEACHER OF PHILOSOPHY: What is the matter here, gentlemen?

JOURDAIN: They have had words over the respective merits of their professions and have nearly come to blows.

TEACHER OF PHILOSOPHY: But gentlemen!—Is this a proper way to behave? Have you not read Seneca's 'Treatise on Anger'? Is there anything lower or more shameful than a passion which makes of man a ferocious beast? And should not reason always govern our actions?

DANCING MASTER: How do you mean? He comes here and starts calling us names, expressing contempt for my art, which is dancing, and for his, which is music—

TEACHER OF PHILOSOPHY: The wise man is above all the names that anyone may call him. And the best answer to make to insults is patient moderation.

FENCING MASTER: But they both had the audacity to compare their professions to mine!

TEACHER OF PHILOSOPHY: Why should that raise your bile? It is unbecoming in man to quarrel about fame and position. The sole distinction between one man and the next is wisdom and virtue.

DANCING MASTER: Still, I maintain that the art of dancing is one which cannot be esteemed too highly.

MUSIC TEACHER: And I that music is an art that has been venerated through the ages.

FENCING MASTER: While I keep telling them that fencing is the greatest and most indispensable of the arts.

TEACHER OF PHILOSOPHY: And what of philosophy, gentlemen? I must say I find all three of you somewhat impertinent to speak in front of me with such arrogance, and to brazenly give the name of arts and sciences to things not even worthy of the name of skill and which really belong under the common name of trades—that of cut-throat, fiddler, and acrobat.

FENCING MASTER: Out with you, pseudo-philosopher!

MUSIC TEACHER: Out, you heavy-handed highbrow!

DANCING MASTER: Out, you vulgar blockhead!

TEACHER OF PHILOSOPHY: What! Bumpkins that you are! *The Philosopher rushes upon them, but all three pummel him in unison.*

JOURDAIN: My dear Philosopher!

TEACHER OF PHILOSOPHY: Loathsome, impudent louts!

JOURDAIN: My dear Philosopher!

FENCING MASTER: Scurvy animal!

JOURDAIN: Gentlemen, please!

DANCING MASTER: Academic ass!

JOURDAIN: Gentlemen!

TEACHER OF PHILOSOPHY: Scoundrels!

JOURDAIN: My dear Philosopher!

MUSIC TEACHER: The devil take the meddler!

JOURDAIN: Gentlemen!

TEACHER OF PHILOSOPHY: Rascals, traitors, rogues, convicts!

JOURDAIN: My dear Philosopher! Gentlemen! My dear Philosopher! Gentlemen! My dear Philosopher! *Exeunt all four, struggling.* Oh, well! Fight to your hearts' content. *I'm* not going to spoil this dressing gown to keep the peace among you. I'd be a fool to interfere and get knocked on the head for my pains.

LE BOURGEOIS GENTILHOMME (1670)

LEO TOLSTOY

An Opera is Rehearsed

*When in the name of simplicity Tolstoy revolted against modern life and art,
he turned first against the most complicated, conventional, and expensive of
the arts—hence the most vulnerable: opera.*

IN every large town enormous buildings are erected for museums,
academies, conservatoires, and dramatic schools, and for performances and concerts. Hundreds of thousands of workmen—
carpenters, masons, painters, joiners, paper-hangers, tailors, hairdressers,
jewellers, moulders, typesetters—spend their whole lives in hard
labour to satisfy the demands of art; so that hardly any other depart-
ment of human activity, the military excepted, consumes so much
energy as this.

Not only is enormous labour spent on this activity, but in it, as in
war, the very lives of men are sacrificed. Hundreds of thousands of
people devote their lives from childhood to learning to twirl their
legs rapidly (dancers), or to touch notes and strings very rapidly
(musicians), or to sketch with paint and represent what they see
(artists), or to turn every phrase inside out and find a rhyme to every
word. And these people, often very kind and clever and capable of
all sorts of useful labour, grow savage over their specialized and
stupefying occupations, and become one-sided and self-complacent
specialists, dull to all the serious phenomena of life and skilful only at
rapidly twisting their legs, their tongues, or their fingers.

But even this stunting of human life is not the worst. I remember
being once at the rehearsal of one of the most ordinary of the new
operas which are produced at all the opera houses of Europe and
America.[1]

I arrived when the first act had already commenced. To reach the
auditorium I had to pass through the stage entrance. By dark entrances
and passages, past immense machines for changing the scenery and

---

[1] This opera, if not imaginary, has not been identified by Tolstoy scholars,
and the scene does not suggest any work described in the histories of the genre.

lighting the stage and the theatre, I was led through the vaults of an enormous building; and there in the gloom and dust I saw workmen busily engaged. One of these men—pale, haggard, in a dirty blouse, with dirty, work-worn hands and cramped fingers, evidently tired and out of humour—went past me, angrily scolding another man. Ascending by a dark stair, I came out on the boards behind the scenes. Amid various poles and rings and scattered scenery, decorations, and curtains, stood and moved dozens, if not hundreds, of painted and dressed-up men in costumes fitting tight to their thighs and calves, and also women, who were, as usual, as nearly nude as might be. These were all singers, or members of the chorus, or ballet dancers, awaiting their turns. My guide led me across the stage and, by means of a bridge of boards, across the orchestra, in which perhaps a hundred musicians of all kinds, from kettledrum to flute and harp, were seated, to the dark pit stalls.

On an elevation, between two lamps with reflectors and in an arm-chair placed before a music stand, sat the director of the musical part, baton in hand, managing the orchestra and singers, and in general the production of the whole opera.

The performance had already commenced, and on the stage was being represented a procession of Indians who had brought home a bride. Besides men and women in costume, two other men in ordinary clothes bustled and ran about on the stage: one was the director of the dramatic part, and the other, who stepped about in soft shoes and ran from place to place with unusual agility, was the dancing master, whose salary per month exceeded what ten labourers earn in a year.

These three directors arranged the singing, the orchestra, and the procession. The procession, as usual, was enacted by men and women in couples with tinfoil halberds on their shoulders. They all came from one place and walked round and round again and then stopped. The procession took a long time to arrange: first the Indians with halberds came on too late, then too soon; then at the right time but crowded together at the exit; then they did not crowd but arranged themselves badly at the sides of the stage—and each time the whole performance was stopped and recommenced from the beginning. The procession is preceded by a recitative, delivered by a man dressed up like some variety of Turk, who, opening his mouth in a curious way, sings, 'Home I bring the bri-i-ide.' He sings, and waves his arm (which is of course bare) from under his mantle. The procession commences. But here the French horn, in the accompaniment of the recitative, does something wrong; and the director, with a shudder as if some catastrophe had occurred, raps with his stick on the stand. All is stopped, and the director, turning to the orchestra, attacks the French horn, scolding him in the rudest terms—as cabmen abuse one another—for taking the wrong note. And again the whole thing recommences. The Indians with their halberds again come on, treading softly in their extraordinary boots; again the singer sings, 'Home I bring the bri-i-ide.' But here the pairs get too close together. More raps with the stick, more scolding, and a recommencement. Again 'Home I bring the bri-i-ide,' and again the same gesticulation with the bare arm from under the mantle; and again the couples, treading softly with halberds on their shoulders, some with sad and serious faces, some talking and smiling, arrange themselves in a circle and begin to sing. All seems to be going well, but again the stick raps and the director in a distressed and angry voice begins to scold the men and women of the chorus. It appears that when singing they had omitted to raise their hands from time to time in sign of animation. 'Are you all dead, or what? What oxen you are! Are you corpses, that you can't move?' Again they recommence, 'Home I bring the bri-i-ide,' and again, with sorrowful faces, the chorus women sing, first one and then another of them raising their hands. But two chorus girls speak to each other—again a more vehement rapping with the stick. 'Have you come here to talk? Can't you gossip at home? You there in red breeches, come nearer. Look at me! Begin again!' Again 'Home I bring the bri-i-ide.' And so it goes on for one, two, three hours. The whole of such a rehearsal lasts six hours on end. Raps with the stick, repetitions, placings, corrections of the singers, of the orchestra, of the procession, of the dancers—all seasoned with angry scolding. I heard the words, 'asses,' 'fools,' 'idiots,' 'swine,' addressed to the musicians and singers at least forty times in the course of one hour. And the unhappy individual to whom the abuse is addressed—flautist, horn blower, or singer—physically and mentally demoralized, does not reply, and does what is demanded of him. Twenty times is repeated the one phrase, 'Home I bring the bri-i-ide,' and twenty times the striding about in yellow shoes with a halberd over the shoulder. The conductor knows that these people are so demoralized that they are no longer fit for anything but to blow trumpets and walk about with halberds and in yellow shoes, and that they are also so accustomed to dainty easy living that they will put up with anything rather than lose their luxurious life. He therefore gives free vent to his churlishness, especially as he has seen the same thing done in Paris and Vienna, and knows that this is the way the best conductors behave, and that it is a musical tradition of great artists to be so carried away by the great business of their art that they cannot pause to consider the feelings of other artists.

It would be difficult to find a more repulsive sight. I have seen one workman abuse another for not supporting the weight piled upon him when goods were being unloaded, or at haystacking, the village elder scold a peasant for not making the rick right, and the man submitted in silence. And however unpleasant it was to witness the scene, the unpleasantness was lessened by the consciousness that the business in hand was necessary and important and the fault for which the elder scolded the labourer was one which might spoil a necessary undertaking.

But what was being done here? For what, and for whom? Very likely the conductor was tired out, like the workman I passed in the vaults; it was even evident that he was; but who made him tire himself? And why was he tiring himself? The opera he was rehearsing was one of the most ordinary of operas for people who are accustomed to them, but also one of the most gigantic absurdities that could possibly be devised. An Indian king wants to marry; they bring him a bride; he disguises himself as a minstrel; the bride falls in love with the minstrel and is in despair, but afterward discovers that the minstrel is the king, and everyone is highly delighted.

That there never were nor could be such Indians, and that they were not only unlike Indians but that what they were doing was unlike anything on earth except other operas, was beyond all manner of doubt; that people do not converse in such a way as recitative, and do not place themselves at fixed distances, in a quartet, waving their arms to express their emotions; that nowhere except in theatres do people walk about in such a manner, in pairs, with tinfoil halberds and in slippers; that no one ever gets angry in such a way, or is affected in such a way, or laughs in such a way, or cries in such a way; and that no one on earth can be moved by such performances—all this is beyond the possibility of doubt.

Instinctively the question presents itself: For whom is this being done? Whom *can* it please? If there are occasionally good melodies in the opera, to which it is pleasant to listen, they could have been sung simply without these stupid costumes and all the processions and recitatives and hand-wavings.

The ballet, in which half-naked women make voluptuous movements, twisting themselves into various sensual wreathings, is simply a lewd performance.

So one is quite at a loss as to whom these things are done for. The man of culture is heartily sick of them, while to a real working-man they are utterly incomprehensible. If anyone can be pleased by these things (which is doubtful), it can only be some young footman or depraved artisan, who has contracted the spirit of the upper classes but is not yet satiated with their amusements, and wishes to show his breeding.

And all this nasty folly is prepared, not simply, nor with kindly merriment, but with anger and brutal cruelty.

It is said that it is all done for the sake of art and that art is a very important thing. But is it true that art is so important that such sacrifices should be made for its sake? This question is especially urgent because art, for the sake of which the labour of millions, the lives of men, and above all love between man and man, are all being sacrificed—this very art is becoming something more and more vague and uncertain to human perception.

For the production of every ballet, circus, opera, operetta, exhibition, picture, concert, or printed book, the intense and unwilling labour of thousands and thousands of people is needed at what is often harmful and humiliating work. It were well if artists made all they require for themselves, but as it is, they all need the help of workmen, not only to produce art but also for their own usually luxurious maintenance. And one way or other they get it, either through payments from rich people, or through subsidies given by the government (in Russia, for instance, in grants of millions of rubles to theatres, conservatoires, and academies). This money is collected from the people, some of whom have to sell their only cow to pay the tax, and who never get those aesthetic pleasures which art gives.

WHAT IS ART? (1898)

JAMES AGATE

Coaching the Aspirant

The incomparable diarist of Ego *was bred to music from the age of seven and was never very far from a piano, a concert hall, or a working musician. The following extract from his autobiography is one of the very few accounts in print of what must be a fairly common scene.*

CAME home and spent the afternoon in a three-cornered wrangle with K. and Leo, who, now that we have got the boy virtually onto the platform at the National Gallery, wants to shove him off with a programme of elusive works which even the highbrows wouldn't stand for. Finally we reached a compromise. But not until I had taken the floor and Trafalgar Square'd K. as blisteringly as I could. Something like this:

'My dear Alexis: There is a quotation from Shakespeare which is so hackneyed that I shouldn't dare to use it in any of my articles. (*J. A. recites the lines from* Julius Caesar *about the tide in the affairs of men.*) Every English schoolboy knows these lines, but you, Alexis, being a Slav, may not know them. They bear directly on your engagement at the National Gallery, for this is the turn of your tide. You must not miss it, Alexis. Remember, you are not a great pianist making assault upon a London which is waiting for you; you are just an unknown pianist begging admission at the doors. (*Alexis grunts.*) Now you must realize that there may be some critics of importance at your concert. You are a virtuoso, and as such belong to what they call the "virtuosic brood." Some of them do accept pianism, it is true; but they only do so when it is a question of some rendering of, say, a theme of Tallis by members of the Dolmetsch family and performed on instruments not later than 1600. You might get the *Times* critic, who, when William Murdoch died last week, told us that he had far too much mind to be a solo pianist. And, by the way, he wasn't talking complete nonsense. Now, the National Gallery people have no interest whatever in you, either as virtuoso or musician. In so far as you exist at all, you are part of their scheme, which is to educate musical taste among the London masses. If you can help, all well and good. As Howard Ferguson hinted to you today, they want some early Beethoven; if you can fill the bill with that you will be a success with them.

'Now please listen carefully, my dear boy. I want you to understand clearly that it is not young Kligerman that they want; it is young Beethoven. And they don't want young Beethoven seen through the eyes of young Kligerman; they want young Beethoven seen through their eyes. In other words, as they want London's masses to see him. If you can give them this, good. It is the price you pay for getting your foot in the magic circle. But a dreadful trap awaits you. Perhaps Leo will tell you what he thinks of your early Beethoven. I make no bones about saying that I think it appalling, and I have listened to you playing early Beethoven for over an hour. Let me give you an analogy taken from the world of horses. In a racehorse, as perhaps you know, all that matters is how quickly the animal can get from one place to another; what he looks like during the process doesn't matter. But with a show harness horse what matters is the majesty, the rhythm, shall I say, the poetry of his motion; how long he takes in covering the ground is of very little account. Do you see this? Now do you understand the trap I speak of? You take your Beethoven at a terrific lick because it is in your blood to feel your Beethoven that way. Personally I think you are wrong, but I know you and therefore don't impute a wrong motive. But the musical critics, who don't know you, will assume that you are using Beethoven as a medium for showing off. And that will be the beginning, and, I fear, the end of Alexis Kligerman.'

There was a silence, and then Leo, who likes to play Eusebius to my Florestan, said quietly, 'I think you ought to be told, Alexis, that if you are going in for the early Beethoven sonatas you ought to accustom yourself to getting a bird's-eye view of each movement as a whole, just as if you were looking at some building from the air. I am afraid you still only consider a piece passage by passage; in that way there will never be any sense of continuity, you will be like those old actors who recited their parts without knowing or bothering to know what the others had said before or were going to say afterwards. . . . I think James is right about your playing too fast. I can understand that; it has something to do with your Slavonic temperament. But don't give way to it in early Beethoven. There was nothing Slavonic there; only German solidity, French elegance, and Italian lyricism exquisitely blended. When you begin your Opus 10, your *Pastorale*, your *Pathétique* . . . leave your Slav ego outside on the mat. Be Western. We are placid, unhysterical people in the West, you know; we don't tear a passion to tatters. Tradition must not be despised, either. If you can bear to hear James read to you how Kean played Othello, how Phelps played Prospero, or Irving Hamlet, then you must listen to people who can tell you how von Bülow, Rubinstein, Stavenhagen, and d'Albert played these early sonatas. Let your presto be a moderato; but let your adagio approach andante.'

It must not be imagined that these orations were uninterrupted. It is only fair to give Kligerman's point of view, and this I reconstruct from his vigorous splutterings and expostulations. Had we given him time for a considered speech it would have gone something like this:

'That what you say is very well. But you suppose I shall make great success with methods which are so reactionary? What will people call me?—they will call me tame, with no life and no fire and no passion. You say "von Bülow." Good. But I am told he played like a volcano extinct. I—I am twenty-two. I am Siegfried, not Wotan. I do not believe that the critics want this, or that, or the other, I believe the critics want a sincerity, an enthusiasm, and I do not think they want the beaten track, a performance like everyone else. To me, my tempi in Beethoven are right. He was young when he wrote these sonatas: you think then one shall play them like an old man? No, no. Beethoven was virtuoso also: shall one then not play quick passages like virtuoso? In "classic" Beethoven I do not believe: I believe only in Beethoven romantic, poetic. Is he not a prince, a prophet, a pioneer? . . . Is he not. . . .' By this time our good Alexis had become so excited that his face had become dead-white, his eyes shone like arc lamps, and he thumped my mantelpiece until I was afraid he would injure his wrist. Then the decanter came to our aid, and thus ended the 'struggle for an artist's soul.' In novels and on the screen this means whether some starving artist should degrade his soul by allowing some rich woman to seduce his body. But Leo and I are not concerned with any such twaddle. The point is: Can we detach this young man's mind from his fingers?

HUGO WOLF

When to Applaud

WHY in the name of heaven and all its angels must the searching fire of enthusiasm always come out through the hands and feet? Why must there be clapping and stamping? Do the public's hands and feet constitute the movable lightning rod for the electrified soul? I ask whether applauding is allowable under all circumstances, whether it is a force of nature—or only a bad and stupid habit.

Yet I do not want to be understood as pleading against applause universally. Let people continue to clap, but only when the work itself in some measure calls for it, when it concludes brilliantly and loud, when its character is festive, gay, warlike, or heroic. Would anyone deny that the close of the *Coriolan* overture affects the soul in a different way from the close of the *Egmont*? The gradually rising dawn of freedom over the grave of Egmont, which shines there at the end like the rays of the sun over an oppressed people, powerfully lifts up the listener's heart. He feels inspirited, elevated, free. He desires to join in the common jubilation, he applauds, he keeps shouting 'Bravo!' We can all join in because we feel at one with liberated peoples: applause is here in its proper place.

But after the frightful tragedy of Coriolan's annihilated ego, does Beethoven's hero awaken no other impulse than the desire to escape at once from so deep an impression? Does not the eye stare madly, as if into a magic mirror in which the gigantic shadow of Coriolan slowly disappears . . . ? I say that if when the last note has barely ceased to resound you are again jolly and pleased, and you babble and criticize and clap, then you have not looked into the magic mirror, you have seen nothing, felt nothing, heard nothing, understood nothing— nothing, nothing: *not a thing!*

COLLECTED CRITIQUES (1885)

DENIS DIDEROT

Rameau's Nephew

Based on fact, this famous dialogue between the French Encyclopaedist and the nephew of the composer Rameau was first made known through Goethe's translation of a manuscript copy that had found its way to Germany. The scene is a café in the Palais Royal.

AFTER a moment's silence on both our parts, during which he paced up and down whistling and singing, I spoke, in order to bring him back to a discussion of his talent. I said:

MYSELF: What are you doing now?

HE: Nothing.

MYSELF: That must be very fatiguing.

HE: I was empty-headed enough to begin with, but I went to hear the music of Duni[1] and our other young composers, and that finished me.

MYSELF: So you like this new genre?

HE: No doubt about it.

MYSELF: You manage to find beauty in these new-fangled melodies?

HE: Do I manage? Ye gods! Don't doubt for a moment that I do! What declamation! What truth of expression!

MYSELF: Every imitative art finds its model in Nature. What is the musician's model when he fashions a melody?

HE: Let's begin with a more general question: What is a melody?

MYSELF: I confess that is beyond me. We are all alike, really, we remember words, which we think we understand from the frequent and even correct use we make of them. But our minds contain only vague notions. When I utter the word 'melody,' I have no clearer idea than you and most of your colleagues when you say, 'Reputation, blame, honour, vice, virtue, modesty, decency, shame, ridicule.'

HE: A melody is a vocal or instrumental imitation using the sounds of a scale invented by art—or inspired by nature, as you prefer; it imitates either physical noises or the accents of passion. You can see

[1] Italian composer of comic operas (1709–75).

that by changing a few words in this definition it would exactly fit painting, eloquence, sculpture, or poetry.

Now to come to your question: What is the musician's model? It is declamation if the model is alive and a thinking being; it is physical noise if the model is inanimate. Consider declamation as one line, and song as another, which twists snakelike about the former. The more the declamation, which is the prototype of song, is vivid and true, the more the song shaped upon it will intersect it at many points. The truer the melody, the more beautiful it will be—and that is what our younger musicians have so well understood.

I say nothing of meter, which is another condition of melody; I dwell on expressiveness. Nothing is more self-evident than the maxim I read somewhere: '*Musices seminarium accentus*'—'Accent is the source of melody.' From this you can infer how difficult and how important it is to know how to handle recitative. There is no beautiful air from which one cannot make a beautiful recitative, and no beautiful recitative from which an able composer cannot make a beautiful air. I would not guarantee that a good reciter will sing well, but I should be surprised if a good singer did not know how to recite well. You must believe all I have been saying, for it's true.

MYSELF: I should like nothing better than to believe you, if I were not prevented by a small difficulty.

HE: The difficulty is?

MYSELF: Only this, that if the new music is sublime, it follows that the music of the divine Lulli, of Campra, of Destouches, of Mouret, and—be it said between us—of your dear uncle, must be a trifle dull.

HE, *coming close and answering in my ear:* I shouldn't like to be overheard, for there are hereabouts plenty of people who know me—but it *is* dull. Not that I worry myself much about the dear uncle—if 'dear' has to come into it. He is made of stone: he could see my tongue hanging out a foot long and he would not give me a glass of water. But try as he will—with the octave, the leading note—*tum-tum-ta-ta-tum, toot-toot-toot, tra-la-toot*—even though he makes a racket like the very devil, some people are beginning to catch on; they will no longer take banging for music—and certainly not *his* banging. The police should forbid any person, of whatever rank, to have Pergolese's *Stabat Mater* performed. That *Stabat* should have been burned by the public hangman.[1] Yes, these confounded *bouffons* with their *Serva Padrona* and

[1] I.e., so that the French might not be won over to the Italian music.

their *Tracallo* have given us a stout kick in the butt. That's why Rebel and Francoeur[1] cry out to heaven. They say all is lost: 'they are ruined; if these fair-ground musicians are allowed to keep on our national music is done for; the so-called Royal Academy—the Opera—might as well shut up shop.' And there is some truth in it. The old fogies who have been going there every Friday for thirty or forty years no longer have a good time. They are bored, they yawn without knowing why. They ask themselves and can't answer. They should ask *me*. As things are going now, Duni's prophecy will come true, and I'm willing to give up living in four or five years if, after *The Painter in Love with His Model*, you find as much as an alley cat in our celebrated Opera house.

The good souls! They've already abandoned their symphonies to hear the Italian ones.[2] They thought they could accustom their ears to these new instrumental pieces without changing their taste as regards the vocal—as if symphonies were not in relation to songs (except for the greater freedom afforded by the range of instruments and the dexterity of the fingers) what songs are to declamation; as if the violin did not ape the singer, who in turn will become the ape of the violin when acrobatics will have replaced beauty. The first one who played Locatelli[3] was the apostle of the new music. Next! Next! We shall all become accustomed to the imitation of passionate accents or of natural phenomena by means of voices and instruments—which is the whole extent of music's purpose. D'you think we'll also keep our taste for flights, dreams, glories, triumphs, and victories? Not so you can notice it, Joe! Did anyone imagine that the public could learn to weep or laugh at tragic or comic scenes when 'musicated,' to respond to the tones of fury, hatred, and jealousy, the true plaints of love, the irony and pleasantries of the Italian or French theatre, and that in spite of all this the public would continue to admire *Ragonde* or *Platée*.[4] You bet your life—go cut it with a knife! That they could once learn how easily, softly, gently the Italian tongue, with its natural harmony, flexible prosody, easy ellipses and inversions, suited the art and motion of music, the turns of song and the measured pace of sounds—and yet would overlook the fact that French is stiff, heavy, pedantic, and monotonous? Well, well, well, they persuaded themselves that after

[1] Directors of the Opera orchestra in Paris.
[2] 'Symphonies' here mean operatic overtures and interludes.
[3] Pietro Locatelli (1693–1764), famous violinist and composer, pupil of Corelli.
[4] Operas by Mouret and Rameau respectively.

weeping with a mother bewailing the loss of her son, and shuddering at the decree of a tyrant committing murder, they would not be bored with their fairyland, their insipid mythology, their saccharine love songs, which show the poet's bad taste no less than the sterility of the music matched thereto. The good souls!

It could not and cannot be. The true, the good, and the beautiful will prevail. Their rights may at first be challenged, but in the end are acknowledged and people do yield their admiration. Inferior things may be esteemed for a time, but the end is a great yawn. Go ahead, gentlemen, yawn away, yawn to your heart's content, don't be afraid! The power of nature and of the trinity that I worship will never be overcome by the forces of darkness—the True which is the father, engenders the Good, which is his son, whence comes the Beautiful, which is the Holy Ghost. Change is gradual. The foreign god takes his place humbly next to the native idol, little by little asserts himself, and one fine day elbows out his fellow—before you can say Jack Robinson, there's the idol flat on its back.

MYSELF: There is some sense in almost everything you've said.

HE: Sense? I'm glad! The devil take me if I've been making any special effort. I speak as it comes. I'm like the opera musicians when my uncle came on the scene. If I'm on the point, well and good. It only shows that a man of the trade will always speak about it more sensibly than any Academy or all the Duhamels in the world.[1]

And now he paces up and down again, humming in his throat some arias from Duni's operas, occasionally raising arms and eyes to heaven: 'It's beautiful, God, but it's beautiful! Why?——How can a man sport a pair of ears and ask such a question?' He was getting into a passion and beginning to sing, his voice growing louder as his passion increased. Next he gesticulated, made faces and twisted his body, and I thought to myself, 'There he goes—losing his wits and working himself up to a scene.' True enough, he suddenly burst out very loud, 'I am but a poor wretch. . . . My lord, my lord, I beg you to let me go! . . . O Earth, receive my gold and keep my treasure safe, my soul, my life, O Earth! . . . There is my little friend . . . *Aspettare e non venire* . . . *A Zerbina penserete . . . Sempre in contrasti con te si sta. . . .*' He jumbled together thirty different airs, French, Italian, comic, tragic—in every style. Now in a baritone voice he sank into the pit; then, straining in

[1] An academic writer on trades he did not practise.

falsetto, he tore to shreds the upper notes of some air, imitating the while the stance, walk, and gestures of the several characters; being in succession furious, mollified, lordly, sneering. First a damsel weeps and he reproduces her kittenish ways; next he is a priest, a king, a tyrant; he threatens, commands, rages. Now he is a slave, he obeys, calms down, is heartbroken, complains, laughs; never overstepping the proper tone, speech, or manner called for by the part.

All the chess players in the café had left their boards and gathered around us. The windows of the place were occupied from outside by passers-by who had stopped on hearing the commotion. They guffawed fit to crack the ceiling. He notices nothing, he keeps on, in the grip of spiritual possession, an enthusiasm so close to madness that it seems doubtful whether he will recover. He may have to be put into a cab and taken to a padded cell, still singing fragments of Jomelli's *Lamentations*.[1] He reproduces with incredible precision, fidelity, and warmth the most beautiful passages of each scene. That magnificent recitative in which Jeremiah describes the desolation of Jerusalem he drenches in tears which draw their like from every onlooker. His art was complete —delicacy of voice, expressive strength, true sorrow. He dwelt on the places where the musician had shown himself a master. If he left the vocal part, it was to take up the instrumental, which he abandoned suddenly to return to the voice, linking them so as to preserve the connection and unity of the whole, gripping our souls and keeping them suspended in the most singular state of being that I have ever experienced.

Did I admire him? Yes, I did admire. Was I moved to pity? I was moved. But a streak of derision was interwoven with these feelings and denatured them.

Yes, you too would have burst out laughing at the way in which he aped the different instruments. With swollen cheeks and a sombre throaty sound, he would give us the horns and bassoons. For the oboes he assumed a shrill yet nasal voice, then speeded up the emission of sound to an incredible degree for the strings, for whose tones he found close analogues. He whistled piccolos and warbled traverse flutes, singing, shouting, waving about like one demented, being in himself dancer and ballerina, singer and prima donna, all of them together and the whole orchestra, the whole theatre; then redividing himself into

[1] A setting of *Jeremiah*. Jomelli (1714–74) was a forerunner of Gluck in operatic reform.

twenty separate roles, running, stopping, glowing at the eyes like one possessed, frothing at the mouth. . . .

HE: Our passions have to be strong. The tenderness of the musician and the poet must be extreme . . . the aria must be the peroration of the scene. We need exclamations, interjections, suspensions, interruptions, affirmations, and negations. We call out, invoke, clamour, groan, weep, and laugh openly. No more witticisms, epigrams, neat thoughts—they are too unlike Nature. And don't get it into your head that the old theatrical acting and declamation can give us a pattern to follow. Not likely! We want it more energetic, less mannered, more genuine. Simple speeches, the ordinary utterance of passion, will be all the more necessary that our French language is more monotonous, less accented. The animal cry or that of man in a passion will supply the accent. . . .

As he spoke, the crowd around us had withdrawn, whether from no longer being able to hear or from having lost interest in the subject; for in general man is like a child and prefers being amused to being instructed. The chess players had resumed their boards and we were alone in our corner. Seated on the bench, his head resting against the wall, his arms hanging and his eyes half closed, he said:

HE: I don't know what's the matter with me; when I came here I was feeling rested and in good form. Now I am exhausted, worn out, as if I had walked thirty miles. It came upon me suddenly.

MYSELF: Should you like something to drink?

HE: With pleasure. My throat feels rough, I am a little faint, and my chest hurts. This happens to me every day and I have no notion of the cause.

MYSELF: What shall you take?

HE: Whatever you say. I am not hard to please. Poverty has accustomed me to everything.

He drank two or three glasses of lemonade without noticing, and would have drowned himself like a spent swimmer had I not moved the bottle, which he sought distractedly, not knowing what he was about. I then said to him:

MYSELF: How is it that with such fineness of feeling, so much sensibility where musical beauty is concerned, you are so blind to the beauties of morality, so insensible to the charm of virtue?

HE: It must be that virtue requires a special sense that I lack, a fibre that has not been granted me. My fibre is loose, one can pluck it forever without its yielding a note. Or else I have spent my life with good musicians and bad people, whence my ear has become very sharp and my heart quite deaf. And then there is heredity. My father's blood is the same as my uncle's; my blood is like my father's. The paternal molecule was hard and obtuse, and like a primordial germ it has affected all the rest.

MYSELF: Do you love your son?

HE: Do I love him? I am crazy about him.

MYSELF: And will you do nothing to thwart in him the effect of his accursed paternal molecule?

HE: I'll try, but (I think) in vain. If he is fated to become a good man, trying won't do any harm. But if the molecule decides that he shall be a ne'er-do-well like his father, the pains I might take to make him an honest man would be very dangerous. Before the molecule could recapture him and reproduce the state of perfect abjection which I have reached, it would take endless time. He would waste his best years. So at the moment I hold my hand, I simply observe him and let him come along. He is already greedy, cozening, rascally, lazy, and a liar: I am afraid he is a pedigreed beast.

MYSELF: And you will make him a musician so that the likeness can be complete?

HE: A musician! A musician! Sometimes I look at him and grind my teeth and say to myself, 'If you ever learn a note, I really think I'll twist your neck.'

MYSELF: But why so?

HE: It leads nowhere.

MYSELF: It leads everywhere.

HE: Yes, if you excel. But who can guarantee that his child will excel? It's ten thousand to one that he will be a wretched note scraper like me. Do you know that it would be easier to find a child able to govern a kingdom than a great violinist?

MYSELF: I think on the contrary that any likely talent, even if mediocre, can lead a man to fortune, provided the country has no morals and lives on luxury and debauch. I myself once heard the following conversation take place between a sort of patron and his would-be protégé. The latter had been recommended to the former as a useful and serviceable man:

'My dear sir, what can you do?'

'I am a fairly good mathematician.'

'Good enough. But after you have taught mathematics for ten or twelve years by running the streets of Paris, you will have only three or four hundred francs a year.'

'I have also studied law.'

'If Puffendorf and Grotius came back to life they would starve in the gutter.'

'I am well versed in geography and history.'

'If there were any parents who really cared about their children's education, your fortune would be made. But such parents do not exist.'

'I am a tolerable musician.'

'Why didn't you say so at once? Just to show you what your gift is worth to you, let me say this: I have a daughter; come every day at seven-thirty and give her a lesson until nine. I shall pay you two hundred and fifty francs a year and give you all your meals at our house. The rest of the day is yours to dispose of for your profit.'

HE: And what happened?

MYSELF: If the man had been clever he would have grown rich—which is all you seem to care about.

HE: No doubt. Gold, gold is everything; and everything, without gold, is nothing. Therefore, instead of having my son's head stuffed with grand maxims which he would have to forget under pain of being a pauper, this is what I do whenever I have a gold piece—not often, to be sure: I plant myself in front of him, draw the piece from my pocket, show it to him with admiring looks, raise my eyes to heaven, kiss the gold in front of him, and to show him still more forcibly the importance of the sacred coin I stammer out the names and point out with the finger all the things one can buy with it—a beautiful gown, a beautiful hat, a good cake; next I put the coin in my pocket, parade before him proudly, pull up my coat-tails, and strike my waistcoat where the money lies. Thus do I make him understand that it is from that coin I draw the self-assurance he beholds.

MYSELF: Nothing could be better. But what if some day, being deeply persuaded of the value of money, he should—

HE: I follow you! One must shut one's eyes to that. There is no principle of conduct wholly without drawbacks. At the worst, one goes through a bad half-hour, then all is over.

MYSELF: Yet in spite of your wise and courageous views, I continue to think it would be a good thing to make him a musician. I know of no better way to approach the rich, to serve their vices and to turn one's own to advantage.

HE: True. But I have projects even more certain of success. Ah, if I only had a daughter! But no man can do as he likes—he must take what he gets and do the best he can with it. For which purpose one must not, like most fathers, stupidly give children who are destined to live in Paris the education of ancient Sparta. One might as well plot their ruin. If the native training is bad, the fault lies with the manners and customs of my country, and not with me. Whoever be responsible, I want my child happy, or what amounts to the same thing, honoured, rich, powerful. I know the easiest ways to accomplish this, and I mean to teach them to my son early in life. If you wise men blame me, the majority (and success itself) will absolve me. He will have gold—it's I who tell you so, I guarantee it—and if he has a great deal, he will lack nothing, not even your admiration and respect.

MYSELF: You might be wrong about the latter.

HE: If so, he can do without, like many other people.

There was in all he said much that one thinks to oneself, and acts on, but that one never says. This was in fact the chief difference between my man and the rest of us. He admitted his vices, which are also ours; he was no hypocrite. Neither more nor less detestable than other men, he was franker than they, more logical, and thus often profound in his depravity. I was appalled to think of what his child would become under such a tutor. It was clear that if he was brought up on a system so exactly framed on our actual behaviour, he would go far—unless he was prematurely cut off on the way.

HE: Never you fear! The important thing that a good father must do is not so much to give his child vices that will bring him wealth and foolish traits that will make him a favourite of the great—everybody does as much: not systematically like me, but by casual precept and example. No, what is more difficult is to teach him the golden art by which he can avert disgrace, shame, and the penalties of the law. These last are dissonances in the harmony of society, which one must know how to use, prepare, and resolve. Nothing is duller than a progression of common chords. One wants some contrast, which breaks up the clear white light and makes it iridescent.

MYSELF: Very good. Thanks. Your comparison brings me back from morals to music. I digressed in spite of myself, for to speak frankly, I like you much better as musician than as moralist.

HE: And yet I am only second-rate in music, whereas I am a superior moralist.

MYSELF: I rather doubt this; but even were it so, I am an honest man and your principles do not suit me.

HE: So much the worse for you. Oh, if I only had your talent!

MYSELF: Leave my talent alone; let's go back to yours.

HE: If I could express myself as you do! But my vocabulary is a damned mongrel—half literary and well bred, half guttersnipe.

MYSELF: Don't think I speak well, I can only tell the truth, and as you know, that doesn't always go down.

HE: It's not for telling the truth that I envy you your gifts. Just the opposite—to tell lies. If I only knew how to throw together a book, how to turn a dedication, intoxicate some fool with praise and make my way among women!

MYSELF: As for all that, you know much more about it than I do; I am not even fit to be your pupil.

HE: Oh, what abilities you are letting go to waste, not even suspecting what they're worth!

MYSELF: I reap whatever I sow, no more, no less.

HE: If that were true, you wouldn't be wearing these coarse clothes —linen coat, woollen stockings, thick-soled shoes, and superannuated wig.

MYSELF: Granted. One must be terribly clumsy if one isn't rich after sticking at nothing to acquire wealth. But there are people like me, you see, who don't consider wealth the most important thing in the world—queer people.

HE: Very queer. No one is born that way. It's an acquired idea; it's unnatural.

MYSELF: Unnatural for man?

HE: Just unnatural. Everything that lives, man included, seeks its well-being at the expense of whoever withholds it. I'm sure that if I let my little savage grow up without saying a word to him, he would of his own accord want to be richly dressed, magnificently fed, liked by men and loved by women, and concentrate on himself all the goods of life.

MYSELF: If your little savage were left to himself and to his native blindness, he would in time join the infant's reasoning to the grown man's passions—he would strangle his father and sleep with his mother.

HE: Which only proves the need of a good education. There's no argument. But what is a good education if it is not one that leads to all the enjoyments without trouble or danger?

MYSELF: I am almost with you there, but let's not go into it.

HE: Why not?

MYSELF: Because I think we are only superficially in agreement, and that if we look into the question of troubles and dangers, we shall no longer be at one.

HE: And what's the harm of that?

MYSELF: Let it go, I say. What I know on the subject I shan't be able to teach you. You will have an easier time teaching me what you know about music, of which I am ignorant. Dear Rameau, let us talk music; and tell me how it is that with your remarkable power for understanding, remembering, and rendering the most beautiful works of the great masters, with your contagious enthusiasm for them and for conveying them, you have never done anything that amounts to anything.

Instead of answering me, he started nodding with his head and, uplifting a finger heavenward, cried out, 'My star! My star! When Nature fashioned Leo,[1] Vinci,[2] Pergolese, Duni, she smiled on them. She put on a grave imposing mien when she made my dear uncle Rameau, who for a dozen years was called "the great Rameau," though soon nobody will have heard of him. But when she slapped together his nephew, she made a face, then another face, and still another.' As he said these words he was making all sorts of faces, depicting contempt, disdain, irony; he seemed to be kneading a ball of dough within his fingers while grinning at the absurd shapes he was imparting to it.

This done, he made a gesture as if throwing the outlandish creation far from him. . . .

RAMEAU'S NEPHEW (1762; publ. 1823)

[1] Neapolitan opera composer (1694–1744).
[2] Of the same Neapolitan school (1690–1730).

BERNARD VAN DIEREN
&
FERRUCCIO BUSONI

What Gives Us Pause

Still insufficiently known as a composer, yet sure of a place in modern music, Bernard Van Dieren (1884–1936) has left a volume of essays that merit attention for their original thought and prose. The other person in the dialogue is Ferruccio Busoni (1866–1924), who was a composer, piano virtuoso, and writer on music. See pp. 19 and 341.

M Y own action once served to bring home to him the roots and the consequences of such misunderstandings. We were together visiting a South German town. Busoni had promised to show me some interesting buildings. In the course of our walk he entered a dark court and then mounted a wide, dimly lit stone staircase. I followed without question. We arrived at what unexpectedly proved a restaurant on the first floor. On the landing he turned round to say:

BUSONI: You are a queer fellow!

MYSELF: What makes you think so?

B.: You never asked where I was going. . . .

M.: Well, are we not 'out for a walk' together?

B.: We are; in fact I took you here for a glass of wine.

M.: It did not look in the least like a place where that could be found: it looked to me more like a coiners' den, but I would naturally follow where you go.

B.: I suppose it does seem natural to you! I would have wanted to know what came next.

M.: Speak of reversed roles! I once felt you did something quite as odd.

B.: And when may that have been?

M.: You remember when you wanted us to hear Liszt's 'Figaro,' which you had just discovered. You asked me to turn the pages. The manuscript was illegible, and you played your own additions that were not marked on it. Not unnaturally, I soon lost my way. Yet by never a whisper or a nod did you tell me when to turn next.

B.: But I played the whole work to a finish!

M.: I admired that as much as I could while feeling so disgruntled. You must realize that you made me feel foolish. It was unkind. . . .

B.: But you said nothing.

M.: I should have had to interrupt you. No, on that occasion it was I who was expecting a word or a sign. And more reasonably, I think.

B.: And you didn't get it! Now I suppose that this time again you think it was for me to speak first?

M.: Not this time. There was nothing here like one page hiding all the following ones. I should soon enough discover where you were leading me. Very much as if I listened—without any impediment— to some of your music. I should not begin arguing before I had seen what you were getting at.

B.: Unfortunately that is what I find people nearly always do. So perhaps your way is best after all. What could not one do if listeners had the patience to reserve critical observations!

M.: Since we are here, let us go in and have the wine. *Seated with the bottle.* You were lamenting that much you could do is left undone. You said people should refrain from mentally formulating their criticisms while you addressed them. That they should surrender for the moment, until they knew where you were leading them. Did I get it right?

B.: That is more or less what I had in mind.

M.: Did you refer to remembered disillusions? Or are you thinking of the future, and of works as yet unwritten?

B.: Of both, but chiefly of so much music I should like to write for which I do not yet trust myself. Perhaps I ought to say, for which I don't trust my public yet—unless I were to adapt my writing to their habits. I should love to set some of those wondrous speeches of Don Quixote. His address to the goat-herds in the first book, for instance. There I feel I could achieve something of real worth.

M.: It seems an exceptionally suitable subject. It is a great pity that you hesitate.

B.: I should want to say so infinitely much that I hardly trust the power of music to convey all that presses itself on my imagination.

M.: It is strange that you should distrust your powers for the task— even counting the limitations of music. As strange as that you distrust my rational mentality when you think I behave in an unexpected way. Honestly, I think it is 'queer' when you say there is something of mystery about me. In the incident I recalled, I showed my confidence in you, as I always should where music is concerned. And that, after all, is what you desire.

B.: What you say sounds flattering. I ought to be pleased. Perhaps most people speak too soon in daily affairs too, and spoil me for the appreciation of your silences.

M.: You would not want me to argue more, or sooner, music or no music?

B.: Mercy! Don't I know that you can beat anybody in debate? Besides, out of my own mouth you have already convinced me.

M.: Granted my debating prowess, why not take it as a compliment if I follow your lead without a word, or listen to your words or your music without itching to interrupt?

B.: Well, perhaps I was slow to see my mistake. Perhaps I did not like having to admit it. Anyhow, you were right. You usually are.

M.: Please! Don't make it too good! You only make me blush. Let us rather empty our glasses and drink to the Don Quixote speeches.

(*They were, alas, never composed, and the more's the pity, for Busoni should have succeeded with their mixture of the fantastic, the burlesque, and mellow wisdom better than anyone.*)

B.: Don't be too sanguine. You will have enough composer's miseries to come to the conclusion that sometimes it is better to leave cherished projects unexecuted.

M.: From choice or from need? Are you thinking of the jealous lover hiding his mistress, or of Berlioz abandoning a symphony after he had calculated the cost?

B.: Both. I am afraid. You ought to make yourself quite independent of composition for your existence. You should, like Rousseau, copy music, for instance.

M.: What on earth brings you to this? You know very well that he did not make anything like a living out of it. Besides, there were no trade unions in his way. I have tried, and found it difficult to enter that closely guarded domain.

B., *reproachfully*: You have been sending in a work for a competition! Did you imagine that any jury would give *you* a prize? Is it likely?

M.: Oh, that is what you were driving at all the time. Do reflect;

I must at least make an honest attempt. You once got a prize yourself, you know.

B.: You don't suppose that I was one-tenth as much of a formed composer then as you are now? A single page of your music will frighten anyone who is ever acceptable as a member of a jury.

M.: But you cannot deny that you are on juries yourself? Wouldn't you give me a chance?

B.: I could not; I should recognize the first bar.

M.: Worse luck! We are turning in a vicious circle. I had hoped that some dishonesty on a jury might bring me a chance some day.

B.: It will! When it is too late! When you don't need it any more for your name. Even then, materially, it won't help you much. And don't forget that a sentimental jury will have other friends. You have nothing to expect from that, I repeat. No, you ought to make a living from something that has nothing to do with music. Then you could afford to write whatever pleased you.

M.: Ouch! Don't you know that I shall be looked upon as an amateur and an interloper, and shunned by all musicians?

B.: Publishers used to accept my works because of my fame as a pianist. But that fame stands in my way with the public.

M.: Because they think you ought to be *only* a pianist. What would they think of 'only an amateur'? *You* despise amateurs.

B.: If you were taken for one, that would not make you one. Still, I admit the objection. I see no way out for you. I should like to give you an income for a number of years so that you could work with complete freedom. Only, honestly, I have been carefully calculating— I cannot manage it. People think I am a wealthy man: I am nothing of the sort. However much I should like to, I simply have not the money.

There are not many composers who would think of such assistance to a confrère, and if Busoni, in this case, was not in a position to do what his feeling prompted, it was because he always had most lavishly given away money, right and left, to pupils and struggling musicians, and sacrificed much of his time to teaching them[1] and performing their works.

If he ever complained of anything, it was that his example had not

[1] It will be remembered that he never accepted remuneration. [Van Dieren's note.]

borne fruit, that younger men, when their successes had made them financially competent, were not in their turn ready to give of what they had acquired, to others less fortunate, whose work might enrich music if not themselves.

He could never understand selfishness, whether reasoning or un-reasoning, and one could not point to a nobler trait in his character, or to one that showed better how loyal and true-hearted an artist he was.

His duty, he felt, was to art, and in every sense.

DOWN AMONG THE DEAD MEN (1935)

APROPOS OF INSTRUMENTS

THOMAS HARDY

The Organ Blower's Complaint

THIS frame of mind naturally induced an amazing abstraction in the organist, never very vigilant at the best times. He would hear the cathedral clock strike one, and go the next minute to see what time it was. 'I never seed such a man as Mr. Julian is,' said the head blower. 'He'll meet me anywhere out-of-doors, and never wink or nod. You'd hardly expect it. I don't find fault, but you'd hardly expect it, seeing how I play the same instrument as he do himself, and have done it for so many years longer than he. How I have indulged that man, too! If 'tis Pedals for two martel hours of practice I never complain; and he has plenty of vagaries. When 'tis hot summer weather there's nothing will do for him but Choir, Great and Swell together, till yer face is but a vapour; and on a frosty winter night he'll keep me there while he tweedles upon the Twelfth and Sixteenth till my arms be scrammed for want of motion. And never speak a word out-of-doors!'

THE HAND OF ETHELBE TA (1876)

ARTHUR SCHOPENHAUER

The Russian Horn

The trenchant philosopher, who did much by his writings to give music intellectual dignity, was himself a good musician and a devotee of Italian opera.

WHOEVER is a whole man, a man par excellence, is no fraction of the human race, but a self-sufficient unit. Ordinary company may in this respect be likened to Russian-horn music. Each horn has only one note, and only by carefully edging in their parts can the instrumentists play a piece.[1] Now this monotone of a Russian horn is precisely what you get from most people's minds. How many of them actually look as if they had at no time more than one and the same thought—incapable of another! This explains why they are so dull, and also why they are so gregarious and always try to forgather in herds. The monotony of his own being makes the lone man intolerable to himself: '*Omnis stultitia laborat fastidio sui*'[2]— only when you bring a number of them together in a group do you obtain anything from them—just like the music from those horns.

On the contrary, a man of brains is like a virtuoso who can give a concert all by himself. Or he is like a piano, which is in itself a small orchestra. Such a man is a small world, and what the others produce by playing all together, he offers in the unity of one consciousness. Like the piano, he is not a part of the symphony but is naturally fitted to play solo. He plays in solitude, perhaps, or if with others, then only as principal, to others' accompaniment—like the piano; or else he gives the true pitch, as in singing—like the piano.

Now those who like company can deduce the rule from this comparison, that deficiency of quality in those we meet must be made up for somehow by quantity. With one intelligent being, though he

[1] The Russian bands often numbered as many as one hundred players. The nstruments are straight conical tubes of varying length, with mouthpieces almost at right angles.

[2] Every kind of idiocy suffers its own disgust.

be the only one, it is possible to have all the social intercourse that may be desired; but when we are forced to deal with none but ordinary people, it is best to collect a crowd of them, so that by collaboration something may result, on the analogy of the horns. And may Heaven grant you patience for the job!

MAXIMS OF WORLDLY WISDOM (1850)

CHATEAUBRIAND

Of Bells

The Genius of Christianity marks a date in the religious history of France after the Revolution. By reviewing in one work all the psychological, social, historic, and artistic merits of the Church, Chateaubriand initiated a revival of faith. Music necessarily concerned him at many points.

IT seems from the outset a rather remarkable thing that a means could be found to awaken by one hammer stroke a single emotion at the same moment in a thousand different hearts, and so compel the winds and the clouds to carry the thoughts of man. Then, considered as harmony, bells undoubtedly possess a beauty of the first order—that which artists call *grandeur*. The sound of thunder is sublime solely because it has grandeur, magnitude. And thus it is with the winds and the sea, with volcanoes, waterfalls, or the voice of a whole people.

With what pleasure would Pythagoras, who gladly heard the blacksmith's hammer, have listened to our bells on the eve of a religious ceremony! The soul may be melted by the strings of a lyre, but it is not fired with enthusiasm as when aroused by the thunderbolts of battle or by an imposing peal that proclaims in the realms above the glory of the Lord of Hosts.

And yet this is not the most wonderful characteristic of the sound of bells, which has so many secret links with our being. How often, in the silence of the night, has not a distant ringing of bells, a faint reverberation, as of a heart expiring in agony, struck and amazed the ear of the adulteress? How often have these echoes not reached even the atheist who, in his impious vigil, was perhaps daring to write that there is no God! The pen falls from his hand as he hears the dreadful knell of death which seems to be saying, 'Is there indeed no God?' Oh, why did not such sounds disturb the sleep of our oppressors! Mysterious religion that by the sole magic of sounding bronze can change pleasures into torments, shake the atheist, and make the assassin drop his knife!

Softer feelings are also linked with the sound of bells. When at dawn in harvest time one hears together with the lark the soft tinklings that rise from our hamlets, one thinks the guardian angel of the crops is rousing the toilers by breathing into some Hebrew instrument the stories of Zipporah or Naomi. It seems to me that were I a poet, I should not disdain the 'bell rung by ghosts' which hangs in the old chapel by the wood, nor that which out of a sacred fear resounds in our villages to avert lightning, nor again that which is heard at night in certain seaports to guide the helmsman through the reefs.

On feast days the carillon adds to the general gladness. But in calamity these same sounds become dreadful to hear. The hair upon the head still rises at the very thought of the days of flame and carnage accompanied by the clangour of the tocsin. Who of us can have lost the memory of the cries, howls, and screams, broken by intervals of silence during which scattered shots or some solitary lamenting voice could be heard, and above all the deep hum of the bell tolling the alarm, or the quiet strokes of the cathedral clock marking the spent hour?

Had bells been attached to any other monument but our churches, they never would have touched the moral sympathies of our hearts. It was God himself who comanded the angel of victory to fling into the ether the peals that proclaim our triumphs, and the angel of death to toll for the leave-taking of the soul He is summoning to Him. Thus does a Christian society communicate by a thousand secret voices with Divinity, and its roots lose themselves mysteriously at the source of all mystery.

Let then the bells call together the faithful; the voice of man is not pure enough to bring to the foot of the altar repentance, innocence, and sorrow.

THE GENIUS OF CHRISTIANITY (1802)

CHARLES DICKENS

The Solitary 'Cello

Hᴇ handed her down to a coach she had in waiting at the door; and if his landlady had not been deaf, she would have heard him muttering as he went back upstairs, when the coach had driven off, that we were creatures of habit, and it was a sorrowful habit to be an old bachelor.

The violoncello lying on the sofa between the two chairs, he took it up, without putting away the vacant chair, and sat droning on it, and slowly shaking his head at the vacant chair, for a long, long time. The expression he communicated to the instrument at first, though monstrously pathetic and bland, was nothing to the expression he communicated to his own face, and bestowed upon the empty chair: which was so sincere, that he was obliged to have recourse to Captain Cuttle's remedy more than once, and to rub his face with his sleeve. By degrees, however, the violoncello, in unison with his own frame of mind, glided melodiously into 'The Harmonious Blacksmith,' which he played over and over again, until his ruddy and serene face gleamed like true metal on the anvil of a veritable blacksmith. In fine, the violoncello and the empty chair were the companions of his bachelorhood until nearly midnight; and when he took his supper, the violoncello set up on end in the sofa corner, big with the latent harmony of a whole foundry full of harmonious blacksmiths, seemed to ogle the empty chair out of its crooked eyes, with unutterable intelligence.

DOMBEY AND SON (1846)

HECTOR BERLIOZ

The Flute

FOR quite a while this instrument remained in many ways most imperfect. But now, thanks to the skill of a few makers and to the device generalized by Boehm from Gordon's invention, it plays as true and as evenly as can be desired. All the woodwind instruments will shortly achieve the same status. It is not hard to understand why up to now their intonation was anything but irreproachable: the distance between the holes bored in the tube was determined by the span of the player's fingers instead of by the rational division of the length of the tube according to the laws of physics. Gordon first, and later Boehm, proceeded to ascertain the points of subdivision of the vibrating body, and to bore the holes at those points regardless of the convenience, or even the feasibility, of playing the instrument. They felt confident of being able somehow or other to make possible the application of the fingers to each of these holes.

Once the instrument had been made 'true' by this procedure, they invented a mechanism of rings and keys which were so placed that the performer's fingers could easily shut or open all the holes out of the normal reach. By this means the old fingering was necessarily changed and the performers had to study new exercises. But after some little practice, the new instruments afforded them so many advantages in return for their effort that there is no doubt a few years more of dissemination through example, and of persuasion by word of mouth, will see the adoption of the new Gordon and Boehm woodwinds, to the entire exclusion of the old.

Within the last few years the compass of the flute has been extended by two half-steps in the bass and three in the treble, which brings the whole range to three octaves. The sonority of the flute is gentle in the medium register, rather piercing in the upper, and strongly characterized in the bass. The timbres of the medium and high notes have no very marked expression of their own. They can be used for melodies and accents of various kinds, but they are unable to rival the naïve gaiety of the oboe or the noble tenderness of the clarinet. Consequently

it seems as if the flute were an instrument almost devoid of characteristic expression, which one may therefore introduce, any and everywhere, for the sake of the ease with which it can perform quick
passages and sustain the high notes of the orchestra in completing high-
register chords.

All this is in general quite true, yet if one studies the flute closely,
one discovers that it possesses an expressiveness of its own, and an
aptitude for rendering certain moods that no other instrument can
compete with. If it is desired to impart to a sad melody an accent of
desolation, though at the same time humble and resigned, the weak
sounds of the medium range, in the keys of C minor and D minor
especially, will unfailingly supply the necessary nuance. Only one
master seems to me to have fully availed himself of this pale colouring:
I mean Gluck. In listening to the air-pantomime in D minor which he
wrote for the scene of the Elysian Fields in *Orpheus*, one perceives at a
glance that only a flute should play the melody. An oboe would have
sounded too childlike, and its voice would not have seemed sufficiently
pure; the English horn is too grave; a clarinet would have done well
enough no doubt, but some of the notes would have been too loud,
and none of the softer notes could have been kept to the mild, veiled,
self-effacing sonority of the F natural in the medium and the first B flat
above the staff, which give so much melancholy to the flute in this key
of D minor where they recur.

Finally, neither the violin, nor the viola, nor the 'cello, whether
alone or in groups, was proper for the plaint, sublime to the highest
degree, of a desperate and suffering shade. It required the very instrument that Gluck chose. And his melody is so conceived that the flute
lends itself to all the anxious moments of this unending pain, still
marked as it is by the passionate accents of earthly life. At first it is a
scarcely audible voice, which seems afraid of being heard; then it
moans quietly, rises to the pitch of repining, then to that of deep
sorrow, as of a heart torn by incurable wounds, and falls back gradually
into plaintiveness, the sweet moaning and murmuring of a soul resigned
to grief—what a poet!

TREATISE ON ORCHESTRATION (1844)

JEREMY COLLIER

An Instrument for War and Peace

Jeremy Collier (1650–1726) was the Royalist bishop who tried to purge English drama after the Restoration by writing his notorious Short View of the English Stage. *His essays on less polemical subjects were widely read and his opinions disseminated, often, through quotation in Addison's* Spectator.

INDEED Musick, when rightly ordered, cannot be prefer'd too much. For it re-creates and exalts the Mind at the same time. It composes the Passions, affords a strong Pleasure, and excites a Nobleness of Thought. But the manner of the Conveyance of Sounds, which is as it were the Basis of Musick, is unintelligible. For what can be more strange, than that the rubbing of a little *Hair* and *Cat-gut* together, shou'd make such a mighty alteration in a Man that sits at a distance?

But this wonder of *Perception* is not peculiar to the *Ear:* For the Operations of all the *Senses* are in some respect incomprehensible. The sense of *Hearing*, as well as that of *Sight*, seems to be of a superior Order to the rest. It commands a satisfaction at a greater distance, strikes a finer stroak and makes a single Object divide itself without Lessening. For instance: A Man may see the light of a Candle, and hear a Voice or Instrument, as well if there be ten in the Room as if he was there alone. The stream of Sounds, though cut into several Rivulets, comes as full to the Ear as if it had but one Channel to feed. The *Tast* and *Touch* are, if one may say so, more narrow Spirited.

The Force of Musick is more wonderful than the Conveyance. How strangely does it awaken the Mind! It infuses an unexpected vigour, makes the impression agreeable and sprightly, and seems to furnish a new Capacity as well as a new opportunity of Satisfaction. Have you not observed a Captain at the Head of a Company, how much he is altered at the Beat of a Drum? What a vigorous Motion, what an erected Posture, what an enterprising Visage, all of a suddain? His blood charges in his veins, his Spirits jump like Gunpowder, and seem impatient to attack the Enemy.

And here it may not be improper to consider, whether there may not be some *Counter-sounds*; which may give the Mind as high a disgust, as the other can a pleasure. For the Purpose: I believe 'tis possible to invent an *Instrument* that shall have a quite contrary effect to those Martial ones now in use. An *Instrument* that shall sink the Spirits and shake the nerves, and curdle the blood, and inspire Despair, and Cowardice, and Consternation, at a surprising Rate. 'Tis probable the roaring of Lions, the warbling of Cats and Scritch-Owls, together with a mixture of the howling of Dogs, judiciously imitated and compounded, might go a great way in this Invention. Whether such Anti-Musick as this might not be of Service in a Camp, I shall leave to the Military Men to consider.

AN ESSAY OF MUSICK (1702)

FREDERIC HARRISON

The Concert Hall

Trained as a historian but dedicated to the spread of Positivism and general culture, Harrison spent his life writing articles, letters, and reviews on a multitude of subjects.

ONE of the leading features of the reorganization of London, as I can conceive it in the future, will be the formation of permanent centres of musical culture. Music is the most social, the most affecting, the purest of the arts; the one most deeply connected with the moral side of civilization. It stands alone in the arts as hardly capable of being distorted to minister to luxury, evil, or ostentation. One can hardly imagine vicious music, or purse-proud music, or selfish music. It is by its very nature social, emotional, and humanizing. Hence I hold music to be the art which specially concerns all social reformers and popular teachers. And, as we have pointed out to Mr. Ruskin and the aesthetic pessimists, these latter ages cannot be called deficient in art, since they have immensely magnified the most human of all the arts of sense.

I am no musician, and do not pretend to say a word about music as an art. But, as one who delights in music, and who has long sought to bring out its social and civilizing mission, I have been very much struck with the fact that music is dependent in a curious degree on the material conditions of our civic life. Pictures, statues, poems, can be sent about and multiplied in various forms *ad infinitum*. The poorest home can contain a Shakespeare, a cast, or an engraving. A great cathedral may impress the spirit of millions, even as they walk to their business under its shadow. But music of a high kind, though it knows no limitations of country, age, or material—though it is free of time, space, and matter—does need trained powers of execution, the combination of suitable hearers and performers, and above all, a place exactly corresponding to the kind of art performed.

Music is peculiarly dependent, both for its artistic and social value, on the material conditions of social organization. It needs three things:

(1) highly trained executants; (2) a permanent and duly trained audience; (3) a *place* of performance, convenient to the audience, and suitable to the artistic conditions.

Now London easily gives us the first. But by its enormous inorganic bulk it makes the second condition very rare and difficult. And strangely enough, in spite of its wealth and energy, perhaps by reason of its wealth and energy, it does not give us the third. I have been from my youth a diligent attendant at many of our best series of concerts; and in days when I had more leisure, I made great sacrifices and underwent great trouble to do so. But the huge floating mobs of London, and the rage of 'undertakers' to collect mobs, have almost driven me out and make me nearly hopeless. I have watched scores of times how all serious music and all serious artists have to educate their audience gradually by a long and conscientious work of cultivation. A great musician has, I hold, more to do to train his audience than to train his orchestra. No audience can become worthy to listen to great music fitly performed unless it is a permanent and painstaking audience; unless it labours honestly to understand the master and his interpreters. And it is just this permanence and this self-educating spirit that the floating mob of London chokes. Just as the audience is pulling itself together and becoming fit to be played to, the series of concerts becomes fashionable, or the season begins; the mob breaks in, and all goes wrong. How delightful the —— day concerts used to be till fine people took them up, and till the balls began. Who can listen to a chaconne whilst a bare-shouldered dowager and her three daughters are hurrying past one to the first dance! No, a permanent self-respecting, art-respecting audience must consist of quiet people, living within a moderate distance of each other and of the concert hall. And this we cannot have till London is grouped into smaller social units.

Besides, London with all its wealth and size does not give us suitable concert halls. They are all either too big, ill shaped for musical purposes, inconveniently placed, or repulsively like a schoolroom. I cannot call to mind one concert hall in London which does not sin in one way or other of these four conditions. To ask us to listen to a great violin in company with three thousand others (some of them talking German, American, or Cockney; some of them hurrying out to a 'crush') is mere torment. No, I will no longer go to hear the finest violin solo on earth with more than four or five hundred of my fellow-beings; and I should greatly prefer three hundred. To give what is facetiously called 'a concert' in a colosseum which holds fifteen thousand people is an impertinence. Time was when I never missed an oratorio. But I have never heard one yet, in an arena which seems designed for a bullfight or a hippodrome. And much as I honour Mr. Manns, I cannot now spend a day in going to Sydenham in order to hear three pieces, the utmost that I care for at the same sitting.[1] There is not one perfect concert hall in London. The —— and the —— are only fit for public meetings; the —— will do for a symphony, but it is too big for a solo or a quartet. The —— is pretty; but its proper purpose is a fancy ball. In the —— and the —— one can hear a quartet to advantage; but then they look like a classroom in a board-school, and the seats are as bad as a third-class box on the South-Eastern Railway. The ideal concert hall should hold five hundred persons comfortably; it should be within an easy walk of their homes; it should have ample passages, exits, cloakrooms, artists' and committee rooms, it should have pure air, cool temperature, no gas, no noise, and no suggestions either of Mohawk Minstrels or fried fish. Lastly, it should be beautiful: architecture, decoration, and fittings should be of an art worthy to invite us to the high art we meet to cultivate. London has no such concert hall; and it is a burning shame.

                                    MEMORIES AND THOUGHTS (1898)

---

[1] The reference is to August Manns (1825–1907) and his famous Crystal Palace concerts.

PRINCESS LIEVEN

The Barrel Organ

I N this unmusical country[1] there are dreadful barrel organs which go up and down the streets—there is one playing under my windows right now, which is so out of tune that it almost makes me weep and I find it nearly impossible to continue this letter to you. When I am forced to listen to discordant sounds, I cannot keep a single clear idea in my head. I feel a physical distress that immediately affects my mental faculties.

LETTER TO METTERNICH, JULY 11, 1820

[1] England.

B. H. HAGGIN

Music on Records

WE hear a piece of music as it comes to us through a player's mind; it sounds different as it comes through different minds; and I judge a performance by considering whether the character, the quality, the significance it imparts to the music is what my own understanding of the composer and the work leads me to believe correct. If I accept Stokowski's performance of the bacchanale from *Tannhäuser* it is because he gives the music the character I think a bacchanale by Wagner should have; if I reject Stokowski's performance of music from *Boris Godunov* it is because the fever and glitter and luxuriance that are eminently suitable to Wagner's bacchanale completely falsify the character and significance of the quietly profound music of Moussorgsky. Or if I object to what Heifetz does in a passage of the third movement of Franck's Violin Sonata, it is because the constant holding back then hurrying, and hurrying then holding back, contradict not only Franck's direction that the passage be played *molto dolce e tranquillo*, but the character and emotional significance which, it is clear from this direction, Franck wants the passage to have.

In the eyes of a record company anything it issues cannot be less than a masterpiece, and the man who performs it is not only a great artist but exactly the right great artist for the work. Actually the company is out to sell records, and the records that sell are the ones made by the currently celebrated players, and of these a very small number indeed are what can be called great artists—that is, men who are endowed not only with fleet fingers but with musical understanding and taste and integrity. Most people understand that an actor can have wonderful gifts of voice and movement and presence, and misuse them; they understand that a painter named Sargent could use a superb technical equipment to achieve slick effects; but they don't understand that an orchestral conductor can have phenomenal technical powers that enable him to produce miraculous sounds with an orchestra, and use these powers to produce miraculous sounds that falsify almost every composer and work he conducts.

Moreover, even a great artist is not equally great in everything he does. An actor plays one role better than another; a conductor does better with the music of one composer than with another. For the music, if it amounts to anything, is not a mere spinning of notes, but in each case a product of human imagination and feeling; and the conductor brings to these his own imagination and feeling, which may match better in one case than in another. But a record company that uses a performer only because of the selling power of his currently celebrated name is not concerned with what, if anything, he does well; and the result is instance after instance of poor matching of performer to music.

The Pro Arte Quartet, which earned its reputation with excellent performances of modern works, now records quartets and quintets of Mozart, for which it has neither the feeling nor even the necessary technical virtuosity. Again, there are conductors who do better than Koussevitzky with Beethoven's *Eroica* and Mozart's G Minor; whereas to hear Koussevitzky's performances of Debussy is to realize that one had never really heard the works before. Yet Koussevitzky records the *Eroica* and the G Minor, but not a note of Debussy; and Debussy's *Iberia* is recorded by Barbirolli, not because he is the right conductor for the work—which he very evidently is not—but because he is the conductor of the New York Philharmonic Symphony Orchestra, and without regard for the fact that he is a good conductor for the music of Haydn and Mozart.

MUSIC ON RECORDS (1938)

TOM S. WOTTON

Notes on Drums

Tom S. Wotton will be remembered as the most thorough student of Berlioz and the compiler of a Dictionary of Foreign Musical Terms *that is in equal degree accurate and inspired. But as this extract shows, Wotton wrote on a variety of musical subjects. He was also the author of a successful comedy praised by Bernard Shaw.*

A DRUM seems to be a simple enough affair. Yet, as we shall see, more confusion has arisen in connection with it than with any other instrument of the orchestra. There are seven kinds specified in modern scores, and, roughly arranged in order of infrequency, they are these:

1. Oriental drums.
2. Tabors.
3. Tenor drums (side drums without a snare).[1]
4. Tambourines.
5. Snare drums (side drums possessing a snare).
6. Bass drums.
7. Kettledrums.

ORIENTAL DRUMS

These include any drum which at present belongs to any country outside Occidental civilization. The drums are of varied shape and size, and the composer seldom deigns to specify them beyond giving them a name which bears little or no resemblance to their native appellation.

In Ippolitov-Ivanov's *Scènes caucasiennes* we find *piccoli timpani orientali* marked in the score. Possibly the instruments are well known to Russian musicians, but there is no description given of them, despite the prominent part they play in No. 2 of the suite.

[1] A snare consists of eight to ten strands of catgut (or its substitutes) which are loosely strung across that head of the drum which is not beaten. The vibrations of the snare produce a characteristic rattling effect.

These drums, of which the Russian name is apparently *timplipito*, may be described as a couple of ginger jars of different sizes, bound together by a strip of rawhide, which also serves to secure the two membranes. The pair are played with a couple of little drumsticks, and cannot be tuned, remaining at the pitch decreed by Providence and the vagaries of the drying hide. The choice of jars of appropriate size may ensure the notes being approximately a fifth apart.

The tarbouka, from the Arabic *darâboukkeh*, is a species of drum used throughout northern Africa, the Egyptian form being shaped like an inverted vase, with a membrane in place of the original bottom. The neck of the vase is tucked under the arm, and the skin struck by both hands, the left beating the edge, and the right, the centre. In the orchestra a small drumstick is used, and the instrument is shaped like a flower pot, with a membrane on the larger end. In both cases the shell is of pottery.

THE TABOR

The French name for the tabor is *tambourin*, and the Spanish, *tamboril*. There is no equivalent in either Italian or German. In the latter the French word is employed, and in the former an Italianized version of it. But unfortunately both *tambourin* and *tamburino* are the ordinary names for the tambourine in the respective languages. Even in France there has been at times some doubt as to the meaning of *tambourin*, e.g. in Kastner's treatise on orchestration (1837) there is a section headed '*Tambourin (Tambour de Basque)*,' in which the latter (the tambourine) is described, with no reference to the tabor. Kastner was, however, an Alsatian, and an inhabitant of northern France might be as ignorant of the tabor (an instrument of the south) as a Devonshire man of the niceties of the bagpipes.

Forsyth, in his *Orchestration*, points out that there is a difference of opinion as to whether a tabor possesses a snare, and, after having quoted Widor's description of the instrument 'as a very long drum without a snare used in Provence,' says, 'the best authorities seem to favour the other view.' Like the two knights who disputed as to whether the shield were of silver or gold, both parties are correct. In this case, however, the difference does not arise from there being two sides to a drum, but because there are two drums.

1. The true *tambourin de Provence*, which has a snare *on the batterhead*, and sometimes on the snarehead as well. (Baggers says that the proper

way to play it is to beat on the snare with the single drumstick—a difficult operation, one would imagine, if the *tambourinaire* were marching, to say nothing of his left hand being engaged with the intricacies of the *galoubet*.) 2. The orchestral form of the tabor, which has no snare, and is perhaps better known to painters than to musicians since it figures in many of Watteau's pictures, and for that reason is sometimes known as *tambourin genre Watteau*. Widor evidently had this second form in mind when writing his description. Where he erred was in adding 'used in Provence.' Pares, in his treatise on military band music, makes the same mistake. That he is referring to the orchestral tabor is proved by his pointing out that the instrument can be tuned, which, as we shall see under 'Snare drum,' is impossible for a drum possessing a snare. He says that, when possible, the tabor should be tuned to the tonic or dominant of the piece. The saving clause is necessary, for to do this for *any* key would mean a compass of an augmented fourth, and the tabor, with its light shell and thin membranes, probably has not a greater range than a third.

Berlioz used a tabor in the '*Pas d'esclaves nubiennes*' of *The Trojans*, and here the instrument, doubling the perpetual quavers of the tarbouka on the stage, is clearly audible. But when Stravinsky, in *Petrouchka*, makes it play fortissimo in unison with a snare drum in the wings, it is another matter. Were not the tabor so carefully specified in the list of instruments heading the score as '*Tambour de Provence (Tambourin)*,' one would imagine that the Russian composer intended some other, more powerful drum. Other composers to employ the tabor have been Auber (*Le Philtre*), Dubois, Vidal, Dukas (*Ariane et Barbe-Bleue*), Debussy (*Rondes de Printemps*) and Wallace (*Villon*).

Although not in the province of this article, a few words must be said as regards the *galoubet*, the companion of the tabor. It is a flageolet, with three vents at the lower end, one at the back for the thumb and two in front for the first and second fingers. That in ordinary use is about twelve inches long, and, since the bore is narrow compared with the length, it is impossible to produce the fundamental notes. As an instance of the confusion attached to the nomenclature of instruments I may add that, in Rousseau's Dictionary, *galoube* (*sic*) is taken as being the name of the *tambourin*, while the *galoubet* itself is termed a *flutet*.

THE TENOR DRUM

The essential distinction between the tenor drum and the snare drum is the absence of a snare in the former. Nowadays it may be said to be larger than the snare drum, but this was not always so. Usually its shell is made of wood, in agreement with the textbooks, but, from the catalogues of the makers, this is not invariably so. Both it and the snare drum are 'side drums,' inasmuch as they are both slung on the left side, and beaten with a pair of drumsticks—occasionally somewhat heavier in the case of the tenor drum. Unfortunately, however, 'side drum' is the ordinary English term for a snare drum, which at once makes for confusion. Why are musicians so careless in their nomenclature? A golfer would cease to be considered as such if he confused his clubs in similar fashion.

THE TAMBOURINE

The French for the tambourine is *tambour de Basque* (with the occasional omission of the *de*)—an inappropriate one since, according to Jacquot (*Dictionnaire des instruments de musique*), the only drum used in the Basque Provinces is the tabor, a statement confirmed by a letter in the *Daily Telegraph* some years ago. I have given already an Italian and a German name, and the possible confusion that may arise from their use. *Tamburello* for the first, and *Schellentrommel* or *baskische Trommel* for the second (all three terms to be found in scores), would avoid this.

The instrument is too well known to need any description, but it must be pointed out that the 'jingles' (the little cymbals strung on wires in the hoop) are not always to be found. Lalo, in his *Le Roi d'Ys* (1888) specifies a tambourine without them, since such a one is used in Brittany, the scene of the opera.

THE SNARE DRUM[1]

Amongst the minor mysteries of life must be placed the fact that when average individuals are asked to describe a kettledrum they immediately move their hands to the left, while they endeavour, with varying success, to imitate the characteristic rattle of the snare drum.

[1] The official name of the instrument is 'side drum,' and, as far as I am aware, no drummer would call a tenor drum by that name. I have used throughout the alternative of 'snare drum' to avoid any possible confusion. [Wotton's note.]

But I do not know whether the average English or German musician rises much above the level of the average individual when he dubs 'any old drum' slung at the side as a 'side drum,' or a *'kleine Trommel,'* as the case may be. The French are much more precise in their nomenclature. With them, a drum with a snare is called a *caisse claire*, as opposed to the *caisse sourde* (dull), an obsolescent name for the *caisse roulante*. The ordinary term for a snare drum—*tambour*—is employed specifically for the military side drum, which nowadays invariably has a snare.

Numerous 'tricks' are possible on the snare drum, though few of them have penetrated into the realm of legitimate music. In *La Tragédie de Salomé*, Florent Schmitt directs his snare drum to play *sur le bois* (on the wood, i.e., on the ropehoop), and in *Catalonia*, Albéniz instructs his drummer to beat on the music desk—a process which some purists might insist was not playing the drum at all! Zandonai, in his *Primavera in Val di Sole*, for one passage directs the performer to play *vicino al metallo*, i.e., on the edge of the membrane near the metal shell, and in another, *sul metallo*, i.e., on the shell itself.

THE BASS DRUM

The correct English name for the *grosse Caisse* (*gran cassa* or *grosse Trommel*) is 'bass drum,' and has been for the past hundred and fifty years at least. It is somewhat necessary to stress the point, because some English authorities have given 'long drum' and 'double drum' as equivalent names for the instrument. A form of tenor drum has been called a 'tambour long,' and with reason, since its length (as with a tabor) greatly exceeded its diameter. Although I should be sorry to assert that a bass drum has never been made of the dimensions of a section of the Channel Tunnel, it obviously could not have been used for marching purposes, when the depth of the instrument is limited by the width of a man's chest. In any case, the bass drum was called so in 1787, as we know from an account for band-fittings sent in by the bandmaster of the Royal Artillery.

Like the tenor one, the bass drum can be tuned to some extent, and possibly an artistic drummer might have a different tension on the skins for depicting the dull sound of distant cannon and in a brilliant march, heavily instrumented. Kastner mentions two apparently unsuccessful attempts to produce a bass drum tunable to definite notes. The only indication as to pitch is, as far as I am aware, in Verdi's

Requiem, where, for the '*Dies Irae,*' the rope is directed to be 'very taut in order that this syncopation may be short and very loud'— chords for full orchestra on the accented beats are followed by strokes on the unaccented ones for bass-drum solo. Verdi, by the way, though he may have abused the instrument at times, was one of the first to employ it for pianissimo rhythmical effects.

Strauss, Mahler, and others have revived the *Rute* (rod or birch), which seemingly was a constant appendage of the bass drum, when it was introduced into Europe by the Turkish Janissaries in the eighteenth century.[1]

KETTLEDRUMS

These instruments are dealt with so exhaustively in the treatises and dictionaries that there is little to remark here. In many modern works chromatic kettledrums, of which the tuning can be altered instantly, are specified. Experiments in this direction have been made for the past hundred years, but none of them have been entirely satisfactory. If animals could be persuaded to grow homogeneous skins, chromatic drums might be a success. Unfortunately, until now they have evinced little interest in their future artistic life, and their skins stretch unevenly, with the result that a drum will possibly require more adjustment at one portion of its circumference than at another. And this can only be achieved by means of the six to ten screws of the ordinary model.

The kettledrums seem to have been regarded as too dignified for many tricks to be played on them. Snare drumsticks are used in *Petrouchka,*[2] first fortissimo in what is practically a roll on F sharp, and secondly mezzo forte on G and B flat alternately. In the score of the *Enigma Variations*[3] we find a similar effect in Number XIII. On the first performance a couple of half-crowns seem to have been used for the pianissimo roll. The directions being also given in German the composer may have hesitated as to which German piece best corresponded to the musical value of a pre-war half-crown; or perhaps he concluded that drumsticks were more likely to be found in an orchestra than coins of the realm.   *MUSICAL TIMES* (1930)

---

[1] Reintroduced—to be quite exact—since the Crusaders brought back from Palestine the bass and other drums. [Wotton's note.]

[2] By Igor Stravinsky (1911).

[3] By Edward Elgar (1899).

ANONYMOUS

The Orchestra

IT is mere folly to talk as the professors talk of a standard orchestra. There never has been a perfect orchestra; there is not a perfect orchestra yet; there is not likely to be a perfect orchestra for many years to come; and instead of regretting that we are moving away from the orchestra of Mozart's and Haydn's time, we should rejoice on that very account. Why two flutes should be right and three flutes shameful extravagance; why the double clarinet should be looked upon as an unauthorized interloper; why the tubas should be thought the inferiors of the trombones merely because they came in later—these and a hundred other things pass the comprehension of everyone who gives ten minutes of serious thought to the orchestra.

The truth is that instead of repelling all the new instruments, we should welcome them, welcome them as helping to make the orchestra a genuine instrument. It is time to be done with the art of faking, which is the only art explained in any book of instrumentation yet written; it is time to say that as there are plenty of players available and we are no longer living around the courts of petty three-square-mile princelets, we should have a complete orchestra. And a complete orchestra would include a complete flute group—a treble, alto, tenor, and bass flute; the complete oboe group that the best bands have at present . . . and so on right through the orchestra. One of the most important things would be to complete the string group. We want a true tenor, running down to the G beneath the tenor C; the violas would then play a true alto part in their best register. We want also the six-stringed double bass with frets, to avoid the present sudden disappearance of the bass part. When these things are done we shall be on the way to getting an orchestra worth writing for.

EDITORIAL, *THE MUSICIAN* (April 1900)

Fantasies
&
Confessions

W. F. APTHORP

Sonata Form in Food

For many years W. F. Apthorp (1848–1913) supplied the notes for the Boston Symphony programmes, setting the genre of mixed anecdote, biography, reminiscence, and criticism. A good musician and facile writer, he often ventured, as is seen below, into the even higher genre of musical fiction.

"STOP monkeying with your chartreuse before you've finished your coffee, like a brute beast that has no soul, and I will prove to you that the regularly planned French dinner is in the sonata form—there can be no doubt about it.'

'Fire away,' said the other, 'I'm quite willing to be educated in the higher gastronomy.'

'Well, then! here it is,' Guloston went on, lighting his cigar at one of the candles on the table, 'here it is. In the first place, you must know that the French dinner of the old school, the good old school, was divided into two parts, two *services*, as the technical name is. The first began with the *relevés*—'

'I always thought the first began with the soup,' put in Harmon, 'or oysters.'

'Not a bit of it! There's where you make a fatal, an unpardonable mistake!' cried Guloston, 'an error that would knock my theory on beam ends! The first *service* begins with the *relevés*, the *grosses pièces chaudes*; then come the *entrées*. The second *service* begins with the *rôts*, plain meat or game, with salad; these are followed by the *entremets*, the vegetables and sweets. Now, both these two *services* must be in equilibrium, they must counterbalance each other exactly; there must be as many *rôts* in the second as there have been *relevés* in the first, as many *entremets* as *entrées*. You understand that?'

'Yes, I see that,' replied Harmon, 'but I must say I'm a bit curious about the soup.'

'Ah! my dear fellow,' went on Guloston enthusiastically, 'the soup and *hors d'oeuvres* belong properly to neither *service*; the soup is nothing more nor less than a free introduction to the whole dinner. As you musical sharps say, the free introduction—in slow tempo—is not a real fact of the form at all; it is only a preparation for what is to follow. As for the *hors d'oeuvres*, their very name shows that they are outside the circle of the form: they are nothing but free light skirmishing, and have no thematic importance. They follow the soup—or, if you take them in the sense of the Italian *antipasti*, as we do our oysters in this country, they come before the soup—and have no influence upon the form whatever. They should be eaten *frei-phantasierend*, just tasted, a bit here and a bit there; not dwelling upon any particular flavour, but skipping daintily from one to another, like eating harlequin-ice. *Hors d'oeuvres*, in the French sense—that is, coming after the soup—might be compared to a free, premonitory transition passage leading over from the introduction to the main body of the movement. You understand so far, Harmon?'

'Yes, I understand so far: the soup, with the *hors d'oeuvres* or *antipasti*, is the free introduction. Now for the sonata form proper!'

'Now for the sonata form proper; exactly!' said Guloston, blowing a ring from his cigar. 'The *relevés*—of which there ought to be two, one of fish and one of meat—are the first and second themes. The *entrées*—of which there should be at least four, if there have been two *relevés*—represent the free fantasia, the working-out in detail of those two leading ideas of fish and meat.'

'Wonderful!' exclaimed Harmon, tossing the stump of his cigarette into the fire, and taking a sip of chartreuse unreproved, before rolling another. 'Wonderful! But how about your working-out of the two principal themes? I see the meat part of it clearly enough; but how about the fish part? The fish once done with, it doesn't return again.'

'There's where you are totally and barbarically wrong,' Guloston replied; 'the idea that fish belongs exclusively to the beginning of the first *service* is that of the British barbarian and of his only slightly more civilized American descendant. There may be, and really should be, an *entrée* of fish, as well as of meat; remember such things as Thackeray lobster, or picked crabs; take little *bouchées* of oysters or clams, or *écrevisses bordelaise*. Any small dish with a sauce and garnish is an *entrée*, and consequently belongs in the second part of the first *service*—in the working-out. You mustn't forget that the *relevés* are essentially *grosses pièces*, big dishes; they, too, have a sauce and garnish, but the little things of a similar kind are *entrées*. Well,

with the *entrées* the first *service*, the first part and free fantasia, comes
to an end.'

'Then comes the Roman punch—with perhaps a cigarette, I suppose,' suggested Harmon. 'Where do you make room for that in
your sonata form?'

'Aha! *tu y es!*' cried Guloston, delighted. 'A pupil who asks intelligent questions is a pupil worth having! Of course, we have Roman
punch, and equally of course, we have a cigarette with it. And, as
you seem to suspect, it is no regular nor necessary part of the form;
only a delightful adjunct. The Roman punch and cigarette form a
free poetic episode, not connected with any of the leading themes;
you find such episodes now and then in symphonic first movements,
though perhaps not so often as in dinners. But we can easily find an
example. Let me see; yes, take the passage for the muted violins with
the tremolo on the violas in the overture to *Euryanthe*: that is the
Roman punch with a cigarette. The parallel could not be more
accurate!'

'Good for you, my boy!' cried Harmon; 'you keep your head and
heels like a true master! Who would have thought of such a parallel!
Well, let's get on to our second *service*, to the third part of the movement—since the first *service* includes the first part and the working-
out.'

'Ah! here you must follow me carefully,' answered Guloston, 'and
for that you had better fill up your glass of chartreuse once more and
pass me the bottle. Here the parallel becomes less exact, I admit; but
it holds good, all the same, if you don't insist upon every i being
dotted and every t crossed, like a mere Philistine pedant. Let us first
consider the *rôts*, of which, as you will remember, there must be as
many as there were *relevés* in the first *service*. These *rôts* represent the
return of the principal themes in the third part of the movement. I
admit that there is no fish in them; also that there is still another
difference between them and their corresponding *relevés*: the *relevés*
were dishes with sauce and a garnish—of mushrooms, truffles, or
some other vegetables—and this same idea of sauce and *garniture*, of a
more or less vegetable nature, was further carried out in the *entrées*;
whereas the *rôts* are plain roast meat or game, without sauce or garnish
—unless you call the salad a garnish, and, if the salad is not of the
vegetable kingdom, what on earth is it? But let that pass for a moment;
we should never ride a simile, or parallel, between two different arts

to death. If we do, we come to grief, and all the poetry of the thing is lost!

'Let us accept the two *rôts* as the second *service* representatives of the two *relevés* in the first; like the *relevés*, they are *pièces de résistance*, solid meat, no matter how delicate; they mean a return to business, just as the return of the first theme does at the beginning of the third part of a symphonic movement. They are followed by the *entremets*—vegetables and sweets—which are equal in number to the *entrées* of the first *service*, and so serve as a sort of ideal counterpoise to them. Now, what are these *entremets*? Evidently they are the coda, the second free fantasia, as Beethoven developed it in the *Eroica*, to counterbalance the first one.

'And note just here how the difference in material between the two *services*—there being a want of perfectly exact correspondence between the *relevés* and the *rôts*, between the *entrées* and the *entremets*—instead of destroying my parallel, makes it ideally stronger and more exact. What is, after all, the main and characteristic difference between the first and third parts of a symphonic movement? Principally a difference in tonality, in key. The first part quits the tonic after the first theme; the third part sticks to the tonic. Now, there is nothing to correspond to the idea of tonality in gastronomy; so our dinner has to mark the difference between its first and second *services* in some other way. And it does this by means that are purely its own, purely gastronomic. The coherent idea that runs through the first *service* is the presentation and working-out of two forms of esculent material—animal and vegetable food—*together*; for the sauces and garnishes are made up largely of vegetable ingredients.

'The idea of the second *service*, on the other hand, is the presentation and working-out of the same, or similar, material—animal and vegetable food—*apart* and *separately*; the *rôts* being all animal, and the *entremets*, all vegetable. In music, symphonic development proceeds from the simpler to the more complex; in gastronomy, it proceeds from the complex to the simple—just the reverse, you see. This is the main difference, depending wholly upon the different media of the two arts. In each of the two, this progression has its own reason of being, based upon the nature of man's receptive power—through the ear in one case, through the gullet in the other. The ear is fatigued in a very different way from the palate; the—'

'Stop! for heaven's sake, stop!' cried Harmon. 'Let's stick to art,

and stop short of metaphysico-physiology! I understand you perfectly; you are right as right can be. Your dinner in sonata form has
entered into my comprehension, and I knock under with the best
grace in the world. You've proved your point to the satisfaction of
anyone whose soul is large enough to take in the delights of the table
and the glories of music! And damned be the musician who has no
love for eating and drinking! But wait a bit; what do you do with
the dessert in your symphonic scheme? It strikes me, now that I think
of it, that the dessert would be the real coda of a dinner.'

'Hm!' said Guloston, looking thoughtfully at the stump of his
cigar, 'dessert—fruit, ices, cheese, nuts, and all that sort of thing—is
something over and above, *par dessus le marché*; very desirable and
even necessary, if you will, but still, like the soup and *hors d'oeuvres*,
lying outside the circle of the form. It has its symphonic equivalent,
too, although, to find it, we may have to leave first movements of
symphonies and turn to the overture—which is, after all, in the same
general form.

'You must know overtures enough that end with a perfectly free
apothéose, as the French say; with a free ending that has no thematic
connection with what has gone before, and merely serves to round
off the whole with a brilliant or soothing farewell. Take the overture
to *Egmont*; that ends in this way. I know that this sort of thing is
technically called a free coda; but you must admit that it has nothing
in common with the sort of coda Beethoven developed, that second
free fantasia to which I have compared the *entremets*. If symphonic
first movements seldom end with a "dessert," it is simply because they
are first movements, and something more is still to come; that is why
we find the "dessert coda" more frequently in overtures: they are
musically complete in themselves. Oh! the dessert presents no real
difficulty: it lies outside the circle of the form.

'And now, if you don't want any more chartreuse, I'll beat you a
game or two at three-ball caroms.'

FROM THE COURT LIBRARY OF UTOPIA (1898)

GIOACCHINO ROSSINI

The Prayer from 'Moses'

'My immortality?' said Rossini; 'do you know what will survive me? (*sais-tu ce qui restera après moi?*) The third act of *Tell*, the second act of *Otello*, and *The Barber of Seville* from one end to the other.'

Strange to say, of the Prayer of Moses,[1] that piece magnificent in its simplicity, he only once spoke to me, but what he then said is well worth repeating. I asked him was he in love, or very hungry and miserable, when he wrote that inspired page; for hunger as well as love has the power of making people write with lofty inspiration.

'I will tell you,' he said, and from his ironical smile I saw some fun was coming; 'I had a little misfortune; I had known a Princess B—g—e, and she, one of the most passionate women living, and with a magnificent voice, kept me up all night with duos and talking, etc. A short time after this exhausting performance, I had to take a tisane which stood before me, while I wrote that prayer. When I was writing the chorus in G minor I suddenly dipped my pen into the medicine bottle instead of the ink; I made a blot, and when I dried it with sand (blotting paper was not invented then) it took the form of a natural, which instantly gave me the idea of the effect which the change from G minor to G major would make, and to this blot all the effect—if any—is due.'

LOUIS ENGEL, *FROM MOZART TO MARIO* (1886)

From Rossini's oratorio *Mosé in Egitto* (1818), later made into an opera.

LEIGH HUNT

Musical Memories

I

MY grandfather, though intimate with Dr. Franklin, was secretly on the British side of the question when the American war broke out. He professed to be neutral, and to attend only to business; but his neutrality did not avail him. . . . My mother at that time was a brunette with fine eyes, a tall, ladylike person, and hair blacker than is seen of English growth. It was supposed that Anglo-Americans already began to exhibit the influence of climate in their appearance. . . . My mother had no accomplishments but the two best of all, a love of nature and of books. Dr. Franklin offered to teach her the guitar; but she was too bashful to become his pupil. She regretted this afterwards, partly, no doubt, for having lost so illustrious a master. Her first child, who died, was named after him. I know not whether the anecdote is new; but I have heard that when Dr. Franklin invented the Harmonica,[1] he concealed it from his wife till the instrument was fit to play; and then woke her with it one night, when she took it for the music of angels.

. . . My mother, though fond of music, and a gentle singer in her way, had missed the advantage of a musical education, partly from her coming of a half-Quaker stock, partly (as I have said before) from her having been too diffident to avail herself of the kindness of Dr. Franklin, who offered to teach her the guitar.

The reigning English composer at that time was 'Mr. Hook,'[2] as he was styled at the head of his songs. He . . . had a real, though small vein of genius, which was none the better for its being called upon to flow profusely for Ranelagh and Vauxhall. He was the composer of 'The Lass of Richmond Hill' (an allusion to a *penchant* of George IV), and of another popular song more lately remembered, ' 'Twas within a mile of Edinborough town.' The songs of that day abounded in

---

[1] The 'musical glasses' encased in a machine.
[2] James Hook (1746–1827).

Strephons and Delias, and the music partook of the gentle inspiration. The association of early ideas with that kind of commonplace has given me more than a toleration for it. I find something even touching in the endeavours of an innocent set of ladies and gentlemen, my fathers and mothers, to identify themselves with shepherds and shepherdesses in the most impossible hats and crooks. . . . The feeling was true, though the expression was sophisticate and a fashion; and they who cannot see the feeling for the mode, do the very thing which they think they scorn; that is, sacrifice the greater consideration for the less.

But Hook was not the only, far less the most fashionable composer. There were (if not all personally, yet popularly contemporaneous) Mr. Lampe, Mr. Oswald, Dr. Boyce, Linley, Jackson, Shield, and Storace, with Paesiello, Sacchini,[1] and others at the King's Theatre, whose delightful airs wandered into the streets out of the English opera that borrowed them, and became confounded with English property. I have often, in the course of my life, heard 'Whither, my love?' and 'For tenderness formed' boasted of as specimens of English melody. For many years I took them for such myself, in common with the rest of our family, with whom they were great favourites. The first, which Stephen Storace adapted to some words in *The Haunted Tower* is the air of La Rachelina in Paesiello's opera *La Molinara*. The second, which was put by General Burgoyne to a song in his comedy of *The Heiress* (1786) is '*Io sono Lindoro*' in the same enchanting composer's *Barber of Seville*.[2] . . . Every burlesque or *buffo* song, of any pretension, was pretty sure to be Italian. When Edwin, Fawcett, and others were rattling away in the happy comic songs of O'Keeffe, with his triple rhymes and illustrative jargon, the audience little suspected that they were listening to some of the finest animal spirits of the south—to Piccinni,[3] Paesiello, and Cimarosa.[4]

. . . I must own that I am heretic enough (if present fashion is orthodoxy) to believe that Arne[5] was a real musical genius, of a very pure albeit not of the very first water. He has set, indeed, two songs of

---

[1] The composers worth identifying are: William Boyce (1710–79), Giovanni Paesiello (1741–1816), and Antonio Sacchini (1734–86).

[2] *C.* 1780.

[3] Niccolo Piccinni (1728–1800).

[4] See p. 133.

[5] Thomas Arne (1710–78). See p. 271 and *n.*

Shakespeare's (the Cuckoo song and 'Where the bee sucks') in a spirit of perfect analogy to the words as well as the liveliest musical invention; and his air of 'Water parted' in *Artaxerxes* winds about the feelings with an earnest and graceful tenderness of regret, worthy in the highest degree of the affecting beauty of the sentiment.

. . . The other day I found two songs of that period on Robinson's music-stall in Wardour Street, one by Mr. Hook entitled 'Alone, by the light of the moon'; the other, a song with a French burden, called '*Dans votre lit*,' an innocent production notwithstanding its title. They were the only songs I recollect singing when a child, and I looked on them with the accumulated tenderness of sixty-three years of age. I do not remember to have set eyes on them in the interval. What a difference between the little smooth-faced boy at his mother's knee, encouraged to lift up his voice at the pianoforte, and the battered grey-headed senior, looking again for the first time on what he had sung at the distance of half a century! Life often seems a dream; but there are occasions when the sudden reappearance of early objects, by the intensity of their presence, not only renders the interval less present to the consciousness than a very dream, but makes the portion of life which preceded it seem to have been the most real of all things, and our only undreaming time.

II

It was very pleasant to see Lord Byron and Moore[1] together. They harmonized admirably: though their knowledge of one another began in talking of a duel. . . . Moore's acquaintance with myself (as far as concerned correspondence by letter) originated in the mention of him in the 'Feast of the Poets.'[2] He subsequently wrote an opera called *The Blue Stocking*,[3] respecting which he sent me a letter at once deprecating and warranting objection to it. I was then editor of the *Examiner*: I did object to it, though with all acknowledgment of his genius.

Moore . . . sang and played with great taste on the pianoforte, as might be supposed from his musical compositions. His voice, which

[1] Thomas Moore (1779–1852), Irish poet and wit, biographer of Byron, and arranger of the ballads of his native land.

[2] Poem by Hunt (1811).

[3] *M.P., or The Blue Stocking* (1811).

was a little hoarse in speaking (at least I used to think so), softened into a breath, like that of the flute, when singing.

[At Pisa] our manner of life was this. Lord Byron, who used to sit up at night writing *Don Juan* (which he did under the influence of gin and water), rose late in the morning. He breakfasted; read; lounged about, singing an air, generally out of Rossini; then took a bath, and was dressed; and coming downstairs was heard, still singing, in the courtyard, out of which the garden ascended, by a few steps, at the back of the house. The servants, at the same time, brought out two or three chairs. My study, a little room in a corner, with an orange tree at the window, looked upon this courtyard. I was generally at my writing when he came down, and either acknowledged his presence by getting up and saying something from the window, or he called out, 'Leontius!' (a name into which Shelley had pleasantly converted that of 'Leigh Hunt') and came up to the window with some jest or other challenge to conversation.

[In Genoa] one night I went to the opera, which was indifferent enough, but I understand it is a good deal better sometimes. The favourite composer here and all over Italy is Rossini, a truly national genius, full of the finest animal spirits, yet capable of the noblest gravity. My northern faculties were scandalized at seeing men in the pit with *fans*! Effeminacy is not always incompatible with courage, but it is a very dangerous step towards it; and I wondered what Doria would have said had he seen a captain of one of his galleys indulging his cheeks in this manner. Yet perhaps they did so in his own times.

It was about this time[1] that I projected a poem of a very different sort, which was to be called 'A Day with the Reader.'

I proposed to invite the reader to breakfast, dine, and sup with me,

[1] 1835.

partly at home and partly at a country inn, in order to vary the circumstances. It was to be written both gravely and gaily, in an exalted
or in a lowly strain, according to the topics of which it treated. The
fragment of 'Paganini'[1] was a part of the exordium—

> So play'd of late to every passing thought
> With finest change (might I but half as well
> So write!) the pale magician of the bow, etc.

I wished to write in the same manner because Paganini with his
violin could move both the tears and the laughter of his audience, and
(as I have described him doing in the verses) would now give you the
notes of birds in the trees, and even hens feeding in a farmyard (which
was a corner into which I meant to take my companion), and now
melt you into grief and pity, or mystify you with witchcraft, or put
you into a state of lofty triumph like a conqueror. That phrase of
'smiting' the chords—

> He smote; and clinging to the serious chords
> With godlike ravishment, etc.—

was no classical commonplace; nor, in respect to impression on the
mind, was it exaggeration to say that from a single chord he would
fetch out

> The voice of quires, and weight
> Of the built organ.

Paganini, the first time I saw and heard him, and the first moment
he struck a note, seemed literally to strike it; to give it a blow. The
house was so crammed that, being among the squeezers in 'standing
room' at the side of the pit, I happened to catch the first sight of his
face through the arm akimbo of a man who was perched up before
me, which made a kind of frame for it; and there, on the stage, in
that frame, as through a perspective glass, were the face, bust, and
raised hand of the wonderful musician, with his instrument at his
chin, just going to commence, and looking exactly as I have described
him—

> His hand,
> Loading the air with dumb expectancy,
> Suspended, ere it fell, a nation's breath.
> He smote; . . .

AUTOBIOGRAPHY (1828–50)

[1] 1844.

JEAN-PAUL RICHTER

The Value of a Deaf Left Ear

THE author of this essay, who has enjoyed precisely this good fortune since childhood, will consider himself fully repaid if through it any readers of *The Fashionable World*[1]—who may for years have been one-eared as Kant was one-eyed, without knowing it—can be induced to shut off one and the other ear alternately so as to discover whether one of the pair possesses the talent which he—the author—boasts of in his left.

Apart from the water shrew which, as everyone knows, is able to shut off its ears under water with a sort of flap; and again, except for bats which have ear muffs, I know of nobody—least of all men—who possesses earlids comparable to eyelids. Nearly every one does hear—and generally not the pleasantest things. But suppose a man, contrariwise, who is endowed with one-sided deafness: he finds it easy with *one* finger to bring about the double-sided boon for as long as may be required. There are four places in particular which the One-eared sees opening before him like four new worlds of joy—the music room, the theatre, the drawing room, and the bed.

. . . In the music room, where one is invited to enjoy artists who are not so much the Tuneful as the Mistuned, the gift of one-sided deafness is possibly as valuable as a good yawn. According to Haller, one is deaf for as long as one yawns, and kind Nature therefore prescribes yawning as the best protection against the influence of boredom. But a one-sidedly deaf person achieves the same end far more courteously when, instead of putting his hand before his mouth, he holds it (under some slight pretext) before his good ear—as I do. This enables one to rest in a pose of attentiveness for as long as the noxious tones continue.

Goethe wished that the performers should be invisible to the audience, that one might not see their contortions. Now if someone can artfully add to this the virtue of inaudibility, all the benefits that may be derived from bad concerts will, I believe, have been brought

[1] The journal in which the essay appeared.

together. From good concerts a man who can move his limbs can benefit still more with one-sided deafness, for whenever the shouts and other expressions of praise, like bad prose, wreck and ruin the poetry of tone, he can easily change his position, withdraw his good ear, and simply turn the dead one toward the barbaric clapping of hands.

MISCELLANEOUS ESSAYS (1806)

P. I. TCHAIKOVSKY

My Taste in Classics

Probably after my death it will not be uninteresting to know what were my musical predilections and prejudices, especially since I seldom gave opinions in verbal conversation.

Shall start gradually and shall speak to the point, touching upon musicians living at the same time with me and about their personalities.

Shall start with Beethoven, whom it is usual to praise unconditionally and whom it is commanded to worship as though he were a god. And so what is Beethoven to me?

I bow before the greatness of some of his works—but I do not *love* Beethoven. My attitude toward him reminds me of what I experienced in childhood toward the God Jehovah. I had toward Him (and even now my feelings have not changed) a feeling of wonder, but at the same time also of fear. He created Heaven and earth, He too created me—and still even though I bow before Him, there is no *love*. Christ, on the contrary, inspires truly and exclusively the feeling of *love*. Though He was *God*, He was at the same time man. He suffered like us. We *pity* Him, we love in Him His ideal *human* side. And if Beethoven occupies a place in my heart analogous to the God Jehovah, then Mozart I love as the musical Christ. Incidentally, he lived almost as long as Christ. I think that there is nothing sacrilegious in this comparison. Mozart was a being so angelic, so childlike, so pure: his music is so full of unapproachable, divine beauty, that if anyone could be named with Christ, then it is he.

Speaking of Beethoven, I come to Mozart. According to my deep conviction, Mozart is the highest, the culminating point that *beauty* has attained in the sphere of music. No one has made me weep, has made me tremble with rapture, from the consciousness of my nearness to *that something* which we call the *ideal*, as he has done.

Beethoven has also made me tremble. But rather from something like fear and the pangs of suffering.

I cannot *discourse* on music and shall not go into details. However, I shall mention two details: (1) In Beethoven I love the middle period, at times the first, but I fundamentally *detest* the last, especially the last quartets. Here there are *glimmers*—and nothing more. The rest is *chaos*, over which, surrounded by an impenetrable fog, hovers the spirit of this musical Jehovah. (2) In Mozart I love *everything*, for we love *everything* in a person whom we love truly. Above all *Don Juan*, for thanks to it I learned what *music* is. Until that time (until my seventeenth year) I did not know any music except Italian, semi-music, however charming. Of course, loving everything in Mozart, I shall not start asserting that every insignificant work of his is a *chef-d'oeuvre*. Yes! I know that none of his sonatas, for example, is a great work, and *still* I *love* every one of his sonatas because it is *his*, because this musical Christ imprinted it with his serene touch.

Concerning the forerunners of both, can say that I play Bach gladly, for to play a good fugue is entertaining, but I do not recognize in him (as some do) a great genius. Handel has for me an entirely fourth-rate significance and he is not even entertaining. Gluck, despite the relative poverty of his creation, is attractive to me. I *like* certain things of Haydn. But all these four Muses are amalgamated in Mozart. He who knows Mozart also knows what is good in these four, because being the greatest and most potent of all musical creators, he was not averse, even, to taking them under his wings and saving them from oblivion. They are rays lost in the sun of Mozart.

DIARIES (1886)

BENVENUTO CELLINI
&
MICHEL DE MONTAIGNE

Music and My Father

Cellini

My father began to teach me to play the flute and to sing at sight, but although I was of a very tender age, when little children usually take pleasure in piping and similar amusements, I felt only the greatest dislike for it, and I sang and played only in order to obey him. At that time my father made the most wonderful organs of wooden pipes, and the finest and best harpsichords that were then to be seen, as well as the most beautiful and excellent viols, lutes, and harps. He was an engineer, and worked miracles in making many sorts of machines such as drawbridges, fulling mills, and so on. In carving ivory he was the first artist who worked really well. But after he had fallen in love with the woman who was to be my mother—perhaps it was piping that brought them together, for to it he gave much more time than he should have—he was asked by the musicians of the Court to join them in performing. Having thus indulged himself a while, he was so strongly urged by them that he became one of their band. But Lorenzo de' Medici and Piero his son, who wished him well and saw him give all his time to piping, and neglect his engineering and artistic work, had him dismissed from the post of musician.

. . . At that time (which was before my birth), these musicians were all distinguished artisans, workers in silk or wool, who belonged to the trades known as the Major Arts, which accounts for my father's not thinking music beneath him. His chief desire in the world as regards myself was that I should become a virtuoso on the flute; but the greatest displeasure in the world for me was when he brought the subject up and told me that if I wanted to apply myself I should become the best man in the world.

As I have said, my father was a great friend and devoted servant of the house of Medici, and when I was still of quite a tender age, he once had me carried pig-a-back to make me play the flute, and I played the treble with the palace musicians in front of the Senate [of Florence]; and I read my notes while one of the ushers held me on his shoulders throughout. Whereupon, Soderini, who was then *gonfalonier*, took much pleasure in making me prattle, gave me candy, and said to my father, 'Master Giovanni, you must teach him your other two great arts, and not only music.' To which my father replied, 'I do not want him to follow any other art but that of performer on the flute and composer. For if God gives him life, I shall make him the greatest man in the world.' To these words, one of the elder statesmen rejoined, 'Ah, Master Giovanni, do as the *gonfalonier* says; why should the boy be nothing more than a good musician?'

AUTOBIOGRAPHY (1558)

Montaigne

Among other things [my father] had been advised to make me enjoy learning and duty by securing the consent of my will and of my desire, as well as to train my mind in full freedom and gentleness without constraint or rigour: I may say he did this with such superstitious regard that, since some hold that it disturbs the tender brains of children to awaken them suddenly in the morning and snatch them violently at one stroke out of their sleep (into which they sink far deeper than we), he had me awakened by the sound of an instrument and never was without an attendant to serve me thus.

ON THE REARING OF CHILDREN (1588)

JONATHAN SWIFT

A Cantata

With Comments by Other Hands

From Sir Walter Scott's biography

The Dean himself did not affect either to be a judge or admirer of music, yet he possessed the power of mimicking it in a wonderful degree. A person regretting at his table that he had not heard Mr. Rosingrave, then just returned from Italy, perform upon the organ; 'you shall hear him now,' said Swift, and immediately started off into a burlesque imitation of the chromatics of the musician. This exploit led to the Dean's composing the celebrated cantata burlesquing the doctrine of imitative sounds in poetry and music. It was set to music by Dr. John Ecclin.

From Dr. Beattie's 'Programme Notes'

Here we have motions imitated, which are the most inharmonious, and the least connected with human affections, as the trotting, ambling, and galloping of Pegasus; the words high and deep have high and deep notes set to them; a series of short notes of equal lengths are introduced, to imitate shivering and shaking; an irregular rant of quick sounds to express rumbling; a sudden rise of the voice from a low to a high pitch to denote flying above the sky, a ridiculous run of chromatic divisions on the words 'Celia dies'; with other droll contrivances of a like nature. The satire of the piece is levelled, not at absurd imitation only, but also at some other musical improprieties, such as the idle repetition of the same words, the running of long extravagant divisions upon one syllable, and the setting of words to music that have no meaning. Swift, though deaf to the charms of music, was not blind to the absurdity of musicians.

Swift's cantata

> In harmony would you excel,
> Suit your words to your music well, music well, music well,

Suit your words to your music well,
Suit your words to your music well.

For Pegasus runs—runs—every race
By gal——loping high or le—vel pace,
Or ambling or sweet Canterbury
Or with a down, a high down derry.

No! no victory, victory he ever got
By jog—ling, jog—ling, jog—ling trot
No Muse harmonious entertains
Rough, roist'ring rustic roar—ing strains
Nor shall you twine——the crack—ling, crackling bays
By sneaking, snivelling round—elays.

Trolloping, lolloping, galloping, trolloping
Lolloping, galloping, trollop;
Lolloping, trolloping, galloping, lolloping,
Trolloping, galloping, lollop.
Now creep——sweep, sweep the deep:
See, see, Ce—lia dies, dies, dies, dies, dies, dies, dies;
While true lovers' eyes
Weeping sleep, sleeping weep, weeping sleep
Bo peep, bo peep, bo peep, bo peep, bo—bo—peeeep.

Now slowly move your fiddlestick
Now tantan, tantan, tantan-tivi,
Now tantan, tantan, tantan-tivi quick—
Now trembling shiv'—ring, quiv'—ring, quak—ing
Set hoping, hoping, hoping hearts of lovers aching.
Fly, fly! above the sky, Ramb—ling, gamb—ling,
        Ramb————ling, gamb—ling.

From George Faulkner, Swift's publisher
   When Arne, the famous composer,[1] was last in Ireland, he made
application to me for this cantata (which I could not then procure),

   [1] Thomas Arne (1710–78), composer of operas and oratorios, author of
'Rule Britannia' and several famous melodies for Shakespeare lyrics.

to set it to music; perhaps he may do it now, and bring it on the stage; which, if he does, will run more than *The Beggar's Opera*; and therefore I would have you get it engraved in folio, with scores for bass, etc., which will make it sell very well.

SCOTT'S *WORKS OF SWIFT* (1814–24)

RUDOLF KASSNER

Musical Brows

A free-lance philosophical writer, Rudolf Kassner, has written about music, intellectual history, and English poetry. He was born in 1873, long resided in Vienna, and was at one time a close friend of Rilke's. He now lives in Switzerland.

I HAVE tried to show at several points in my works on Physiognomy that the so-called 'musical brow,' which stretches from ear to ear in a beautiful curve highly arched toward the middle, is the peculiarity not so much of the creators of music as of the mere performers, that is, the great conductors or executants on violin or piano. In other words, the creative musicians possess a physiognomy of the Eye-type no less than of the Ear-type; they are Eye-men as well as Ear-men. I find, to be sure, an exception in Mozart's face, but it is due, as I think, to absolute genius, which in his case makes use of the creature as a tool, or, indeed, as a plaything. Mozart, to put it paradoxically, could have had any face whatever. His uncontested genius appeared most truly incognito or cloaked in the manner of the gods when they tread the earth. Everything about him, including his death, is as it were mythic, just as everything about Beethoven is human and dramatic.

Nothing in the study of Musical Physiognomy strikes me as so fascinating, and at the same time fruitful, as a comparison of the three brows of Bach, Beethoven, and Richard Wagner. Bach's brow is immobile, towering, *plane*—like the tablets of the law or like one of his scores engraved with failing eyes—all in immediate contact with the Ear. It is as when a person high placed in government or business has a private wire through which to speak at will, without switchboards or intermediaries. Another comparison: I [once] . . . looked up and saw how the summit of a mountain, stony and eternally snow-clad, towered ever higher than the clouds by which I had believed it was hidden; I ceased wondering and merely closed my eyes, for they were filled with tears. Just so is Bach's brow compared to Beethoven's, over which storms pass with blasting bolts, but which does not invariably tower above the clouds, as is true of the image before us.

As for Richard Wagner's brow, it forms but one piece with his occiput. It begins at the root of the nose and goes all the way back to the nape of the neck. Who, on looking at Bach's face, would ever think of his occiput? In Beethoven likewise it is of no importance. In Bach's world heaven and earth are two separate realms; in Beethoven's they are at strife with each other. Richard Wagner's world would be tottering, it would be pure agitation without the stage. Richard Wagner's world would go astray in the Infinite, were it not enabled to make continually fresh starts through the stage or the means of staging. That is how I interpret this brow which reaches from the root of the nose all the way back to the nape of the neck.

DER GRÖSSTE MENSCH (1946)

MODESTE MOUSSORGSKY

My Life and Works[1]

MODESTE (Piotr) Moussorgsky, Russian composer, born in 1839, the sixteenth of March, province of Pskov, county of Toropetz; son of an ancient Russian family. Under the direct influence of his nurse, he became familiar with Russian fairy tales. This acquaintance with the spirit of the folk life was the main impulse of musical improvisations before he had learned even the elementary rules of piano playing. His mother gave him his first piano lessons, and he made such progress that at the age of seven he played small pieces by Liszt, and at nine played a grand concerto by Field before a large audience in his parents' house. His father, who worshipped music, decided to develop the child's ability—and entrusted his further musical education to An[ton] Herke in Petersburg. The professor was so satisfied with his pupil that when he was twelve he had him play a 'Concerto Rondo' by Herz at a private charity concert in the home of the Court Lady-of-Honour, Ryumina. The success and impression made by the young musician's performance was such that Professor Herke, ever a severe critic of his pupils, presented him with a copy of Beethoven's Sonata in A Flat. At thirteen young Moussorgsky entered the Cadet School of the Guards and was honoured by the particularly kind attention of the late Emperor Nikolai. It was then that Moussorgsky composed a little piano piece and dedicated it to his comrades. This piece was published by his father with the help of An. Herke. This was the first work of the young (talented) musician to appear in print. In school he visited a great deal with the religious instructor, Father Krupsky, thanks to whom he acquired a profound knowledge of the very essence of ancient Greek and Catholic church music. At the age of seventeen he entered the Preobrazhensky regiment. In the regiment his comrade Vanlyarsky introduced Moussorgsky to the genius Dargomizhsky. In the home of Dargomizhsky, Moussorgsky became friendly with the

[1] Written for a dictionary of musicians, this note anticipates the completion of certain works.

prominent workers of musical art in Russia, C. Cui and M. Balakirev.[1] With the latter the young nineteen-year-old composer studied the whole history of the development of musical art—with examples, with severe systematic analysis of all the most important musical creations by the composers of European art in their historical sequence, this study proceeded during regular readings together of the musical works on two pianos. Balakirev brought Moussorgsky close to the family of one of the most important connoisseurs of arts in Russia, the well-known art critic Stassov,[2] and with the sister of the genius-creator of Russian music Glinka. On his part Cui introduced Moussorgsky to the famous Polish composer Moniuszko. Shortly thereafter the composer came close and became friendly with other such talented composers, such as the present well-known professor of the Petersburg conservatory, N. A. Rimsky-Korsakov. This closeness to a talented circle of musicians, regular discussions, and the establishment of firm contacts with a wide circle of Russian scholars and writers, such as Vladimir Lamansky, Turgenev, Kostomarov, Grigorovich, Kavelin, Pisemsky, Shevchenko [Dostoyevsky], and others, particularly stimulated the mental activity of the young composer and gave it a serious, strictly scientific direction. The result of this fortunate closeness was a whole series of musical compositions on Russian folk life, and the friendly companionship in the home of Shestakova with Professor V. Nikolsky caused the creation of the grand opera *Boris Godunov*, based on a subject by the great Pushkin. In the family circle of Privy Councillor Purgold, a great lover of art, and with the collaboration of his nieces A. and N. Purgold, serious and talented interpreters of music, *Boris Godunov* was performed for a large gathering, in the presence of the distinguished Petrov, Platonova, Kommissarzhevsky, and Associate Director Lukashevich. Directly thereupon it was decided to stage three scenes of this opera, although this very opera not long before had been rejected by the theatre directorate. With the participation of the distinguished artist D. Leonova, the opera, supported on the shoulders of the above-named artists, was staged, finally, in its entirety with stupendous success. The impression it made on the audience, the artists, and the orchestra was astonishing. The success of the opera was a complete triumph for its author. Following this opera there were planned, with the assistance of the critic Stassov, Professors Nikolsky and Kostomarov, two more operas simultaneously: *Khovanshchina* and

[1] See pp. 142–43.   [2] See p. 173.

The Fair at Sorochintzi, based on Gogol. As a relaxation from this work there were composed the *Album Series* on the exhibition of the works of the genius-architect Hartmann, *Danse macabre* (five scenes) on a text by the author's friend Count Golenishchev-Kutuzov, and several songs with text by Count Al[exei] Tolstoy. In 1879 the distinguished Russian dramatic singer Leonova invited Moussorgsky to undertake a grand artistic tour of Russia and Little Russia, the Crimea and along the Don and the Volga. This journey, taking three months, was a genuine triumphal procession for the two important Russian artists: the talented composer and the well-known singer. On tour the author conceived the idea of transposing into music one of the as yet untouched, from the musical point of view, creations of the great Goethe: Song of Mephistopheles, in Auerbach's Cellar, about the Flea.[1] As an impression of the tour through the Crimea, Moussorgsky published two caprices for piano: 'Baidari' and 'Gursuf'; then there was composed and played by the author himself at several concerts a large musical picture, 'Storm on the Black Sea.' He is bringing to completion both grand operas—*Khovanshchina* and *Fair at Sorochintzi*, which are on the press, as well as a large suite on themes of the Trans-Caspian region. Several of the most sharply original pictures for singing—'Savishna,' 'The Orphan Girl,' 'The Naughty Boy,' 'Gopak' (Shevchenko), struck the author's friend von Madeweiss, who handed them over for safe-keeping to the Strasbourg library with explanatory letters on these pieces by the author.

Two scherzi: B flat major and C sharp minor; the former was performed by an orchestra under the direction of A. Rubinstein, which was the first opportunity the author had to hear his work played by an orchestra, *Impromptu*, *Prélude* and *Menuet monstre*, 'Savishna,' 'Gopak,' 'Gathering Mushrooms' (Mey), 'Jewish Song' for orchestra and chorus, *The Destruction of Sennacherib* (Byron), *Jesus Navinus* [Joshua] (on ancient Israelite themes, recorded by the author), 'The Naughty Boy,' 'The Magpie' (Pushkin), *Intermezzo symphonique*, *Kinderscherz*, *La Fileuse*, 'King Saul' (after an Israelite text), 'Jewish Song,' 'The Nurse's Child's Song,' *Album from Childhood*, 'Forgotten' (from the Central Asiatic war), 'Night—A Fantasy' (from Pushkin), 'Yeremushka' (Nekrasov); the polemical pieces: 'The Classicist,' *Penny Paradise*, 'The Seminarist'—prohibited and circulated in a mass of handwritten copies, published abroad.

[1] In *Faust*; but Moussorgsky's claim to originality here is contrary to fact.

Moussorgsky cannot be classed with any existing group of musicians, either by the character of his compositions or by his musical views. The formula of his artistic *profession de foi* may be explained by his view, as a composer, of the task of art: art is a means of communicating with people, not an aim in itself. This guiding principle has defined the whole of his creative activity. Proceeding from the conviction that human speech is strictly controlled by musical laws (Virchow, Gervinus[1]) he considers the task of musical art to be the reproduction in musical sounds not merely of the mood of the feeling, but chiefly of the mood of human speech. Acknowledging that in the realm of art only artist-reformers such as Palestrina, Bach, Gluck, Beethoven, Berlioz, and Liszt have created the laws of art, he considers these laws as not immutable but liable to change and progress, like the entire spiritual world of man.

Under the influence of such developed artistic views of the composer on the tasks and character of his creative work—was a whole. . . . [The manuscript breaks off.]

AUTOBIOGRAPHIC NOTE (JUNE 1880)

[1] German physiologist and Shakespeare scholar, respectively.

BRILLAT-SAVARIN

Sing for Your Life

Jurist, diplomat, and exile in the United States (where he left his name attached to sauces and restaurants), Jean-Anthelme Brillat-Savarin (1755–1826) was never suspected of being a gastronomist until the publication of his great work in 1825.

IT was in the worst days of the Revolution, and I was on my way to Dôle, to see the local representative Prot and obtain from him a safe-conduct which might prevent my being imprisoned and doubtless subsequently guillotined.

On reaching Dôle, I found Representative Prot very much prejudiced against me. He looked at me ominously and I thought I was going to be arrested. But my fright was quite wasted, for after some explanations he seemed to me to be softening a little.

I am not one of those whom fear renders cruel, and I may say I think the man was not a bad fellow. But he was a man of very limited capacities and did not know what to do with all the power that had been entrusted to him: he was like a child wielding Hercules' club. An acquaintance of mine whose name I am happy to set down here, M. Amondru, had a great deal of trouble to persuade him to accept an invitation to a dinner which I was to attend as well. Prot finally gave in, though he greeted me in a manner that was far from reassuring to me.

I was received somewhat better by Mme Prot, whom I then approached to pay my respects. My circumstances must have at least aroused her curiosity. Among the first words that she said, she asked me if I loved music. What unexpected luck! She was passionately fond of it, and as I am myself a pretty fair musician, from that moment on our hearts beat in unison.

We talked before supper and discussed everything thoroughly. She mentioned certain treatises on composition—I knew them all. She spoke of the most fashionable operas—I had them by heart. She named the best-known composers—I had met most of them. She could not stop talking, not having run into anyone for quite a while with whom to discuss this favourite subject of hers. Though she talked as an amateur, I heard afterward that she had taught singing.

After supper she sent for some of her music. She sang, I sang, we sang. I never applied myself more strenuously, nor did I ever enjoy it more. M. Prot had already remarked several times that he was leaving, but she took no notice, and we were sounding like a pair of bugles in the duet from *La Fausse Magie*[1]—

'Do you recall the festive time?'—

when he notified her that they were leaving.

We concluded perforce. But in taking leave Mme Prot said to me, 'Citizen, a man who cultivates the fine arts as you do cannot be a traitor to his country. I know you have asked some favour of my husband. You shall have it. I give you my word: it is a promise.'

Hearing these comforting words, I kissed her hand with heartfelt warmth, and, sure enough, the next morning I received my safe-conduct, duly signed and magnificently sealed. The purpose of my journey had been fulfilled. I returned home with head erect; and, thanks to Harmony, genial daughter of Heaven, my ascension was postponed for a period of years.

PHYSIOLOGY OF TASTE (1825)

---

[1] An opera by Grétry (1741–1813), first produced in 1775.

Correspondence

JOHANN SEBASTIAN BACH

To Georg Erdmann, Russian envoy at Danzig

Leipzig, October 28, 1730

EXCELLENCY:

Your Excellency will excuse an old friend and faithful servant who takes the liberty of intruding upon you. It is now four years since Your Excellency has favoured me with a reply to my letter. . . . You have known me and my doings since youth and up to the time of my chapel-mastership at Cöthen.[1] I found there a noble prince who knew music and loved it, and there I hoped to end my days. But it so happened that His Highness married a princess from Bernburg, and it seemed to me that my master's love of music was cooling off, his lady being quite muse-less. It pleased God that I should be called here as musical director and cantor of St. Thomas's School,[2] even though at first it seemed to me intolerable to descend to the rank of cantor after having been chapel-master. That is why for three months I held back my decision. But the post was so favourably recommended to me that finally, and chiefly because my sons appear to be inclined toward study, I dared, in the name of the Almighty, to go to Leipzig. I passed an audition and then moved to the new place where, by the grace of God, I am still.

But as I find that (1) the duties are by far not so agreeable as they were described to me originally; and (2) that quite a few of the bonuses attached to the post have been withdrawn; that (3) the cost of living is very high here; and (4) that the authorities are rather strangely hostile to music; that I have to live in a state of almost constant struggle; that envy prevails and vexations are numerous; I find myself, so help me God, compelled to seek my fortune elsewhere. If Your Excellency knows of any suitable position for an old faithful servant in your city, I should be deeply obliged for your help and recommendation in securing it. I in turn will not fail to live up to the promise implied by your gracious intercession. I will truly do my best in the discharge of duty.

My salary here is seven hundred thalers, and when there are more burials than usual, the added fees raise this proportionately higher. But whenever the air is a little more healthful, the loss is great. Last year the fees for common burials showed a deficit of a hundred thalers.

[1] I.e., up to 1717.   [2] In 1723.

With four hundred thalers I could support myself in Thuringia more comfortably than here with twice that amount, for the cost of living in Leipzig is exorbitant.

I should also give you some details about my family. I remarried after the death of my first wife in Cöthen. From my first marriage I still have three sons and one daughter, as you may remember from seeing them at Weimar.[1] From my second, one son and two daughters are alive. My eldest boy is studying law; the other two are in the top two classes; my eldest daughter is not yet married. The children of my second marriage are still quite little, the eldest being only six. All are born musicians, which enables us to have family concerts with voice and instruments, for my wife has a nice soprano voice and my eldest daughter also does pretty well.

I would be overstepping the bounds of courtesy if I bored you with further details. I therefore close and remain, ever respectfully,

Your Excellency's most devoted servant,

Joh. Seb. Bach

---

[1] Between 1707 and 1717.

LORD CHESTERFIELD

To his son

London, June 22, 1749

DEAR BOY,

. . . I approve of your going to Venice, as much as I disapprove of your going to Switzerland. I suppose that you are by this time arrived, and, in that supposition, I direct this letter there. But if you should find the heat too great, or the weather offensive at this time of the year, I would have you go immediately to Verona, and stay there till the great heats are over, before you return to Venice.

The time you will probably pass at Venice will allow you to make yourself master of that intricate and singular form of government, which few of our travellers know anything of. Read, ask, and see everything that is relative to it. There are likewise many valuable remains of the remotest antiquity, and many fine pieces of the *antico moderno*; all which deserve a different sort of attention from that which your countrymen commonly give them. They go to see them as they go to see the lions, and kings on horseback, at the Tower here; only to say that they have seen them. You will, I am sure, view them in another light; you will consider them as you would a poem, to which indeed they are akin. You will observe whether the sculptor has animated his stone, or the painter his canvas, into the just expression of those sentiments and passions which should characterize and mark their several figures. You will examine likewise whether, in their groups, there be an unity of action or proper relation; a truth of dress and manners. Sculpture and painting are very justly called liberal arts; a lively and strong imagination, together with a just observation, being absolutely necessary to excel in either; which, in my opinion, is by no means the case of music, though called a liberal art, and now in Italy placed even above the other two: a proof of the decline of that country. The Venetian school produced many great painters, such as Paul Veronese, Titian, Palma, etc., by whom you will see, as well in private houses as in churches, very fine pieces. . . . A taste of sculpture and painting is in my mind as becoming as a taste of fiddling and piping is unbecoming a man of fashion. The former is connected with history and poetry, the latter, with nothing that I know of but bad company.

MARIA THERESA, EMPRESS OF AUSTRIA,[1] & COUNT DE MERCY-ARGENTEAU

The Imperial family trusted Gluck and used him as secret envoy whenever he travelled between Vienna and Paris. Sometimes he carried political news, sometimes intimate information from the young queen, Marie Antoinette, indicating that her hoped-for pregnancy was not yet a fact. This eighteenth-century simplicity was matched by the duplicity embodied in Mercy-Argenteau, for he was little more than a spy set by Maria Theresa on her daughter, who never suspected his role.

Count de Mercy to the Empress

Paris, April 19, 1774

Today our celebrated chapel-master Gluck gives the first perform-ance of his opera, *Iphigénie en Aulide*, which Mme la Dauphine[2] will attend. The music has been greatly applauded at the rehearsals, and it is expected to mark an epoch in the reformation of French harmony, for this last is, as you know, very insipid and monotonous.

Maria Theresa to Count de Mercy

Vienna, November 15, 1774

Count de Mercy, I also want to tell you in secret of the plan I have in mind, to see the French opera *Iphigénie* produced here for the arrival of my son Ferdinand and his wife.[3] They are coming here next year. The performers—and I want rather good ones—would have to be here by the end of August, and I think I would detain them until the end of November. You would be doing me a kindness to find out quietly whether I can count on such persons, and whether they would be satisfied with reasonable fees for their trip here (where I should see them taken care of) instead of making extravagant demands. But since I want this opera production to be a surprise to the Emperor, to my daughter, and to the public, it matters greatly to me that the business be prepared secretly, and although I think you could talk about it

---

[1] Properly Maria Theresia, but English usage has prevailed.

[2] Marie Antoinette, daughter of Maria Theresa; the Dauphin being the future Louis XVI.

[3] Fourth son of Maria Theresa, Duke of Modena.

with Gluck, it would have to be done cautiously, because I do not want to entrust too much to his taciturnity.

Count de Mercy to the Empress

Paris, January 15, 1775

. . . The queen[1] came to the Opera in Paris on Friday the thirteenth. The people, heavily congregated along the line of her passage, gave extraordinary and most lively evidence of their love for their queen. The same was true of Her Majesty's entrance into the theatre, which was filled to overflowing. The opera represented was *Iphigénie*, composed by Gluck. In the second act of that piece occurs a chorus, of which Achilles sings the first verse while turning to his suite—

'Now sing in honour of your queen!'

Instead of this, the actor, moving forward toward the parterre and boxes, said—

'We sing in honour of our queen,
The union which binds her to our lord,
Will make us happy evermore!'

This was taken up by the public with incredible enthusiasm; nothing could be heard but shouts and handclapping, and what has never before happened at the Opera, the audience made the singers repeat the chorus while the public joined in with cries of 'Long live the queen!' It stopped the play for nearly fifteen minutes, and the queen was so moved that she shed a few tears.

Count de Mercy to the Empress

Paris, January 19, 1775

Your Sacred Majesty, the two very gracious letters dated last November 15, which Count de Fossières gave me, require a separate answer, together with a few remarks on the means of carrying out Your Majesty's intention as regards producing the French opera *Iphigénie* in Vienna.

The undeserved importance which the Paris public ascribes to its Opera is no doubt the reason why the government has given a very special character to it, and to whoever is connected with it, thus making

[1] Louis XV had died in May 1774, which made the Dauphin and Dauphine king and queen.

it into a national institution, regular and permanent. It is according to this notion that by letters patent of Louis XIV the acting troupe of the Opera constitutes a Royal Academy of Music, and that among several privileges which are as extraordinary as they are absurd, the profession of opera singer is declared to be compatible with the rank of nobility, so that a nobleman born may practise this calling without losing his rights or title—a privilege, however, which extends only to the singing actors, and from which the dancing actors are excluded.[1]

All these actors are on fixed salaries, paid by the City of Paris, and are guaranteed a retirement pension equal to half their salary. In addition, these same persons belong also to the King's Music and receive the fees assigned to such a post. The result is that the actors of the Paris Opera, being doubly bound, in perpetuity, to the service of the Court and of the City of Paris, may not contract any other engagements of their talents, nor absent themselves save by express order or permission of the King.

The foregoing means nothing but difficulties; yet since all difficulties must yield to the wishes of Your Majesty, I have given all my mind to resolving them. And first I conferred with Chapel-Master Gluck, enjoining him in such a manner to keep the secret that I am assured he will not violate it. Since at no time can the Paris Opera remain unoccupied, I suggested to Gluck that he compose at once a new work, so contrived that it should be playable by the weaker performers, and by the understudies who are provided (in cases of necessity) to replace the leading actors which are essential to the *Iphigénie*. This new work, which Gluck has already begun, will perhaps require him to stay here a few weeks longer than his permission allows, but Your Majesty will deign not to consider this improper, since it comes about solely with a view to an expedient for carrying out your intentions.

To reduce the difficulty as far as possible, Gluck has managed things so that five leading actors and twelve voices for the chorus will suffice to produce his opera *Iphigénie*. Hence only seventeen persons will need transportation to Vienna. The only way, however, will be by an express order from the King. There is no doubt that the monarch will deem it a pleasure to serve Your Majesty in the contemplated object, about which such arrangements will have been made that the Paris performances will not be interrupted.

[1] These letters patent were issued to Lulli, March 29, 1672; they gave him a monopoly and made his fortune. See p. 94.

As for the expenses connected with this project, the outlay will be all the greater that the actors' fees will depend entirely on Your Majesty's pleasure and munificence. For as explained above, it is not possible to enter into contracts with the aforesaid actors. When Your Majesty will please to order it, I shall lay before your eyes an estimate of the likely cost. I close with the comment that the public here will surely be greatly flattered at the thought that Your Majesty should want to see a show of which the French nation has always felt proud—more so, I suspect, than the thing itself deserves.

Maria Theresa to Count de Mercy

Vienna, February 4, 1775

Count de Mercy, after the information you have given me about the circumstances of the actors of *Iphigénie* at the Paris Opera, I find that the project of having them brought here would be as awkward as it would be expensive. We will therefore not say another word about it.

P.S.—except in case Gluck may be able to bring a couple with him and give us an idea of the show between June and October; but I do not want to spend any money on it, nor have too many additional persons on my hands.

Count de Mercy to the Empress

Paris, February 20, 1775

I shall let Gluck know Your Majesty's intentions as regards giving in Vienna a sketch of the French operas, but I believe it could be done without bringing from here any singing persons. They could easily be replaced by a few French actors from the travelling comic opera troupes; Gluck's cleverness could manage with them, and that would save expense, for the outlay would be great even if only a very few actors of the Paris Opera were to travel.

Maria Theresa to Count de Mercy

March 4, 1775

Count de Mercy, I deem it proper to abandon the project of having Gluck engage a few French actors to come here.

Leopold Mozart to his wife

Rome, April 14, 1770

. . . You have no doubt often heard of the famous *Miserere*, which is so highly treasured that the musicians of the Chapel are forbidden, under pain of excommunication, to take a single part out of the Chapel, to copy it, or give it to anyone. *We now have it:* Wolfgang wrote it down,[1] and we would have sent it to Salzburg, with this letter, were our presence not required to produce it; for the style contributes more than the composition itself.[2] Accordingly we shall bring it with us, and it being one of the secrets of Rome, we do not want it to fall into other hands, lest we should incur directly or indirectly the censure of the Church.[3]

. . . Wolfgang is well and sends a *contredanse*. He would like Herr Hofmann[4] to make up the steps to it, and in such a way that when the two solo violins play, only two persons should dance as principals, and then whenever the band joins in with all the instruments, the whole company can dance. What would be most beautiful would be for five couples to dance the piece—the first pair taking the first solo, the second next, and so on, for there are five solos and five tuttis.

Mzt

Wolfgang to his sister Maria Anna (Nannerl)

Rome, April 21, 1770

Cara sorella mia! I beg you to find me the arithmetic lessons; you know you wrote them out yourself for me, and now I have lost them. So I have quite forgotten what I knew about it. Please copy them out with other examples and send them to me.

Manzuoli is under contract with the Milanese to sing my opera.[5] With this in mind he sang me four or five arias in Florence, including a few which I had to compose in Milan because people have not heard a single thing of mine for the theatre which would enable them to

---

[1] Wolfgang was then in his fourteenth year.

[2] But see p. 360.

[3] This last clause is written in Latin.

[4] Dancing master at the Salzburg Court.

[5] *Mitridate, Rè di Ponto* (1770), Mozart's first opera seria.

judge whether I was capable of writing an opera. . . . I am now at work on the air '*Se ardire, e speranza.*'

The same to the same[1]

Rome, April 25, 1770

Cara sorella mia! . . . Please do what I asked you to do the last time I wrote and answer me about it. I have played in two concerts and tomorrow shall play in one more. . . . This letter done, I shall finish a symphony of mine which I have begun, the aria is finished, another symphony is with the copyist (who happens to be my father) because we do not want to give it out to be copied, for then it would be plagiarized. To all my friends give my greetings, kiss my mother's hand for me, since I am (tra-la-lira) the

Wolfgango in germania e amadeo
Mozartt in italia

In Leopold's hand: I kiss you both.

Maria Anna Mozart to her husband Leopold

Augsburg, October 14, 1777

We left Munich on the 11th at noon and arrived safe in Augsburg at nine in the evening; the journey was done in nine hours with a hired coachman who moreover fed his horses for an hour.

[*Wolfgang continues:*] So we made no mistake about the date. We wrote in the morning and will be off again (I think) next Friday, that is, day after tomorrow. Now hear how mightily generous these good Augsburgers have been! Nowhere have I been so overwhelmed with marks of honour as here. My first visit was to the mayor, Longotabarro.[2] . . . He gave me no peace but I must go with him upstairs to his son-in-law . . . while my cousin had the honour of waiting, sitting on a stool in the vestibule. I had to take hold of myself most manfully, otherwise I should have—most politely—said something. Upstairs I had the honour of playing for about three-quarters of an hour on a good clavier by Stein in the presence of the stiff-bosomed son and the long-legged young wife and the stupid old lady.

. . . Although I had asked them not to say who I was, Herr von Langenmantel thoughtlessly blurted out to Herr Stein, 'I have the

---

[1] The original is in Italian.
[2] Mozart italianizes the name of Herr von Langenmantel.

honour of introducing to you a virtuoso on the clavier,' and began to snicker. I at once protested, saying I was only an unworthy pupil of Herr Siegl of Munich, who had charged me with a thousand compliments to him. He nodded negatives with his head and finally: 'Is it possible that I have the honour of seeing Herr Mozart before me?' 'Oh, no,' I replied, 'my name is Trazom and I have a letter for you.' . . . I began to play. He could hardly open the letter in his eagerness to find out; he read only the signature. 'Oh,' he shrieked, and embraced me. He kept crossing himself and making faces and was terribly pleased. I'll tell you later about all his claviers. He then took me to a coffeehouse. When I stepped in I thought I would fall down overcome by the stench and fumes of tobacco. But for God's sake I had to stand it for an hour and pretend to enjoy it all, though I felt as if I were in Turkey.

He then talked a great deal about a certain Graf, a composer, but who has only written flute concertos.[1] He said, 'Now there is a man who is really remarkable'—and other such exaggerations. I was sweating with apprehension, head, hands, my whole body. . . . My host would not yield but took me to Graf on the spot. Graf is indeed a fine figure of a man. He had on a dressing gown such as I should not be ashamed to wear on the streets. His words are all mounted on stilts and he usually opens his mouth before he knows what one is going to say; and often it shuts again without having done anything. After many compliments he performed a concerto for two flutes. I had to play the first violin part. . . . When it was over I praised him highly, for he really deserves it. The poor man must have taken great pains over it; he must have studied hard. At length they brought in a clavier . . . quite good though full of dust. Herr Graf, who is music director here, stood there like a man who had always thought himself very unusual in his wanderings from key to key and who now finds that one can be still more unusual, and yet not offend the ear. In short, they were all astounded. . . . I am

Wolfgang Mozart

Wolfgang to his father

Paris, May 1, 1778

. . . At last the Duchesse de Chabot appeared and asked me very

---

[1] Friedrich Graf (1727–95) was a flute virtuoso who also composed for other instruments and achieved considerable renown in his day.

courteously to make the best of the clavier in the room because none
of her own was in condition—would I try it? I said I'd gladly play
something but that it was impossible just then, for I could hardly feel
my own fingers for the cold. I asked her whether I might be taken at
least to a room where there was a fire. 'Why, yes, of course, you are
right.'[1] was all the answer I got. She then sat herself down and began
to draw for a whole hour, in company with some gentlemen who sat
around a large table, while I had the honour of waiting for that whole
hour. The doors and windows were open and my whole body was
frozen as well as my hands and feet. I began to have a headache.
There was deep silence,[2] and I hardly knew what to do, what with
the cold, headache, and boredom. I kept thinking, 'If it weren't for
Mr. Grimm,[3] I'd leave at once.' Finally, to make a long story short, I
played on that miserable wreck of a pianoforte. But what was more
irritating was that Madame and all the gentlemen did not interrupt
their drawing for a moment, but kept right on, so that I had to play to
the chairs, table, and walls.

. . . Give me the best clavier in Europe with listeners who understand nothing, or won't understand and won't feel with me what I
am playing, and I shall lose all pleasure and interest. I told Grimm all
about it afterward. . . . People pay plenty of compliments but there it
ends. They appoint a day, I play, they shout, 'Oh, it's prodigious,
inconceivable, amazing!'[4]—then good-bye. . . . Paris has greatly
changed; the French are not nearly so polite as fifteen years
ago. Their manners verge on boorishness and their condescension is
abominable.

. . . As far as music is concerned I am among sheer brute beasts.
How can it be otherwise? In all their actions, feelings, and passions
they are just the same—there is no place in the world like Paris. You
mustn't think I exaggerate when I speak of the music here in this way.
Ask anyone you like except a born Frenchman, and if he is at all
reliable he will tell you the same. But here I am and I must stick it out
for your sake. . . .

Wolfgang Amadè Mozart

[1] French in the original.
[2] Latin in the original.
[3] Baron Friedrich Melchior Grimm (1723–1807), German literary correspondent—and for a short time Mozart's sponsor—in Paris.
[4] French in the original.

Wolfgang to his father

Paris, September 11, 1778

I have duly received your three letters of the 13th, 27th, and 31st of August, but I shall reply only the last because it is the most important. As I read it . . . I trembled with joy, for I saw myself already in your arms. To be sure—you will admit it yourself—no great fortune awaits me there,[1] but when I think once more of kissing and hugging my dearest father and sister,[2] I know of no other good fortune. That is in fact the one thing I can say in excuse to the people here who keep shouting in my ears that I must stay. I tell them, 'What do you mean? If I am satisfied, that should be enough.' There is one place I can call home and be in peace and quiet with the best of fathers and sisters—I can do what I want, for apart from my duties I am my own master—can count on a regular income—can go off when I like—can travel every second year. What more could I want?

The only thing, I tell you frankly, that makes me disgusted with Salzburg is that one cannot go about freely with everybody there, and that the musicians are not held in higher consideration, and—that the Archbishop puts no faith in intelligent, well-travelled people. For I assure you that people who do not travel—at least people in the arts and sciences—are pretty sorry creatures, and I promise you that if the Archbishop does not allow me to travel every other year, I cannot accept the appointment. A man of ordinary talent will always be ordinary, whether he travels or not; but a man of superior talent (which I cannot deny myself to be without being impious) will go to pieces if he remains forever in the same place. . . .

I hope to have an answer soon so as to be able to leave soon. Your most obedient son

Wolfgang Amadè Mozart

Wolfgang to his father

Vienna, May 19, 1781

Mon très cher Père: I too do not know how to begin this letter, for I cannot get over my astonishment and shall never be able to as long as you continue to think and write as you do. I must tell you there is not a single remark in your letter in which I can recognize my father—a

[1] In Salzburg.

[2] Mozart's mother had been with him in Paris and had died there two months before.

father indeed, but not the dearest and best of fathers who cares for his own and his children's honour—in short, not *my* father. The whole thing must have been a dream. You are awake now, and need no reply from me on your arguments in order to be more than convinced that—*now more than ever*—I cannot change my decision.[1]

Yet I must take up some of the points in which my honour and character are most cruelly attacked. You say it was not right that I should resign from Vienna. I believe rather that if one is so minded (though at the time I was not, else I would have done it the first time) the most sensible thing to do is to do it from a place where one is contented and has the brightest prospects. No doubt you won't approve of this in the presence of the Archbishop, but to me you cannot but approve it. You say the only way to save my honour is to reverse my decision. How can you contradict yourself so! You must have forgotten, when you wrote this, that if I went back on my resolve I should be the lowest of the low. All of Vienna knows that I have left the Archbishop—and knows why—knows it was because my honour was wounded—and what's more, that it was for the third time. And now I am to give public evidence of the contrary—I am to make myself out a snivelling cur and the Archbishop a noble prince? No man can bring about the former, I least of all, and only God the latter—if he chooses to let him see the light.

Then you say I am wanting in affection for you, and therefore ought now to show it for the first time. Can you really be saying that? That I will never sacrifice my pleasures for your sake. What kind of pleasures have I here? The pleasure of worrying and toiling to fill my purse! You seem to think that I wallow in bliss and amusements. How you deceive yourself! That is, for the time being! Right now I have only just enough for my needs. But the subscription for my six sonatas is under way and then I shall have some money. All goes well, too, with the opera,[2] and in Advent I am to give a concert; then things will get better and better, because the winter season here is quite good. If you call it *pleasure* to be rid of a prince who does not pay and hounds one to death, then it is true my pleasure is great.

. . . All I can say to you is that on your account—solely on your account—I am very sorry that I was driven so far—I wish that the Archbishop had behaved more sensibly—if only in order that I might

[1] To leave the Archbishop's employ.
[2] *The Abduction from the Seraglio.*

devote my whole life to you. To please you, dear father, I would sacrifice my fortune, my health, and my life—but my honour, that is to me beyond reach and it must be so to you. . . . Had I not thought of you, I should not have waited for him to say for the third time 'Clear out of here!' without taking him at his word. What am I saying: Waited! *I* should have said it, and not he. . . . Dearest and best of fathers, ask of me anything you want but not that—anything but that—the mere thought makes me tremble with rage. I kiss your hands a thousand times and hug my sister with all my heart. Ever your most obedient son

Wolfgang Amadè Mozart

Wolfgang to his father

Vienna, October 13, 1781

. . . Now as to the libretto of the opera.[1] You are quite right as regards Stephanie's work.[2] Still, the poetry is in keeping with the character of the dumb, rude, and wicked Osmin. I know perfectly well that the versification is not of the best, but it fitted in so well with the musical ideas that were already knocking about my head that it could not fail to please me, and I'm willing to bet that in performance nothing will be amiss. As for the poetry of the original piece, I really can't complain. Belmont's aria, 'Oh, what anxiety!' could hardly be better for music. Except for the 'Hui' and 'Sorrow rests in my heart' (as if sorrow could rest!), the aria is not so bad, especially the first part.

Besides, I should say that in an opera the poetry must be the obedient daughter of music. Why do the Italian comic operas please everybody, in spite of their wretched words, even in Paris, where I saw their success? Because in them Music reigns supreme and one forgets the rest. All the more will an opera succeed when the plot is well worked out, the words expressly written for the music and not twisted around for some miserable rhyme (which God knows never contributes to the value of a show but rather detracts from it)—I mean words or stanzas that distort the composer's whole conception. Verse is no doubt indispensable to music, but rhyme—for the sake of rhyme—is a curse. The pedants who follow that system will always come to grief, and their music too. What is best is for a good composer who under-

[1] Still *The Abduction from the Seraglio.*

[2] Gottlieb Stephanie (1741–1800), opera director who arranged the text of the *Abduction.*

stands the stage and is able to make useful suggestions to join a clever poet—that true phoenix. Then you needn't worry about success, even with the ignorant. But poets remind me of trumpeters with their tricks to show off. If we composers were to stick so faithfully to our rules (which were good enough when no one knew better), why, we'd manufacture music almost as useless as their librettos! . . .

W. A. Mozart

CHRISTOPH WILLIBALD GLUCK

Even more than today, the eighteenth century managed its musical affairs in print, by direct polemic, of which the following is a fair sample. La Harpe (1739–1803) was a self-made man and a miscellaneous writer of severely academic views.

To M. de la Harpe

Paris, October 1777

Sir:

I find it is impossible for me not to yield assent to the very judicious remarks that you have just published upon my operas in your *Literary Review* of the 5th instant. I have nothing, absolutely nothing, to offer in rejoinder.

Hitherto I had been naïve enough to believe that music was like the other arts in being allowed to take all the passions as its domain, and that it should not give the less pleasure when it expressed the ravings of a madman or the cries of one in pain than when it depicted the sighings of love.

> There are no monsters, no enormities
> Which art by showing may not cause to please.[1]

I had thought this maxim true for Music as for Poetry. It had been my creed that if song was to be marked throughout with the colouring appropriate to the sentiments it was required to express, then it must be modified whenever these changed and take on as many different accents as they present different nuances. I believed, finally, that voices, instruments, and all possible sounds—even silence itself—must tend toward one goal, which is expression; and that the union between words and music must be so close that the poem should seem no less moulded on the music than the music on the poem.

These were not my only errors. I thought I had noticed that the French language was but slightly accented, and did not, like the Italian, make use of quantity. I had, moreover, been struck by another difference between the singers of the two nations. The ones seemed to have softer, more flexible voices; but the others had greater strength and put more energy into their performance; whence I concluded that Italian melody would not suit the French. And in going over the score

[1] From Boileau's *Art Poétique*, Canto III, 1–2.

of your older operas, I found enough real beauties—despite an excess of trills, cadences, and other faults of song writing—to persuade me that the French had a sufficient tradition of their own.

Such, sir, were my ideas when I read your strictures. At once your light dissipated my darkness. I was aghast to discover that you had learned more about the art of my choice in a few hours' reflection than I had been able to master in forty years of practice. Your words demonstrate that it is enough to be a man of letters in order to speak well of everything. I am now convinced that the music of the Italian masters is music *par excellence*, is Music itself; that in order to charm, melody must be regular and four-square, and that even in moments of confusion in which the dramatic hero passes from one emotion to another, the composer must throughout repeat the identical melodic motive.

I agree with you that, of all my works, *Orpheus* is the only tolerable one. I sincerely beg pardon of the god of taste for having *deafened* my hearers by means of my subsequent works. The number of times these other operas have been played, and the applause which the public was good enough to accord them, do not blind me to the fact that they are in truth pitiable. I believe this so strenuously that I am about to revise them, and since I note that you are all for tender strains, I am planning to make the raging Achilles sing in a manner so pathetic and soothing that the audience will be dissolved in tears.

As regards *Armide*, I am certainly not going to keep the poem as it is. For as you judiciously remark, 'The librettos of Quinault,[1] although full of beautiful passages, are not properly constructed for music; they are superb poems, but bad operas.' At the risk of turning into very bad poems, they shall become beautiful operas in the manner you prescribe, and I would ask you to introduce me to some versifier who will take *Armide* apart and put it together again with two airs in each scene. He and I shall confer about the number and meter of the lines, and provided he gives me enough syllables, I shall leave the rest to him. On my side, I will get to work on the music so as to banish from it all the noisy instruments, such as the kettledrum and the trumpet. There shall be heard in my orchestra only oboes, flutes, French horns, and violins—these last with mutes, of course. My only task shall be to fit the words to the airs, which will not be difficult since both will be ready-made according to measure.

[1] See pp. 43 and 94.

As a result, the part of Armide will cease to be 'a monotonous and wearisome screaming.' She will be an enchantress, and I will see to it that she sings an air of such regularity and squareness—to say nothing of tenderness—that the most flighty belle in the audience will be able to hear it without the slightest feeling of annoyance.

If some pedant should come to me and say, 'Please take care that Armide outraged does not express herself like Armide intoxicated with love,' I shall retort, 'I do not want to *frighten the ear* of M. de la Harpe; I do not want to *parody Nature*—rather would I embellish it; hence instead of making Armide *scream*, I will make her lull you.' He may insist and remind me that Sophocles did not scruple to show the Athenians an Oedipus with bloodstained eyes, and that the recitative or sung declamation of this beautiful tragedy must have exhibited the eloquent sorrows of this unfortunate king in the accents of acute suffering; but I shall tell my critic that M. de la Harpe 'does not want to hear the cries of a man in pain.'

Have I not, sir, truly caught the meaning of your teaching? I have shown your remarks to several of my friends, one of whom said to me in returning them, 'You should be grateful. M. de la Harpe gives you excellent advice. He has written his musical credo; do the like for him. Read his poetical and critical works and note down whatever displeases you. Now some people maintain that criticism has no effect but to wound the artist whom it concerns; and to prove this they say that poets have never been so much criticized as now, and have never been worse. But ask the journalists about this and see whether they think anything more useful to the State than their reviews. Some, again, may object that it is not your business as a musician to judge of poetry, but no one can find this more surprising than to see a poet and man of letters dogmatize about music.'

Thus my friend. His reasoning seemed to me very sound. But despite the gratitude I owe to you, Sir, I feel that after all I cannot reciprocate as I should. I am too afraid of incurring the fate of the lecturer who, in Hannibal's presence, made a long speech on the art of war.

JOSEPH HAYDN

To Fräulein Leonore ——?, later Frau Lechner

Esterhazy, July 6, 1776

Mademoiselle!

You will not take it in bad part if I hand over to you a hodgepodge in place of what you requested:[1] to describe such things in orderly fashion takes time, which I have not got; hence I did not dare write direct to Mons. Zoller himself,[2] and I hereby beg forgiveness.

I send only a crude sketch, for neither pride nor fame causes me to comply with the request but only the extreme kindness and the persuasive satisfaction expressed by such a truly learned *National* Society about my earlier works.

I was born on the last day of March 1733[3] in the small market town of Rohrau in Lower Austria, near Bruck on the Leitha. My late father, a wheelwright by trade and a subject of Count Harrach's, was by nature a great lover of music. He played the harp without knowing a note, and I, as a boy of five, was able to sing correctly after him all his simple little pieces. This led my father to send me to a relative of ours, the school director at Hainburg, where I was to learn the rudiments of music, together with other youthful essentials. God Almighty, to whom alone I owe these immeasurable blessings, gave me especially in music so much facility, that already in my sixth year I could sing with confidence some few masses in the choir, as well as play a little on the violin and clavier.

In my seventh year the late Herr Kapellmeister von Reutter, who was travelling by chance through Hainburg, heard my still feeble yet pleasing voice. He took me at once with him in the Chapel house, where together with ordinary studies I learned under very good masters the arts of singing, clavier, and violin. I sang soprano both at St. Stephen's and at the Court until my eighteenth year, and was much applauded. When I finally lost my voice, I had to scurry about painfully, devoting myself to the instruction of the young for eight full

---

[1] For transmission to Ignaz de Lucca, who was compiling a Who's Who, *Das gelehrte Oesterreich.*

[2] Possibly the landscape painter Franz Carl Zoller (1748–1829), who had conveyed the request.

[3] It seems that Haydn, though an eyewitness, mistakes here: he was born in 1732.

years. *N.B.*: in this miserable breadwinning many a genius is ruined, having no time for study.

This experience was unfortunately mine. I should never have accomplished the slightest thing if I had not zealously kept composing at night. I wrote diligently, though I was not thoroughly trained, until I had the good fortune to study the genuine fundamentals of composition with the renowned Herr Porpora, who was at that time in Vienna.[1] Finally, on the recommendation of the late Herr von Fürnberg (who was especially good to me), I was appointed music director at Count von Morzin's, and thereafter Kapellmeister at the Prince's,[2] where I hope to live my days and die.

Among my works the following have had the best reception: the operas—*Le Pescatrice*, *L'incontro improviso*, which has been produced before her Imperial Majesty, *L'infedeltà delusa*; the oratorio *Il ritorno di Tobia*, performed in Vienna.

The *Stabat Mater*, about which I received from a good friend the written (but undeserved) praise of our great master Hasse.[3] As long as I live I shall keep that written word like precious gold, not for what is said in it, but as coming from so great a man.

In the chamber style I have had the good fortune to please almost all the nations of the earth except the people of Berlin—as is shown by the public prints and other writings that have reached me. My only wonder is that the otherwise reasonable Berliners seem to find no happy medium when criticizing my works. In one weekly sheet they raise me to the skies; in another they hurl me sixty fathoms deep into the sea; and all this without explaining why. I know very well why: it's because they are not in a position to perform this or that of my works properly; from self-esteem they do not take the trouble to penetrate them truly. And there are still other causes which with God's help I shall account for at the proper time.

Herr Kapellmeister von Dittersdorf[4] of Silesia wrote to me not long ago begging me to refute their harsh attitude. I answered that

---

[1] Nicola Antonio Porpora (1686–1766), opera composer of the Neapolitan school.

[2] Prince Nikolaus Joseph Esterhazy.

[3] Johann Adolf Hasse (1699–1783); pupil of Alessandro Scarlatti and Porpora; composer of operas and sacred music; long musical director at Dresden.

[4] Karl Ditters von Dittersdorf (1739–99).

one swallow does not make a summer: it may be that soon enough their mouths will be stopped by impartial people, and they will change their tune from sheer boredom. In spite of all this they go to much trouble to procure all my works, as the Imperial Ambassador to Berlin, Baron van Swieten,[1] assured me when he was in Vienna this past winter.

Enough of this.

Dear Mademoiselle Leonore!

You will be good enough to submit the present letter to Mons. Zoller, for his sound judgment, adding my best compliments:

my greatest ambition consists only in being justly considered by all the world an honest man—which is what I am. Any tributes of praise I dedicate to Almighty God, to whom alone I am indebted for them:

and my sole wish is never to offend my neighbour or my gracious Prince—still less my infinitely merciful God.

For the rest I remain, Mademoiselle, with all respects,
                    Your sincere friend and obedient servant,
                              Josephus Haydn in his own hand

---

[1] Austrian diplomat (1734–1803) who translated for Haydn the text of *The Creation* and *The Seasons*.

NAPOLEON

To Fouché, Minister of Police

Potsdam, October 25, 1806

I enclose my approval of the voucher for the expense of putting on the ballet *Ulysses' Return*. Get a report on the details of this work and go to the first performance to make sure there is nothing wrong in it —you understand what I mean. The subject incidentally strikes me as excellent. It was I who suggested it to Gardel.

N.[1]

To Cambacérès, Arch-Chancellor

Berlin, November 21, 1806

While the army does its best to honour the nation, the men of letters, it would seem, do their best to dishonour it. I read yesterday the wretched verses that were sung at the [Paris] Opera. Really, it is a mockery. Why do you allow such improvisations to be sung there— they are only fit for vaudeville. Convey my displeasure to M. de Luçay. It was the business of M. de Luçay and the Minister of the Interior to see to it that something decent be performed. To accomplish this, it must of course be commissioned three months in advance, and not played any sooner. I hear a complaint that we have no literature. It is the fault of the Minister of Interior. It is absurd to order an eclogue from a poet as if one were ordering a new dress. The Minister should have taken steps toward the preparation of hymns for December Second.[2] If he has not already done so for this year, tell him to start making his arrangements now for next year.

N.

To M. de Rémusat, First Chamberlain

Paris, March 2, 1810

There should be given on May 26, *The Death of Abel*;[3] on Easter Monday the ballet *Perseus and Andromeda*;[4] then *The Bayadères*;[5] two

---

[1] Napoleon's signature has been reproduced in facsimile in the centre of each endpaper of this book.

[2] The anniversary of the Coronation.

[3] Opera by Rodolphe Kreutzer.

[4] By Gardel, music by Méhul.

[5] By Catel.

weeks after *Sophocles*,[1] *Armide*[2] in midsummer, *The Danaïdes*[3] in the autumn, and *The Sabine Women*[4] by the end of May. In general, my plan is to provide as many novelties as possible during the month of Easter, since there will be a large number of visitors in Paris for the festivities.

N.

---

[1] By Fiocchi.
[2] By Gluck.
[3] By Salieri.
[4] Ballet by Milon, music by Berton.

LORD BYRON

To John Murray

Venice, February 20, 1818

. . . Tomorrow night I am going to see *Otello*, an opera from our *Othello*, and one of Rossini's best, it is said. It will be curious to see in Venice the Venetian story itself represented, besides to discover what they will make of Shakespeare in music.

To Samuel Rogers

Venice, March 3, 1818

. . . They have been crucifying *Othello* into an opera (*Otello*, by Rossini): the music good but lugubrious; but as for the words, all the real scenes with Iago cut out, and the greatest nonsense inserted; the handkerchief turned into a *billet-doux*, and the first singer would not *black* his face, for some exquisite reasons assigned in the preface. Scenery, dresses, and music very good.

To John Cam Hobhouse

Venice, May 17, 1819

There has been a splendid opera lately at San Benedetto, by Rossini, who came in person to play the harpsichord. The people followed him about, cut off his hair 'for memory'; he was shouted, and sonnetted, and feasted, and immortalized much more than either of the Emperors. . . . Think of a people frantic for a fiddler, or at least an inspirer of fiddlers.

I doubt if they will do much in the liberty line.

LUDWIG VAN BEETHOVEN

To Therese von Malfatti

[1807]

Here, honoured Therese, you have what I promised you, and were it not for most serious impediments you would be receiving even more, if only to show you that I always perform more for my friends than I promise. I hope and trust that you are pleasantly occupied and are having an agreeable time, though not too agreeable, so that you may also think of us.

It would probably be asking too much of you, or presuming too far on my own value, if I imputed to you the sentiment, 'People are not together only when side by side; even the absent one lives in us still.' Who would think of ascribing such a thing to the sprightly T. who takes life as it comes?

Amid your occupations, don't forget the piano or, indeed, music in general. You have such a talent for it, why not cultivate it thoroughly? You who have such an instinct for all that is beautiful and good, why not put it to use, and thus come to discern in this high art the perfection which shines down even on such as we.

I live very quietly and alone. Though now and then lights might arouse me, since you all left I feel in me a void here which nothing can fill. Over this feeling even my hitherto faithful art has been powerless. Your piano is ordered and you will soon have it. What a difference you will find between the theme I improvised one evening and the way I recently wrote it down for you! Make this out for yourself, but don't drink punch to help you. How lucky you are to be in the country so early! I shan't be able to enjoy that happiness till the eighth. I rejoice like a child at the thought of wandering among woods, copses, trees, grass, rocks. No man loves the country more than I do; for woods, trees, and rocks echo the thing man yearns for.

Soon you will receive some new compositions of mine, whose difficulties will not cause you to complain very much. Have you read Goethe's *Wilhelm Meister* or Schlegel's translation of Shakespeare? One has so much leisure in the country that you might like me to send you these to read.

By chance it happens that I have an acquaintance in your neighbourhood, so perhaps you'll see me appear some morning early, spend half a hour with you, and be off again. You see that I plan to cause you the shortest period of boredom possible.

Remember me kindly to your father and mother, though I have as yet no right to claim this privilege—also to your cousin Mm.[1] Farewell, my honoured T., I wish you all that is good and beautiful in life. Remember me with gladness, forget my mad deeds, and be assured that no one more than I can wish to know you happy and prospering, and this even though you have little concern for

Your most devoted servant and friend
Beethoven

N.B. It would be really nice of you to drop me a line saying how I can be of service to you.

To George Thomson in Edinburgh[2]

Vienna, July 17, 1810

Sir:

Here, Sir, are the Scottish airs, the greater part of which I composed *con amore* as a token I wished to give of my esteem for the Scottish and English nations by cultivating their national songs. As regards the repeat in the songs I composed for two voices, you may omit them at will and have them sung *senza replica*. Since I did not know whether or not any of those airs had more than one stanza, I had to compose them in such a way that they could be repeated if need be. Hence you will have to adjust them—to leave the repeats in the airs for more than one stanza and omit them for the rest.

I should greatly like to have the words of these Scottish songs, so as to make use of them in Germany as soon as you have published them in Scotland. You could even send them to me at once; I would have them translated and then wait for the notice of publication in Scotland. I would ask you to write out the words under the notes—just the melody.

As for the three quintets [?] and three sonatas, I accept your offer and trust they will suit you. You can have the hundred and twenty pounds sterling or the two hundred and forty ducats paid in two instalments and in specie—the first half when I shall deliver the three quintets, the second half on delivery of the three sonatas, or vice versa.

---

[1] This is said to allude to the Baroness Magdalene Gudenus.
[2] The original is in French.

As regards the airs with English words, I shall make you a very low price, to show you how much I want to serve you. That is why I am asking only twenty pounds sterling or forty ducats in cash for these airs. I could not compose them for less without being out of pocket, for I am offered more here for a dozen airs on German words, which present no language difficulties, whereas I have to have the English ones translated and look up questions of pronunciation, all of which is always a burden to me.

And lastly, about the length of time after which I would be allowed to dispose of these works in Germany, I think that six months for the quintets and sonatas and three months for the airs would suffice, counting from the day when you will publish them in Scotland. I must ask you, however, to answer me on this point.

Be assured, Sir, of the high esteem with which I have the honour to be, Sir, your most obedient servant

Ludwig van Beethoven

P.S. I do not want to forget to let you know that I have just received the sum of one hundred and fifty ducats for fifty-three Scottish airs[1] at Fries' banking house.

Several of my symphonies are arranged as quartets or quintets; if these arrangements suited you, I would send them at once. . . .

To Bettina Brentano[2]

Vienna, August 11, 1810

Dearest Friend!

No finer spring than this one—I say that and feel it because I have made your acquaintance. You must have noticed that in society I am just like a fish out of water, who twists and turns helplessly until a well-wishing Galatea throws him back into the mighty ocean. Yes, I was gasping on dry land, dearest Bettina, you caught me at a time when bad humour possessed me quite. But at sight of you it disappeared, I saw at once that you belonged to another world than this absurd one, to which with the best will one cannot listen. I myself am a miserable wretch and yet complain of others!! Of course you forgive me out of the goodness of your heart, which one sees in your

[1] More of these were Irish than Scotch, but, as Thayer has remarked, 'For Beethoven everything was Scotch.'

[2] Later Bettina von Arnim (1785–1859). As a young girl she earned, and returned, the passionate devotion of both Beethoven and Goethe.

glance; and out of your understanding, which lies in your ears—at least your ears know how to flatter when they listen.

My ears, alas, are a blank wall through which I cannot easily hold friendly communication with men. If it were not so!—possibly!— I should have confided more in you. Could I but interpret the deep understanding look in your eyes which moved me so that I shall never forget it. Dear Bettina, dearest girl!—Art! Who understands it? With whom can one converse about this great goddess——!

How I cherish the few days when we gossiped together, or rather, corresponded: I have kept all the little notes that contain your sweet, clever, darling answers. So I can at any rate thank my bad hearing for the fact that the best part of our fugitive talks was noted down. Since you went away I have spent depressing hours, hours of darkness, in which one can do nothing; after you had left I must have walked up and down the Schönbrunner Allee for a full three hours, but I met no angel who could take such a hold on me as you, angel— forgive me, dearest friend, this departure from the key; I must be allowed such skips in order to relieve my heart.

Now, you have written to Goethe about me, haven't you? Oh that I might stick my head in a sack where I would hear and see nothing of the world's goings-on, since you, dearest angel, will not join me. But I shall surely have a letter from you? I feed on hope—it feeds half the world—and has been my nearest neighbour all my life; otherwise, what would have become of me? I send you, written out in my own hand, '*Kennst du das Land*,'[1] in memory of the hour when I met you. I also send you the rest of what I have composed since I parted from you, dear darling heart!—

> *Herz, mein Herz, was soll das geben,*
> *Was bedränget dich so sehr;*
> *Welch ein fremdes, neues Leben*
> *Ich erkenne dich nicht mehr.*[2]

Yes, dearest friend, you must answer me, you must write and say what will happen to me now that my heart has become such a rebel. Write to your most faithful friend

Beethoven

[1] Mignon's song in Goethe's *Wilhelm Meister*.
[2] 'Oh my heart, what is it that oppresses thee so?
What is this strange new feeling—I recognize thee not.'

To Louis Schlösser[1]

Vienna, May 6, 1823

Herewith, my dear Schlösser, a letter to Cherubini[2] and one to Schlesinger, the publisher.[3] The latter's address you must find out by asking here at Steiner's in Paternostergässerl. Just say that I am sending you there with a recommendation to Herr Haslinger.[4] Tell Cherubini all the kind things you can think of, tell him my most ardent wish is that we should soon have a new *opera* by him, and that, altogether, I respect him above all our contemporaries. I hope he received my letter and I am really eager to have a few lines from him. Also ask Schlesinger whether he received and delivered my letter to Cherubini and why I have not received my author's copies of the Sonata in C Minor.[5] I do beg you to write to me at once from Paris on both matters, i.e., Cherubini and Schlesinger.[6] At the Paris post office, where letters are simply put in a letter box, one must especially not forget to add the postage, otherwise the letters are kept there and cannot be obtained except by writing to Paris for them.[7] Heaven grant you all good things, I shall always be happy to know what you are doing.

Your devoted

Beethoven

To Anton Schindler

May [?] 1824

Papageno, don't talk of what I said about Prussia.[8] It is of no importance—only something like Martin Luther's *Table Talk*. I likewise

---

[1] Darmstadt Kapellmeister who was then in Vienna and on friendly terms with Beethoven.

[2] Italian composer, long resident in Paris, where he headed the Conservatoire from 1822 till his death in 1842.

[3] German music firm with offices in both Berlin and Paris.

[4] Tobias Haslinger, assistant, later head, of Steiner's, Beethoven's publisher.

[5] Opus 111.

[6] Beethoven had written to Cherubini on March 15 asking him to induce the King of France to subscribe to the publication of the *Missa Solemnis*.

[7] Postage stamps were not yet in use, though prepaid mailing was displacing the original system of charge-on-delivery.

[8] In retaliation for what Beethoven took to be ill usage by the Secretary of the Prussian Embassy. 'Papageno' and the sentence at the end of the paragraph about Beethoven's brother are a double allusion to Mozart's *Magic Flute*.

request my brother not to give the sign and say nothing about it, whether at the upper or lower end of the Selchwurstgasse.

. . . Inquire of that arch-scoundrel Diabelli when the French copy of the Sonata in C Minor¹ is to be printed, so that I can have proofs to correct. I have stipulated as well that there shall be four copies for myself, of which one is to be on fine paper for the *Cardinal*.² If he acts in his usual stiff-necked way, I will sing to him personally the bass aria in his own ancestral hall so that the vault and the ditch shall both resound with it.³

Your most obedient servant
Beethoven

*To King George IV of England*⁴

[*c.* 1823]

In the year 1813, at the desire of a number of English gentlemen residing here, the undersigned took the liberty of sending to Your Majesty his work entitled *Wellington's Battle and Victory at Vittoria*, which at that time no one else possessed. Prince Razoumovsky, who was then ambassador here, undertook to forward the work to Your Majesty by courier.

For many years the undersigned nursed the sweet hope that Your Majesty would most graciously let him know that the work had been duly received; but to this date he has not been able to boast of this good fortune and has had to content himself with the brief message of his excellent pupil, Herr Ries,⁵ who informed him that Your Majesty had most graciously condescended to hand over the aforesaid work to the music directors, Mr. Salomon and Mr. Smart,⁶ with a view to having it publicly performed in Drury Lane Theatre. The

---

¹ Opus 111. Beethoven had already revised his own text several times but wanted it back once more.

² Beethoven's pupil, Archduke Rudolph of Austria, became Cardinal-Archbishop of Olmütz in 1819.

³ Diabelli adroitly replied that he would note down this 'aria,' publish it and pay for it—which pacified the composer.

⁴ Rough draft, not given here in full. The letter was sent but not acknowledged.

⁵ Ferdinand Ries (1784–1838), see pp. 165ff.

⁶ J. P. Salomon, a native of Bonn, settled in London, where he died in 1815, so highly esteemed as a musician that he was buried in Westminster Abbey. Mr. Smart (later Sir George) was a violinist, an organist, and a composer (1776–1867).

English newspapers announced this and added, as did Herr Ries, that this work was received with extraordinary success in London and everywhere else.

Since it has been vexing to the undersigned that he should learn of all this only indirectly, Your Majesty will surely forgive him on account of his sensitiveness, and graciously allow him to observe that he has spared neither time nor expense to present this work to Your Majesty in as worthy a way as possible, with a view to affording Your Majesty pleasure.

From the foregoing facts the undersigned concludes that matters may have been placed before Your Majesty in a wrong light, and as the present most submissive request gives him another opportunity to approach Your Majesty, he takes the liberty of forwarding to Your Majesty the enclosed engraved copy of the *Battle of Vittoria* in full score. It was already prepared for this very purpose in the year 1815, and has been held back for this long time solely owing to the uncertainty in which the undersigned felt about this whole matter.

Convinced of the great wisdom and grace with which Your Majesty has always shown esteem and favour to art and artists, the undersigned flatters himself that Your Majesty will take this into account and will feel disposed to grant his most humble request.[1]

---

[1] Presumably to subscribe to the publication of the *Missa Solemnis*.

THOMAS LOVELL BEDDOES

To Bryan Waller Procter

Milan, June 8, 1824

Dear Procter,

If I do not dream, this is the city of Sforza, and today I have seen a picture of his wife by Leonardo da Vinci. Paris, Lyons, Turin, and Novara, and beautiful Chambéry in its bed of vines, they have passed before me like the Drury Lane diorama, and I almost doubt whether I have been sitting in the second tier or on the top of the diligence. Paris is far preferable to London as a place of amusement, and the manner of the lower orders is strikingly superior to that of their island equals. I saw the opera; the ballet much better than ours, but the music was French; the house is not nearly so commodious or elegant as Drury Lane, and the painting and mechanism of their scenery is not so dexterous and brilliant. The Teatro della Scala in this city I have not yet seen; it is considered only inferior to the San Carlo at Naples. . . .

June 9. Since I began this letter I have been to the top of the cathedral, and in the pit of the Teatro della Scala. The former is the finest church externally which I have seen; but the interior of Westminster's old Abbey is triumphant over the marble simplicity of the Milanese's conclave. . . .

Now for Della Scala. It is a vast theatre—six tiers of boxes, all hung with silk, disposed like our window curtains, of a light blue or yellow colour; the pit, I should think, almost twice as large as Covent Garden's. The opera was *Tancredi*[1]—Madame Sesta, the prima donna, old but generally preferred to Pasta; the primo basso a most extraordinary singer, with tones more like those of an organ than any human creature. The scenery is not, in my opinion, equal to the best at our theatres. One of the drops was a sort of Flemish painting, the subject a village carnival, very well executed. Such a thing would be novel at C.G.[2] if it could be well, but it must be very well done. Now that silk is so cheap too I think they might be a little more lavish of draperies; but we are not managers yet. The ballet, *i baccanali aboliti*[3] incalculably

[1] By Rossini (1813). Mme. Sesta eludes further identification.
[2] Covent Garden opera house in London.
[3] Author and composer untraceable.

superior to ours or the French in the exquisite grace of the grouping, the countless abundance of dancers, and the splendours and truth of costume and decoration. The house was about one-third full, and the people all talking, so that there was a buzz outbuzzing the Royal Exchange all night, except during '*di tanti palpiti.*'[1]

And what else have I seen? A beautiful and far-famed insect; do not mistake, I mean neither the Emperor of Austria nor the King of Sardinia, but a much finer specimen of creation—the firefly. Their bright light is evanescent, and alternates with the darkness; as if the swift wheeling of the earth struck fire out of the black atmosphere. . . . Tonight at twelve I leave Milan and shall be at Florence on Saturday long before this letter tastes the atmosphere (*pardonnez*—I mean the smoke) of London.

There and here,

Yours truly T.L.B.

P.S. If you see Mrs. Shelley, ask her to remember me, and tell her that I am as anxious to change countries with her, as she can be. If I could be any use in bringing the portrait[2] etc., it would be a proud task, but most likely I only flash over Florence: entering on the flood of the stars, and departing with their ebb.

[1] 'O agitated heart,' contralto aria from *Tancredi*.
[2] Of Shelley, to be used in the posthumous edition of his poems.

THE MENDELSSOHNS

Abraham Mendelssohn-Bartholdy to his children

Paris, July 2, 1819

You, my dear Felix,[1] must say precisely what kind of music paper you want—ruled or not ruled, and if the former, you must tell me exactly how it is to be ruled. When I went into a shop the other day to buy some, I found I had no idea myself what I was trying to buy. Read over your letter before sending it, and ask yourself whether, supposing it sent to you, you could understand what it says and could do the errand required.

Salomon-Bartholdy to his brother-in-law Abraham

1821

I cannot wholly agree with you about not indicating positively to Felix the calling he must follow. It would not interfere with his talent for music, which everybody acknowledges. A professional musician—the idea sticks in my throat. It is no career, no life, nothing to aim at. A man is no farther off at the beginning than at the end, and knows it. In fact, you are usually better off at first than at last. Let the boy study in the regular way and then prepare himself for the Civil Service by studying law at the university. His art will remain his friend and companion. If I understand the way things are going at present, there is more than ever a demand for people who have gone through the university. Should you intend to put him in business, let him enter a counting house early.

Felix to his family

Weimar, November 6, 1821

Now listen, all of you. Today is Tuesday. On Sunday, the Sun of Weimar, Goethe, arrived. We went to church in the morning and heard half of Handel's music to the Hundredth Psalm. The organ, though large, is feeble. The one at St. Mary's [Berlin], small as it is, is much more powerful. The one here has fifty stops, forty-four notes, and one thirty-two-foot pipe.

After church I wrote you that little word dated the fourth, then went to the Elephant Hotel, where I made a sketch of Lucas Cranach's

---

[1] The composer, then aged ten years and five months.

house. Two hours later Professor Zelter came[1] calling out, 'Goethe's come; the old man is here!' We hurried down at once and went to Goethe's house. He was in the garden, just coming around a hedge. Isn't it odd, dear father, that's how it was with you! He is very affable, but I do not think any of his portraits look like him. He then went through his interesting collection of fossils, which has recently been arranged by his son, and he kept repeating, 'H'm, h'm, I'm quite satisfied.'

After that I walked in the garden with him and Professor Zelter for about half an hour. Then to dinner. He does not look like a man of seventy-three, more like fifty. After dinner, Miss Ulrike, Goethe's sister-in-law, asked him for a kiss, and I did too. Every morning I have a kiss from the author of *Faust* and *Werther*, and every afternoon two kisses from my good fatherly friend Goethe. Just think of it!

In the afternoon I played to Goethe for about two hours, Bach fugues and my own improvisations. In the evening they made up a table for whist, and Professor Zelter, who took a hand in the beginning, said, 'Whist means—you're to shut up!' That's one of his clinchers for you.

Zelter at the private rehearsal of Felix's opera The Two Nephews

February 3, 1824[2]

My dear boy, from this day forward you are no longer an apprentice but a journeyman in the brotherhood of musicians. I proclaim your emancipation in the name of Mozart, Haydn, and old father Bach.

Felix to his sister Fanny

Paris, May 9, 1825

Your last letter made me furious—rather! . . . You talk of prejudice and preconceived ideas, of my being morose and querulous, and of the 'land of milk and honey' as you call this Paris. Please stop and think a moment: are you in Paris or am I? Now, then, isn't it likely that I know what's what better than you? Is it my habit to let my judgment of music be influenced by prepossessions? But suppose it

[1] Felix's music teacher as well as an old friend of Goethe's.

[2] Felix's fifteenth birthday. The opera was his fourth. It is in three acts and its subtitle is 'The Uncle from Boston.'

were, is Rode[1] prejudiced when he says to me, 'This place is a musical shambles'? Is Neukomm[2] prejudiced when he says, 'This is no country for orchestras'? Is Herz[3] prejudiced when he says, 'Here the only thing the public likes and understands is variations on popular tunes'? And are ten thousand others prejudiced who damn Paris? . . . Read the *Constitutionnel*: what do they give at the Italian opera except Rossini? Read the catalogues: what do they publish and sell except romances and potpourris? Come and hear *Alceste*[4], come and hear *Robin des bois*;[5] hear the soirées (which, by the way, you've confused with the *salons*: soirées are concerts at which you pay, and salons are musical parties); hear the music in the Royal Chapel—*then* pass judgment and call me down, but not now when *you* are the one who is full of preconceptions and blind with prejudice!

Felix to his family

Heidelberg, September 20, 1827

'O Heidelberg, O wondrous town, where all the day the rain pours down!' That's the sophisticated line, but what care I, a student, a rake-hell, if it rains or not. There are grapes, instrument-makers, newspapers, inns, Thibauts—no, I'm exaggerating—there is *one* Thibaut left, but he's worth six: what a man![6]

. . . It is odd—the man does not know much about music, even his knowledge of musical history is rather limited, he judges mostly by instinct and I understand more than he does, and yet I have learned a great deal from him and am much indebted to him. For he revealed to me the merits of old Italian music and has kindled in me his own enthusiasm for it. His words are aglow with enthusiasm, in fact I must say his language is really flowery. I have just left him, and as I had told him a good deal about Sebastian Bach, and said that he still did

[1] Pierre Rode (1774–1830) French prodigy on the violin and composer of études still in use.

[2] Sigismund von Neukomm (1778–1858), pupil of Haydn, pianist in Talleyrand's household, and composer—it is said—of one thousand works.

[3] Heinrich Herz (1806–88), brilliant German pianist long established in Paris; ridiculed by Schumann.

[4] Gluck's opera.

[5] Weber's *Freischütz* in garbled form.

[6] Anton Friedrich Thibaut (1772–1840), distinguished German jurist and patron of music, collector of ancient Italian scores and author of a treatise on purity in his favourite art.

not know the fountainhead and the principal—which are all to be found in Sebastian—he said as I left, 'Farewell! We shall found our friendship on Luis de Vittoria[1] and Sebastian Bach, as do two lovers who pledge each other to look at the moon and so feel in that way that they are close together.'

Felix to his parents

Cologne, October 2, 1827

[My friends found that they] must be in Berlin by the sixth . . . so that even though I had virtually promised Schelble[2] to go back via Frankfort and attend the performance at the St. Cecilia Society of a Handel oratorio which I did not know, I made up my mind to return with them, the weather being so bad that at Horchheim I could hardly go outdoors. I was about to start last evening when suddenly the clouds left the hills, the mist vanished, the moon rose shining, and news came that on the right bank of the Rhine, all the way from Horchheim to Ehrenbreitstein, the gathering of the grapes would begin day after tomorrow.

At that point Uncle put in a word.[3] He gave me a glowing account of the pleasures and wonders of the grape gathering, and said that two days after it is over he goes himself to Frankfort, where he means to attend the St. Cecilia performance. If I stayed to cheer him and Auntie he would see me back in Berlin. When I argued that I had to finish my piano score,[4] he brought me the most beautiful music paper and demonstrated what a good quiet place I had to work in. So—I gave up. I'm finishing my tedious chore at Horchheim and shall have it behind me when I get home. I shall hear the St. Cecilia concert, to which Schelble is sending out special invitations in my honour. I shall take part in the grape gathering—dear God, forgive me, it is all too beautiful!

[1] Tomás Luis de Victoria (1535?–1611), Spanish composer of sacred music, usually associated with the Roman school of Palestrina.

[2] Johann Nepomuk Schelble (1789–1837), close friend of Beethoven, founder and director of St. Cecilia concerts at Frankfort until his death.

[3] Joseph Mendelssohn, older brother of Felix's father.

[4] Of still another opera, *The Wedding of Camacho*, which had brought forth cabals and criticism.

ROBERT SCHUMANN

To D. G. Otten, Music Director at Hamburg

Dresden, April 2, 1849

Honoured Sir:

You must think very badly of me for having waited so long to answer your kind note. I have in fact thought both of you and of your letter quite often—and gratefully—but will now make no more excuses, except the old one of the musician's laziness about writing words. We all prefer to deal with notes.

I wrote the symphony[1] in December 1845, when I had scarcely got over my illness, and it seems to me that my music betrays as much. Only in the last movement did I begin to feel like myself again, and I really began to recover only after I had finished the whole work. Otherwise it reminds me of a dismal period; that you should nonetheless take a sympathetic interest shows that even such gloomy sounds can find a receptive ear. Everything you say certainly proves that you thoroughly understand the music, and the fact that the doleful bassoon which I took particular pleasure in placing in the adagio did not escape you pleased me best of all.

I have long heard of your energy in promoting good music, especially through your Concertverein. Anything really good gets to be known without articles in the newspapers. Invisible good-natured sprites convey the news by air. For about a year I too have derived much enjoyment from a similar concert society. I refresh myself there with Palestrina, Bach, and other things that one does not hear elsewhere.

Do you know Bach's *Passion According to St. John*, the so-called little one? I'm sure you do! Now, don't you think it is much bolder, more powerful and poetical than the one according to St. Matthew? To me the latter seems to have been written some five or six years earlier. I think it contains tedious parts and is inordinately long. But the other—how compact and full of genius, especially the choruses— and what consummate art! If the world could only attain a solid grasp of such works as that! But no one writes about it. The musical journals make the attempt now and then, but give it up again, because critics lack the needful knowledge and true conviction. That's how it is

[1] In C Major, Op. 61. Otten had performed it and written about the 'melancholy bassoon' in the adagio.

and always will be. But something has to be reserved for the few, scattered artist spirits, and they have indeed Palestrina, Bach, Beethoven's last quartets, etc.

So I greet you with the cordial cry 'Forward together!'—i.e., we will not cease to make known, as far as in us lies, all that we recognize to be great and true. It brings its own reward.

With best regards,

Yours sincerely,

R. Schumann

JOHANN WOLFGANG VON GOETHE

To Carl Zelter[1] in Berlin

Weimar, November 9, 1829

I too have now heard Paganini, and immediately thereafter, the same evening, I had your letter, which gave me to believe that my estimate of these marvels was quite reasonable. I thought they gave something less than enjoyment—which with me is always intermediate between sensation and understanding; something was lacking—a base to this pillar of flame and cloud. . . . This time I felt the lack of the necessary foundation, for both my mind and my ear. I heard only something meteoric, and could give no further account of it to myself. Yet it is curious to hear people, women especially, talk about it. Without any hesitation they give utterance to what are in fact confessions.

[1] See p. 317.

NICOLO PAGANINI

When Paganini arrived in Paris in February 1831—his first visit—he found lithographs on display which depicted him as a convict in chains, as a murderer caught in the act, and other discreditable guises. He addressed his defence to the musicologist, composer, and critic who was also his friend, F.-J. Fétis (1784–1871).

To F.-J. *Fétis, editor of the* Revue Musicale

Paris [1831]

Sir:

The French public has shown me such kindness and has been so generous with its applause that I am forced to believe in the renown which, it is said, preceded me in your city. I am also led to hope that my concerts have not fallen too far below their reputation. But had I any doubts about my notoriety, it would be dispelled by the zeal which I see your artists have used in portraying me and placarding with my name the walls of your capital. Unfortunately, they have not stopped at mere portraits, for walking one day on the Boulevard des Italiens, I saw in an engraver's window a lithograph purporting to depict 'Paganini in Prison.'

Well, said I to myself, here are honest folk using for their profit a certain slander which has dogged me for fifteen years. While I gazed and laughed at this travesty which the artist had tricked out with full details drawn from his imagination, I noticed that a large circle of passers-by had collected around me and, while audibly comparing my features with those of the youth in the picture, were remarking how much I had changed since my prison term.

I then saw that the affair was being taken seriously by those you call, I believe, 'rubbernecks,' and I inferred that the forgery was indeed a good business venture. It occurred to me that since everyone must live, I might as well furnish a few more anecdotes to the portraitists who are good enough to use me in this fashion, and so enlarge their repertory. It is to this end, Sir, that I beg you to publish the present letter in your *Revue Musicale*.

The gentlemen in question have depicted me in prison, but they do not know how I came there; as to which they know exactly as much as I, or as those who first circulated the tale. There are several versions, which could supply as many different subjects for art. It has been said, for example, that having surprised my rival with my mistress, I courageously slew him from behind, at the moment when he was least capable of self-defence. Others have maintained that my jealous fury wreaked itself on my mistress alone, but there is no agreement about the mode of my dispatching her. Some say a dagger, others affirm that I chose to enjoy her sufferings by administering poison. Each has followed his free fancy, and I would extend the same liberty to the lithographers.

At any rate, this is what befell me at Padua about fifteen years ago: I had given a concert there with considerable success. The next day I was seated at the table d'hôte among sixty others—no one had noticed my entrance—when someone expressed his enthusiasm about the effect I had produced on the audience the day before. His neighbour seconded this praise, adding that *'there was nothing surprising in Paganini's virtuosity. It is the result of his being eight years in prison with only his violin to mitigate his solitary confinement. He was convicted for the cowardly murder of one of my friends who happened to be his rival in love.'*

Everyone was indignant, as you may imagine, at the baseness of the crime. Whereupon I spoke up and, addressing myself to the person who was so familiar with my history, begged him to tell me in what place and year this adventure had occurred. Everyone's eye turned to me in astonishment at discovering the chief actor of the tragedy. The narrator was much put out. It was no longer his friend who had perished—it had merely been said—he had been told—or rather he had believed—but no doubt he had been misled—. Thus, my dear Sir, does the reputation of an artist become the plaything of idle talk—the sport of people who are too lazy to imagine that a man can as readily study and practise of his own free will in his room as locked up in a cell.

In Vienna a still more ridiculous rumour arose to test the credulity of some enthusiasts. I had played there some variations entitled *Le Streghe* (*The Witches*). They had proved rather effective; so that a gentleman (who was described to me as pale, melancholy, and rapt of gaze) asserted that he found nothing amazing in my technique, for all through my playing of the variations he had distinctly seen the Devil near me, guiding my bow arm. The Devil's striking resemblance to myself sufficiently proved my ancestry. The Devil was dressed in red, bore horns, and carried his tail between his legs. You can conceive, Sir, that after so minute an identification it was impossible to doubt the report, and many persons were persuaded that they had at last found the secret of what is called my *tours de force*.

My peace of mind was long at the mercy of these stories. I vainly tried to show their absurdity. I pointed out that since the age of fourteen I have never ceased to play before public audiences; that for sixteen years I was orchestra conductor and music director at Lucca; that accordingly if I had spent eight years in prison for killing rival or mistress, it must have been at an earlier time and hence that I must have had this mistress and rival at the age of seven.

In Vienna I called on my ambassador, who testified that he had known me for nearly twenty years as a man of standing and probity, and this did quell for a time the course of slander. But it can never be wholly stilled, and I was scarcely surprised to find it springing out again in Paris. What, Sir, am I to do? I see nothing open to me but to resign myself and let malice do its worst. Perhaps, though, I should apprise you of yet another anecdote that has lent colour to the libellous attacks made upon me.

This is it: a violinist named D——i, resident in Milan, became friendly with a pair of shady characters and was persuaded to join them in an attack on the curate of a neighbouring village, who was reputed to keep a large sum in his house. Fortunately, one of the trio lost heart and denounced the plot to the police, who seized D——i and his accomplice just as they reached the curate's house. They were condemned to twenty years in irons. But General Menou, after he became Governor of Milan, set the musician free after two years. Incredible as it may seem, that is the canvas for the embroidery fashioned to discredit me. A violinist whose name ends in *i* must be Paganini. The plot became the murder of my mistress or rival, so that none but myself could plausibly have been in prison. Still, since I was supposed to develop my new technique there, the irons had to be dispensed with and my arms left free.

I repeat: since they wish it so, against all probability, I must yield. But I cling to one hope, which is that after my death Calumny will let go its prey, and that those who have so cruelly avenged themselves for the reality of my fame will leave my ashes in peace.

Yours, etc.,

Paganini

JOHANNES BRAHMS

This document is made all the more poignant by the likelihood that at the time of writing Brahms and Clara Schumann were lovers.

To Julius Otto Grimm[1]

Heidelberg, September 1856

My dear Julius,

What must you think of me for not answering? Don't be angry! Had you been bright and a little more —— and written to Frau Klara [Schumann], you wouldn't have had to wait.

Rather than make excuses and so on, I'll give you some particulars about those days.

I had spent Schumann's birthday with him—June 8—and found him remarkably changed, suddenly, compared with the previous time. Then Frau Klara came back from England, and just as she arrived so did worse news from Endenich.[2] A week before his death, on the Wednesday, we had a telegraphic dispatch. I barely read, it said roughly this: 'If you wish to see your husband while he still lives, come at once. His appearance is frightful to behold.'

We drove over. He had had an attack which the doctors thought would be fatal. I don't know the right name—an asthmatic seizure? I went to him, saw him in fact in an attack, and so greatly agitated that I, and the doctors too, dissuaded Frau Schumann from going to him and urged her to make the return trip.

Schumann just lay, taking nothing but an occasional spoonful of wine and jelly. Frau Schumann's misery was so great all this while that on Saturday evening I *had* to suggest that she come back again and see him.

Now we give thanks to God that it happened so, for it is now absolutely indispensable for her peace of mind. She saw him again on Sunday, Monday, and early Tuesday. He died in the afternoon about four o'clock.[3]

I cannot ever again experience anything so touching as the reunion of Robert and Klara.

At first he lay a long time with closed eyes, and she kneeled in

---

[1] Organist, conductor, teacher, musicologist, and composer (1827–1903). Brahms roomed with him in Leipzig and they were friends till death.

[2] In the asylum in which Schumann was confined.

[3] July 29, 1856.

front of him, more quietly than one would have thought possible. But he recognized her and again on the following days. Once he desired clearly to embrace her and threw his arms around her.

Of course he was no longer able to speak; one could only make out single words (perhaps imagine them), but even that must have pleased her. He often refused the wine that was offered him, but took it eagerly from her finger, for so long at a time and so ravenously, that one was convinced he recognized the finger.

Tuesday noon Joachim[1] from Heidelberg, which held us up a while in Bonn, otherwise we would have arrived before his death, but we were half an hour too late. He died as easily as you read these words. We should have breathed more freely once he had been released but could hardly believe it.

His death was so gentle that it almost passed unnoticed. His body looked calm, as if all were for the best. It would have been impossible for a woman to stand it much longer.

They buried him Thursday afternoon. I carried the wreath before the coffin, with Joachim and Dietrich.[2] The members of a choral society were pall bearers. There was trumpeting and singing.

The town had prepared ahead of time a beautiful spot for the event and had it decorated with five plane trees. Madame Klara found another kind of consolation in the institution itself. It set at rest all the evil rumours which had come to her ears about things—for example through Bettina—.[3] I might and could write it all to you—somehow —but it wouldn't do. You can imagine for yourself on the strength of these bare facts, how sad, how beautiful, how moving this death was.

We (J[oachim], Kl[ara], and I) have put in order the papers that Schumann left: and that includes all he ever wrote! One comes to love and honour the man more and more as one has these closer dealings with him.

I shall delve deeper and deeper into all this.

Farewell. Forgive the hurried scrawl: there is no peace here for a peaceful letter. We are now in Heidelberg, after a few weeks on Lake Vierwaldstätter.[4]

---

[1] Famous violinist (1831–1907).
[2] Pupil of Schumann's.
[3] Bettina von Arnim (see p. 309) thought Schumann's doctor inadequate.
[4] In Switzerland.

If you write to Frau Schumann and me, address us at Düsseldorf, to which we are returning very soon.

But still here for another week!

My next one will be longer and calmer. Regards to your dear wife. And don't be angry with me.

Affectionately yours,

J. Brahms

(Notwithstanding—I send heartfelt greetings to you and your wife. Kl. Sch.)[1]

P.S. Frau Klara is as well as can be expected, but not so well as one could wish. I forgot that you would ask about her.

Added by Clara Schumann in her own hand.

CHARLES BAUDELAIRE

To Richard Wagner

Paris, February 17, 1860

Dear Sir:

I have always imagined that however used to fame a great artist may be, he cannot be insensible to a sincere compliment, especially when that compliment is like a cry of gratitude; and finally that this cry could acquire a *singular* kind of value when it came from a Frenchman, which is to say from a man little disposed to be enthusiastic, and born, moreover, in a country where people hardly understand painting and poetry any better than they do music. First of all, I want to tell you that I owe you *the greatest musical pleasure I have ever experienced.* I have reached an age when one no longer makes it a pastime to write letters to celebrities,[1] and I should have hesitated a long time before writing to express my admiration for you, if I did not daily come across shameless and ridiculous articles in which every effort is made to libel your genius. You are not the first man, sir, about whom I have suffered and blushed for my country. At length indignation impelled me to give you an earnest of my gratitude; I said to myself, ' I want to stand out from all those imbeciles.'

The first time I went to the Italian Theatre in order to hear your works,[2] I was rather unfavourably disposed and indeed, I must admit, full of nasty prejudices; but I have an excuse: I have been so often duped; I have heard so much music by pretentious charlatans. But you conquered me at once. What I felt is beyond description, and if you will be kind enough not to laugh, I shall try to interpret it for you. At the outset it seemed to me that I knew this new music, and later, on thinking it over, I understood whence came this mirage; it seemed to me that this music was *mine*, and I recognized it in the way that any man recognizes the things he is destined to love. To anybody but an intelligent man, this statement would be immensely ridiculous, especially when it comes from one who, like me, *does not know music,*

---

[1] Baudelaire was thirty-nine, but still obscure, or else unfavourably known for his *Fleurs du Mal* published three years earlier.

[2] Wagner had just given three concerts there, consisting chiefly of overtures and choral excerpts from his earlier operas. The *Tristan* prelude was the only recent work.

and whose whole education consists in having heard (most pleasurably, to be sure) some few fine pieces by Weber and Beethoven.

Next, the thing that struck me most was the character of grandeur. It depicts what is grand and incites to grandeur. Throughout your works I found again the solemnity of the grand sounds of Nature in her grandest aspects, as well as the solemnity of the grand passions of man. One feels immediately carried away and dominated. One of the strangest pieces, which indeed gave me a new musical sensation, is the one intended to depict a religious ecstasy.[1] The effect produced by the Entrance of the Guests and the Wedding Fête[2] is tremendous. I felt in it all the majesty of a larger life than ours. Another thing: quite often I experienced a sensation of a rather bizarre nature, which was the pride and the joy of understanding, of letting myself be penetrated and invaded—a really sensual delight that resembles that of rising in the air or tossing upon the sea. And the music at the same time would now and then resound with the pride of life. Generally these profound harmonies seemed to me like those stimulants that quicken the pulse of the imagination. Finally, and I entreat you not to laugh, I also felt sensations which probably derive from my own turn of mind and my most frequent concerns. There is everywhere something rapt and enthralling, something aspiring to mount higher, something excessive and superlative. For example, if I may make analogies with painting, let me suppose I have before me a vast expanse of dark red. If this red stands for passion, I see it gradually passing through all the transitions of red and pink to the incandescent glow of a furnace. It would seem difficult, impossible even, to reach anything more glowing; and yet a last fuse comes and traces a whiter streak on the white of the background. This will signify, if you will, the supreme utterance of a soul at its highest paroxysm.

I had begun to write a few meditations on the pieces from *Tannhäuser* and *Lohengrin* that we listened to; but I soon saw the impossibility of saying everything.[3]

Similarly, this letter could go on interminably. If you have been able to read it through, I thank you. It only remains for me to add a few words. From the day when I heard your music, I have said to

[1] Baudelaire means the overture to *Lohengrin*.

[2] From *Tannhäuser*, Act II, and *Lohengrin*, Act III, respectively.

[3] Baudelaire did publish an article on Wagner and his music about a year later, reproducing verbatim some of the remarks in this letter.

myself endlessly, and especially at bad times, '*If I only could hear a little Wagner tonight!*' There are doubtless other men constituted like myself. After all, you must have been pleased with the public, whose instinct proved far superior to the false science of the journalists. Why not give us a few more concerts, adding some new pieces? You have given us a foretaste of new delights—have you the right to withhold the rest? Once again, Sir, I thank you; you brought me back to myself and to what is great, in some unhappy moments.

Ch. Baudelaire

I do not set down my address because you might think I wanted something from you.

EMMANUEL CHABRIER

To the publisher Costallat

[*c.* 1883]

'I now know *The Tempest* by heart; there are many good things in it, but Blau[1] is right to want some expanding of the love story, otherwise Papa Prospero would get to be a bore. As for *drama*, properly so called, where is it? Are they really dramatic, those conspiracies among old ward-heelers—Alonzo, Antonio, Gonzalvo, Stefano? And those two crapulous rakes, Caliban and Interpocula[2]—who cares a rap about their backtracking across that island?

So—the business will have to be spiced up on t'other side. But we have, first, the idyll between Ferdinand and Miranda—of the finest colour; second, the whole nuptial atmosphere and the spirits of the air in Act IV; not to mention, thirdly, a good bit of buffoonery with all the topers. Is that enough to make an opera? We'll see. But the fellow's first scene, at sea, is a poser: it's exactly *The Flying Dutchman* overture, which, alas, is not by me. It's a terror to do over again. Tempests and shipwrecks—*brr!* And after Wagner and Beethoven—*double brrr!* We must wait!

[1] The librettist.
[2] 'Between-cups,' i.e., Shakespeare's Trinculo.

SYDNEY SMITH

My dear Lady Holland,[1]

I have not the heart, when an amiable lady says, 'Come to *Semiramis* in my box,' to decline; but I get bolder at a distance. *Semiramis* would be to me pure misery. I love music very little—I hate acting; I have the worst opinion of Semiramis herself, and the whole thing (I cannot help it) seems so childish and so foolish that I cannot abide it. Moreover, it would be rather out of etiquette for a Canon of St. Paul's to go to an opera, and where etiquette prevents me from doing things disagreeable to myself, I am a perfect martinet.

All these things considered, I am sure you will not be a Semiramis to me, but let me off.

Sydney Smith

---

[1] Charming and tyrannical leader of the famous Whig salon, Holland House. She was then a widow, the third Baron Holland having died in 1840. Sydney Smith's daughter, also Lady Holland, was the wife of the eminent physician Sir Henry Holland. *Semiramis*: Rossini's opera (1823).

GIUSEPPE VERDI

To Giuseppina Appiani[1]

Paris, August 22, 1847

I owe you a great many letters, but you'll forgive me when I tell you all I have had to do here. Quite another thing than London, the Opera here! Just imagine being all day between two poets, two managers, two publishers—they always come in pairs; getting a prima donna engaged; working up the subject of a libretto, etc., etc., I tell you it's enough to drive one mad—But I have no intention of going mad, and I defy the whole tribe of opera-mongers, all the Parisians, all the papers *pro* and *con*, as well as the comic squibs in the *Charivari* and *Entr'acte*. Speaking of *Entr'acte*, you will find there a very funny article about me. I think Emanuele Muzio[2] took it with him to Milan —get him to show it to you.

I shall be here until about November 20, and at the end of that month I shall be admiring the cupola of the Duomo.

My health is better than in London. I enjoy Paris less than London and I have in fact an extreme dislike for the boulevards (hush! let no one hear my heresy!).

You ask for some account of Donizetti,[3] and I shall give you the news as it is, however painful. I have not seen him yet, having been advised not to, but I assure you I very much want to see him and if opportunity offers without its being known by anyone, I shall certainly do so. His physique is in good shape, except that he always holds his head bent over his chest and his eyes closed; he eats and sleeps well and says hardly a word, or if he does it is quite indistinct. When someone approaches, he opens his eyes for a moment, and if he is told 'shake hands,' he does it. It seems this is a sign that his mind is not all gone; and yet a doctor who is also his very close friend was telling me that these acts are done from habit and that it would be better if he were lively and even violently mad. There might then be some hope; as he is now, only a miracle could help. But on the other hand he is still as he was six months ago, a year ago—no better, no worse. Such is Donizetti's actual condition now. It is dreadful, it is

[1] Née Contessa Stripelli, friend and confidante of Verdi's early years.

[2] See p. 172.

[3] Composer of many operas. Born in 1797, his mind gave way in the mid-forties and he died in 1848.

just too dreadful! If there is any cheerful news I shall write to you instantly.

To Giuseppe Mazzini

Paris, October 18, 1848

I am sending you the hymn, even if a little late, but I hope it will arrive on time. I have tried to make it as popular and easy as I could. Do with it what you like; burn it if you think it not worthy. If you publish it, have the poet change some of the words at the beginning of the first and second stanzas, in which it would be good to have phrases of five syllables, with different meanings each time, as in the other stanzas—'We swear it,' 'Sound the trumpets,' etc., etc. And of course, end the verse with a slide. In the fourth line of stanza two, the question must be altered to a positive and the meaning stopped with the verse. I could have set it as it stands, but then the music would have been less easy, hence less popular, and we would have missed our aim.

May this hymn, amid the music of cannon, soon be sung on the plains of Lombardy!

To Tito Ricordi[1]

October 24, 1855

... I know you can say 'I have the right to do this; the law allows it.' I know, I know. But I had hoped you would never use that kind of nonsense against me—me who have so often performed more than I promised or was obliged to; me who am to such a large extent the source of your colossal fortune. ... Now, the sole condition—I asked no money whatever—was to have my scores printed correctly and properly published, and the latest ones are perfect travesties. ...

But who cares about an artist's reputation! I can't help remarking on a discouraging fact, which is that during my already long career I have always found managers, publishers, etc., etc., hard, unyielding, implacable, ready to appeal to the contract or the law-book—honeyed words and harsh deeds. I've never been considered anything but an object, a tool, to be used as long as it produces. It is sad to say but true.

[1] Head of the Milan publishing firm of the same name, lifelong friend of Verdi.

To Signor Filippi

Genoa, March 4, 1869

Dear Sir:

I cannot possibly be offended by your article in *Perseveranza* on *La Forza del Destino*. If you felt obliged, amid much praise, to add a little blame, this was wholly within your rights and you did well so to write. You must know, in any case, that I never complain of attacks, any more than I send thanks (perhaps there I am wrong) for favourable reviews. I love my own independence in all things, and I respect it in others. I am particularly grateful to you for your reserved attitude during my stay in Milan. Since you were to write about my opera, it was best not to let yourself be influenced by a handshake or a visit paid or received. As regards your article, since you ask me about it, I am free to tell you that it did not, and could not, displease me.

I knew nothing of the incident between you and Ricordi, but it may be that Giulio, who, I believe, prefers Donna Leonora's aria to many other compositions, was a little put out to find it impugned as an imitation of Schubert. If it is indeed that, then I am as surprised as Giulio, for, musical ignoramus that I am, it's years since I have heard Schubert's 'Ave Maria,' and it would have been hard for me to copy it. Don't think that when I speak of my *extreme ignorance of music* I am pretending. It is the simple truth. In my house there is hardly any music to be seen; I have never stepped into a music library, nor gone to a publisher's to read a piece. I keep up with the best contemporary operas, not by study, but by hearing them occasionally at the theatre. In all this, I have a purpose that you will easily guess. Hence I repeat to you that of all composers, past or present, I am the least erudite. Let us be clear about this—and I say again, I am not 'putting on' anything—when I refer to *erudition* I do not mean musical *knowledge*. I should be lying if I pretended that in my youth I did not study long and hard. That is why I now have a hand strong enough to shape sound as I like, and sure enough to obtain, usually, the effects that I imagine. And when I write something contrary to the rules, that is because the strict rule does not give me what I want, and because I do not really believe that the rules hitherto in force are all good. The textbooks of counterpoint need revising.

What a long letter! And what's worse, much of it is useless! Forgive me, please, and accept my sincere greetings.

FRANZ SCHUBERT

Vienna, November 12, 1828

Dear Schober:[1]

I am ill. I have had nothing to eat or drink for eleven days now, and can only stagger feebly and uncertainly between armchair and bed. Rinna[2] is treating me. If I take food I cannot keep it down.

So please be good enough to help me out in this desperate state with something to read. I have read Cooper's *Last of the Mohicans*, *The Spy*, *The Pilot*, and *The Pioneers*. If by any chance you have anything else of his, do please leave it for me with Frau von Bogner at the coffeehouse. My brother, who is responsibility personified, will bring it over to me without fail. Or indeed anything else.

Your friend,
Schubert

[1] Franz von Schober, a well-born youth only a few months younger than Schubert, became his devoted friend, patron, and room-mate.

[2] Ernst Rinna von Sarenbach, Court physician. Schubert died of typhus on the nineteenth.

Maxims
&
Good Stories

WISDOM & FAITH

Music has always been interwoven with my life—so much so that I can hardly imagine the one without the other. I am not sure that this is altogether a good thing, but it is too late now to change. With the passing of time I have learned to wean myself away from certain musical influences, and especially not to think of music as a refuge in times of trouble. On the contrary, it is just at those times that I avoid it. I no longer want to hear music except when I am serene and, if possible, happy. But to coddle one's melancholy by feeding it with the accumulated sadness of the Nocturnes—none of that!

JULIAN GREEN, *Journal* (1938)

I felt that besides wanting to hear music, I wanted to know things about music. I likewise felt that there was much to learn from other people's musical experiences and study of music. In due course, I learnt to take nothing on trust, not even praise or blame emanating from the writers whom I considered soundest and most sensitive and thoughtful; for I encountered a bewildering discrepancy of views. Here were two authors who agreed in their appraisement of Beethoven and Wagner but disagreed in their appraisement of Berlioz; another two agreed on Beethoven, Wagner, and Berlioz, but disagreed on Liszt; others, agreeing on Beethoven, Wagner, Liszt, and Berlioz would disagree on Strauss or Hugo Wolf, and so on.

M. D. CALVOCORESSI, *Musical Taste* (1925)

In every period the alarm sounds: 'Today we have no great musicians, poets, painters.' This is due to the fact that traditionally one keeps looking at the sequence of geniuses, which appears like an avenue of trees seen in foreshortened perspective, much thicker than in reality. Between one genius and the next is an average distance of half a century. They represent in fact the results acquired along the way. Between one genius and the next the talents are at work; they represent the links joining the two end points.

Let it therefore be the task and care of the contemporaries to recognize and appreciate the worth of these men of talents who conserve and connect. The geniuses, whatever the contemporaries may say, stand solid and rear their heights in full view. But contemporaries see only what they believe in and what they wish to believe; and they may not believe in what they see and what they hear.

FERRUCCIO BUSONI, Reflections (1921)

. . . Nothing is more a fashion then musick; no not cloathes, or language, either of which is made a derision to after times. And so it is of all things that belong to the pleasures of sence. For allowing that there is somewhat preferable in right reason, as some cloathes may be more convenient, and language concise, and significant: yet there is a great deal indifferent, and so much, that the prejudice of custome will get the better of it. And the grand custome of all is to affect novelty, and to goe from one thing to another, and despise the former. And it is a poorness of spirit, and a low method of thinking, that inclines men to pronounce for the present, and allow nothing to times past. Cannot wee put ourselves in *loco* of former states, and judge *pro tunc*? Therefore as to all *bon gusto* wee ought to yield to the authority of the proper time, and not determine comparatively where one side is all prejudice. It is a shallow monster that shall hold forth in favour of our fashions and relishes, and maintaine that no age shall come wherein they will not be despised and derided. And if on the other side, I may take upon me to be a fidling prophet, I may with as much reason declare that the time may come when some of the present celebrated musick will be as much in contempt as *John come kiss me now*, now, now, and perhaps with as much reason, as any is found for the contrary at present.

ROGER NORTH, Memoirs of Musick (1728)

You want my opinion on the following questions: What I require of the modern opera house . . . and also, what I hope for and expect, as a composer, from opera managers. As to the first, I want the classical operas produced as if they were modern, and vice versa. And as the composer of *Wozzeck*, I naturally hope that this opera of mine will be produced—but I do not expect it.

ALBAN BERG, Interview (1928)

[Is there not] a rudimentary redundancy in grand opera as exemplified in simultaneously showing a sword on the stage, speaking about a sword in the book, singing about a sword, and introducing a pre-arranged labelled sword motive in the orchestral part? In 1960 this will, surely, long ago have proved simply too insulting to the imagination of the least-educated spectator-auditor.

SIR WALFORD DAVIES, *The Pursuit of Music* (1944)

It is a great error to say, 'Such and such a composer is a good orchestrator; such and such a work is very well instrumented.' For orchestration is one of the aspects *of the very soul of the work*. The work is thought orchestrally and from its very conception carries with it a certain orchestral colouring proper to it and to its author. Is it possible to separate Wagner's music from its actual orchestration? That would be tantamount to saying of a painting by a given master, 'What an admirable drawing with colours!'

NIKOLAI RIMSKY-KORSAKOV, *Principles of Orchestration* (1891)

Mahler had a very delicate ear for all natural sounds and could not help paying attention to them. Thus the call of the cuckoo in his First Symphony is given a pert, gay part; likewise the cry of peacocks, hens, and roosters. . . . In his little working house, which he greatly liked, there were none the less quite frequent causes of disturbance: the birds bothered him with their song, in spite of scarecrows and random discharges of shot. And then there were barking dogs, barrel organs, and brass bands. . . . He writes: 'We are ever surrounded on all sides by barbarism which it is beyond man's power to overcome. The majority have no notion of what it means to respect another man's privacy. I tend more and more to think that only the deaf and blind are fortunate, cut off as they are from this miserable world, and I can well imagine that a musician might voluntarily deprive himself of his hearing, as Democritus is said to have made himself blind.'

NATALIE BAUER-LECHNER, *Recollections of Gustav Mahler* (1923)

An artist can easily enough slip from sheer love of art into hatred of mankind.

JEAN-PAUL RICHTER, Introduction to Hoffmann's *Tales* (1813)

A splendid brass band has just been playing a few pieces on the street, in the rain. It felt like velvet to one's inner being. O Pythagoras, if music thus transports us into the skies, it is because music is harmony, harmony perfection, perfection our dream, and our dream is heaven. This world of strife, bitterness, selfishness, ugliness, and misery makes us sigh involuntarily for eternal peace, for boundless adoration and love without end. It is not so much the infinite that we long for as the beautiful. It is not Being nor the confines of Being that hem us in; it is evil, within us and without. There is no need to be great if we can only be in harmony with the order of the universe.

H.-F. AMIEL, *Journal*, March 17, 1870

This is Eros as the ancients felt him—seductive, playful, malicious, demonic, invincible. To perform this you need a real witch: I know of no song quite like it—and it must be sung in the Italian way, *not* the German!

FRIEDRICH NIETZSCHE, marginal note to the 'Habanera' in *Carmen* (1881)

If I were to begin life again, I would devote much time to music. All musical people seem to me happy; it is the most engrossing pursuit, almost the only innocent and unpunished passion.

SYDNEY SMITH (*c.* 1840)

If ever you become a musical critic, Gemel, . . . you've got to realize that music is only one thing in the world. That the painter is a better man than the person who looks at his painting only in so far as painting goes. That the bricklayer is *in point of bricklaying* vastly superior to Beethoven, me, or anybody else who can't lay one brick on top of another. You must never let your work as an artist override your humanity. It is not a crime for a man to know nothing about art and care less.

JAMES AGATE, *Gemel in London* (1934)

Whenever a new composer comes along, the unanimous opinion of sober judges is that he doesn't know how to write for the voice. If he is successful—after his third opera—the sober judges have nothing more to say. 'Sound opinions' are nothing but clichés, parrot cries.

EMMANUEL CHABRIER, *Letters* (1885)

The Germans, who make doctrines out of everything, deal with music learnedly; the Italians, being voluptuous, seek in it lively though fleeting sensations; the French, more vain than perceptive, manage to speak of it wittily; and the English pay for it without meddling.

STENDHAL, 'Raison, Folie' (n.d.)

There never was a more imbecile notion than the twentieth-century cult of Pure Music, for the simple reason that although in one sense all music must be programme music, since it is concerned with human emotions, in another sense music, in so far as it *is* music, can never be anything but pure.

W. H. MELLERS, 'The Textual Criticism of Music' (1939)

I have tried . . . to prove that the formation of scales and of the web of harmony is a product of artistic invention, and is in no way given by the natural structure or by the natural behaviour of our hearing, as used to be generally maintained hitherto. . . . Just as peoples whose tastes are differently inclined fashion very different buildings out of identical stones, so in the history of music we see the identical peculiarities of the human ear serve as the basis of very different musical systems.

HERMANN VON HELMHOLTZ, *Theory of Sound* (1862)

I can discover from a poet's versification whether or not he has an ear for music. To instance poets of the present day: from Bowles's and Moore's, I should know that they had fine ears for music; from Southey's, Wordsworth's, and Byron's, that they had no ears for it.

SAMUEL ROGERS, *Table Talk* (1856)

If I were in Berlin I should rarely miss the performances of the Moser Quartet. Of all the instrumental genres, I have always been able to follow this one best. You listen to four sensible persons conversing, you profit from their discourse, and you get to know the peculiar properties of their several instruments.

JOHANN WOLFGANG VON GOETHE, *Letters* (1829)

Numbers in music do not govern but merely enlighten. The hearing is the only channel through which their force is impressed upon the innermost soul of the attentive listener. . . . Hence the true target of music is not the eye, nor yet the reason properly so called, but simply and solely the Hearing, which imparts to the soul and to the understanding whatever enjoyment it experiences.

JOHANN MATTHESON, *Das neu-eröffnete Orchestre* (1713)

All the worst things happen in the best works, and the worst music appears to be streaked all through with the most luscious bits.

BERNARD VAN DIEREN, *Down Among the Dead Men* (1935)

I have spoken frequently in Parliament, and not always without some applause; and therefore I can assure you, from my experience, that there is very little in it. The elegancy of the style, and the turn of the periods, make the chief impression upon the hearers. Give them but one or two round and harmonious periods in a speech, which they will retain and repeat, and they will go home as well satisfied, as people do from an opera, humming all the way one or two favourite tunes that have struck their ears and were easily caught. Most people have ears, but few have judgment; tickle those ears, and, depend upon it, you will catch their judgments, such as they are.

LORD CHESTERFIELD, *Letters* (1749)

If I have time, I shall rearrange some of my violin concertos and shorten them.[1] In Germany we rather like length, but after all it is better to be short and good.

WOLFGANG AMADEUS MOZART, *Letters* (1778)

The artist must yield himself to his own inspiration, and if he has a true talent, no one knows and feels better than he what suits him. I should compose with utter confidence a subject that set my blood going, even though it were condemned by all other artists as anti-musical.

GIUSEPPE VERDI, *Letters* (1854)

As I looked at a portrait of Wagner, I wondered how a head which looks like that of a stingy landlord could ever have produced *Siegfried*.

JULIAN GREEN, *Journal* (1932)

Only this much is certain, that as no mother bears children to see them blown to rags or choked in poison gas, so no composer plans his works for the monstrous fate of falling into the conventional concert programme, to hang there like a soldier's body on the barbed wire.

BERNARD VAN DIEREN, *Down Among the Dead Men* (1935)

[1] Five works composed in 1775.

Good music isn't nearly so bad as it sounds.

HARRY ZELZER, Chicago impresario

If an inhabitant of another planet should visit the earth, he would receive, on the whole, a truer notion of human life by attending an Italian opera than he would by reading Emerson's volumes. He would learn from the Italian opera that there were two sexes; and this, after all, is probably the fact with which the education of such a stranger ought to begin.

JOHN JAY CHAPMAN, *Emerson and Other Essays* (1909)

The prosaic fallacy that the essence of Music is vague namable expressiveness, instead of definite unnamable impressiveness, is only carried out by making the expressiveness itself mechanical and independent of any impressiveness whatever.

EDMUND GURNEY, 'Wagner and Wagnerism' (1883)

Emotion is specific, individual, and conscious; music goes deeper than this, to the energies which animate our psychic life, and out of these creates a pattern which has an existence, laws, and human significance of its own. It reproduces for us the most intimate essence, the tempo and the energy, of our spiritual being; our tranquillity and our restlessness, our animation and our discouragement, our vitality and our weakness—all, in fact, of the fine shades of dynamic variation of our inner life. It reproduces these far more directly and more specifically than is possible through any other medium of human communication.

ROGER SESSIONS, 'The Composer and his Message' (1941)

Music is the imagination of love in *sound*. It is what man imagines of his life, and his life is love.

W. J. TURNER, *Orpheus, or The Music of the Future* (1926)

DERISION & INVECTIVE

Hell is full of musical amateurs: music is the brandy of the damned.

BERNARD SHAW, *Man and Superman* (1903)

Those things that act through the ears are said to make a noise, discord, or harmony, and this last has caused men to lose their heads to such a degree that they have believed God himself is delighted with it.

BARUCH SPINOZA, *Ethics* (1677)

One who opened Jowett's version [of Plato] at random and lighted on the statement that the best guardian for a man's 'virtue' is 'philosophy tempered with music,' might run away with the idea that, in order to avoid irregular relations with women, he had better play the violin in the intervals of studying metaphysics.

F. M. CORNFORD, *The Republic of Plato* (1941)

Amidst all the follies of the age, there never was a greater than the immoderate passion of the people for music. Though amusement and recreation are sometimes necessary, yet when carried to excess they become vicious. Now so far did the luxury of this kingdom extend at the time when this plate[1] was first published, which was in the year 1741, that Italians (as being supposed to be the greater proficients) were brought over at considerable expense; and the poorest and least skilled among them, who from a want of ability or a want of means, could not continue in their own country, soon discovering our folly, gathered here in flocks and took possession of the place. When here, they were encouraged, and their wretched abilities looked upon as supernatural; they introduced a new style of music, which suited well the growing levity of this nation. The noble and elevated was immediately transformed into the trifling and insignificant: and the solemn and majestic sounds of British harmony gave place to the tinkling frippery of Italian singsong.

To ridicule this immoderate passion of the age for music, Mr. Hogarth published this print; in it he represents an Italian professor of music, at his study, enraged to the greatest degree at the astounding noise the motley group collected beneath the window are making,

[1] 'The Enraged Musician,' described in the next paragraph.

which seem assembled in order to annoy and distress him. By the inscription on the house over the way, he is also supposed to live in the neighbourhood of a pewterer, whose constant hammering is no trifling annoyance to him. Our artist seems in this plate to have let none of the material or customary noises of London streets escape him. In front are some children at their sports, one of whom is hallooing and beating of a drum; another dragging a tile upon the stones, while a third is winding a racket. On the right is a ballad singer bawling out 'The Lady's Fall,' with a squalling infant in her arms; on the left, a man grinding a cleaver, whose machine is standing on the foot of a dog, and sets him yelping.

ANONYMOUS NOTE in early nineteenth-century reprint of Hogarth's *Works*

A certain skilful action of his fingers as he hummed some bars and beat time on the seat beside him seemed to denote the musician; and the extraordinary satisfaction he derived from humming something very slow and long, which had no recognizable tune, seemed to denote that he was a scientific one.

CHARLES DICKENS, *Dombey and Son* (1846)

The expression consisted in being very soft on the words *love*, *peace*, etc., and then bursting into roars of triumph on the words *hate*, *war*, and *glory*. To this pattern Mr. Braham[1] composed many of the songs written for him; and the public were enchanted with a style which enabled them to fancy that they enjoyed the highest style of the art, while it required only the vulgarest of their perceptions.

LEIGH HUNT, *Autobiography* (1850)

I shall never be able to say: 'What a chorus! What an orchestra! This theatre ranks first in the whole world!' It sticks in my throat. Again and again I have heard people say one after another in Milan (especially when I was putting on *La Forza del Destino*): La Scala is the first theatre in the world. In Naples: the San Carlo is the first theatre in the world. In Venice it was: La Fenice is the first theatre in the world. In Petersburg: the first theatre in the world. In Vienna: the

[1] John Braham (1774–1856), English tenor. An example might be his once famous show-piece, 'The Death of Nelson.'

first theatre in the world (and that I would say too). And in Paris: the Opera is the first theatre in two or three worlds.

GIUSEPPE VERDI, Letters (1879)

Italian music, its orchestration: the oboes play with the flutes,[1] the clarinets with the oboes, the flutes with the violins, the bassoons with the lower strings, the second violins with the first, the viola with the bass. The voices are ad lib., the violins as in the score.

CARL-MARIA VON WEBER (1818)

It has been said that because today more people hear Beethoven in twenty-four hours (on the radio) than heard him in his whole lifetime, the people have music. Momentarily disregarding the question of the quality of the emanations from the radio, we can say: yes, and a citizen doubtless sees more policemen now in twenty-four hours than Beethoven saw in his whole lifetime. The people hear more music, and *ipso facto* they are more musical? The people have more law, and *ipso facto* they are more lawful?

The analogue is not so absurd. . . . Hearing more music—ninety-nine per cent of which is not Beethoven but the equivalent of the radio vibrations of frankfurters—accomplishes just one thing: ennui in the eardrum.

HARRY PARTCH, Genesis of a Music (1949)

The first thing to do on arriving at a symphony concert is to express the wish that the orchestra will play Beethoven's Fifth. If your companion then says 'Fifth what?' you are safe for the rest of the evening.

DONALD OGDEN STEWART, Perfect Behaviour (1922)

To know whether you are enjoying a piece of music or not, you must see whether you find yourself looking at the advertisements of Pears' soap at the end of the programme.

SAMUEL BUTLER, Note-Books (c. 1890)

What most people relish is hardly music; it is rather a drowsy reverie relieved by nervous thrills.

GEORGE SANTAYANA, Reason in Art (1917)

[1] I.e., the same notes.

It's Prussian blue—it fades!

    Attributed to JOHANN SEBASTIAN BACH about the music of his son
    EMANUEL.

Weber wanted a drama with which to unite his noble, spiritual
melody. Meyerbeer, on the other hand, wanted an irresistibly
mongrel, historico-romantic, diabolico-religious, emotionally fickle,
bigoted-voluptuous, frivolously sacred, mysterioso-shameless hodgepodge to serve as subject for an extraordinarily strange music, which,
owing to the leathery texture of his musical mind, never quite came
off.

                RICHARD WAGNER, *Opera and Drama* (1850)

The essential lack in Wagner is after all a want of sanitary plumbing.
No amount of sentiment or passion can wholly make up for this.
One feels all the time that the connection with the main is fraudulent.

                JOHN JAY CHAPMAN, *Letters* (1895)

Do you think me so devoid of taste that I would stand there in front
of the orchestra, violin in hand, but like a listener, while the oboe
plays the only melody in the entire work?

    PABLO SARASATE to EDOUARD LALO apropos of Brahms' Violin
    Concerto (1879)

There is a definite limit to the length of time a composer can go on
writing in one dance rhythm. This limit is obviously reached by Ravel
toward the end of *La Valse* and toward the beginning of *Bolero*.

                CONSTANT LAMBERT, *Music Ho!* (1934)

Brahms' *Song of Triumph* came at the end of the concert—a Handelian
impersonation, unfortunately rather tiresome, like all of Brahms' im-
personations. The programme notes of the Friends of Music speak
of this *Song of Triumph* as a 'powerful work.' Sheer puffing! Why has
the free-handed author of these notes not blared it forth that Bruckner's
Te Deum is a powerful work? Why these delicate distinctions? Or does
the epithet 'powerful' apply only to the voluminosity of the score?
Is the public being prepared for a more prolonged torture? These
warning signals at performances of Brahms might be valued as boons

to a suffering humanity, were it not that there is a still more effective
means of avoiding discomfort—the reader understands me!

HUGO WOLF, concert review, January 16, 1887

The case was aggravated when the fanatical Wagnerian was a professional composer: being incapable of imitating what belongs solely
to genius, he would cling desperately to whatever lay within the
reach—whether because it was false or artificial—of any simple mortal
of ordinary intelligence; thinking thereby to appropriate the glittering
treasure which showed through the intermittent darkness. As for the
non-musicians, I myself have known more than one whose mouth
filled with anathemas and who *tore their raiment* at the least unfavourable
judgment aimed at the idol they deemed sacrosanct.

MANUEL DE FALLA, 'Notes on Wagner' (1933)

Ah, it's a pretty trade we're in! I'm writing piano pieces for four
hands. Why do I do it? you ask. How in hell should I know, my poor
d'Estaleuse! It's stupidity, of course—my publisher won't even take
them. One will be too long—never too short, you'll observe; another
too difficult—never too easy; and none of them *practical*!

EMMANUEL CHABRIER, *Letters* (1884)

Lord! will the time ever come when nobody asks us what we were
up to in our divine compositions! Pick out the fifths and leave us in
peace!

ROBERT SCHUMANN, concert review (1838)

The study of old music, both sacred and profane—yes. But it would
be a good idea to remember that not all the old music is beautiful
either.

GIUSEPPE VERDI, *Letters* (1871)

No one, I conclude, would wish to see literature discoursed about in
the same pinchbeck and affected style as are painting and music; yet
this is what will happen if the prolific weed of sham admiration is
permitted to attain its full growth—the well-nigh universal habit of
literary lying and pretence of admiration for certain works of which
in reality we know very little, and for which, if we knew more, we
should perhaps care even less.

JAMES PAYN, *Some Private Views* (1881)

TARADIDDLE

Music makes for exuberance and hyperbole, and this is sometimes aped by those whose blood stays cool but who would like excitement too. The point of the extravagant examples that follow in illustration of this fact is not that they are foolish, but that they are the foolishness of sensible men—a source of amusement and a warning, alike unintended, but worthy of all gratitude.

The first publication in English to supply enlightenment about The Ring was written and published in Germany in 1879 by the Wagnerites Hans and Ernst von Wolzogen. The present extract does not include the remarkable description of the 'brangling and brustling' effects, which was omitted from the second and later editions of the Guide.

The bird warns again and again, when Mime with his old praise of his education, with the dusky harmonies of the cooking motive, and with the coaxing-crawling motive, or even with the charming tune of Nature's life, tries to obtrude his poisonous brewage upon the dragon killer. . . .

But to what end all precaution? As Siegfried with scorn and menace refutes the Walhall theme which is held up against his impatience, there, in the second half of the scene, Wotan's motive of wrath rises more and more, and between its most urgent repetitions cites—in vain—the horrors of the fiery blaze.

. . . With the accords of the Walhall-march the proud passage of the godly power once more rises and then descends in several repetitions of the world's destruction, closely following each other. Her lay becomes dark and low: 'Holda's apples' are cited in vain. Gloomily the Walhall-theme dies away, the Rhinegold slowly arises in Wotan's resigned mind.

Thereupon ceases this excitement and a new lively, pompous symphonic set begins.

For the last time we hear Siegfried's motive, but the wild rush of the Götterdämmerung motive overpowers it with the utmost force: flames cover the picture of the old gods and the melody of salvation through love waves *dim.* under ethereal harp sounds, as the freed and blessed spirit of love of the whole world's tragedy ascends to the eternal regions of his heavenly home!

HANS AND ERNST VON WOLZOGEN, *Guide through Wagner's Ring*
(1882)

On Handel's Messiah in Boston

I walked in the bright paths of sound, and liked it best when the long continuance of a chorus had made the ear insensible to the music, made it as if there was none; then I was quite solitary and at ease in the melodious uproar. Once or twice in the solos, when well sung, I could play tricks, as I like to do, with my eyes—darken the whole house and brighten and transfigure the central singer, and enjoy the enchantment.

This wonderful piece of music . . .

RALPH WALDO EMERSON, *Journal*, December 25, 1843

We need not seek farther whom we must put down on the title page of the *Eroica*. We musicians dedicate and consecrate with heart and brain, with hand and lips, the *Eroica* symphony to the greatest hero that has seen the light of day since Beethoven. We dedicate it to Beethoven's twin, the Beethoven of German politics, the Prince Bismarck. Prince Bismarck, hail!

HANS VON BÜLOW, speech after the Berlin Philharmonic Concert of March 28, 1892

On Beethoven's Fourth Piano Concerto

At the beginning the piano emerges gently from dreams; this is truly Beethoven improvising. Two romantic themes, renunciation and hope, are gradually developed. When, after an orchestral interlude, the piano is heard again solo, it is as if a butterfly rose ecstatically from its cocoon. There are no fortissimos here, and when the call to new adventures sounds, the butterfly sinks back, dreaming. The whole thing is wrapped in dark-red velvet; at times it is as if one were caressing it with one's hands.

EMIL LUDWIG, *Beethoven, Life of a Conqueror* (1943), translated by George Stewart McManus

Weber may not have been a great composer, but he was without doubt a great opera composer. . . . Weber never produced a prize bloom nor perfected a single species, but the luxuriance of his colours is supreme, and ranges from delicacy to exoticism.

DENNIS ARUNDELL in *The Heritage of Music* (1934)

On Sir Thomas Beecham

'A Dean of Dignity'

What a scene in the vast crowded hall where thousands sat thick upon their chairs, so close and mingled and motionless as the music held them that they looked like painted frescoes. What a wonderful silence, the silence of that throng, whence no rustle nor cough nor murmur came to taint the beauty of the song nor mar the orchestra's luminous flow!

What a moment . . . when Sir Thomas Beecham, while the audience broke into applause, came smiling to his place, bowing to his public, bowing to his orchestra, a dean of dignity, a marvel of men, a figure straight from the Prado, specially released by Velázquez for the occasion. What a man! What a master of music! Till you have seen him conduct you do not know what movement can be.

He stands there and spreads his arms as if he were about to take a deep, deep dive, stands poised on the edge of melody, and then plunges, and then all the currents of sound swirl him about, and all its broad waves bear him nobly on their spread; his arms toss with the foam of notes, his fingers flash like silvered bubbles, as he cleaves the vocal waters.

All the gestures that man has ever known seem to be his under the sway of the music at once gushing from his own baton and drunk by his own heart. The delicacies and reverences of the eighteenth century, the sabre cuts of a captain of Napoleon's cavalry charging across Europe, the pleadings of an advocate, the prayers of a saint, the very kiss of a lover—all these he conjures up and draws upon and delivers as messages to his orchestra.

Sometimes he puts aside his baton and conducts with his hands alone, throws himself back and flings some divine missile at his players on the orchestra's edge, pommels the rhythm into his violins, and then flutters again into gentleness, and his fingers flicker and flicker, flicker and interweave, till they seem to be but running oil.

His singers tore at our hearts as we listened, to his orchestra I bow an untutored head for the joy they gave it, but him himself, the great conductor I shall never forget, and would adjure all to see him and swim with him where the great operas flow into the eternal sea.

J. M. N. JEFFRIES, *Daily Mail* (London), October 31, 1927

On the centenary performance of Beethoven's Missa Solemnis

Whatever may be said this year about the greatest musician that the heavens ever inspired on this earth will be no match for the respectful hearing of his own voice, for the flights of a pure and ardent soul, which arose from a human crowd in tears and which, in the heavenly light of the stained glass two hundred feet above the ground, touched divinity.

Le Matin (Paris), March 18, 1927

On Corelli

In the portrait by Howard painted about 1700 he has large regular features, bright deep-set eyes, and a general expression of calm and nobility. When he played upon the violin, however, his eyes blazed and he threw himself into convulsions.

On Maugars

He has left no indication of his repertory, but it probably consisted of well-known airs on which he devised brilliant variations.

On Gesualdo

Related to the great aristocratic families of Italy, Gesualdo was of a violent nature. In 1590 he ordered the murder of his wife Marie d'Avalos and her lover Fabrizio Carafa; after which tragic event he composed six books of madrigals, married Eleonora d'Este, and devoted himself to music.

HENRY PRUNIÈRES, *A New History of Music*, translated by Edward Lockspeiser (1941)

We live in an age of remarkable progress, in which all the arts are being daily perfected. Mechanics especially is advancing fast and will soon bring you relief as regards performing upon your instruments.

THE FRENCH MINISTER OF FINE ARTS, addressing the Faculty of the Conservatoire, January 3, 1896

Tonight I go to another musical party at Marshall's, the late M.P. for Yorkshire. Everybody is talking of Paganini and his violin. The man seems to be a miracle. The newspapers say that long streamy flakes of music fall from his string, interspersed with luminous points of sound which ascend the air and appear like stars. This eloquence is quite beyond me.

T. B. MACAULAY to his sister, May 27, 1831

CLASSIC TALES

This past winter, wishing to complement the programme of the Conservatoire (inadequately enough, owing to lack of time), I devoted several concerts to the performance of the piano duets, trios, and quintets of Beethoven. I was almost sure they would bore my audiences, but I was equally sure no one would dare to object. As things turned out, there were some lively expressions of enthusiasm by which it would have been easy to be taken in, and hence to believe the crowd overcome by the power of genius.

But at one of the last concerts a change in the order of the pieces played put an end to that illusion. Without notice we performed a trio by Pixis[1] in place of Beethoven's and vice versa. The Beethoven was found feeble, commonplace, positively boring, and M. Pixis was deemed impertinent to risk comparison before an audience which had come solely to admire the work of the great master. I am far from suggesting that it was wrong to applaud the Pixis trio; but he himself can only smile with pity at the bravos of a public incapable of distinguishing the styles of such different compositions.

FRANZ LISZT, *Gazette Musicale*, July 16, 1837

Byron, to his childhood friend, Elizabeth Pigot: 'I don't know how it is, I sing a great deal better to your playing than to other people's.'

Elizabeth Pigot: 'That's because I play to your singing, while others make you sing to their playing.'

THOMAS MOORE, *Notes for the Life of Byron* (c. 1820)

The two great masters of poetry and music, Goethe and Beethoven, were taking a walk along the path through the woods one day in order to be able to exchange world-shaking ideas without hindrance. Wherever they went, the people on their path made way for them and saluted them with great respect. Goethe, annoyed by this continual interruption, said, 'What a nuisance! I don't seem ever able to avoid this kind of thing.' To which, with a calm smile, Beethoven answered,

---

[1] French composer of songs and chamber music (1788–1874).

'Don't let it bother Your Excellency: the greetings are probably meant for me.'

Traditional in Teplitz since 1812

A Frenchman in Munich asks Giuseppe dall'Abaco:[1] Have you been to Paris?

Abaco: Yes.

F.: Did you go to the concert of sacred music?

A.: Yes.

F.: What do you think of the attack with the bow, did you hear the first attack with the bow?

A.: Yes, I heard the first and the last.

F.: What did you say? The last? What does that mean?

A.: Why, just that—the first and the last—and I may say the last gave me even greater pleasure.

WOLFGANG AMADEUS MOZART,
retelling it from Raaf,[2] Letters (1778)

First Rival Composer, while clapping: 'What do you think of his piece?'

Second Rival Composer: 'I think it's glorified dinner music.'

Third Rival Composer: 'Dinner music! It not only dines but it whines!'

One evening in Moscow, in E. P. Pyeskovskaya's flat, Lenin was listening to a sonata by Beethoven being played by Isaiah Dobrowein, and said, 'I know nothing which is greater than the *Appassionata*; I would like to listen to it every day. It is marvellous, superhuman music. I always think with pride—perhaps it is naïve of me—what marvellous things human beings can do!'

Then, screwing up his eyes and smiling, he added rather sadly, 'But I can't listen to music too often. It affects your nerves, makes you want to say stupid, nice things, and stroke the heads of people who could create such beauty while living in this vile hell. And now you mustn't stroke anyone's head—you might get your hand bitten off. You have to hit them on the head, without any mercy, although

[1] Italian musician at Bonn (1709–1805).
[2] Anton Raaf, famous tenor (1714–97).

our ideal is not to use force against anyone. H'm, h'm, our duty is infernally hard.'

MAXIM GORKY, Days with Lenin (1924)

You have heard of Mozart's celebrated feat of giving a notation of Allegri's Miserere.[1] But here is a good instance of the partial interpretation of happenings. It was not done at a first hearing, but after careful preparation. He heard it six times, helped and prompted by his very capable father, and even then his notation was so full of mistakes that his father destroyed the tentative score after the Pope had explained to the Archduke that the singers relied on memory and tradition. There were, therefore, legitimate excuses for Mozart, but nonetheless we see that it is wise to be wary about reputed feats of technical prowess in music.

BERNARD VAN DIEREN, A Berlioz Conference (1929)

'When in doubt, play what's written!'—Harold Bauer to a pupil struggling over a passage. But later in the same piece: 'Ah, but the right notes won't help you there!'

Rossini, strolling on the Paris boulevards, runs into the director of the Opera, who tells him that the composer's William Tell has just been chosen for revival. It will be put on next month. Rossini: 'What? All of it?'

Young and handsome, Liszt was first introduced to English society at the salon of Lady Blessington. At the end of the musical evening he wished to know from a third party her opinion of him. 'Why, only this, that it's a shame to put a fine man like you at the piano!'

Cheerful Philistine to the leader of a new string quartet still struggling for recognition: 'Well, here's hoping your little organization will grow!'

[1] This famous work in four, five, and nine parts, was sung in St. Peter's at Rome during Holy Week. The full score was not available, so that when Mozart's father took the boy, aged fourteen, to Italy, he arranged to have the young prodigy note the work down during the performance. See p. 290.

James Agate, meeting a friend, a member of the B.B.C. orchestra:
'Who conducted this afternoon?'

Alec Whittaker, First Oboe: 'Sorry, James, I forgot to look.'

ENVOY

From continually shifting key, music may get to such a persistently
enharmonic condition as to be never at any moment in less than two
keys at once, and hence IN NO KEY AT ALL!

What next? Why, this next!

W. F. APTHORP (1898)

Sources & Acknowledgments

List of Sources & Acknowledgments

The page numbers following each work indicate the passages used or excerpted from in the text. Chapter or section references are given when a book exists in many editions, and letters dated in the text are marked as 'under date.'

The Editor thanks the owners and publishers of copyright materials for permission to reprint. The details of these obligations are given after the titles to which they apply.

AGATE, JAMES. *Ego 6* (London, 1944), pp. 35–37.
  Whittaker story, in *Ego* (London, 1946), p. 42.
  On Gemel, in *Ego 8* (London, 1947), p. 208.
  Courtesy of George G. Harrap & Co., Ltd.
AMIEL, H.-F. *Fragments d'un Journal Intime*, ed. Bernard Bouvier (3 vols., Geneva, 1922). Vol. II: pp. 158–59.
ANONYMOUS. Editorial on 'The Orchestra,' in *The Musician*, April 1900, p. 114.
ANONYMOUS. Letter on 'Clouc,' in J. Tiersot, *Lettres de musiciens écrites en français*, etc. (2 vols., Turin, 1924). Vol. I: pp. 55–56.
APTHORP, W. F. *By the Way: Being a Collection of Short Essays on Music and Art . . . from the Programme Books of the Boston Symphony Orchestra* (2 vols., Boston, 1898). Vol. II: pp. 162–73; Envoy, in Vol. I, p. 157.
ARUNDELL, DENNIS. 'Weber,' in *The Heritage of Music*, ed. H. J. Foss (London, 1934), pp. 133–34.
BACH, JOHANN SEBASTIAN. *Gesammelte Briefe*, ed. Erich H. Müller von Asow (Regensburg, 1938), under date. Epigram on his son's music, in *Musical Quarterly*, Oct. 1950, p. 506.
BALZAC, HONORÉ DE. 'Gambara,' in *Oeuvres Complètes* (50 vols., Paris: Ollendorff, 1901). *Etudes Philosophiques*, Vol. III: pp. 347–70 and 412–17.
BAUDELAIRE, CHARLES. Letter to Richard Wagner, in *Revue Musicale*, Nov. 1, 1922, pp. 2–4.
BAUER-LECHNER, NATALIE. *Erinnerungen an Gustav Mahler* (Leipzig, 1923), pp. 81 and 138–39.
BEAUMARCHAIS, P.-A. CARON DE. *Oeuvres Complètes* (Paris, 1861), pp. 205–209.
BEDDOES, THOMAS LOVELL. Letter to Procter, in *Works*, ed. H. W. Donner (London, 1935), under date.
  Courtesy of Mr. Donner.
BEETHOVEN, LUDWIG VAN. Letters, in *Sämtliche Briefe*, ed. A. C. Kalischer (5 vols., Berlin and Leipzig, 1908), under dates. On 'Beethoven's Third and Fifth,' see Prodhomme and Berlioz. On his conversation with Goethe, see Goethe.
BERG, ALBAN. Interview, in Willi Reich, *Alban Berg* (Vienna, 1937), p. 173.
BERLIOZ, HECTOR. 'An Interview with the Police' and 'Beethoven and Lesueur,' in *Mémoires* (2 vols., Paris, 1926). Vol. II: pp. 171–73; Vol. I: pp. 112–13.
  'An Artist from the Grocer's,' in *Soirées de l'Orchestre* (Paris, 1852 ff.), Third and Fourth Evenings.
  'The Limits of Music,' in *Gazette Musicale*, Jan. 1 and 8, 1837, and in *A Travers Chants* (Paris, 1862 ff.), pp. 152–58 and 189.

BERLIOZ, HECTOR. 'The Flute,' in *Traité d'Orchestration* (2nd ed., Paris, 1856), pp. 151–53.

BLESSINGTON, MARGUERITE, COUNTESS. On Liszt, in *Correspondance de Liszt et de la Comtesse d'Agoult* (Paris, 1933), p. 433.

BRAHMS, JOHANNES. *Briefwechsel mit J. O. Grimm*, ed. Richard Barth (Berlin, 1908), pp. 43–46.

BRILLAT-SAVARIN, JEAN-ANTHELME. *Physiologie du Goût ou Méditations de gastronomie transcendante* (Paris, 1847). Part II: chap. 23.

BROWNE, SIR THOMAS. *Religio Medici*, in *The Works*, ed. Charles Sayle (3 vols., Edinburgh, 1927). Vol. I: Part II, Sec. 9, pp. 100–101.

BÜLOW, HANS VON. On Bismarck, in *Hans von Bülows Leben in seinen Briefen dargestellt*, ed. Marie von Bülow (2nd ed., Leipzig, 1921), p. 548.

BURNEY, CHARLES. *An Account of the Musical Performances in Westminster Abbey . . . in Commemoration of Handel* (London, 1785). Part I: pp. i–iv; Part II: pp. 25–41.

BURTON, ROBERT. *The Anatomy of Melancholy* (11th ed. corrected, 2 vols., London, 1813). Vol. I: Part 2, Sec. 2, Mem. 6, Subs. 3, pp. 449–53.

BUSONI, FERRUCCIO. *Scritti e pensieri sulla Musica*, ed. L. Dallapiccola and G. M. Gatti (Florence, 1941). 'The Unity of Music,' pp. 70–71; the other fragment, pp. 62–63.

BUTLER, SAMUEL. *The Note-Books*, in *Works* (Shrewsbury ed., 20 vols., London, 1926). Vol. XX: pp. 107–12 and 209.
Courtesy of the Executors of Samuel Butler, and Jonathan Cape, Ltd.

BYRON, GEORGE GORDON, LORD. *Letters and Journals*, ed. R. E. Protheroe (6 vols., London, 1898–1904). Vol. IV: pp. 204 and 214.
Correspondence, ed. John Murray (2 vols., London, 1922). Vol. II: pp. 111–12.
Courtesy of John Murray, Ltd.

CALVOCORESSI, M. D. *Musical Taste and How to Form It* (London, 1925), pp. 2–3.

CELLINI, BENVENUTO. *La Vita*, ed Carlo Cordié (2 vols., Milan, 1944). Vol. I: Bk. I, chaps. V–VI, pp. 11–13.

CHABRIER, EMMANUEL. 'Lettres Inédites,' in *Bulletin de la S.I.M.*, Jan.–Feb. 1909. On composing 'The Tempest,' p. 122; two others, p. 6.

CHAPMAN, JOHN JAY. *Emerson and Other Essays* (New York, 1909), p. 83.
Letters, ed. M. A. DeWolfe Howe (Boston, 1937), p. 102.

CHATEAUBRIAND, RENÉ DE. *Le Génie du Christianisme*, ed. Guizot (2 vols., Paris, 1885). Vol. II: Part IV, Bk. I, chap. 1, pp. 151–53.

CHESTERFIELD, PHILIP DORMER STANHOPE, FOURTH EARL OF. *Letters*, ed. Bonamy Dobree (6 vols., London, 1932). Vol. IV: pp. 1360–61 and 1458.

CHESTERTON, G. K. 'Music with Meals' ('On Misunderstanding'), in *Generally Speaking* (New York, 1929), pp. 103–109.
Courtesy of Dorothy Edith Collins, Methuen & Co., Ltd., and A. P. Watt & Son.

COLLIER, JEREMY. *Essays upon Several Subjects* (5th ed., 2 vols. in one, London, 1702–1703). Vol. II: pp. 19–24.

CORNFORD, F. M. *The Republic of Plato* (Oxford, 1941), pp. v–vi.

DAVIES, SIR WALFORD. *The Pursuit of Music* (London, 1944), p. 390.

DEBUSSY, CLAUDE. *M. Croche, Anti-Dilettante* (Paris, 1921), pp. 135–37.

DELACROIX, EUGÈNE. 'Mozart,' in *Journal, 1853-1856*, ed. André Joubin (3 vols., Paris, 1932). Vol. II: pp. 24, 42, 71, 102, 124, 154 ff., 317-18, 438-39, 481.

DE QUINCEY, THOMAS. *Works* (2nd ed., 17 vols., Edinburgh, 1862-78). Vol. XIII: 'The *Antigone* of Sophocles,' pp. 208-11.

DICKENS, CHARLES. 'The Solitary 'Cello,' in *Dombey and Son*, chap. LVIII.
On the scientific musician, *ibid.*, chap. XXXIII.

DIDEROT DENIS. 'Le Neveu de Rameau,' in *Oeuvres Choisies*, ed. F. Tulou, Paris, 1932, 2 vols. Pp. 68-86.

D'INDY, VINCENT. *César Franck* (6th ed., Paris, 1912), pp. 76-77.

EMERSON, RALPH WALDO. *Journals*, ed. E. W. Emerson and W. E. Forbes (10 vols., Boston, 1909-14). Vol. VI: p. 479.

ENGEL, LOUIS. *From Mozart to Mario* (2 vols., London, 1886). Vol. II: Rossini, p. 72; Verdi, pp. 134-38.

FALLA, MANUEL DE. 'Notas sobre Wagner en su Cincuentenario,' in *Cruz y Raya* (Madrid), Sept. 1933, pp. 67-80.

GLUCK, CHRISTOPH WILLIBALD VON. Letter to La Harpe, in J.-G. Prodhomme, *Ecrits de Musiciens* (Paris, 1912), pp. 414-19.

GOETHE, JOHANN WOLFGANG VON. *Briefwechsel zwischen Goethe und Zelter*, ed. Max Hecker (3 vols., Leipzig, n.d.), under date; on Möser Quartet, *ibid.* Beethoven anecdote, from various sources, e.g., August Frankl, 'Schiller, Beethoven, und Goethe in Karlsbad' (Carlsbad, 1862), pp. 9-10 and 16.

GORKY, MAXIM. *Days with Lenin* (New York: International Publishers, 1932), p. 52.

GOUNOD, CHARLES. *Mémoires d'un Artiste* (Paris, 1896), pp. 99-104.

GREEN, JULIAN. *Journal* (3 vols., Paris, 1938-46). Vol. I: on Wagner, p. 111; Vol. II: on music, p. 188.

HAGGIN, B. H. *Music on Records* (New York, 1938), pp. viii-xi.
Copyright 1938 by the Oxford University Press, Inc.
Courtesy of the Oxford University Press, Inc.

HANSLICK, EDUARD. *Concerte, Componisten und Virtuosen: 1870-1885* (Berlin, 1886), pp. 224-27.

HARDY, THOMAS. *Under the Greenwood Tree* (London, 1872, 1912), chaps. III and IV.
The Hand of Ethelberta (London, 1876, 1912), chap. XLIV continued.
Courtesy of Macmillan & Company Ltd.

HARRISON, FREDERIC. 'The Concert Hall' ('Music in Great Cities'), in *Memories and Thoughts* (New York, 1906), pp. 299-302.
Courtesy of Macmillan & Company Ltd.

HAYDN, JOSEPH. Letter, in Willi Kahl, *Selbstbiographien deutscher Musiker des XVIIIten Jahrhunderts* (Cologne, 1948), pp. 83-86.

HEARN, LAFCADIO. 'L'Arlésienne,' in *Editorials*, ed. C. W. Hutson (Boston, 1926), pp. 306-11.

HEINE, HEINRICH. *Gesammelte Werke*, ed. Gustav Karpeles (9 vols., Berlin, 1887). Vol. VII: 'Letters on the French Stage,' Nos. 9 and 10, pp. 132 and 145-53.

HELMHOLTZ, HERMANN VON. *Die Lehre von Tonempfindungen* (6th ed., Brunswick, 1913), pp. 587-88.

HESELTINE, PHILIP. Editor's Foreword, in *The Sackbut* (London), May 1920, pp. 7–9. ·

HOFFMAN, E. T. A. [W]. *Gesammelte Schriften* (12 vols. in six, Berlin, 1844–45). Vol. VII: pp. 91–108; comment by Jean-Paul Richter, p. 6.

HOGARTH, WILLIAM. 'The Enraged Musician,' in *Marriage à la Mode and Other Engravings* (New York: Lear, 1947), no pl. number.

HUNT, LEIGH. *Autobiography*, ed. Thornton Hunt (London, 1860). 'Musical Memories,' pp. 21–22, 41–45, 323–24, 355; on 'expression,' p. 124.

JEFFRIES, J. M. N. [J.M.N.J.]. 'A Dean of Dignity,' in *Daily Mail* (London), Oct. 31. 1927, p. 9.
Courtesy of Mr. Jeffries and the *Daily Mail*.

KASSNER, RUDOLF. *Der grösste Mensch: Auswahl aud den Schriften* (Amandus ed, Oesterreichische Vereinigung, Vienna, 1946), pp. 93–944

LAMBERT, CONSTANT. *Music Ho! A Study of Music in Decline* (London, 1934). pp. 206–207; on Ravel, pp. 197–98.
Courtesy of Faber & Faber, Limited.

LANIER, SIDNEY. *Centennial Edition of the Works* (10 vols., Baltimore, 1945). Vol. II: *Essays on Music*, ed. P. F. Baum, pp. 333–34.
Courtesy of The Johns Hopkins Press.

LIEVEN, PRINCESS DOROTHEA. *Private Letters to Prince Metternich*, trans. Peter Quennell and Dilys Powell (New York, 1938), pp. 49–50.

LISZT, FRANZ. *F. Chopin* (Paris, 1852), pp. 146–48.
Pixis story, in *Gazette Musicale*, July 16, 1837, p. 341. See also Blessington.

LUDWIG, EMIL. *Beethoven, Life of a Conqueror*, trans, by George Stewart McManus (New York, 1943), p. 185.

LUTHER, MARTIN. *Gedanken über die Musik*, ed. F. A. Beck (Berlin, 1825), pp. 17, 18–23.

MACAULAY, T. B. From *Life and Letters*, by G. O. Trevelyan (2 vols., London, 1876), under date.

MARIA THERESA. *Correspondance secrète entre Marie-Thérèse et le Comte de Mercy-Argenteau, avec les lettres de Marie-Antoinette*, ed. A. Arneth and A. Geffroy (2nd ed., 3 vols., Paris, 1875), under dates.

MATTHESON, JOHANN. *Das neu-eröffnete Orchestre* (3 vols. in two, Hamburg, 1713–21). Vol. I: pp. 126–27.

MAZZINI, GIUSEPPE. 'Filosofia della Musica,' in *Scritti, Editi ed Inediti* (Edizione Nazionale, 94 vols., Imola, 1906–43). Vol. 8: *Letteratura*; Vol. II: pp. 121–65.
Additional note of 1867, in *The Life and Works of Joseph Mazzini* (6 vols., London, 1864–70). Vol. IV: pp. 52–55.

MELLERS, W. H. 'The Textual Criticism of Music,' in *Scrutiny*, March 1939, p. 480.

MENDELSSOHN-BARTHOLDY, FELIX. Letters to and by, in *Die Familie Mendelssohn: 1729-1847*, ed. S. Hensel (7th ed., 2 vols., Berlin, 1891). Vol. I: pp. 93, 106–107, 147–48, 159, and 161–62.

MERCY-ARGENTEAU, COUNT DE. See Maria Theresa.

MOLIÈRE (J.-B. POQUELIN). *Le Bourgeois Gentilhomme*, in *Oeuvres* (2 vols., Paris: Didot, 1862). Vol. II: Acts I and II, pp. 338 ff.

MONTAIGNE, MICHEL EYQUEM DE. *Essais*, ed. J.-V. Leclerc (4 vols., Paris, 1925). Vol. I: Bk. I, chap. xxv, p. 186.

MONTEVERDI, CLAUDIO. Preface to *Madrigali guerrieri e amorosi*, in Domenico De Paoli, *Claudio Monteverdi* (Milan, 1945), pp 247–49.

MOORE, THOMAS. 'Notes for the Life of Byron,' in *Prose and Verse*, ed. R. H. Shepherd (London, 1878), p. 420.

MOSCHELES, IGNAZ. *Aus Moscheles Leben*, ed. by his wife (2 vols., Leipzig, n.d. [1873], Vol. II: p. 28.

MOUSSORGSKY, MODESTE. 'Autobiographic Note,' in *The Musorgsky Reader: A Life . . . in Letters and Documents*, ed. and trans. by Jay Leyda and Sergei Bertensson (New York, 1947), pp. 416–20.
Also in *The Musorgsky Reader:*
Stassov, Vladimir. On *Boris Godunov*, p. 349.
Copyright 1947 by W. W. Norton & Company, Inc.
Courtesy of W. W. Norton & Company, Inc.

MOZART, W. A. *Briefwechsel*, ed. Hedwig and E. H. Mueller von Asow (Lindau im Bodensee, 1949); 2 vols. published, through the year 1778; under dates. *Briefe*, ed. Ludwig Nohl (Salzburg, 1865), under dates and p. 161.

NAPOLEON I. Letters, in J. Tiersot, *Lettres de musiciens écrites en français*, etc. (2 vols., Turin, 1924). Vol. I: pp. 532–33.

NIETZSCHE, FRIEDRICH. *Gesammelte Werke*, ed. 'Musarion' (23 vols., Munich, 1922). Vol. VII: *Thoughts out of Season*, No. IV, Secs, 1, 2, 3, and 5; Vol. XVII: *Nietzsche contra Wagner*, Sec. 2. The note on the 'Habanera,' from *Friedrich Nietzsches Randglossen zu Bizets 'Carmen,'* ed. Hugo Daffner (Deutsche Musikbuecherei, I; Regensburg, n.d.), p. 27.

NORTH, ROGER. *Memoirs of Musick*, ed. Edward F. Rimbault (London, 1846), pp. 115–17; on musical fashions, pp. 91–92.

PAGANINI, NICOLÓ. Letter, in F.-J. Fétis, *Biographie Universelle des Musiciens* (2nd ed., 8 vols. in four, Paris, 1864). Vol. VI: pp. 410–12.

PARTCH, HARRY. *Genesis of a Music: Monophony* (Madison, Wis., 1949), p. 58.
Courtesy of The University of Wisconsin Press.

PAYN, JAMES. *Some Private Views* (London, 1881), pp. 40–43.

PEACOCK, THOMAS LOVE. *Gryll Grange*, ed. George Saintsbury (London, 1896), chaps. XIV and XV.
'Mangled Operas and the Star System,' in *Works* (Halliford ed., 12 vols., London, 1926). Vol. IX: pp. 225–50.

PRODHOMME, J.-G. *Les Symphonies de Beethoven* (Paris, 1906). On 'Beethoven's "Third" and "Fifth," ' pp. 113–14, 206–207, 220, and 221–22.

PROKOFIEV, SERGEI. 'Statement,' in American-Russian Institute publication, *On Soviet Music: Documents and Discussions* (Hollywood, 1948), pp. 9–11. Translated by Alexandra Groth.

PRUNIÈRES, HENRY. *A New History of Music*, trans. by Edward Lockspeiser (New York, 1943), pp. 119, 242, and 260.

RADCLIFFE, ANN (WARD). *The Italian: or, The Confessional of the Black Penitents*, in *Novels, to which is prefixed a Memoir by Sir Walter Scott* (London, 1824), chap. XV.

RAVEL, MAURICE. See Renard, Jules.

RENARD, JULES. *Journal* (5 vols., Paris, 1927). Vol. V: p. 1343.

RICHTER, JEAN-PAUL. *Werke*, ed. Eduard Berend (5 vols., Berlin, 1923). Vol. V: pp. 778–79. On artists hating the world, see Hoffmann.

RIMSKY-KORSAKOV, N. *Principes d'Orchestration*, trans. by M. D. Calvocoressi (2 vols., Paris, 1914), Vol. I: p. 2.

ROGERS, SAMUEL. *Recollections of His Table Talk*, ed. Alexander Dyce (2nd ed., London, 1856), pp. 223–24.

ROLLAND, ROMAIN. *Jean-Christophe à Paris*. Part II: *La Foire sur la Place* (Vol. V of *Jean-Christophe*, Paris, 1908), 'Making the Rounds,' pp. 65–69; on Bach, pp. 259–60.
  Courtesy of Editions Albin Michel.

ROUSSEAU, JEAN-JACQUES. *Oeuvres* (17 vols., Paris, 1830). Vol. VI: *La Nouvelle Héloïse*, Part II, Letter 23, pp. 332–35.

SAINT-SAËNS, CAMILLE. 'The Composer as Psychologist,' in *Portraits et Souvenirs* (Paris, 1903), pp. 206–17, and *Ecole Buissonnière* (Paris, 1913), pp. 116–19.

SAND, GEORGE. 'Lettres d'un Voyageur,' No. IV, in *Revue des Deux Mondes*, June 1835, pp. 698–736.

SANTAYANA, GEORGE. *Reason in Art* (New York, 1917), p. 51.

SARASATE, PABLO. Letter, in Marc Pincherle, *Les Musiciens peints par eux-mêmes* (Paris, 1939), p. 182.

SCHOPENHAUER, ARTHUR. *Sämmtliche Werke*, ed. Julius Frauenstädt (2nd ed., 6 vols., Leipzig, 1877). Vol. V: *Parerga und Paralipomena*, Part I, 'Aphorismen zur Lebensweisheit,' chap. v, pp. 450–51.

SCHUBERT, FRANZ. *Briefe und Schriften*, ed. Otto Erich Deutsch (2nd ed., Munich, 1922), pp. 32–34 and 97.

SCHUMANN, ROBERT. *Gesammelte Schriften über Musik und Musiker*, ed. F. Gustav Jansen (4th ed., 2 vols., Leipzig, 1891). Vol. I: pp. xxiii–xxiv and 3–5; Vol. II: p. 178.
  Leben aus seinen Briefen (2 vols. in one, Berlin, 1887), under date.

SESSIONS, ROGER. 'The Composer and His Message,' in *The Intent of the Artist*, ed. Augusto Centeno (Priceton, 1941), pp. 123–24.
  Courtesy of the Princeton University Press.

SHAW, G. B. *Love Among the Artists* (New York, 1910), chap. ix.
  'Sir George Grove,' in *Pen Portraits and Reviews* (London, 1931), pp. 106–109.
  Man and Superman (New York, 1904), Act III, p. 99.
  Courtesy of The Public Trustee and The Society of Authors.

SMITH, SYDNEY. *A Memoir of the Reverend Sydney Smith by his daughter Lady Holland, with . . . Letters*, etc. (2 vols., London, 1855). Vol. II: under date.
  Anecdote, in George W. E. Russell, *Sydney Smith* (English Men of Letters series; New York, 1905), pp. 206–207.

SPINOZA, BARUCH. *Ethica ordine geometrico demonstrata*, in *Opera*, ed. C. Gebhart (4 vols., Heidelberg, 1926). Part I: Appendix.

SPOHR, LOUIS. *Selbstbiographie* (2 vols., Cassell, 1861). Vol. II: pp. 77–88.

STASSOV, VLADIMIR. See Moussorgsky.

STENDHAL [HENRI BEYLE]. *Vie de Rossini*, ed. Henry Prunières (2 vols., Paris, 1922), chaps. XVI and XL; on the nations, in 'Raison, Folie,' Vol. I, p. 230, ed. Henry Martineau, *Oeuvres Complètes* (Le Divan), 79 vols., Paris, 1927–37).

STEWART, DONALD OGDEN. *Perfect Behaviour* (New York, 1922), p. 94.

SWIFT, JONATHAN. *Works*, ed. Sir Walter Scott (2nd ed., 19 vols., London, 1884). Vol. XIX: pp. 254–57.

TCHAIKOVSKY, P. I. *The Diaries*, ed. and trans. by Wladimir Lakond (New York, 1945), pp. 247–49.
Copyright 1945 by Wladimir Lakond.
Courtesy of W. W. Norton & Company, Inc.

TOLSTOY, LEO. *War and Peace*, authorized trans. into French (3 vols., Paris, 1885). Vol. I: Part I, chap. IV, Sec. XV, pp. 378–81.
What is Art?, trans. by Aylmer Maude (World's Classics; London, 1930), chaps. I and II.
Courtesy of the Oxford University Press.

TURGENEV, IVAN. *Smoke*, French ed. by Charles Sarolea (Paris, Nelson, n.d.), pp. 125–28.

TURNER, W. J. *Berlioz, The Man and His Work* (London, 1934), pp. 133–35.
Orpheus, or The Music of the Future (London, n.d. [1926]), p. 9.

VAN DIEREN, BERNARD. *Down Among the Dead Men and Other Essays* (London, 1935). 'What Gives Us Pause,' pp. 96–99, aphorisms, pp. 247 and 267. Mozart anecdote, in *Berlioz . . . the report of a discussion* (London, 1929), p. 25.
Courtesy of Mr. Bernard van Dieren, Jr.

VERDI, GIUSEPPE. *I Copialettere di Giuseppe Verdi*, ed. G. Cesari and A. Luzio (Milan, 1913), under dates.

VERNON, P. E. 'Non-Musical Factors in the Appreciation of Music,' in *Musical Times*, Feb.–Apr. 1929, pp. 123 ff.
Courtesy of Mr. Vernon.

VOLTAIRE [F.-M. AROUET]. *Le siècle de Louis XIV*, ed. René Groos (2 vols., Paris, 1929). Vol. II: pp. 330 and 348–49.

WAGNER, RICHARD. *Gesammelte Schriften und Dichtungen* (3rd ed., 10 vols. in five, Leipzig, 1883 ff.). Vol. I: 'A Pilgrimage to Beethoven,' pp. 90–114; Vol. III: on Meyerbeer, p. 300; Vol. IX: Beethoven's Day, pp. 96–97.

WEBER, C.-M. VON. *Sämtliche Schriften*, ed. Georg Kaiser (Berlin and Leipzig, 1908). Novel outline, 439–510; on Italian music, p. 510.

WOLF, HUGO. *Musikalische Kritiken*, ed. R. Bakta and H. Werner (Leipzig, 1911), pp. 222–24, 228, and 334.

WOLZOGEN, HANS VON. *Guide through the Music of R. Wagner's 'The Ring of the Nibelung,'* tr. by Ernst von Wolzogen (2nd ed., Leipzig and London, n.d. [1882]), pp. 45–79.

WOTTON, TOM S. 'Drums,' in *Musical Times*, July–Sept. 1930, pp. 602 ff.
Courtesy of Mrs. Florence M. Wotton.

Diderot
amadeo Wolfgango Mozart
G. Bernard Shaw
Richard Wagner
Fr Nietzsche
J. B. P. Molière
R W Emerson
Leon. Tolstoy
Charles Baudelaire
G. Rossini
H. Heine.